Practical Statistics

Practical Statistics

A Quick and Easy Guide to IBM® SPSS® Statistics, STATA, and Other Statistical Software

David Kremelberg

Los Angeles | London | New Delhi
Singapore | Washington DC

For information:

SAGE Publications, Inc.
2455 Teller Road
Thousand Oaks,
    California 91320
E-mail: order@sagepub.com

SAGE Publications Ltd.
1 Oliver's Yard
55 City Road, London EC1Y 1SP
United Kingdom

SAGE Publications India Pvt. Ltd.
B 1/I 1 Mohan Cooperative
    Industrial Area
Mathura Road, New Delhi 110 044
India

SAGE Publications Asia-Pacific Pte. Ltd.
33 Pekin Street #02-01
Far East Square
Singapore 048763

Printed in the United States of America

Library of Congress Cataloging-in-Publication Data

Kremelberg, David.
Practical statistics: a quick and easy guide to IBM® SPSS® Statistics, STATA, and other statistical software/David Kremelberg.
    p. cm.
Includes bibliographical references and index.
ISBN 978-1-4129-7494-3 (pbk.)
  1. SPSS for Windows. 2. Stata. 3. Statistics—Computer programs. I. Title.

HA32.K74 2011
005.5'5—dc22   2009043892

This book is printed on acid-free paper.

11   12   13   14   10   9   8   7   6   5   4   3   2   1

Acquisitions Editor:	Vicki Knight
Associate Editor:	Lauren Habib
Editorial Assistant:	Ashley Dodd
Production Editor:	Brittany Bauhaus
Copy Editor:	QuADS Prepress (P) Ltd.
Typesetter:	C&M Digitals (P) Ltd.
Proofreader:	Dennis W. Webb
Indexer:	Diggs Publication Services, Inc.
Cover Designer:	Candice Harman
Marketing Manager:	Stephanie Adams

BRIEF CONTENTS

DETAILED CONTENTS

About the Author

David Kremelberg works as a statistical consultant and writer. He has held research positions at the North American Jewish Data Bank at the University of Connecticut and at the Institute for Community Research in Hartford, Connecticut. He has a strong interest in statistics and quantitative methods and spends his time writing, conducting research, and working with clients. He received his BA in psychology from the University of Binghamton, his MA in sociology from the University of Miami, and his PhD in sociology from the University of Connecticut. During his doctoral program, he also earned a certificate in quantitative methods through the University of Connecticut's Department of Psychology. He can be contacted for statistical consulting services through his Web site, www.dkstatisticalconsulting.com, where he also hosts a statistics blog and a number of statistics resources for students.

PREFACE

My motivation for writing this book came from the challenges I experienced trying to learn quantitative methods and statistics during my time as both an undergraduate in psychology and as a graduate student in sociology. I, as well as many other students that I've known, have experienced much difficulty in learning how to use statistical software programs, not because we lacked the ability but due to a severe lack of simple, step-by-step guides to running statistical analyses, either in book form or on the Internet. The aim of this book is to help fill this gap. While this book cannot be said to be comprehensive enough to make you an expert in statistical methods, it will give you a very good start, as well as give you the ability to run a number of advanced tests that can be particularly difficult to learn on your own.

Chapter 1 serves as a brief introduction to quantitative methods and statistics. Chapter 2 serves to introduce you to two very popular general-purpose statistical software programs; IBM® SPSS® Statistics, an IBM company†; and Stata. Chapter 3 focuses on descriptive statistics, which consists of a number of methods that can be used to describe your data. Chapter 4 discusses a number of simpler but very commonly used statistical tests: Pearson's correlation coefficient, chi-square, the *t*-test, and the ANOVA. Next, Chapter 5 focuses on linear regression, which is a very commonly used and somewhat more advanced statistical method. Chapter 6 discusses other forms of regression: logistic, ordered, multinomial, negative binomial, and Poisson regression. Chapter 7 focuses on factor analysis, which is a method that is used to reduce a larger number of variables to a smaller number of factors. Chapter 8 discusses time-series analysis, which is a series of methods that are used to model or predict data over time. Next, Chapter 9 discusses hierarchical linear modeling, which is a specialized statistical model that can be used to model nested data, which are data that can be grouped in some way. Finally, Chapter 10 focuses on structural equation modeling, which is a very advanced yet very general statistical model. Finally, the appendixes describe the statistical tests presented in this book, list significance tables (which will be explained later on), and include a series of additional tests and equations.

---

†SPSS was acquired by IBM in October 2009.

will simply be its percentage divided by 100. Also, you'll get rid of the percentage sign (%).

For example:

The chance of flipping a coin and getting heads = 50%.

$$50\%/100 = .50 \text{ or } 0.50$$

Here, the probability of flipping a coin and getting heads is .50.

The chance of rolling a die and getting "6" = 16.67%.

$$16.67\%/100 = .1667 \text{ or } 1/6$$

Here, the probability of rolling a die and getting "6" is .1667 or 1/6.

Shortly, I will present a small **data set** I constructed for this example, followed by the results of a statistical analysis (don't get scared!) testing whether there is a gender difference in income. This data set consists of 10 males and 10 females, and as you can see from the data, I made it a point that males on average have higher incomes than females. Besides illustrating the concept of the probability level in statistics, this section will also give you an introduction to **IBM® SPSS® Statistics** and data sets.

Just as a note, I will try throughout this book to have examples that use actual data. Also, I will as much as possible (beginning now) include actual screenshots and results from the software that you'll be using when you do your statistical analyses. The software that is covered in this book includes IBM SPSS and **Stata**, which are two very popular general-purpose statistical analyses programs; **HLM**, which is a program that is used solely for **hierarchical linear modeling**, a specialized type of statistical test; and **AMOS**, which is used for **structural equation modeling**, an advanced statistical model.

So here is our data set. This screenshot comes from IBM SPSS. While we will cover these different statistical software packages more later on, I will include some basic notes here as we go along. You may find that IBM SPSS is more convenient than Stata for entering data (e.g., if you gave a survey, we would first have to enter the data into a software program before you can do an analysis).

So let's take a look at this. You can see that on top there are two variables, "sex" and "yincome." In your data sets, as in this one, each variable will have its own column. On the left, we see a column of numbers, with the numbers 1 through 20. The 20 numbers (called "case numbers" when discussing data sets) correspond to the 20 individuals whose data we have.

gender and income.sav [DataSet1] - PASW Statistics Data Editor

File   Edit   View   Data   Transform   Analyze   Applications   Graphs   Utilities   Add-ons   Window   Help

1 : sex   0

	sex	yincome	var	var	var	var	var
1	0	12578					
2	0	11478					
3	0	14574					
4	0	12545					
5	0	9854					
6	0	11452					
7	0	14523					
8	0	8965					
9	0	17854					
10	0	12014					
11	1	15879					
12	1	19875					
13	1	20451					
14	1	14545					
15	1	22545					
16	1	24545					
17	1	28545					
18	1	21015					
19	1	17874					
20	1	15145					
21							

The first variable, "sex," measures the person's sex (in statistics, we call the individuals who make up a data set "respondents" or "participants"). In data sets, to run an analysis, everything needs a numerical or number code, even things such as sex, the region of the country you live in, or the highest degree you have. In this case, we chose "0" to stand for females and "1" to stand for males. In the case of "yincome," the number represents the respondent's yearly income in dollars. You may find it more convenient to give variables short (eight characters or less) but descriptive names, as older versions of Stata only support variables with eight characters or less in their name. If you were to import a file from IBM SPSS into an older version of Stata that contains variables with more than eight characters in their names, everything will work, but the names of the variables will be truncated to eight characters, which might make things confusing. AMOS and older versions of IBM SPSS have this same limitation. In general, it is a good rule to always limit variable names to eight characters or less.

OK, now for the analysis. For now I'll skip over how to do the analysis, as I will cover this in much detail in a later chapter. However, I will include a screenshot of results to illustrate the concept of the probability level. Just as a note, to analyze this data, we will conduct what is called a *t*-test (Figure 1.1).

Don't let this scare you: By the time you have finished reading this book, you will easily understand the meaning of this output. In this example, we find that the probability level under the fifth column of numbers, labeled "Sig. (2-tailed)." Here, it is ".000." However, in statistics, the probability level can never be 0, because there is always some chance that our findings are due to error. What IBM SPSS means is our probability level is very very low, below .001. When IBM SPSS finds the probability to be below .001, it gives ".000" as your result. Keep in mind that this is just a minor "bug" in IBM SPSS; in reality, your probability level can be extremely small, but it can never be 0.

So we know that our probability level is less than .001. But that mean? It means that the probability that the differences in income that we saw based on gender are due to chance, or random variation, is less than .001. Conversely, there is a greater than .999 probability that the differences we saw based on gender in income are due to a real, genuine difference (due to, say, differences in level of education, discrimination, etc.). Basically, there's a greater than .999 probability that this difference is *not* due to our having happened to have picked males who had very high incomes and/or females who had very low incomes. In social science, you will see these three standards for the probability level: .05, .01, and .001. A probability level of .05 means that there is a 95% chance that there is a real relationship between the variables and a 5% probability that the difference is due to error or chance. The .05 standard is the one most commonly used in the social sciences;

→ **T-Test**

[DataSet1] T:\Books\Practical Statistics\#Data\Chapter 1\gender and income.sav

Group Statistics

	sex	N	Mean	Std. Deviation	Std. Error Mean
yincome	0	10	12583.70	2557.644	808.798
	1	10	20041.90	4424.846	1399.259

Independent Samples Test

		Levene's Test for Equality of Variances		t-test for Equality of Means						95% Confidence Interval of the Difference	
		F	Sig.	t	df	Sig. (2-tailed)	Mean Difference	Std. Error Difference	Lower	Upper	
yincome	Equal variances assumed	2.445	.135	-4.615	18	.000	-7458.200	1616.193	-10853.696	-4062.704	
	Equal variances not assumed			-4.615	14.410	.000	-7458.200	1616.193	-10915.359	-4001.041	

Figure 1.1   Probability Levels: Example of a *t*-test in SPSS

however, if your probability level is lower than one of the stricter standards (.01 or .001), then that is what would be noted in a research paper or study. To illustrate, in the example above, we had a probability level of less than .001. If we were writing these results in a research paper, we could say something such as the following: The relationship between gender and income was **statistically significant**, with males tending to have higher incomes than females ($p < .001$). The term *statistically significant* simply refers to the fact that our probability level was less than .05, the standard. We have also noted that our calculated probability level, represented as p, was less than .001. We note that the probability level is less than .001 instead of using the .05 or .01 standards as it is customary to include only the strictest standard that is met.

In statistics, the probability level will always refer to the probability that the difference or relationship that you see is due to chance. To come up with the probability that the difference or relationship is *not* due to error or chance, you just need to subtract the probability level from 1.

For example:

If our probability level (the probability it was due to chance) = .07 (or 7%).

The probability that the difference is a real effect = $1 - .07 = .93$ (or 93%).

△ HYPOTHESES AND TESTS

In the example above, where we tested gender differences in income based on a hypothetical data set, we also tested a **hypothesis**. When you run a statistical analysis, you'll typically be testing one or more hypotheses. A hypothesis is a prediction about the relationship between two or more variables. For example, when we tested the relationship between gender and income, our hypothesis may have been: *Males are more likely to have higher incomes than females.*

Here are some more examples of hypotheses:

It is predicted that males are more likely to vote Republican than females.

It is predicted that high levels of frustration lead to heavy alcohol use, which in turn leads to unprotected sex.

We can use statistical tests to test these and all sorts of other hypotheses. A very important point here is that a particular type of statistical test will be most appropriate depending on your hypothesis and the nature of your data.

While several different types of statistical tests may be appropriate, there will be some that will be very inappropriate. It is important to consider your hypotheses and data and come to a correct decision based on your hypothesis and the nature of your data. While I'm simply noting this now as part of the introduction, a guide to determining which test to use on the basis of the nature of your hypothesis and data is included in Appendix A. This is a crucial issue and one which can lead to serious errors if not considered appropriately.

As a quick example, in the analysis above, I chose to do a *t*-test; more specifically, an **independent samples *t*-test**. This type of test happens to be appropriate because we're looking at the difference between two groups, males and females (if you're looking at the difference between three or more groups, you would do an **ANOVA**), and because the **dependent variable**, the variable we're trying to predict (income), is continuous (not a number of categories). Variables that we use to predict our dependent variable are called **independent variables**. In this case, our independent variable is sex or gender. If our data were different, or our hypothesis (what we were trying to test) was different, we would probably use a different statistical test. This issue will be covered throughout the text.

GENERALIZATION AND REPRESENTATIVENESS △

The concepts of **generalizability** and **randomness** are the most important, yet some of the most neglected, in the field of statistics. First, we will cover the concept of a **random sample**. A random sample does not mean you got a group of "random people" that you gave a survey to on the street or in a mall. In statistics, a random sample means a very specific and particular thing. A random sample means that every person in your **population** has an equal chance of being selected for participation in your study. When conducting research, a sample refers to the group of people you select for study, while a population refers to a larger body of individuals from whom you selected your sample and who you wish to be able to describe using the results of your study. For example, say that your population is adults living in the United States. In doing your study, you wish the results of your study to be generalizable to this population. If your study was to be generalizable to all adults living in the United States, it would mean that you can apply the results of your study to *all adults living in the United States.* This is one of the most powerful elements of statistics. Your study may only consist of 50 or 100 individuals; however, if it is a random sample, you can apply your results to the entire population (in this example, all the adults living in the United States). In this way, our sample is **representative** of our population.

Take as an example, the analysis between gender and income that was presented earlier in this chapter. If this sample of nearly 20 individuals was a random sample of adults in the United States (i.e., if every adult living in United States had an equal chance of being selected for the survey), we could say that not only do these 10 males have a significantly higher income than the 10 females we selected in our survey, but that on average, adult males *in the United States* have higher incomes than adult females. By using this method of sampling combined with statistical tests, we are able to extend our results based on 20 individuals to millions of individuals.

Keep in mind that representativeness and generalizability work both ways. If you do not have a random sample (if it is not true that every member of the population has an equal chance of being selected for your study), then your sample is not representative of the population and you cannot generalize your results to the population at hand. So if you stand on a busy sidewalk and recruit 40 people to fill out a survey, when you discuss your results, you can *only* talk about those 40 people, because you did not have a random sample. You cannot generalize the results to people in general, Americans in general, adults in general, the population of that town, and so on. This is a crucial point that even some famous researchers do not take into account, and it is a grievous error.

△   CORRELATION AND CAUSATION

A very important concept in quantitative methods is the distinction between correlation and causation. The term *correlation* refers to the relationship between two variables (i.e., how related they are). A distinct concept is that of causation, which signifies that one variable causes another one to change. Just because two variables are correlated (i.e., related) does not necessarily mean that they are related causally (i.e., that one causes the other). This is an extremely important concept in quantitative methods. Take the example of the relationship between watching violent television and being violent among youth. Say you found that there was a relationship between watching violent television and expressing violent behavior such that children who spend more time watching violent television also express more violent behavior. Here, we know that these two factors are correlated: that there is a relationship between the two variables of time spent watching violent television and violent behavior. However, we know nothing about whether watching violent television in fact causes violent behavior. Therefore, we cannot say whether these two factors are causally related. Providing evidence for a correlation or relationship between two variables is very easy, but providing evidence that two variables are causally related (that one in fact causes the other) is significantly more difficult. The key concept to remember here is a phrase that you might hear in your first statistics course: "Correlation does not imply causation." This phrase simply means that having a relationship or correlation between two variables says nothing about whether one in fact causes the other.

THE NORMAL DISTRIBUTION △

A **normal distribution** describes data that are distributed in a certain type of way. In essence, in data that are **normally distributed**, the majority of cases (e.g., of years of education, attitude measurements, etc.) will be close to the average value, and the further away you get from the average value, the fewer cases you will see. An example of something that is normally distributed is height. The height of most people is around the average, which is approximately 5 feet 7 inches when including both males and females. While the majority of individuals have a height close to this value, there are still a fair degree of individuals who are substantially taller or shorter than this average, say around 6 feet 6 inches or 4 feet 8 inches. As you continue traveling further from this average, you see fewer and fewer individuals. There are some individuals who are 7 feet tall or 4 feet tall, but they are very rare. Likewise, there are even some individuals who are 8 feet tall or 3 feet tall, but they are even more rare. Pictorially, a graph of human height versus the number of individuals with that height would look like Figure 1.2.

The shape of this graph is called a "bell curve" and resembles what any normally distributed variable would look like. As the graph illustrates, the majority of people are around the average height of 160 cm. As you get further and further away from this average, we see fewer and fewer people. IQ (intelligent quotient), which is also a normally distributed variable, would look like Figure 1.3.

Here, we see that the average is 100, and the further we get away from this average, the fewer people there are.

A number of the statistical tests that are discussed in this book make the assumption that the dependent variable, the variable that you are trying to predict, is normally distributed. If you use one of these tests with data that are not normally distributed, it may or may not be an issue. The area of assumptions, testing assumptions, and what to do when an assumption has been violated is a very complex and nuanced area and is not the focus of this book. In statistics classes that you take, you may be given the simple instruction of performing an alternative test when an assumption has been violated. This is

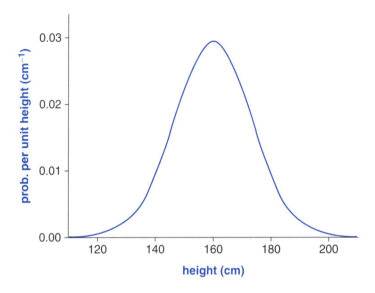

Figure 1.2   The Normal Distribution: Height

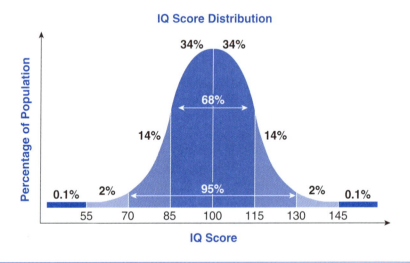

Figure 1.3   The Normal Distribution: IQ Scores

an overly simplistic view of the issue of assumptions and assumption violation and really does more harm than good. In regard to certain assumptions of certain tests, violation may not really be an issue at all. In other cases, it may be. Whether it is or not depends on the particular assumption and the particular test and how badly the assumption has been violated.

If you are more interested in the subject of testing variables for normality (whether they are normally distributed or not), please see Section 3 of Appendix C.

SUMMARY   △

This chapter provided a brief but important introduction to statistics and quantitative methods. First, the purpose of statistical tests was discussed. Statistical tests are used to provide evidence for or against a relationship between two or more variables. Variables can consist of anything that can be measured. Most analyses consist of a single dependent variable and multiple independent variables. Your dependent variable is the variable which you are trying to predict or explain, while your independent variables are the variables that you use to predict your dependent variable. Next, the concept of the probability level was introduced. The probability level is an indicator that measures the level of certainty that a finding was in fact due to a real relationship between variables versus the probability that it is simply due to error or chance. Next, the concept of the hypothesis was introduced, which is a prediction about the relationship between two or more variables. Based on your hypothesis and the nature of your data, you will select the appropriate statistical test to perform in order to test your hypothesis. Selecting the appropriate statistical test is vital to avoid errors, and while this process is simple even with a basic knowledge of statistics, it is commonly incorrectly done. The next section of this chapter introduced the concept of generalizability. To be able to generalize your findings to the larger population, you must use a random sample that is representative of the larger population. Finally, many variables in the social sciences are normally distributed, in which most cases are close to the average score, and the further you get from the average the fewer cases you see (the "bell curve").

The next chapter will introduce the reader to two very popular, general-purpose statistical software packages, IBM SPSS and Stata. Chapter 2 will also present directions on how to enter data into both of these programs, which would be the first step of your data analysis if you were not using a preexisting data set.

RESOURCE

This book's Web site can be found at the following location: www.sagepub.com/kremelstudy

CHAPTER 2

An Introduction to IBM® SPSS® Statistics and Stata

OUTLINE OF CHAPTER

In this chapter, I will introduce you to two very popular statistical software packages: IBM SPSS and Stata. As you begin using these programs yourself, you'll likely find that you may prefer either IBM SPSS or Stata, both in general and when conducting particular statistical tests. From my experience, I prefer IBM SPSS for data entry and some **charts** and **graphs**, while I prefer Stata for almost everything else (virtually all statistical analyses). IBM SPSS tends to be more user-friendly and is more suited to data entry than Stata. While being more difficult to use as a beginner, Stata is more versatile, powerful, and easier to use once you become familiar with it, hence its greater value when performing statistical analyses. After introducing you to these two statistical software packages, I will show you how to create new variables, enter data, and modify or recode variables. I'll show you how to do this both in IBM SPSS and Stata, as well as how to do this both through the programs' menus and through what is called **syntax**.

Syntax looks like computer code (e.g., BASIC or C++), and in our case, syntax is the instructions that IBM SPSS or Stata can use to create new variables, recode variables, create charts and graphs, run analyses, and so on. Many new users find that it is easier to do these things through the program's menus (e.g., in Microsoft Word, you would create a new file using the program's menus by clicking on "file" and then clicking on "new"). However, especially with experience, you will find that using syntax will save you much time because it becomes extremely simple and quick to make changes to your analyses, which may take a very long time if you had to go through the menus all over again to make these changes. With the syntax file, all you need to do is to make whatever modifications you need to the syntax, and then run the entire file. For example, if you wanted to add a single variable to an analysis, using a syntax file, all you would need to do would be to go to that particular line in the syntax file and add that variable to the appropriate point in that line. However, if you did everything through menus, you would spend a while clicking through the menu system, wasting a lot of time. While if you only needed to make one or two minor changes to your analyses, it wouldn't make much of a difference either way, typically you'll end up making a lot of changes, and doing a lot of recoding of variables. So much more likely than not, you will find that using syntax, while having a slower learning curve than using menus, will save you great amounts of time in the long run. If you are interested in becoming proficient in running statistical analyses, I strongly suggest that you become proficient in writing Stata syntax.

△   SECTION 2: IBM SPSS

Introduction to IBM SPSS

In this section, I'll introduce you to IBM SPSS. You can find more information about IBM SPSS and how to purchase it by navigating to the following Web site: www.spss.com/software/statistics/.

Below is a screenshot of what you'll see when you open the IBM SPSS program.

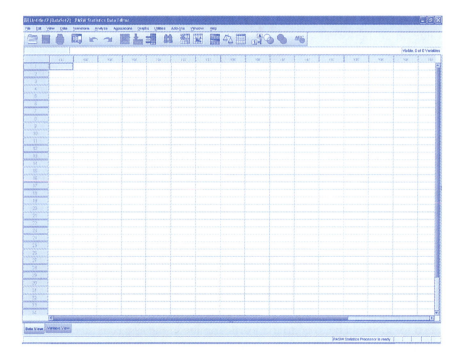

This is the screen that you will see when you go to enter data into IBM SPSS later on. At the top of every column, you see *var*—this stands for "variable." Each variable will have its own column. When you go to enter data, you'll first need to create a number of variables; for example, *sex* for the respondents' sex, *educ* for the respondents' level of education, and so on. Since we just opened IBM SPSS, this is a new data file and does not contain any variables or any data.

The leftmost column contains numbers, starting at 1 and counting upward. Each of these numbers, and likewise each row, represents a single **case**. In most data sets, the case will be an actual person: a respondent from a study, a participant in an interview, and so on. However, a case can also represent things such as a school, a classroom, a state or province, a year or another unit of time, and so on.

At the top of the window you see the **menu bar**, which starts with *File* and goes through *Help*. As I mentioned earlier, you can choose to either navigate through the menu bar to do analyses and other things, or you can use syntax. While I will cover both menu-driven statistical analyses as well as syntax-driven analyses in this book, as I mentioned earlier, I highly recommend learning and using syntax, most especially Stata syntax.

At the bottom of the screen in the picture shown on the previous page you see that the tab *Data View* is highlighted. In IBM SPSS, there are two main windows: the data window, which is open in the screenshot above, and the variable window. The variable window will be open when you are creating new variables or modifying them (e.g., if you wanted to change a variable that was set to use eight decimal places to two decimal places). The data window will be open when you are entering data. When you are doing analyses, either through the menus or by using syntax, it doesn't matter which of these windows you have open. Below I have a screenshot of the variable window.

In this window, each variable gets its own row, and the numbers on the left correspond to each variable instead of each case. The columns correspond to different characteristics of the variables. *Name* is simply the name of the variable, which you specify. For example, you might name the variable for the region of the United States in which the respondent is living as *region*. *Type* refers to whether the variable is a number (numeric) or consists of letters or words (string). While IBM SPSS allows for other data types, you can simply stick to these two, *numeric* if your variable contains only numbers, and *string* if it contains numbers and words or only words. *Width* refers to how many places your variable has as its maximum. For example, if you have a variable that measures IQ (intelligent quotient) scores, you can specify "3" as the width, as you'll never have a score of 1,000 (four places) or more. *Decimals* refer to how many decimal places your variable has, as its maximum. *Label* is a more descriptive title you can give to your variable, which is helpful as the length of the variable name is limited.

Under *values*, you can specify what the different values of the variable mean. If your variable is IQ score, you probably won't need to use this. However, this is very useful when the values for your variable represent something else. For example, if our variable is sex, we may choose "0" to stand for males and "1" to stand for females. You can specify this coding scheme in the *values* field. It is much more convenient to do this within IBM SPSS, so you have all the information right there, than to write it down separately or try to remember it. I will describe how to do this in detail later in this chapter.

The next column is *missing*. When you do a survey, give interviews, and so on, you'll always have what is called **missing data**. For example, if you ask respondents their income, many will not want to answer that question, and leave it blank. This is called missing data. If you simply do not enter any value for a respondent under that variable (e.g., if respondent number three did not answer "income," so you do not enter anything), IBM SPSS will code it as missing by default. However, you can also specify a particular number to stand for missing data, and you can specify this in the "missing" column. While you can choose any number to stand for missing data, the number "–999" is popularly used. The most important point is to not use a value that might represent actual data. For example, in the case of IQ scores, using "–999" to represent missing data would be appropriate, but using "99" would not be appropriate as there likely would be cases of respondents who had 99 as their IQ score. This would be problematic because if you told IBM SPSS, in the missing column, that 99 represents missing data, then respondents who had an IQ score of 99 would be considered by IBM SPSS to have missing data. Accurately labeling missing data as missing, either by default by IBM SPSS or by giving missing data a particular numerical code is very important so that IBM SPSS will appropriately ignore these cases when doing analyses.

The second to last column, *measure*, allows you to specify whether the variable is a scale, **nominal**, or **ordinal** variable. A scale variable is a **continuous** variable. Continuous variables are variables that do not consist of a number of discrete categories. Examples of continuous variables are age, IQ, height, weight, and years of education completed. However, variables that are "counted" are not considered continuous variables. **Count variables** measure the number of times the respondent (or something else) has done something. An example would be the number of times you went to a doctor in the past year. In IBM SPSS, you can simply specify these variables as scale variables. *Nominal* and *ordinal* variables consist of variables that are measured as a number of discrete categories. The difference between nominal and ordinal variables is that nominal variables are unordered, while ordinal variables can be ordered. Variables that would be considered nominal variables include race, college major, sex, region of residence in the United States, and religion. Examples of ordinal variables include highest degree completed and social class. Also, if you were to recode continuous variables into a series of categories (e.g., if you coded age by decade, with people under 10 coded "0," people between 10 and 20 coded "1," etc.), this new variable would also be considered an ordinal variable. The two columns in IBM SPSS before the "measure" column, which are "columns" and "align," you do not need to worry about.

IBM SPSS: Creating New Data Sets

In this section, I will cover how to create a new data set in IBM SPSS. The next section will cover creating new variables, and the next will cover entering data. The section after that will cover recoding and otherwise modifying variables. This is followed by a section that will cover saving data sets, as well as a section on selecting cases. Next, all this will be covered in Stata. The final section of this chapter will cover transferring data sets between IBM SPSS, Stata, Excel, and other programs.

In IBM SPSS, you can create a new data set in one of two ways. If IBM SPSS is not open, you can create a new data set simply by launching the program. At that point, you could immediately start creating variables and entering

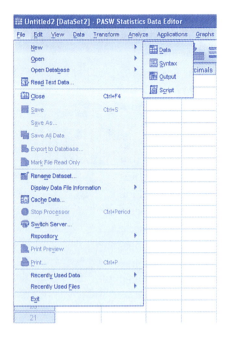

new data, just as you could create a new file in Microsoft Word simply by launching the program and starting to type. However, if IBM SPSS is open and another data set is loaded, you would first want to save the data set if necessary, and then select "file," "new," and "data." See the following screenshot for the location of this selection:

You can see from the previous screenshot that you have several other options when creating a new file. The only options that you need to concern yourself with are the *Data* and *Syntax* selections. You will select *Data* when you want to start entering data into a new file, and you'll select *Syntax* when you want to start writing a new syntax file to analyze your data with.

After you click on *Data*, you'll be prompted whether or not to save your file if you have one already open in IBM SPSS. After you make your selection, you will see this screen:

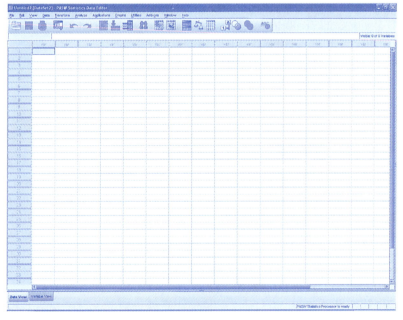

At this point, you'll start creating new variables and entering data. We will pick up from this point in the next section of this chapter, which covers creating new variables.

IBM SPSS: Creating Variables

This section will cover how to create new variables in IBM SPSS. First, if you are starting with a new data file, you must first create a new file—this is covered in the previous section. In short, a new file can be created in IBM SPSS by simply launching the program. After this is done, you will want to click on the *Variable View* tab near the bottom-left-hand corner of the IBM SPSS window. This will give you the following screen:

Now, we will begin by creating variables. Say we are interested in studying gender differences in income and level of education, so we gave a survey to 20 males and 20 females, which just asked for their gender, their yearly income in dollars, and how many years of education they completed. For these variables, we can choose the obvious names of *sex*, *income*, and *educ*. I suggest always restricting your variable names to eight characters or less, as some older versions of IBM SPSS (which are still commonly used), Stata, as well as some other programs limit variable names to only eight characters or less. Simply sticking to eight characters or less in your variable names and giving them more descriptive names in the label field if necessary will save you many potential difficulties.

After clicking in the first box (the white box in the extreme upper-left-hand corner), we can simply type "sex," and then click on the box directly below that to enter our next variable name. In this second box, we will enter "income," and then enter "educ" in the third box. After we have finished with that, we will see the following screen:

Next, we can make a few changes. First, we can change *Decimals* to "0" for all our variables, as *sex* will be either coded as "0" or "1"; we will keep income rounded to the nearest dollar, and education will be measured as the number of years completed. This step isn't necessary, but it will make the data set look cleaner (under the data view) when we start entering data as we won't have all those unnecessary decimal points and zeros. Please take note that the newest version of PASW/SPSS, Version 18, will do this for you automatically. However, if you have an earlier version, to make this change manually, first click on the *Decimals* box for *sex*. See below:

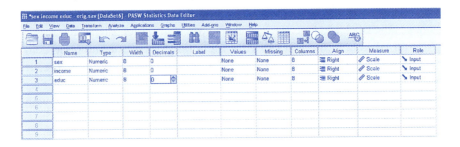

As you can see, little up and down arrows popped up on the right side of this box. By clicking on either the up arrow or down arrow, you can change the number of decimal places that this variable will have. We will click on the down arrow twice. Then, we will click on the *Decimals* box for *income*, and also change this to 0. Finally, we will click on the *Decimals* box for *educ*, and again change this value to 0. When we are finished, our screen should look like this:

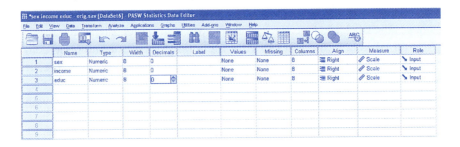

So we have just changed all our variables to have zero decimal places (i.e., to simply be whole numbers, or more correctly, integers). Next, we'll give our variables more descriptive names. While this isn't as necessary in this case because our variable names are rather self-descriptive as they are, this will come in handy when you start to work with larger and more unwieldy data sets. To do this, we simply need to click on the label box for each variable and then enter a short description. This is what I wrote:

Here, I have increased the width of the *Label* column by clicking and holding on the line between *Label* and *Values* and sliding it to the right. Next, we will want to specify the values for our sex variable, but this will not be necessary for our income or level of education variable. We only need to do this for sex because we need to come up with a number that will stand for "male" and another number that will stand for "female." Income simply stands for the respondent's yearly income and education simply stands for the respondent's level of education in years. However, since the numbers for sex will represent something else (either male or female), we want to specify that in IBM SPSS. This again is not required to do analyses but is very strongly recommended so that results of analyses you do later on will be easier to understand (i.e., when looking at results, "female" is much explanatory than "1"). It simply makes it much easier to keep track of what means what. So first we will click on the *Values* box for *sex*. This is what you will see:

You can see that, by default, nothing is included in this box. You'll also see a small gray box with three periods appear after clicking on the values box for sex. Next, we will click on the small gray box. After that, this screen will appear:

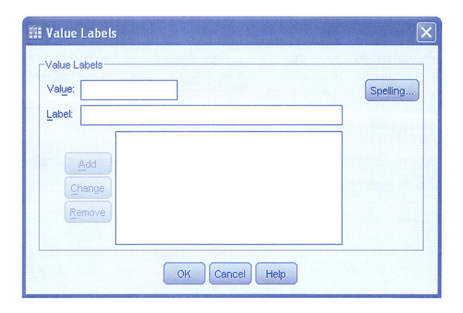

In this box, we can specify our values and value labels for *sex*. We will choose "0" to stand for "male" and "1" to stand for "female." First, you'll click on the white box next to *Value* and type "0." Next, we will click on the white box next to *Label* and type "male." Next, we will click on the *Add* button. After clicking the *Add* button, this is what you will see:

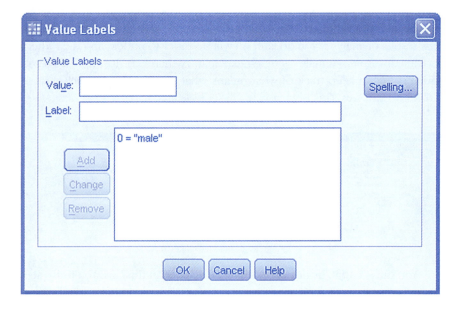

Next, you'll type "1" under *Value* and "female" under *Label* then click on *Add*. After that, you will see this:

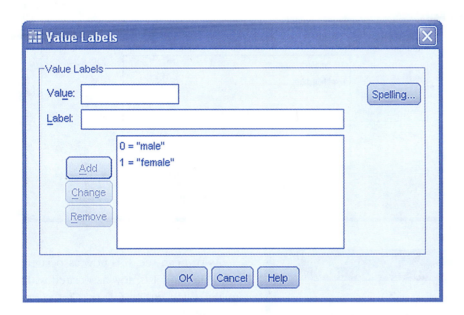

Now we are done. Click *OK* to finish. We can see how the values box for *sex* has changed:

Now, this is what we will see if we click on the values box for sex again, and click on the small gray square:

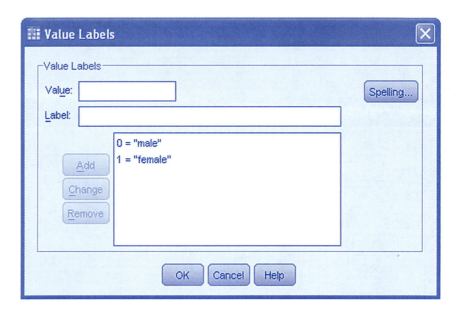

As you can see, 0 is now associated with male, and 1 is now associated with female. Click either *OK* or *Cancel* to close out this box. At this point, we are nearly finished and can start entering data soon. The final columns that we need to go over are the *Missing* column and the *Measure* column.

Just like with the *Values* box, if you click on the *Missing* box for any variable, a small gray box with three periods will appear on the right-hand side of the box. Try this by clicking on the *Missing* box for *sex*. You'll see this screen:

By default, *No missing values* is selected. As you can see IBM SPSS gives us two other options. *Discrete missing values* lets you define up to three specific numbers to represent missing data points (a *data point* is one particular piece of data: e.g., gender for respondent number 13 or level of education for respondent number 27). *Range plus one optional discrete missing value* allows you to specify a range of numbers all of which represent missing values along with a single discrete value, which also represents missing data. Typically, you will only select one discrete number to represent missing data. If, for example, we wanted to select "999" to represent missing data, we would click on the button next to *Discrete missing values* and then type in "999" in the first box. Then, we would click OK. If we chose to do this, we would then see the following screen:

As you can see, under missing values for *sex*, "999" is displayed. Now, if we encounter any missing data for sex, we would simply enter "999" for that data point. Now, in any analyses that you run, data points that are coded "999" for sex will be considered missing data by IBM SPSS. By clicking on the small gray box again, we can edit or change what is defined as missing values, just as with the *Values* box.

Finally, we will work with the *Measure* column. While not necessary when running analyses, you may find it useful to specify the nature of your variables within SPSS. As discussed previously, IBM SPSS defines variables as scale, nominal, or ordinal variables. Continuous variables are called "scale" variables in IBM SPSS. Nominal and ordinal variables retain the standard terminology, with nominal variables being variables that consist of a number of unordered categories, and ordinal variables being variables that consist of a number of ordered categories. "Sex" is a variable that consists of categories (just two: male and female) that are unordered, making it a nominal variable. Both income and years of education would be considered continuous variables or scale variables within IBM SPSS.

To modify the measure of a variable, first click on the *Measure* box for that variable. Try this with the *sex* variable. You'll see a menu appear, as displayed in this screenshot:

After selecting this, you will see the following dialog box:

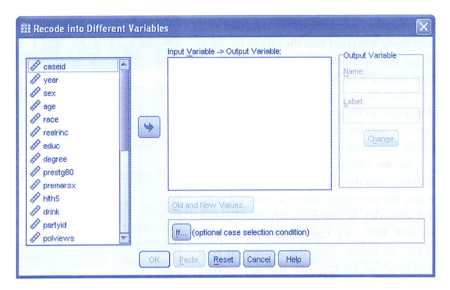

For example, let's say we want to recode the age variable into two categories: individuals under the age of 30 and those aged 30 or older. First, you would select age and click the arrow pointing to the right. After doing that, you would get the following result:

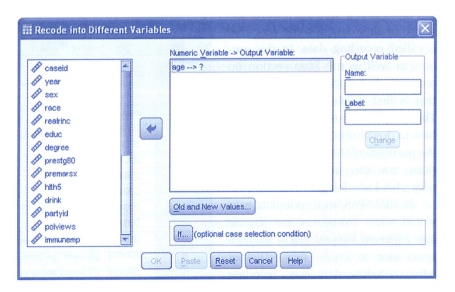

Next, you would have to assign a name to your new variable. I'll call the new variable *age2* and label it as "Age: recoded." After that, clicking the *Change* button will give you the following result:

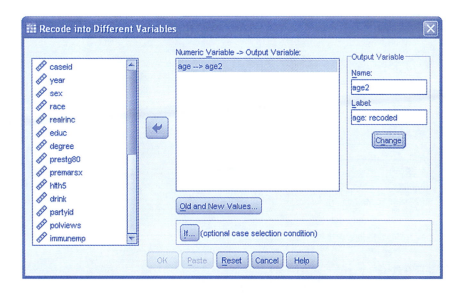

Next, you would need to click *Old and New Values*:

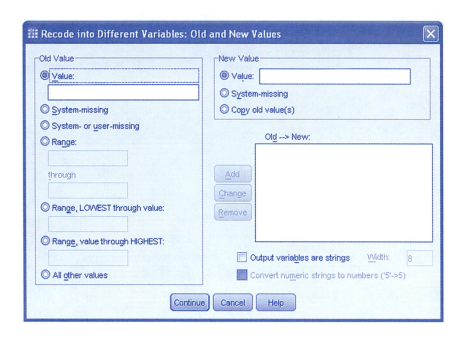

First, we will click the first *Range* button and specify the range as 0 through 29. Next, we will specify the new value, under *Value* as 0. That will result in the following screen:

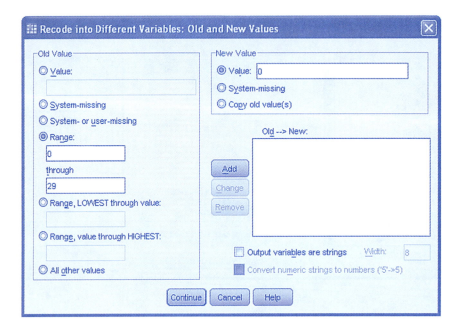

Next, we will click the "Add" button:

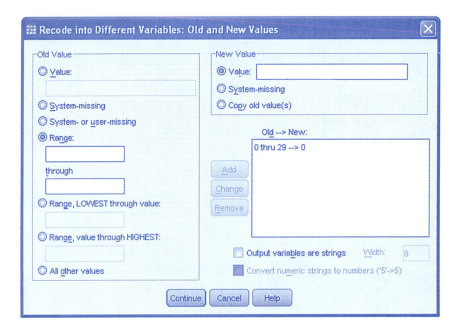

Here, we can now see that all individuals who currently have values of 0 through 29 for their age will have the new value of 0 for our new variable, *age2*. Now, we will specify 30 through 150 as the range (150 just being an arbitrarily high number, most likely there are no individuals in our data set much older than 100). We will also specify 1 as the new value. Then, clicking *Add* will result in the following screen:

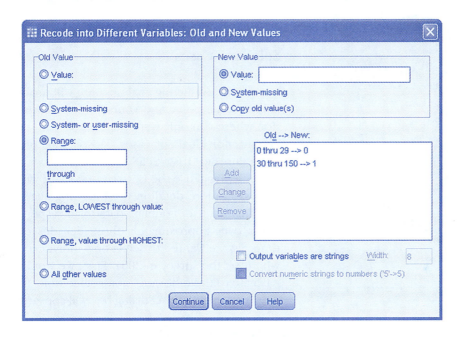

Now, we can also see that individuals who currently have values of 30 through 150 for their age will be recoded as "1" for the new *age2* variable. Finally, click *Continue* and *OK*. This will run the commands you have specified and your new variable, *age2*, will have been created.

The following is the equivalent syntax of what we have just run using the menu system:

```
RECODE age (0 thru 29=0) (30 thru 150=1) INTO age2.
VARIABLE LABELS age2 'age: recoded.'
EXECUTE.
```

As you can see, the first line specifies that we are recoding variables, specifically stating that *age* is the variable that we are going to recode. The "INTO age2" command specifies that we are recoding *age* into a new variable named *age2*. This line also specifies exactly how to recode the variable. Here, individuals under age 30 are recoded into 0, while those

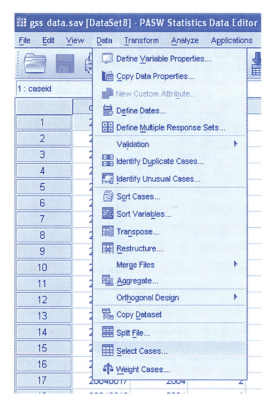

aged 30 or older are recoded into 1. The second line labels our new variable. Finally, our third line contains the EXECUTE command followed by a period, executing the syntax.

IBM SPSS: Selecting Cases

When conducting analyses, you will probably at some point find yourself in the situation where you only want the analysis run on certain individuals or cases. This is a simple procedure in IBM SPSS. In the following example, I will use the GSS data set that I will discuss in more detail in the following chapter. This data set contains data from respondents over approximately three decades of time. Say we wanted to select only individuals who took the survey in 2004. First, we would navigate to the following menu selection:

Next, the following dialog box will appear:

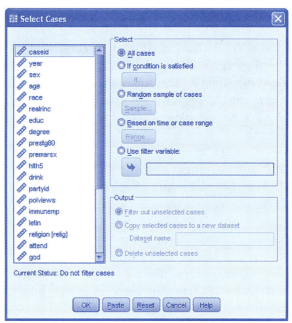

Next, we will select *If condition is satisfied*, and click *If . . .* :

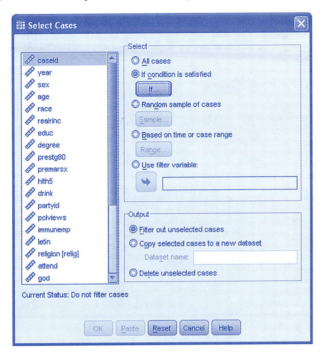

This will open the following dialog box:

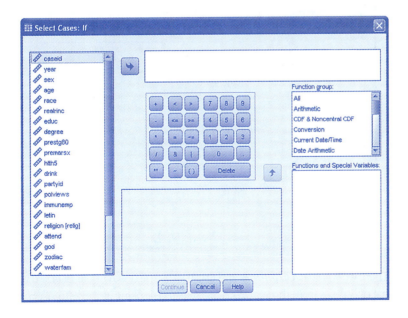

Next, we will select the *year* variable and move it to the right by clicking on the arrow:

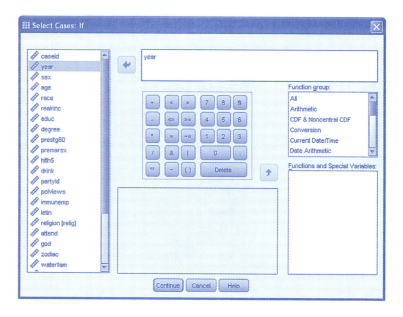

Finally, setting it equal to 2004, we get the following:

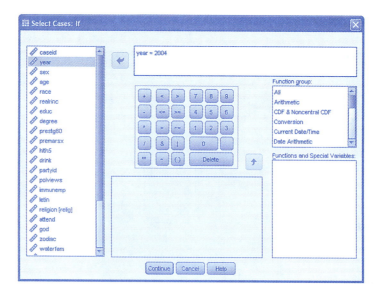

Then, we will select *Continue* and *OK*. If we scroll down in our data set, we can see that only cases from the year 2004 are selected, looking at the leftmost column:

Finally, to go back to selecting all cases, go back to the same initial menu selection:

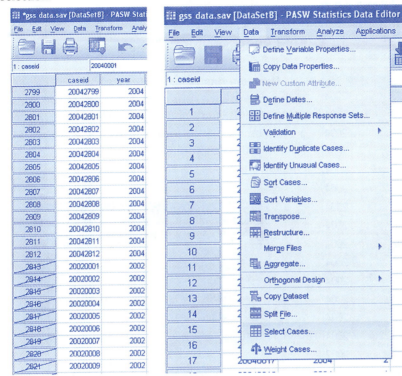

Then simply select *All cases*:

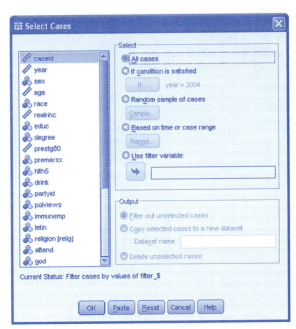

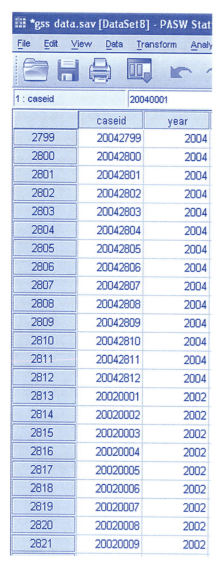

Then click *OK*, and everything will be back as it was originally.

IBM SPSS: Saving Data Sets

After entering or modifying data, you will want to make sure to save your data set for future use. This is as simple as saving a document you have just written in a program such as Microsoft Word. If you are working on a new file that you have never saved before, select *File* and *Save As . . .* as shown below:

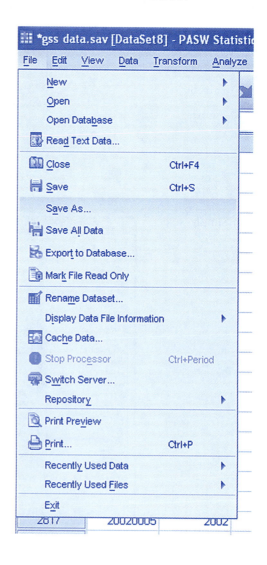

Next, the following dialog box will pop up:

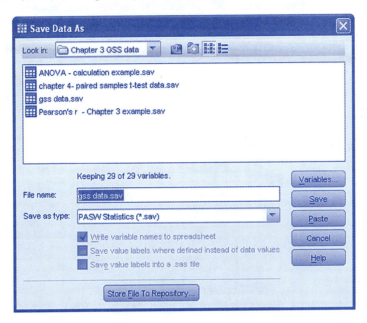

Here, you simply select the directory in which you would like to save your file as well as specify the filename, just as you would with a newly written Word document. Next, clicking *Save* will save your file.

If we had opened a previously saved data set and were, for example, adding additional cases to it as we continued the process of entering data, we could instead select the *Save* option:

This option would simply save over your previously saved data set.

When selecting the *Save As . . .* option, IBM SPSS will allow you the option of only selecting certain variables to keep in your saved data set. This option can be accessed by clicking on the *Variables* button before saving your file in the dialog box shown below:

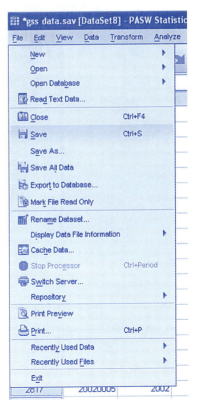

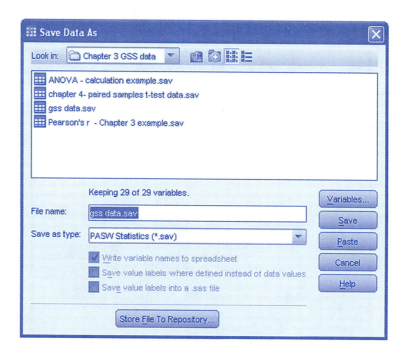

Selecting *Variables* would present the following dialog box:

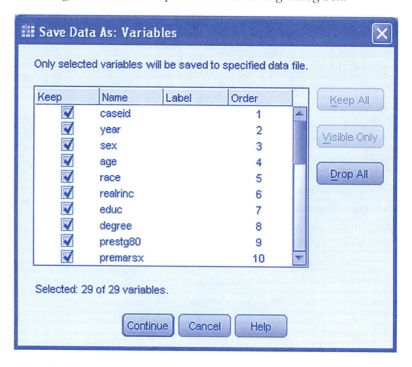

Here, all variables that are being kept in the saved data set are marked with a checkmark under *Keep*. On the right, you see the *Keep All* button, which specifies that all variables be kept, as well as the *Drop All* button, which specifies that all variables be dropped. Using the *Drop All* button is useful when selecting only a small number of variables to keep in your final saved data set, as you can first click this button, dropping all variables, then one by one select only the variables that you want to keep in your final data set, saving time.

In the dialog box below, I have deselected three variables simply by clicking on their respective checkmarks:

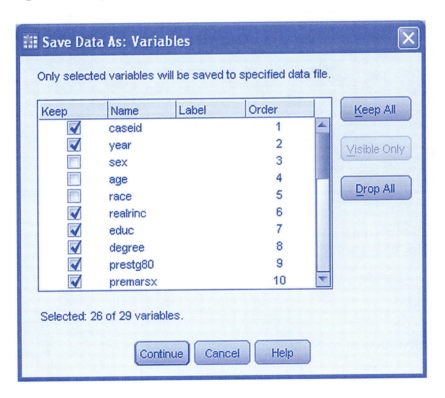

Next, I will click continue, getting the following dialog box:

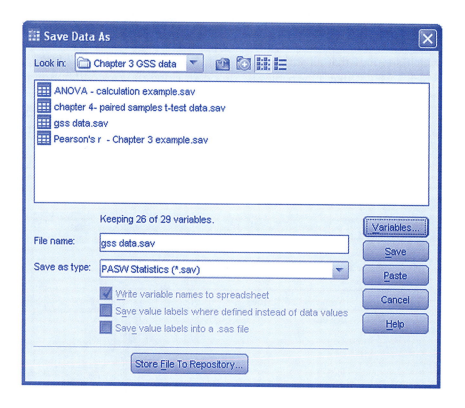

As you can see, IBM SPSS now indicates that we are keeping 26 of 29 variables, dropping three. Clicking *Save* will save this data set.

△   SECTION 3: STATA

Introduction to Stata

In this section, I'll introduce you to Stata. You can find more information about Stata and how to purchase it by navigating to the following Web site: www.stata.com

Below is a screenshot of what you'll see when you open Stata.

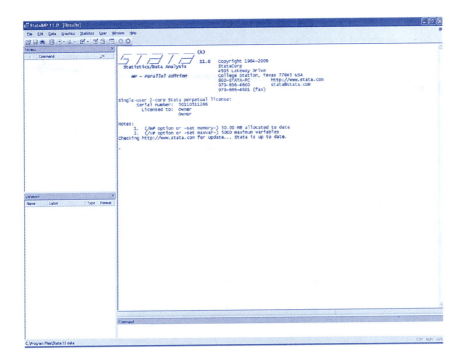

Stata, along with IBM SPSS, is one of the most popular general-purpose statistical software packages. Just like in IBM SPSS, there is a menu bar on top. Also, just as in IBM SPSS, you can do analyses through the menus or by using syntax. However, Stata syntax is different from IBM SPSS syntax, as you will see. The main window, which has a black background, is the window in which all your results will be shown. When using syntax, you also have the option of saving all your results to a log file. The bottom *Command* window is the window in which you will type your commands. In this case, your commands will be the same commands as you will use when writing syntax. For example, if you type gen age=0 in the command window and hit enter, a new variable will be created (gen stands for generate) called age, which will be set equal to 0 initially for all your cases.

The *Variables* window will contain a list of all the variables in your data set. Because we just opened Stata, and no data set is loaded, this window is empty. Finally, you see a *Review* window in the upper-left-hand corner. If you type a command in the *Command* window and hit enter, that command will automatically be copied into the *Review* window. This is simply for convenience, as you'll be able to click on that command within the review window and have it appear in the command window. This is useful in case you want to make a slight alteration to a previously entered command or if you have made a typographical error and want to correct it and run the command again. For example, this is what you will see after you type `gen age=0` into the command window and hit enter:

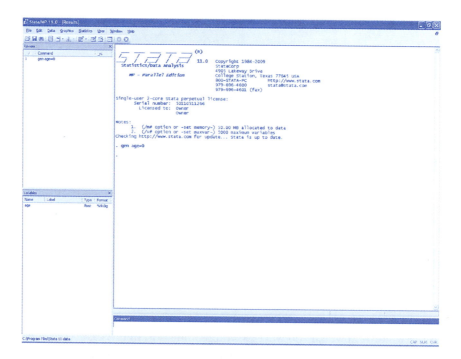

First, you can see that the command was copied into the *Review* window. Second, you see that there is a new variable, age, in the *Variables* window. Finally, you can see in the main *Results* window that this command has been executed. Also, because there is no error message in the main window, you also know that this command was executed correctly.

Finally, I'll show you Stata's version of the data window (data view) from IBM SPSS. To get to this window, you need to type `edit` or simply `ed` in the command window and hit enter. When you do that, this is what you'll see:

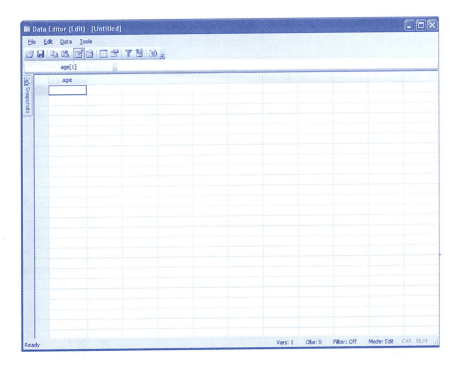

Here, you can see that there is only one variable, *age*. This is the window that you would see if you were to use Stata to enter data. To save your changes, simply close out the data editor window.

You may notice that while we had set age equal to 0 in our syntax, all the data **cells** for our new age variable are empty. This will be the case in situations like this where we have no cases. If, for example, we had entered results from a survey that was administered to 20 people, and then typed the command gen age=0, we would see values of "0" for our 20 cases.

Stata: Creating New Data Sets

Now, we will cover the procedure for creating a new data file in Stata. If there is a data file already open, make sure to save your work, then type clear in the command window, and hit enter. This will clear the loaded data file out of memory (after you type this command, you'll see the variable list in the *Variables* window disappear). Alternatively, if you simply go to open a new file while having one already open, Stata will prompt you on what to do if you have made changes to the data that you have not already saved. At this point, you would begin creating new variables as necessary (this was covered in the previous section) and then just type `edit` or `ed` in the command window and hit enter to start entering data for your new variables. As a note, as you gain more experience using Stata, you will find that Stata incorporates many abbreviations for syntax commands. For example, here, we can simply type `ed` instead of `edit` to open the data editor. While it is not necessary to know them, they do save a bit of time in the long run.

Stata: Creating Variables

This section will explain how to create new variables in Stata. In both IBM SPSS and Stata, but especially in Stata, I'll try to focus on syntax as opposed to menu-driven methods of working with data and doing analyses. I say "especially in Stata" because in general, syntax is quicker and more efficient than using menus within Stata. While this may be true also in IBM SPSS, I feel that the IBM SPSS program is somewhat more menu-focused than syntax-focused and that IBM SPSS syntax tends to be considerably more lengthy and involved as compared with Stata syntax.

To create a new variable using the menus within Stata, click on *Data*, *Create or change data*, and finally *Create new variable*. This is shown in the following screenshot.

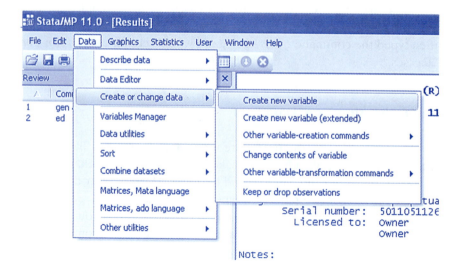

Next, the following box will pop up:

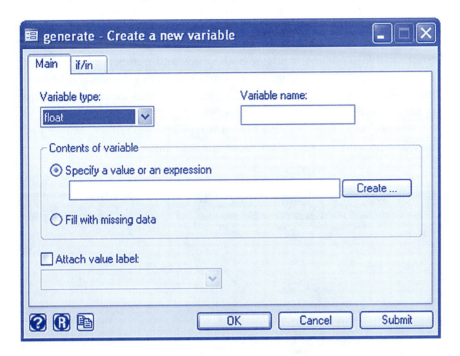

Next, all we need to do is specify the new variable name in the appropriate field and give it a value. As mentioned previously, I strongly recommend limiting variable names to eight characters or less, as earlier versions of IBM SPSS and some other programs, such as AMOS, limit variable names to eight characters or less. Even if you have a newer version of IBM SPSS, keeping this limitation in mind will help prevent future difficulties if you then go to analyze your data on another computer that has an older version of IBM SPSS, Stata, AMOS, and so on.

The data that we are going to enter can simply be specified as missing data initially, not giving it any specific value. Within Stata, you would enter a period (.) under the *Specify a value or an expression* option to do this, or simply select *Fill with missing data*. Then, as we enter data, we would enter the values from the results of our survey or what have you, replacing the periods (representing missing data) with our real data points. This will save some time as data points that are truly missing (i.e., the respondent refused to answer) can simply be left alone, kept as periods, which both IBM SPSS and Stata interpret as missing data. Furthermore, beginning with periods helps prevent errors during data entry, which would be more likely if you specified a new variable as having a value (e.g., if you specified age as equal to 50 initially, how would you differentiate whether the respondent was actually 50 or that this was simply the initial value you had assigned?).

We can leave the contents of *Variable type* alone as long as our new variable is numeric (contains numbers only). However, if our new variable is a string variable (contains words or both words and numbers), then we will want to change this field from *float* to *str* (*str* standing for string). As mentioned previously, we always want to give numeric values for any variable that we plan to analyze in any statistical analysis.

So if we were entering data from a survey and wanted to create a new variable representing political attitudes, our box might look like this:

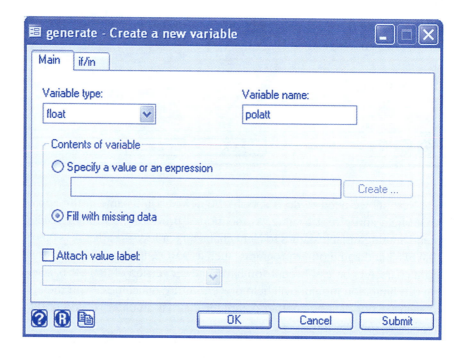

And then, if we pressed OK, we would see this in our results screen.

Because there is no error message, we know that this was done successfully. If we type *edit* in the command screen to open the data editor, we will get this as the result:

```
. generate polatt = .

.
```

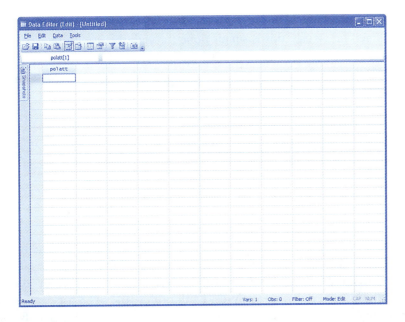

Again, we see no values because we have not specified any cases yet. If we had done this same sequence to a preexisting data set, for example, one that contained data on the sex and age of 10 respondents, we would see the following result, which shows that "polatt" was indeed defined as being equal to missing for all cases:

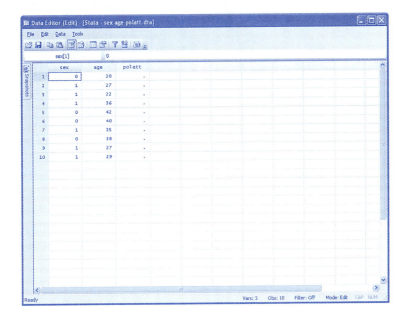

The second way to create a new variable within Stata is to use syntax. As mentioned previously, this is simply done through the use of the *gen* command. To create the same *polatt* variable using syntax, we would simply type this into the command window:

```
gen polatt=.
```

This would have exactly the same effect as creating a political attitudes variable through use of the menus.

Stata: Entering Data

Next, I will cover how to enter data within Stata. I have found through experience that IBM SPSS is more user-friendly in regard to data entry than Stata. While I prefer Stata over IBM SPSS for almost everything, especially for analyses, I still prefer IBM SPSS for data entry. Microsoft's program Excel, which is also quite user-friendly, can also be used for data entry. However, if you have data or enter data into Excel, it would have to be converted into an IBM SPSS or Stata file for analyses using StatTransfer. IBM SPSS is also superior to Excel in regard to creating and naming variables. Thus, I would recommend IBM SPSS for data entry.

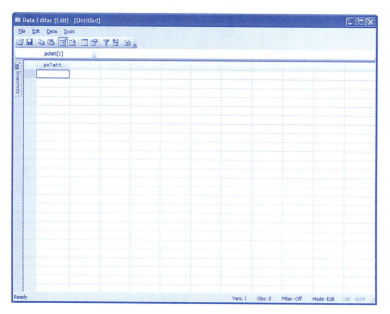

In this section, let us continue with the *polatt* example for simplicity's sake. So we have just opened Stata and have appropriately defined a new *polatt* variable. Next, we would type edit or ed in the command window and hit enter. Also, this could be achieved through the menu system by clicking on *Data, Data Editor, and Data Editor (Edit)*. Either method would lead you to the screen presented on the previous page.

As you can see, this is very similar to IBM SPSS's screen for data entry. From this point on, in regard to data entry, Stata works rather identically to IBM SPSS. When you have finished, closing out the data editor will automatically save your changes.

Stata: Recoding Data

In this section, I will cover recoding data within Stata. In Stata, it is easiest to simply use syntax to recode variables. In this section, I will present the Stata syntax version of the *age* recode example from the IBM SPSS section on recoding data. First, we will want to create a new variable called *age2* so that we're not modifying our original variables. To do this, we will type the following syntax:

```
gen age2=age
```

Here, we have created a new variable called *age2* that is identical to the original *age* variable. Next, we will want to recode this new *age2* variable. Following from the original example, individuals under the age of 30 were recoded as 0, and individuals aged 30 or older were recoded as 1. This would require the following syntax:

```
recode age2 0/29=0 30/150=1
```

Here, the slashes specify a range of values. For example, the term 0/29 means all values from 0 through 29. This syntax would be similar if you wanted to change one specific value to something else. For example, say that in the original data set, individuals with missing data were coded as "500." If you wanted to change this to something more typical, such as "999," we would use the following syntax:

```
recode age2 500=999
```

Stata: Selecting Cases

In Stata, it is easiest to simply specify which cases to include in your syntax command if you wish to include only certain cases in your analysis.

For example, if you are conducting an ANOVA (which will be discussed in a later chapter) on education and race, but only wanted to run it on cases from the year 2004, you could use the following command:

```
oneway educ race if year==2004
```

Make sure to include two equals signs. This is a Stata particularity, and you'll generally need to include two equals signs in your syntax instead of just one. We could include a similar command in most of the analyses that can be run within Stata. For example, if we had included the term if age>30 in the syntax for a **regression**, only cases in which the individual's age was greater than 30 would be included in the analysis. All the following syntax commands are possible within Stata:

```
regress income age gender if age >30
```

In this regression analysis, which is covered later in this book, the variables *age* and *gender* are used to predict income. Only cases in which the age of the respondent is greater than 30 are included in this analysis.

```
regress income age gender if age <30
```

In this analysis, only cases in which the age of the respondent is less than 30 are included.

```
regress income age gender if age >=30
```

In this analysis, only cases in which the age of the respondent is greater than or equal to 30 are included.

```
regress income age gender if age <=30
```

In this analysis, only cases in which the age of the respondent is less than or equal to 30 are included.

```
regress income age gender if age !=30
```

In this analysis, only cases in which the age of the respondent is not equal to 30 are included.

Stata: Saving Data Sets

The process of saving data sets within Stata is similar to the process used in IBM SPSS. After working on a new data set, or to save the file that you are currently working on under a new name, select *File* and *Save As . . .* , as shown here:

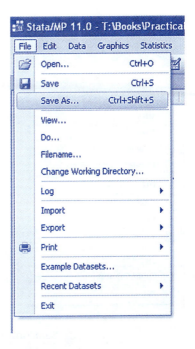

Making this selection will present the following dialog box:

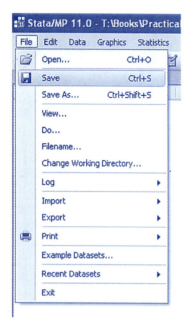

Here, just as within IBM SPSS, you will simply specify the directory in which to save the file as well as the filename. Then, clicking *Save* will save your file.

Once again, if you are saving a preexisting data set in which you perhaps added some cases and wanted to save over it with the identical filename, you could select *File* and *Save*, as shown below:

Just like in IBM SPSS, selecting this option will allow you to save over your current data set with whatever changes you have made. Unlike IBM SPSS, Stata will first present you with a prompt:

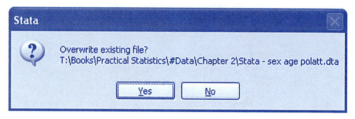

Selecting *OK* will overwrite your existing file of any changes that you have made.

Just like in IBM SPSS, Stata allows you the option of only selecting certain variables to keep in your saved data set. First, I would suggest that you save your current data set under a different name in case you need some of the variables that you are deleting in the future. Next, you can use the `keep` and `drop` commands to specify what variables to keep in your saved data set. The `keep` command tells Stata to only keep certain variables. This is more efficient if you only want to keep a small number of variables in your final, saved data set. The `drop` command tells Stata to drop certain variables, and is more efficient in situations where you want to keep the majority of your variables in your saved data set, only dropping a few.

Say, for example, you want to drop the politically oriented variables from a data set. In this example, I will use the data set that you'll be able to download if you follow the directions in the following chapter. In this data set, the two politically oriented variables are *partyid* and *polviews*, which measure the respondents' political party affiliation and degree of liberalism/conservatism, respectively. To drop only these two variables, after saving your file under a different name, type the following command in the *Command* window of Stata like this:

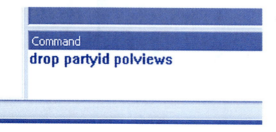

Next, hitting enter will give you the following result:

As you can see, your command has disappeared from the *Command* window and is now displayed in the *Results* window. As no error message has been presented, your command dropping those two variables was run successfully. If you check your variables window, as shown below, you will see that these two variables are no longer present:

. **drop partyid polviews**

.

Variables			✕
Name	Label	Type	Format
caseid		long	%12...
year		int	%8.0g
sex		byte	%8.0g
age		byte	%8.0g
race		byte	%8.0g
realrinc		long	%12...
educ		byte	%8.0g
degree		byte	%8.0g
prestg80		byte	%8.0g
premarsx		byte	%8.0g
hlth5		byte	%8.0g
drink		byte	%8.0g
immunemp		byte	%8.0g
letin		byte	%8.0g
relig	religion	byte	%8.0g
attend		byte	%8.0g
god		byte	%8.0g
zodiac		byte	%8.0g
waterfam		byte	%8.0g
xnorcsiz		byte	%8.0g
region		byte	%8.0g
abany		byte	%8.0g
antirel		byte	%8.0g
closebk		byte	%8.0g
partyidr	recode party id	byte	%8.0g
female		float	%9.0g

C:\Program Files\Stata 11 data

Now, beginning with the original data set, say that you only wanted to keep these two variables in your final, saved data set. First, you would type the following command:

Command
keep partyid polviews

`. keep partyid polviews`

`.`

Next, hitting enter will give you the following result:

You can see, the command has been run successfully both through the fact that no error message was presented as well as by looking at the variables window, which is displayed below:

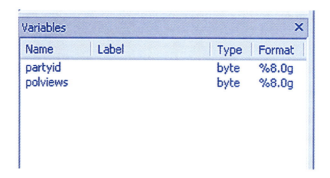

As you can see, now only these two variables remain in your data set.

After removing unneeded variables by using the drop or keep commands, you'll select *File* and *Save* to save over your current file. I suggest when dropping variables in Stata to first save your file under a new filename, then dropping your variables, then saving over this new file as opposed to first dropping your variables then saving under a new filename, as when using this latter technique, it is fairly easy to accidentally save over your original file with this new version that omits certain variables.

△   SECTION 4: STAT/TRANSFER

Transferring Data Sets Between
IBM SPSS, Stata, Excel, and Others

It is important to remember that you cannot simply save a data file in IBM SPSS or Stata and open it in a different data analysis program (typically). The program that I always use to transfer data files, especially between IBM SPSS, Stata, and Excel, is called **Stat/Transfer**. Honestly not plugging the program, Stat/Transfer makes it very simple and easy to transfer data sets between these different data file formats. When Stat/Transfer is opened, you will see the following screen:

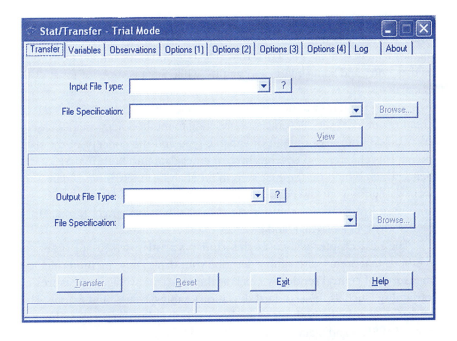

Here, all you need to do is specify the input file type and the file itself. For example, if you are transferring a Stata data file into an IBM SPSS data file, you simply select "Stata" under *Input File Type*. Next, you click on *Browse* under *File Specification* (right under *Input File Type*) and locate and select your data file. Then, you would select "SPSS for Windows" under *Output File Type*. Then you can *Browse* for the location in which Stat/Transfer will create and place your file. When clicking *Browse* this second time, you will also specify a filename for your output file. Finally, you'll click on *Transfer*, and Stat/Transfer will perform the conversion and create a new data file, placing it in the folder and giving it the name you specified. Viola! All done.

SECTION 5: SUMMARY ▲

This chapter served to introduce the reader to two very popular, general-purpose statistical software packages: IBM SPSS and Stata. You will most likely find yourself relying on these two programs when conducting the majority of your statistical analyses. When conducting analyses using these programs, you can choose to use either the menu system or syntax, which are written commands similar to computer code. While it takes longer to learn initially, you'll find that using syntax saves much time in the long run as it takes much less time to make minor modifications to analyses you have already run. In general, I feel that IBM SPSS is superior for simpler tasks such as data entry and some charts and graphs, while Stata is superior for statistical analyses. After discussing both of these programs, I introduce the reader by showing them how to do simple tasks in both IBM SPSS and Stata such as creating new data sets. Several issues relating to methodology are discussed, such as level of measurement or variable type and the concept of the data point. This chapter also covered how to enter data into both IBM SPSS and Stata, which would be the first step in an analysis in situations where you were gathering your own data. Finally, Stat/Transfer is discussed, which is a very useful program for transferring data sets between Excel format, IBM SPSS format, Stata format, and a variety of other formats.

The next chapter will cover **descriptive statistics**, which are statistical methods that are used to simply describe your data. These methods include **measures of central tendency** (such as the mean, or average), **measures of variability** (such as the **standard deviation**), **tables**, charts, and graphs. The chapter will describe both these methods as well as how to perform them in both IBM SPSS and Stata.

RESOURCES

You can find more information about IBM SPSS and how to purchase it by navigating to the following Web site: www.spss.com/software/statistics/

You can find more information about Stata and how to purchase it by navigating to the following Web site: www.stata.com

This book's Web site can be found at the following location: www.sagepub .com/kremelstudy

CHAPTER 3

DESCRIPTIVE STATISTICS

OUTLINE OF CHAPTER

◬　SECTION 1: INTRODUCTION AND THEORETICAL BACKGROUND

Introduction

In this chapter, I will show you how to perform what are called **descriptive statistics**. Descriptive statistics are statistical methods that are used to simply describe your data. Here, you will not be testing hypotheses in regard to the relationship or lack of relationship between two or more variables. Those methods will be covered in later chapters; they are called **inferential statistics**. Descriptive statistics include the following:

- *Measures of central tendency:* These measures attempt to get at the "middle" or "average" score. In statistics, the most common measures of central tendency used are the **mean**, **median**, and **mode**.
- *Measures of variability:* These measures show the degree of variability or range within your data. The most common measures of variability are the **range**, **standard deviation**, and **variance**. I will also cover the **interquartile range**.
- *Tables:* Tables are used to summarize your data by category. For example, with level of education, if measured by highest degree achieved, your table may list the different **response categories** (e.g., no degree, high school diploma, bachelor's degree, master's degree, PhD/MD/JD) and then list the number of people within that category and/or the percent of people in that category. As another example, if level of education was measured in years, you may choose to come up with the following categories for your table: less than 12 years, 12 to 16 years, and more than 16 years. Then you would list the number of people within those categories and/or the percent of people within those categories.
- *Charts and graphs:* Charts and graphs can also be used to summarize data. For graphs, you may choose to simply summarize data on one particular variable just as you would with a table. For example, you can use a **bar chart** to illustrate level of education, based on the groupings we gave in the previous paragraph. Other graphs, such as **pie charts**, can also be used. Graphs can also be used to illustrate the relationship between two variables. Since you would not be performing a statistical test, this would still be considered descriptive statistics. In this case, you may choose to graph one variable along the ***x*-axis** and another variable along the ***y*-axis** to see if they have a relationship pictorially. Also, you can chart one variable along the *y*-axis and *time* along the *x*-axis to see trends over time. If you do not understand this terminology (*x-axis*, *y-axis*, *bar charts*, *pie charts*, etc.) don't worry, as I will explain all of them within this chapter.

This chapter and the next few chapters will consist of three main parts. The first will be a short introduction to that particular method or statistical test. The second part will consist of a short theoretical background to that test. Because the focus of this book is on practical statistics, the second section will not be particularly lengthy. Furthermore, if you are not mathematically inclined, or are not particularly interested in knowing the mathematical backgrounds to these tests, you are free to skip these sections. Also, I will focus on these theoretical/mathematical sections mainly for the more simple statistical tests, in which these mathematical backgrounds will be more useful. This is due to the fact that the mathematical bases for more advanced tests (regression onward) become more complex and difficult to understand and thus are less helpful to focus on as a method to expand your understanding of a particular test. The third part of each section will focus on the practical use of these methods or tests. This third part will be divided into two: an IBM SPSS section and a Stata section, with each of these two sections being divided into a section focused on syntax and a section focused on menu-driven analyses. Depending on the particular test and software package, I may focus more highly on syntax or the menus or even totally omit one of the two, depending on the practicality.

Measures of Central Tendency:
Mean—Introduction and Mathematical Background

Measures of central tendency attempt to get at the "middle" or "average" score. In this section, we will cover mean, median, and mode. We will also start using actual data sets in our examples. When someone speaks of an "average," they are typically referring to the mean. To calculate the mean, you simply add up all the scores and divide that sum by the total number of scores.

This is the equation for the mean:

$$\bar{x} = \frac{1}{n} \sum_{i=1}^{n} x_i = \frac{1}{n}(x_1 + \cdots + x_n)$$

Let me explain this equation step by step. First, the x with the bar over it is just a mathematical symbol that stands for the mean of a sample. You may also see the symbol μ (mu), which stands for the mean of a population. As it is typically impossible to have data on an entire population, our data sets will typically comprise a sample, or subset of the population. The second and third terms are both equations for calculating the mean. Let's start with the third, which is more simple:

$$\bar{x} = \frac{1}{n}(x_1 + \cdots + x_n)$$

First, we can see that the mean (what I will refer to as *x bar*) is equal to the equation on the right. First, we have $1/n$. Here, n is equal to the number of total cases. For example, if we had five people with intelligence quotients (IQs) of 92, 98, 103, 115, and 130, our n would be 5. In the parentheses we have a sum, starting with x_1 and ending with x_n. This just means that we add up all the values from the first to the last. In this IQ example, this just means to add the first through the fifth scores. This would be

$$92 + 98 + 103 + 115 + 130 = 538$$

This is what we would get for the mean:

$$\bar{x} = \frac{1}{5}(92 + 98 + 103 + 115 + 130) = \frac{1}{5}(538) = 107.6$$

In this example, our mean is an IQ of 107.6.

Now, to tackle the part of the equation with the giant "*E*":

$$\bar{x} = \frac{1}{n}\sum_{i=1}^{n} x_i$$

First, we begin with $1/n$, which again is simply one divided by the total number of cases. The big "*E*" symbol is called a *summation*, meaning that it represents a sum. The actual name of the symbol is *sigma*, which is a Greek letter. In this case, the summation stands for the sum of x_i, from $i = 1$ to $i = n$. So, just as before, this means that we add up all of our scores from the first through the last. The mean would be calculated in the same way, by multiplying $1/n$ by the sum of our scores. Of course, this is equivalent to simply adding up all our scores and then dividing by n.

Measures of Central Tendency: Median—Introduction and Mathematical Background

Median is another measure of central tendency. Median, along with mode, is sometimes preferred to the mean, as these measures are not as influenced by **outliers**. Outliers are scores that are very high or very low as compared with the average. For example, if you had a group of 10 students, 9 of whom had IQ scores between 90 and 110, and one individual who had an IQ of 175, the inclusion of this one individual's score would greatly inflate the mean. However, this one outlier would not influence median or mode. In this way, median and mode are sometimes preferred as measures of central tendency as compared with the mean.

The median is simply the middle score. Let's continue with this example of 10 IQ scores. To calculate the median by hand, we would first arrange the scores in numerical order, from lowest to highest. For example,

81, 83, 89, 97, 101, 107, 115, 119, 175

Next, we would calculate the median by simply choosing the middle score. As you can see, as we have an even number of scores, there is no one middle score. When we have an even number of cases such as this, we simply average (take the mean of) the two middle scores to arrive at the median. In this case, the two middle scores are 101 and 107. The mean of these two scores is 104, which would be the median of this group of scores.

If we had an odd number of scores, as in this example,

76, 83, 97, 115, 146,

the median would simply be the middle score. In this case, the middle score and median is 97.

Measures of Central Tendency:
Mode—Introduction and Mathematical Background

As mentioned previously, mode, along with median, is sometimes preferred to the mean as a measure of central tendency due to the fact that it is less influenced by outliers. Mode is simply the most common score. Take this example:

79, 86, 93, 93, 93, 97, 101, 105, 105, 109, 113, 127

The mode would be 93, as it is the most common score. In this example, there are three individuals who have an IQ of 93, two individuals who have an IQ of 105, with every other score only being held by one individual. Therefore, the most common score and mode would be 93. If there were two or more different values, all of which were the most common, you would list all of them as modes. For example, if your scores were 93, 107, 107, 111, and 111, you would list both 107 and 111 as your modes.

Measures of Variability: Mathematical Background

Measures of variability show the degree of variability or range within your data. The most common measures of variability are the range, standard deviation, and variance. In this section, I will also cover the interquartile range.

Range is the most simple measure of variability. Range simply is the difference between your highest score and your lowest score. Let's say we were looking at the age of respondents, with the youngest respondents being 18 years of age, and the oldest respondents 89 years of age. As you can see from the definition, the equation for range is simply this:

$$\text{Range} = \text{Highest score} - \text{Lowest score}$$

So in this case, this would be our range:

$$\text{Range} = 89 - 18 = 71$$

Both variance and standard deviation measure the amount of dispersion in your data. If your data tend to be very highly clustered around the mean, you'll get a low value for both the variance and standard deviation. However, if your data have a lot of dispersion (they are not clustered around the mean), you'll get high values for both the variance and standard deviation. This is the equation for variance:

$$s^2 = \frac{\sum_{i=1}^{n} \left(x_i - \bar{x} \right)^2}{n - 1}$$

To calculate the variance by hand, you'll subtract the mean from each individual score to obtain a difference. These differences will all be squared, and they will all be summed together (the sigma [Σ] symbol from before). Then, this sum will be divided by $n - 1$, your total number of cases minus one. In reality, we would use a program such as IBM SPSS or Stata to calculate the variance. However, knowing the equation and how it is calculated will give you a better understanding of the concept. As a note, when reading some texts, you may encounter the symbol σ^2 when reading about variance. This symbol, σ^2, refers to the variance of a population, while s^2 refers to the variance of a sample.

Here's an example of the calculation:

For example, pretend we have five IQ scores: 86, 89, 94, 115, and 132.

First, we need to calculate the mean. This would be,

$$\bar{x} = \frac{1}{n}\sum_{i=1}^{n}x_i = \frac{1}{n}(x_1 + \cdots + x_n) = \frac{1}{5}(86 + 89 + 94 + 115 + 132)$$

$$= \frac{1}{5}(516) = 103.2$$

And our variance would be

$$s^2 = \frac{\sum_{i=1}^{n}(x_i - \bar{x})^2}{n-1}$$

$$= \frac{(86 - 103.2)^2 + (89 - 103.2)^2 + (94 - 103.2)^2 + (115 - 103.2)^2 + (132 - 103.2)^2}{5-1}$$

$$= \frac{295.84 + 201.64 + 84.64 + 139.24 + 829.44}{4} = \frac{1550.8}{4} = 387.7$$

Standard deviation is another measure of variability that measures the amount of dispersion within your data, and it is easier to work with compared with the variance, as values for the variance tend to be very high. Standard deviation is simply the square root of the variance. It is computed as follows:

$$s = \sqrt{\frac{\sum_{i=1}^{n}(x_i - \bar{x})^2}{n-1}}$$

One may find it easiest to first simply calculate the variance using the equation at the top of the page and then simply take the square root of this value to obtain the standard deviation.

To continue our example,

$$s = \sqrt{\frac{\sum_{i=1}^{n}(x_i - \bar{x})^2}{n-1}} = \sqrt{387.7} = 19.69$$

Standard deviation is not quite the average distance between your data and the mean, but it does measure this concept. Here, when referring to the standard deviation, I am using the symbol s, which refers to the sample standard deviation. The population standard deviation is symbolized by σ.

Take our IQ example. IQ tests are set up specifically so that the standard deviation equals 15 points, and the mean, of course, is 100 points. It is important to keep in mind that both variance and standard deviation talk about how dispersed your data are, or how clustered they are, in a general way. In this IQ example, there are of course individuals who have average IQs of 100, individuals who have IQs less than one standard deviation away from the mean (i.e., greater than 85 and less than 115), as well as individuals who have IQs greater than one standard deviation away from the mean (i.e., lower than 85 or greater than 115).

Finally, I will discuss the interquartile range. Calculating the interquartile range is similar to calculating the range, but instead of using the highest and lowest points in your calculation, you'll use the 25th percentile and the 75th percentile. The interquartile range is also called the *middle fifty*, as it gives you the range for this middle 50% of scores. While calculating the interquartile range would be difficult to do by hand, it would be very simple to do using IBM SPSS or Stata. However, I will give a quick example here just so you can see how it would be done.

The equation would be as follows:

Interquartile range = 75th percentile score – 25th percentile score

Say we had these scores: 12, 15, 18, 22, 34, 37, 39, 44, 47, 55, 57.
We would first order them in this way, from lowest to highest:

12

15

18: 25th percentile

22

34

37: 50th percentile

39

44

47: 75th percentile

55

57

We can see that the 50th percentile, or the median, is 37. The 25th percentile (the score halfway between the median and the lowest score) is 18. The 75th percentile (the score halfway between the median and the highest score) is 47. So, plugging these values into our equation,

Interquartile range = 75th percentile
score – 25th percentile score = 47 – 18 = 29

Tables: Introduction

Tables show you the number of respondents or cases in each response category of a variable. Typically, tables are only used for **categorical variables**, but they can also be used for continuous variables. When making a table for a continuous variable that has a large number of response categories (such as age), it is typical for researchers to first come up with a number of categories (e.g., under 18, 18 to 30, 31 to 40, etc.), and to construct the table with these new categories. Tables, graphs, and charts are all used simply to summarize and illustrate data, not to test statistical relationships between variables.

Charts and Graphs: Introduction

Charts and graphs, along with tables, are useful in illustrating and displaying your data in an easy-to-read format. Just as with tables, when making charts or graphs of continuous variables, you may find it more useful to first recode these variables into a number of discrete categories instead of leaving them as continuous.

There are many different types of charts and graphs, and you may wish to experiment with other types that are not included in this book in IBM SPSS or Stata in the future. In this chapter, we will cover bar charts and **histograms**, **pie charts**, **line graphs**, and **scatter plots**. With line graphs and scatter plots, I will show you how to make charts comparing two different variables. I will also illustrate how to show the change in one variable over time using a line graph.

The only real difference between bar charts and histograms is that bar charts are used for categorical variables and histograms are used for continuous variables. The main difference you'll find is that bar charts have spaces between each bar while histograms do not. In both of these types of charts, the height of the bar corresponds to the number or percentage of cases within that category. This allows you to compare the frequencies of cases that reside within each category. Pie charts are similar to bar charts and histograms in that they also allow you to compare a number or percentage of cases that reside within each response category. Line graphs may also be used to show the average of one variable over the change in another variable or to show the change in the average score over time, as with scatter plots. The difference between scatter plots and line graphs is that while line graphs typically use the average score in the graph, scatter plots mark each individual data point with a symbol, such as a "+."

△ SECTION 2: IBM SPSS

Measures of Central Tendency:
Mean, Median, and Mode—IBM SPSS

As mean, median, and mode are all contained within the same dialog box within IBM SPSS, they will all be covered within this one section. I will try to make it a habit to first cover the use of the menus, followed by the use of syntax. Starting in this section, I will make use of actual data sets in our examples. Here, I will use data from the General Social Survey (GSS). The GSS is a very large, biannual survey that covers a very large multitude of topics. It is representative of nonincarcerated, nonhomeless American adults. Data from the GSS are free and available to the public. Currently, you can access data from the GSS on this Web site: http://gss.norc.org/.

To obtain the data set, you can also go to the following Web site, which allows you to download a selected subset of variables from the GSS: http://sda.berkeley.edu/cgi-bin/hsda?harcsda+gss04.

After going to this Web site, scroll your mouse over to "download" and click on "customized subset." Under "Enter names of individual variables (original or created) to include," you can enter

year sex age race realrinc educ degree prestg80 premarsx hlth5 drink partyid polviews immunemp letin relig attend god zodiac waterfam xnorcsiz region abany antirel closeblk

to get the identical data set to the one I will be using. You can look up what each of these variable names refer to (including the particular question asked on the survey as well as the different response categories) by going to the following Web site, which contains the GSS codebook: www.norc.org/GSS+Website/Browse+GSS+Variables/.

You will find that it is much easier to use a data set that only includes the variables you need from the GSS as opposed to the full data set, which is extremely large and unwieldy.

Let's find the mean, median, and mode for age. Keep in mind that right now, our data set contains data for the years 1972 (the first year of the GSS) through 2004. For now, we will use the full data set in our example, which will include all respondents from 1972 through 2004. However, in some later analyses, we will choose to select only one year or a subset of years.

To find the mean, median, and mode in IBM SPSS using the menus, click on *Analyze*, *Descriptive Statistics*, and *Frequencies*, like the following:

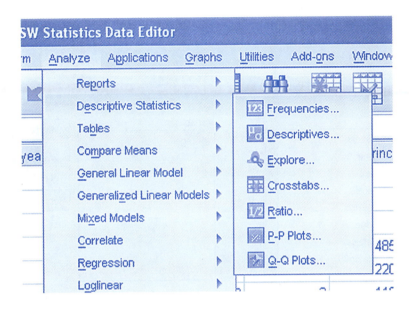

At this point, you will see the following dialog box:

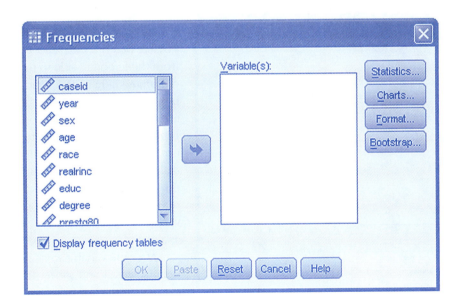

Next, you'll select the variable from the list on the left that you want to include. In this example, we will find the mean, median, and mode of age. To do this, we first select *age* from the list on the left-hand side of dialog box and then click on the arrow pointing to the right. If you have done this, your screen should look like this:

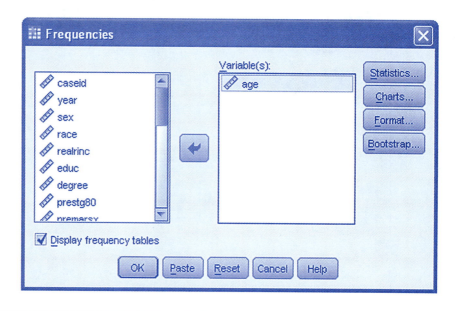

As you can see, the variable *age* has been moved from the left-hand side to the right-hand side of the dialog box. Also, we see that the arrow has reversed direction. Highlighting a variable that is on the right-hand side of the dialog box and then clicking on the arrow again will remove it from the list of variables included in the analysis.

After the variable *age* has been selected and moved to the right-hand side of the dialog box, you'll click on *Statistics*. Doing this will reveal the following dialog box:

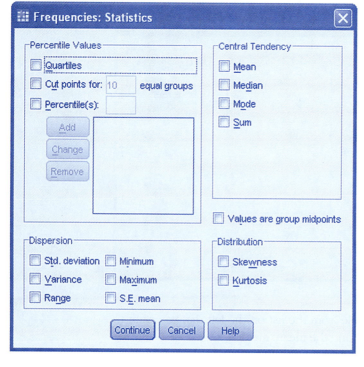

This dialog box will come up later when we get into the topics of standard deviation and variance. However, for now, we will simply select *Mean*, *Median*, and *Mode*, which are located within the *Central Tendency* box in the upper-right-hand corner of the dialog box. After you have selected these (you will see small check marks in their boxes), click on *Continue*, and then click *OK*. Clicking *OK* will run the analysis.

After the analysis has been run, you will see IBM SPSS's output. It will look like this:

➡ Frequencies

[DataSet9] T:\Books\Practical Statistics\#Data\Chapter 3 GSS data\gss data.sav

Statistics

age

N	Valid	46344
	Missing	166
Mean		45.26
Median		42.00
Mode		28

age

		Frequency	Percent	Valid Percent	Cumulative Percent
Valid	18	159	.3	.3	.3
	19	655	1.4	1.4	1.8
	20	697	1.5	1.5	3.3
	21	791	1.7	1.7	5.0
	22	821	1.8	1.8	6.7
	23	962	2.1	2.1	8.8
	24	956	2.1	2.1	10.9
	25	1052	2.3	2.3	13.1
	26	1034	2.2	2.2	15.4
	27	1056	2.3	2.3	17.7
	28	1123	2.4	2.4	20.1
	29	994	2.1	2.1	22.2
	30	1091	2.3	2.4	24.6

Finally, here are our results for mean, median, and mode. As you can see, the mean, or average score, for age is 45.26 years. Our median age, or middle score, is 42 years. The mode, or most common age, is 28. You also see two numbers under *Valid* and *Missing*. Under *Missing*, we have 166, which represents the fact that in our data set, we have 166 cases with missing data for age. *Valid* refers to cases in which we have actual data (not missing data), and in this case, we have 46,344 valid cases, or cases with actual data.

Following this table, we see another table labeled "age." The leftmost column contains individual response categories. In this case, for age, response categories go from 18 (representing 18 years of age) through 89. Next to the response categories, we first see a *Frequency* column. This column represents the number of individuals who fell into that particular response category. For example, we have 159 individuals who are aged 18 years. Next to this column is the *Percent* column. This column represents the percentage of individuals falling into that particular response category. In this example, 0.3% of all individuals are aged 18 years. Next to this column is the *Valid Percent* column. This calculates the percentage of respondents falling into that category but does not include cases with missing data in the total number of cases. Finally, *Cumulative Percent* represents the percentage of the total of all the response categories up to that point. So, for example, 1.8% of all individuals are aged either 18 or 19 years. A total of 10.9% of all individuals are between the ages of 18 and 24.

If we wanted to omit this table from our results, we would simply uncheck the *Display frequency tables* checkbox within the first dialog box:

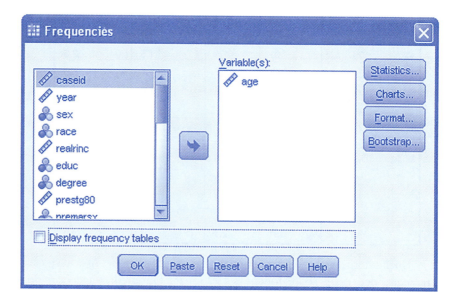

Now we do the same thing but with syntax. One trick within IBM SPSS is that if you ever click *Paste* within a dialog box, IBM SPSS will paste the equivalent syntax of whatever it was you were going to do into the IBM SPSS syntax editor. For example, look at the dialog box above. IBM SPSS will save the options you have chosen, so as we have selected only mean, median, and mode, they will continue to be the only options selected under *Statistics*. However, you can click on the *Statistics* button if you want to make sure. Also, you can see in the dialog box above that *Display frequency tables* has not been selected. Therefore, our output will only give us the mean, median, and mode of *age*. Now, let's click *Paste*. Doing so will give you the following:

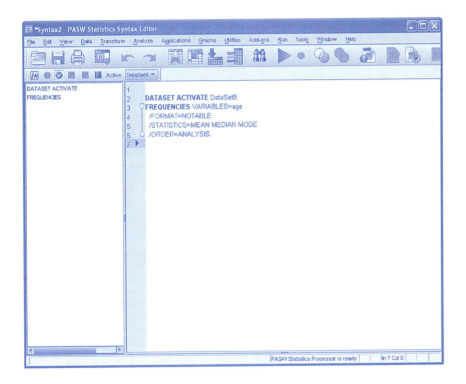

This syntax is the equivalent of using the menus in that running it will get you exactly the same output as you would've gotten if you had clicked *OK* in the previous dialog box. To illustrate, click on *Run* and then *All*. Doing so will give you the following output:

→ **Frequencies**

[DataSet9] T:\Books\Practical Statistics\#Data\Chapter 3 GSS data\gss data.sav

Statistics

age

N	Valid	46344
	Missing	166
Mean		45.26
Median		42.00
Mode		28

As you will probably notice, these results are exactly the same as the results we got when we did this analysis using the menus. Therefore, you can choose either to use the menus, or to use the syntax, whichever is more convenient or easier for you. While I stress the importance and value of becoming adept at writing Stata syntax, IBM SPSS is more suited for menu-driven use. Because of this, I will not focus strongly on the use of IBM SPSS syntax. However, it remains useful when you need to run slight modifications of descriptive or inferential statistics, as well as when you are running many instances of very similar tests (e.g., a large set of *t*-tests). In these cases, it will save time to get IBM SPSS to paste a copy of the syntax, then to modify it or copy/paste/edit it as necessary. It would also be a good idea to have a copy of the syntax of analyses that you run—especially important ones—so that you can refer to them later.

Measures of Variability: IBM SPSS (Menus)

Now I will show you how to run the four measures of variability within IBM SPSS using the menus. In these examples, I'll use the same data set from the GSS as used previously. However, I will use the respondent's income in these examples. In the GSS data file, this variable is called *realrinc*.

In IBM SPSS, range, variance, standard deviation, and interquartile range can all be found within the same menu, which is the same menu that we used when we calculated the mean, median, and mode. This menu can be found by clicking on *Analyze*, *Descriptive Statistics*, and *Frequencies*:

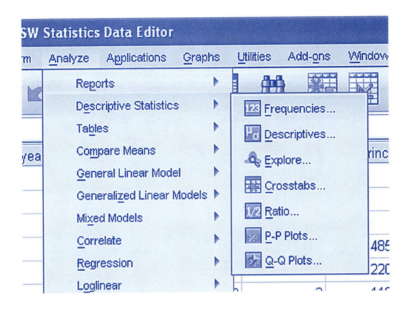

In the dialog box that pops up, we will first move *realrinc* to the right as we did before with *age* when calculating the mean, median, and mode:

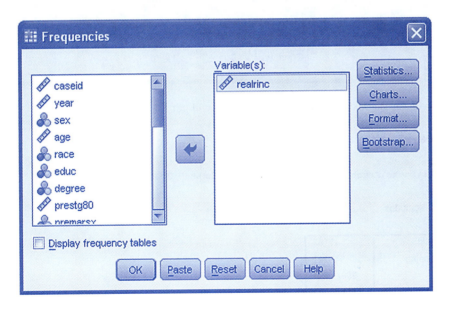

We can also uncheck the *Display frequency tables* checkbox, as we will not be needing this. If a warning pops up, you can simply ignore it. Next, we will click on *Statistics* and check *Quartiles* under *Percentile Values* and *Standard Deviation*, *Variance*, and *Range* under *Dispersion*:

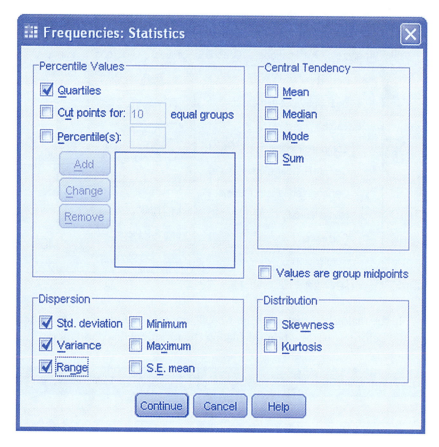

After clicking *Continue* and *OK*, we will get the following result:

➡ **Frequencies**

[DataSet1] T:\Books\Practical Statistics\#Data\Chapter 3 GSS data\gss data.sav

Statistics

realrinc

N	Valid	27163
	Missing	19347
Std. Deviation		20871.594
Variance		4.356E8
Range		201346
Percentiles	25	8156.00
	50	16363.00
	75	26538.00

As you can see, both our standard deviation and variance are very large. SPSS has calculated our variance to be 4.356E8, which stands for $4.356 * 10^8$, which is scientific notation. This means 4.356 times 10 to the eighth power, or 10 followed by eight zeros, or 4.356 * 100,000,000, or 435,600,000. Whenever you see numbers written in this fashion (2.3E5, 7.2E+9, etc.), they can always be interpreted in this way. Our standard deviation is 20871.594, or approximately $20,871.

Our range, the lowest score subtracted from the highest score, is 201,346. To get our interquartile range, we'll have to do a subtraction. We see that the 75th percentile is 26538.00, and the 25th percentile is 8156.00. To get our interquartile range, we simply subtract 8,156 from 26,538, obtaining 18,328, our interquartile range.

Measures of Variability: IBM SPSS (Syntax)

To obtain these measures of variability in IBM SPSS through use of syntax, I will cheat and use the *Paste* button in the dialog box to paste the syntax into the IBM SPSS syntax editor. Doing so gives the following:

```
FREQUENCIES VARIABLES=realrinc
/FORMAT=NOTABLE
/NTILES=4
/STATISTICS=STDDEV VARIANCE RANGE
/ORDER=ANALYSIS.
```

As you can see, the syntax is rather simple. The first line simply specifies that we are running frequencies and which variables we are running the frequencies on. The second line simply specifies to not include a table. The third line specifies four percentiles, which you will use in the calculation of the interquartile range. The fourth line specifies to include standard deviation, variance, and range as statistics in your table. The final line you can copy and paste into your syntax editor and leave alone. Make sure to include the period at the end of this command. Running this syntax from within the IBM SPSS syntax editor will give you exactly the same results as if you had done the same thing through the use of the menus.

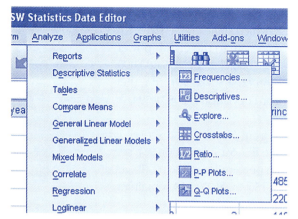

Tables: IBM SPSS

This section will cover how to make tables in IBM SPSS using both the menus and syntax. A good example of a variable that would be used unaltered in a table would be race, which is the example that we're going to use now. These examples, both for tables and graphs and charts, will use the same GSS data set as used previously.

To create a table, first click on *Analyze*, *Descriptive Statistics*, and *Frequencies:*

In the following dialog box, all you need to do is to move race to the right-hand side and make sure that *Display frequency tables* is checkmarked. Also, you can click on the *Statistics* button to make sure that nothing is selected:

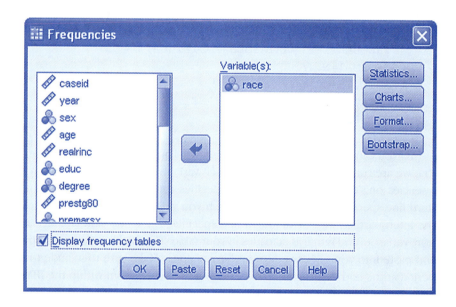

Clicking *OK* will give you the following result:

➜ Frequencies

[DataSet9] T:\Books\Practical Statistics\#Data\Chapter 3 GSS data\gss data.sav

Statistics

race

N	Valid	46510
	Missing	0

race

		Frequency	Percent	Valid Percent	Cumulative Percent
Valid	White	38480	82.7	82.7	82.7
	Black	6399	13.8	13.8	96.5
	Other	1631	3.5	3.5	100.0
	Total	46510	100.0	100.0	

Looking at the results, we can first see that we have 46,510 valid cases and 0 missing cases on the *race* variable. In the "race" table, we can see the different response categories followed by a "Total" row. We can see that 38,480 respondents, or 82.7% of all respondents, are white, and 6,399 respondents, or 13.8%, are black. Finally, 1,631 respondents, or 3.5% of all respondents, are members of other races. As you can see, as we have no missing cases, the *Valid Percent* column is identical to the *Percent* column. Also, the *Cumulative Percent* column sums the percentages of that category with every previous category. For whites, the percentage of whites (82.7%) in the cumulative percent column is the same as in the percent column, as it is the first response category. For blacks, the cumulative percent is 96.5% (82.7% plus 13.8%), and the cumulative percent for members of other races is 100% (82.7% plus 13.8% plus 3.5%).

Also, under the first column, we see that the different response categories are labeled (White, Black, and Other). If you may recall from before, this would be done by entering the different response categories under the *Values* column within the *Variable View* tab within IBM SPSS. If this was not done, instead of labels, we would have numerical values. For example, if you entered data from a questionnaire that you conducted in which you coded whites as 1, blacks as 2, and people of other races as 3 (as the GSS does), but neglected to add these labels into the *Values* column, you would see the following result:

➼ **Frequencies**

[DataSet9] T:\Books\Practical Statistics\#Data\Chapter 3 GSS data\gss data.sav

Statistics

race

N	Valid	46510
	Missing	0

race

		Frequency	Percent	Valid Percent	Cumulative Percent
Valid	1	38480	82.7	82.7	82.7
	2	6399	13.8	13.8	96.5
	3	1631	3.5	3.5	100.0
	Total	46510	100.0	100.0	

The results are identical to the previous table, but you do not have the response categories labeled in the first column under the "race" table. This is one of the reasons why it's a good idea to label response categories.

To get the IBM SPSS syntax for this same command, we can use the "paste" trick:

```
FREQUENCIES VARIABLES=RACE
        /ORDER=ANALYSIS.
```

Make sure to include the final period on the second line, otherwise IBM SPSS will give you an error.

Charts and Graphs: IBM SPSS

In this section, I will discuss how to make all different types of charts and graphs within IBM SPSS, using both the menus and the syntax. First, I will cover bar charts and histograms. As mentioned previously, bar charts are used for categorical variables, whereas histograms are used for continuous variables. Besides this minor distinction, both bar charts and histograms display the same sort of information: the number, or percentage, of cases falling within a certain category or range of scores.

Let's try a bar chart using religion as an example, from the same data set we have been using. Using the menus, select *Graphs*, *Legacy Dialogs*, and *Bar*:

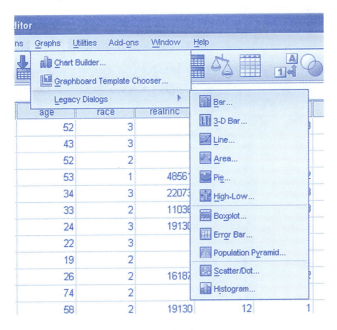

Next, you will see the following dialog box:

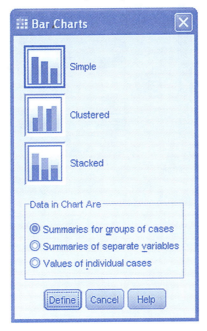

We can leave the default settings as they are: *Simple* and *Summaries for groups of cases*. *Summaries for groups of cases* means that you'll get separate bars for Protestants, Catholics, and so on.

Next, click *Define*. This will give you the following dialog box:

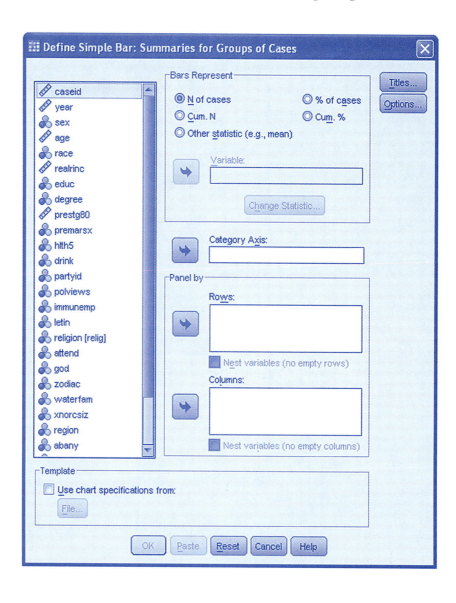

Here, we will allow the bars to represent the *N*, or number, of cases. You can also select percentage of cases. Click on *relig* followed by the arrow next to "Category Axis" to move this variable into the *Category Axis* box, like the following:

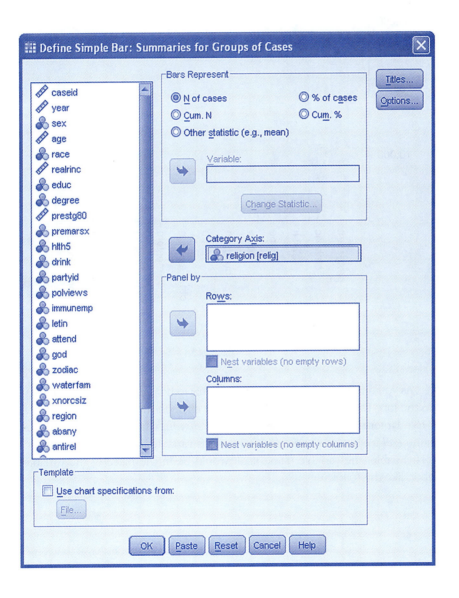

Next, click *OK*. This will give you the following output:

→ Graph

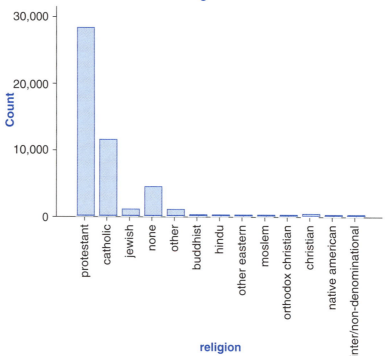

As you may notice, IBM SPSS does not have the prettiest graphs, but they do the job. The image will be clearer if you click on the graph and then drag it to a larger size. At the bottom, you see *religion*, which is not our variable name (*relig*), but the label I have given this variable. If you had not labeled this variable, the variable name itself would be in the place of the variable label, like the following:

➜ Graph

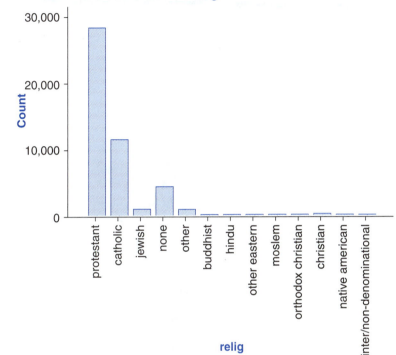

Under the bars, you can see the different religions represented. If these different religions were not associated with their numeric counterpart (i.e., if the response categories for religion were not labeled) under the *Values* column in the *Variable View* tab within IBM SPSS, you would instead simply see the numerical codings instead of the religious categories. The height of the bar represents the number of respondents within that category. Protestants are the largest group, with almost 30,000 respondents. Catholics are the second largest group, with a little more than 10,000 respondents.

Again using the "paste" cheat, this is the corresponding syntax for the bar chart:

```
GRAPH
/BAR(SIMPLE)=COUNT BY relig.
```

Income will be used in an example of a histogram. First, click on *Graphs*, *Legacy Dialogs*, and *Histogram*:

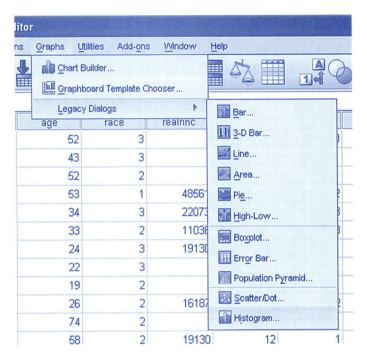

This will bring up the following dialog box:

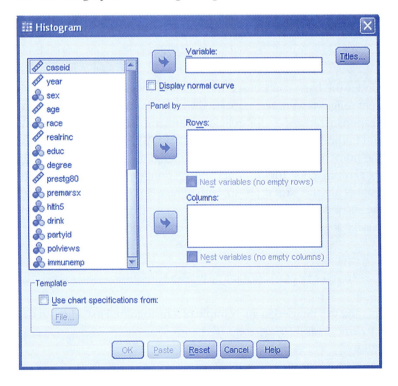

Next, simply move *realrinc* (the respondent's yearly income in dollars) into the *Variable* box:

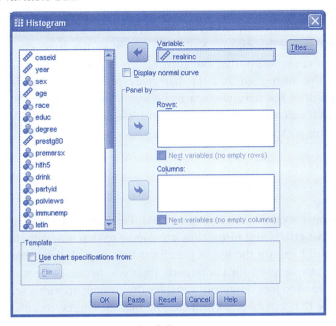

Next, click *OK*. You will see the following output:

→ Graph

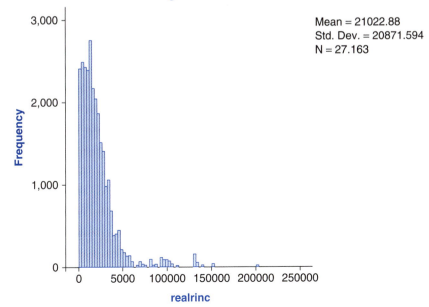

[DataSet9] T:\ Books \Practical Statistics\#Data\Chapter 3 GSS data\gss data.sav

With histograms, IBM SPSS automatically comes up with a number of categories for our variable, in this case, income. From the histogram, you can see that the majority of people have a low or middle-range income, with only a few outliers (cases with scores very much below or above the mean, in this case, high above the mean). Again, the height of the bars represents the number of cases within that category. Also notice that the only difference between this histogram and the bar chart presented earlier is that the histogram does not have any spaces between the bars, while the previous one—which was run on a categorical variable—did.

And this is the corresponding syntax:

```
GRAPH
/HISTOGRAM=realrinc.
```

This next section will cover pie charts. Pie charts are used in the same way that bar charts and histograms are used—to describe data. In this section, we will focus on the use of pie charts for categorical variables, though they also can be used for continuous variables, in the same way that histograms are used for continuous variables (by coming up with a series of categories for that variable). We will use the highest degree completed as the example in this section.

First, click on *Graphs*, *Legacy Dialogs*, and then *Pie*:

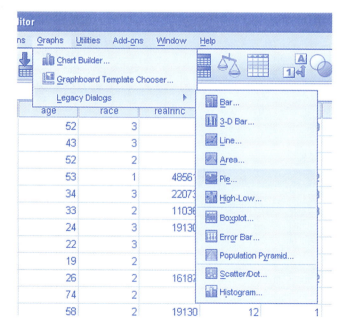

In the following dialog box, select *Summaries for groups of cases*; then click *Define*:

After clicking *Define*, you will see the dialog box shown below. Here, you only need to select the *degree* variable and move it into the *Define Slices by* box:

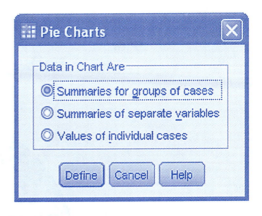

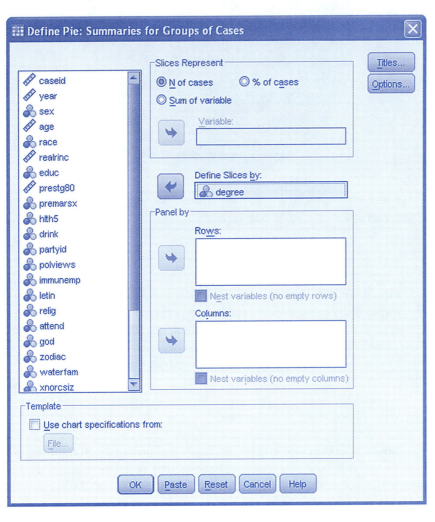

After clicking *OK*, you will see the following output:

➔ Graph

[DataSet9] T:\ Books \Practical Statistics\#Data\Chapter 3 GSS data\gss data.sav

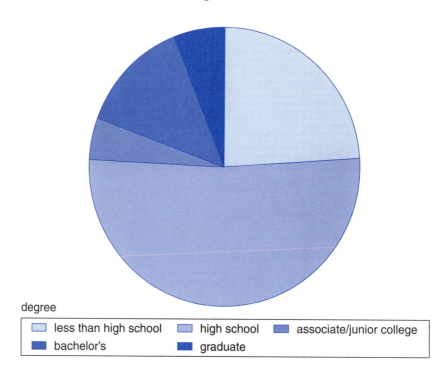

degree

- less than high school
- high school
- associate/junior college
- bachelor's
- graduate

Finally, our pie chart. As you are probably aware, the width of the "slice" represents the number or percentage of respondents in that category. In this example, the largest percentage of respondents, slightly more than 50%, have a high school diploma as their highest degree.

This is the corresponding syntax:

```
GRAPH
/PIE=COUNT BY degree.
```

Now, I will cover line graphs. As mentioned previously, in this section I will cover both how to create line graphs that plot one variable against another as well as showing the change in a variable over time. As an example, let's say we want to plot income over years of education. First, click on *Graphs* and *Chart Builder*:

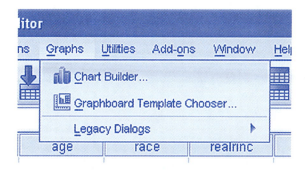

In the following dialog box, you can simply click *OK*:

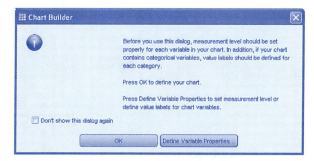

In the next dialog box, select *Line* and then select the first option on the left:

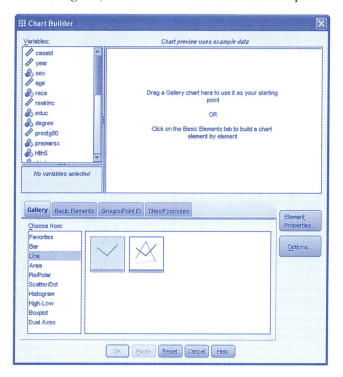

Next, click and drag the image into the large white area that says "Drag a Gallery chart here." When finished, the dialog box should look like the following:

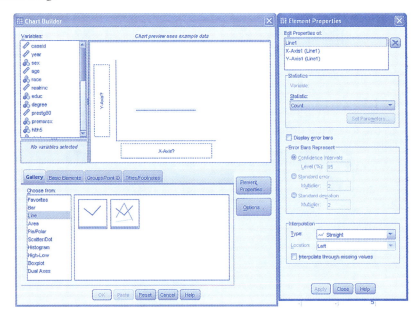

Next, drag the *educ* variable into the *X-Axis* box, and drag the variable *realrinc* into the *Y-Axis* box, like the following:

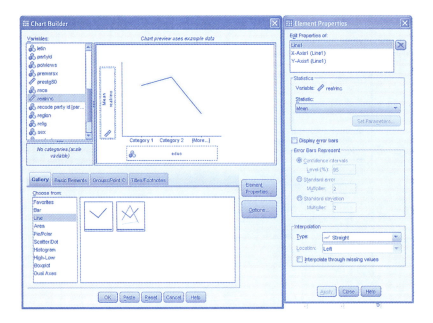

Finally, click *OK*. This will give you the following output:

Then, click on the rectangle representing income, select "Mean" in the *Statistic:* box, and click "Apply".

➔ GGraph

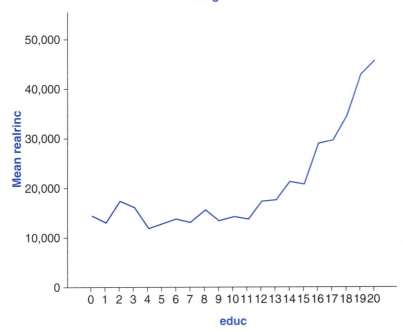

As the output notes, the line represents the mean of income depending on level of education. This can be changed to other values, such as the mode or standard deviation, in the previous dialog box (in the "Statistics" box under "Element Properties"). Education occupies the *x*-axis, and ranges from a value of 0 (0 years of education) to 20 (20 years of education). On the *y*-axis is income, which ranges from 0 to slightly more than 45,000. As you can see, in general, the average income increases as years of education increase. As a note, we call the relationship that you see between level of education and income as being exponential. This is exponential due to the fact that the line representing mean income increases its slope at an increasing rate.

This is the syntax for this graph:

```
* Chart Builder.
GGRAPH
/GRAPHDATASET NAME="graphdataset" VARIABLES=educ
MEAN(realrinc)[name="MEAN_realrinc"]
```

```
MISSING=LISTWISE REPORTMISSING=NO
/GRAPHSPEC SOURCE=INLINE.
BEGIN GPL
SOURCE: s=userSource(id("graphdataset"))
DATA: educ=col(source(s), name("educ"),
unit.category())
DATA: MEAN_realrinc=col(source(s),
name("MEAN_realrinc"))
GUIDE: axis(dim(1), label("educ"))
GUIDE: axis(dim(2), label("Mean realrinc"))
SCALE: linear(dim(2), include(0))
ELEMENT: line(position(educ*MEAN_realrinc),
missing.wings())
END GPL.
```

Next, I will give an example of a change in the mean of a variable over time. A good example for our purposes will be the change in average incomes over time. This will definitely show a relationship due to the effect of inflation. To do this, go to the same dialog box as before by clicking *Graphs* and *Chart Builder*. Next, select the same line graph as before and specify *year* to occupy the *x*-axis and *realrinc* to occupy the *y*-axis:

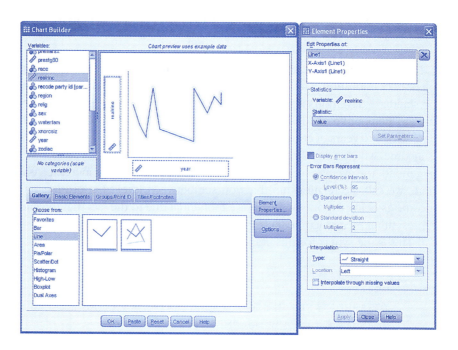

Next, select *Mean* under *Statistic* after highlighting (clicking on) the blue square for *realrinc*:

Next, click on *Apply*:

Now, the main screen will be updated to reflect this change:

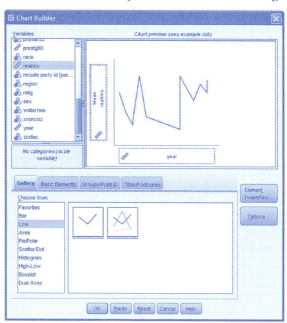

Finally, clicking *OK* will give the following output:

➔ GGraph

[DataSet9] T:\ Books \Practical Statistics\#Data\Chapter 3 GSS data\gss data.sav

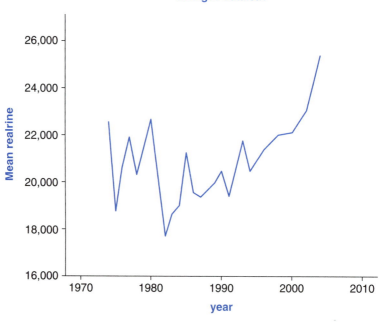

As you can see, from about 1972 through 1982, there is no direct relationship between year and income. After 1982, and especially after the mid-1990s, income generally increases with year.

This is the syntax for this graph:

```
* Chart Builder.
GGRAPH
/GRAPHDATASET NAME="graphdataset"
VARIABLES=year
MEAN(realrinc)[name="MEAN_realrinc"]
MISSING=LISTWISE REPORTMISSING=NO
/GRAPHSPEC SOURCE=INLINE.
BEGIN GPL
SOURCE: s=userSource(id("graphdataset"))
DATA: year=col(source(s), name("year"))
DATA: MEAN_realrinc=col(source(s),
name("MEAN_realrinc"))
GUIDE: axis(dim(1), label("year"))
GUIDE: axis(dim(2), label("Mean realrinc"))
ELEMENT: line(position(year*MEAN_realrinc),
missing.wings())
END GPL.
```

Finally, I will show you how to do scatter plots within IBM SPSS. As mentioned previously, scatter plots mark each individual data point with a symbol, such as a "+." They can be described best by simply showing you one. You'll find scatter plots to be more useful when you have a limited number of cases. So, before running a scatter plot, I will tell IBM SPSS to only select cases from the year 2004. To do this, select *Data* and *Select Cases*. Next, you will see the following dialog box:

Within this dialog box, click on *If condition is satisfied* and then click on *If . . .* In the next dialog box, click on the variable *year* and move it to the right, or simply type "year" in the large white box. Next, click on or type an "=" and then click or type "2004," as shown below:

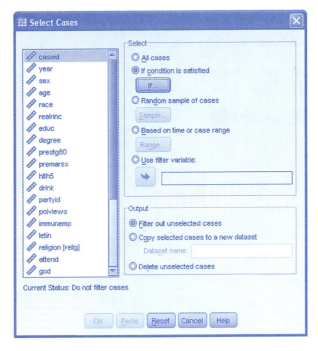

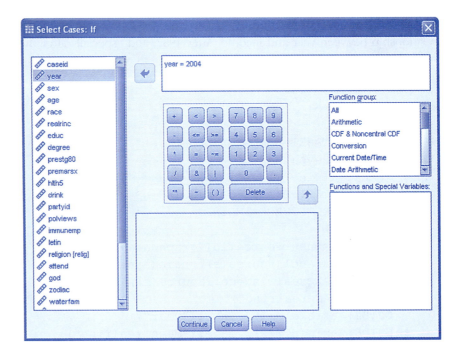

Then, click *Continue* and *OK*. Now, only cases from the year 2004 are selected, and only those cases will be included in any analyses that you do. You can verify this by looking along the leftmost column of IBM SPSS: cases

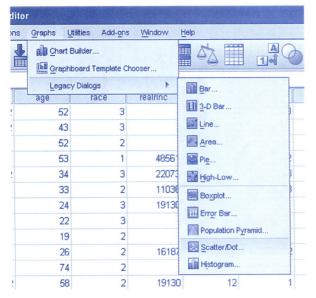

from the year 2004 appear as normal, while cases from any other year are crossed out. To go back to having all cases selected, simply go back to the first dialog box by clicking on *Data* and *Select Cases*. Then, click on *All Cases* and click *OK*. Now, all cases will be selected and included in your analyses, and this also can be verified in the leftmost column: Now, no cases will be crossed out.

Now for the scatter plot. First, I have only selected cases from the year 2004, as described in the previous paragraph. To run a scatter plot comparing two variables, click on *Graphs*, *Legacy Dialogs*, and *Scatter/Dot*:

In the following dialog box, simply select *Simple Scatter* (the default) and click *Define*:

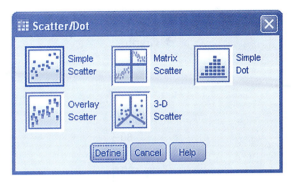

In the scatter plot, I will look at the relationship between years of education and occupational prestige. Occupational prestige is a variable that measures how prestigious people believe an occupation to be. As would be expected, jobs that have a high occupational prestige include professions such as physician, lawyer, and professor. Jobs that have a low occupational prestige include many manual labor and low-paying jobs. In the next dialog box, I will specify *educ* to occupy the *x*-axis and *prestg80* to occupy the *y*-axis, as shown below:

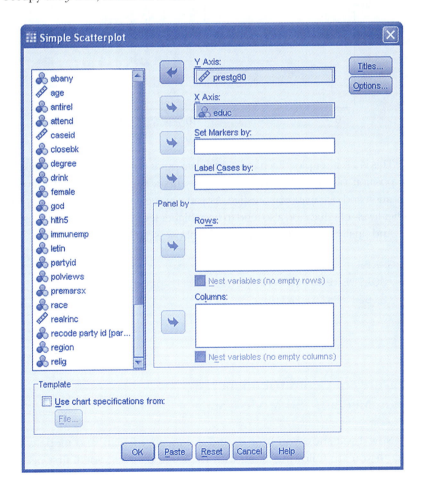

Next, clicking *OK* will give the following output:

➔ Graph

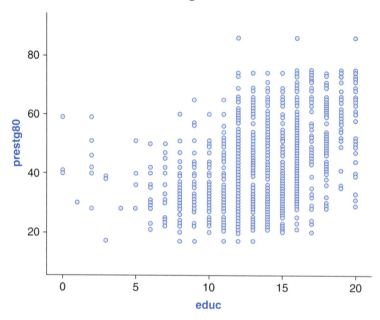

[DataSet9] T:\ Books \Practical Statistics\#Data\Chapter 3 GSS data\gss data.sav

This is a scatter plot. Each individual data point is represented by a circle. So the position of any individual circle represents a single respondent's level of education and occupational prestige. As you can see, in general, individuals with higher levels of education also tend to have higher levels of occupational prestige.

And finally, this is the syntax for the above scatter plot:

```
GRAPH
/SCATTERPLOT(BIVAR)=educ WITH prestg80
/MISSING=LISTWISE.
```

△ SECTION 3: STATA

Measures of Central Tendency: Mean, Median, and Mode—Stata

Now, I will show you how to find the mean, median, and mode within Stata. If you are following along with the same data set, you'll first need to convert the IBM SPSS file into a Stata file as discussed in the Stat Transfer section of Chapter 2. When you open a file in an older version of Stata (Version 9 or older), you may see this screen:

To fix this, you need to set Stata to use more memory. This is a very simple command. All you need to do is to type in the command window,

```
set memory 25M
```

And this will set the memory to 25 MB. You can also simply type `set mem  25M`. This should be enough memory, but if it is not enough for your data set, you can increase this number.

Now, you can just click *File* then *Open* to open the data file again. Afterwards, you should see this screen within Stata:

This means that everything is working correctly. You can see in the *Variables* box all the variables of the data set. For now, we will continue with the example of *age*, finding the mean, median, and mode of *age* within Stata. First, the menus.

First, to find the mean and median, we click on *Data*, *Describe data*, then *Summary statistics*:

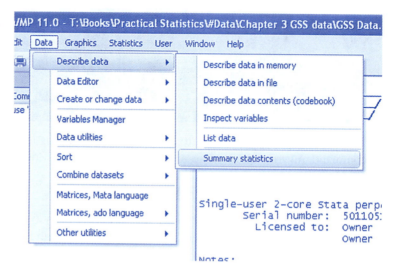

After clicking on *Summary statistics*, we will see the following dialog box:

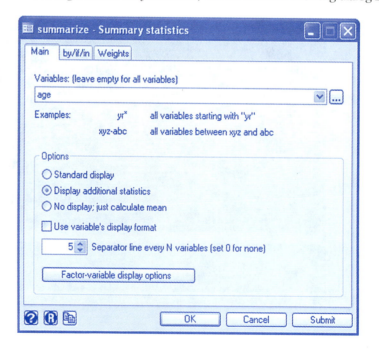

As you can see, I have entered *age* in the *Variables* box. Also, you will want to select *Display additional statistics* under *Options*. This will also display the median. Finally, click *OK*. As a note, clicking *Submit* will run the analysis but will also keep the dialog box open. Clicking *OK* will yield the following output:

```
. summarize age, detail

                              age

        Percentiles      Smallest
 1%          19             18
 5%          22             18
10%          24             18        Obs                46344
25%          31             18        Sum of Wgt.        46344

50%          42                       Mean            45.26474
                          Largest     Std. Dev.       17.48464
75%          58             89
90%          71             89        Variance        305.7126
95%          77             89        Skewness         .471595
99%          86             89        Kurtosis        2.253091

.
```

Our result for the mean is on the right-hand column, the third entry down, approximately 45.26. As you may notice, this is the same result as we got when finding the mean in IBM SPSS. However, sometimes Stata and IBM SPSS will give us slightly different answers due to the fact that they sometimes use slightly different procedures. However, in those cases, both answers can be considered to be correct. Continuing on, the median is under the 50th percentile, again age 42. The 50th percentile means that half of the respondents got a higher score than that number and half got a lower score than that number. As you can see, this is the same as the median, the middle score.

Stata does not have a direct way to find the mode of a variable. If you wanted to find the mode within Stata, you would have to tabulate the variable (create a table of the variable, as we did in IBM SPSS previously, where each response category has its own row), making sure to sort the table by frequency. To do this in Stata through the menus, we click on *Statistics*; *Summaries, tables, and tests; Tables;* and *One-way tables*:

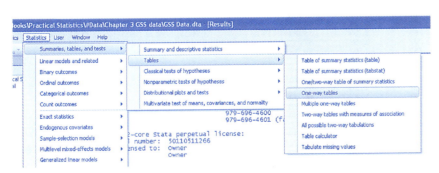

Doing so will result in the following dialog box:

. tabulate age, sort

age	Freq.	Percent	Cum.
28	1,123	2.42	2.42
32	1,092	2.36	4.78
30	1,091	2.35	7.13
34	1,065	2.30	9.43
27	1,056	2.28	11.71
25	1,052	2.27	13.98
35	1,046	2.26	16.24
26	1,034	2.23	18.47
33	1,033	2.23	20.70
38	1,021	2.20	22.90
36	1,017	2.19	25.09
31	1,009	2.18	27.27
29	994	2.14	29.42
37	993	2.14	31.56
23	962	2.08	33.64
24	956	2.06	35.70
40	954	2.06	37.76
43	901	1.94	39.70
41	884	1.91	41.61
39	882	1.90	43.51
42	872	1.88	45.39
44	835	1.80	47.19
22	821	1.77	48.97
45	808	1.74	50.71
46	797	1.72	52.43
21	791	1.71	54.14
49	785	1.69	55.83
48	777	1.68	57.51
47	752	1.62	59.13
51	734	1.58	60.71
52	708	1.53	62.24
50	699	1.51	63.75
20	697	1.50	65.25
56	681	1.47	66.72
53	674	1.45	68.18
19	655	1.41	69.59
54	655	1.41	71.00
58	642	1.39	72.39
60	609	1.31	73.70
57	601	1.30	75.00
59	594	1.28	76.28
55	583	1.26	77.54

Here, I have simply entered *age* in the *Categorical variable* box and have also checked the *Display the table in descending order of frequency* option. Next, simply click *OK*. That will give you the following output:

Now, to find the mode, we simply look at the first row in this output. Here, we see that the response category with the greatest number of cases is 28 years of age. In this example, there are 1,123 individuals who are 28 years of age, making 28 the mode for this variable. Again, this is the same result that we got when using IBM SPSS. As you can also see, Stata has displayed the syntax for this command in the main window:

```
tabulate age, sort
```

So typing `tabulate age, sort` or simply `tab age, sort` in the command window and hitting *Enter* will give you exactly the same result. Since the Stata syntax for these commands are quite simple, I will simply review them here. You can also use the abbreviated commands as shown:

For mean and median:

```
summarize [variable name], detail
    sum [variable name], det
```

For mode:

```
tabulate [variable name], sort
    tab [variable name], sort
```

As one final section, what if you want to summarize or tabulate two or more variables? If you're using the summarize commands, simply type it like this:

```
sum [variable name 1] [variable name 2]
        [variable name 3], det
```

simply putting spaces in-between the variable names.

If you're using the tabulate command, you need to simply add a "1" after the tab command, without a space:

```
tab1 [variable name 1] [variable name 2]
            [variable name 3]
```

Measures of Variability: Stata (Menus)

This section will cover how to find the measures of variability within Stata using the menus. To do this, you'll click on *Statistics; Summaries, tables, and tests; Tables;* and *Table of summary statistics (tabstat)*:

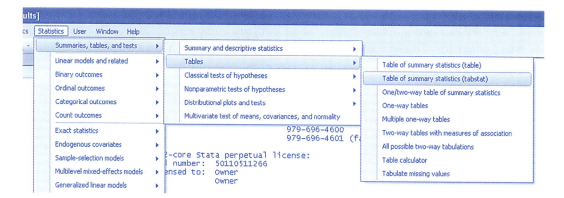

Clicking on this will give you the following dialog box:

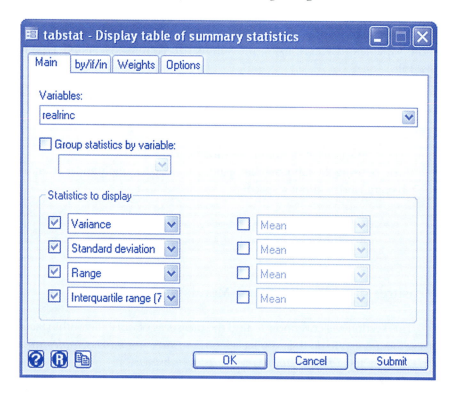

Here, you can see that I have specified *realrinc* as the variable and have selected variance, standard deviation, range, and interquartile range under *Statistics to display*. Clicking *OK* will give you the following output:

```
. tabstat realrinc, statistics( var sd range iqr ) columns(variables)

    stats |   realrinc

 variance |   4.36e+08
       sd |   20871.59
    range |     201346
      iqr |      18382
```

As you can see, the variance is 4.36e + 08, which is equal to 4.36×10^8, or 436,000,000 (the difference between this value and the value we obtained in IBM SPSS is due to rounding). Also, the standard deviation is 20871.59. The interquartile range is 18382, and the range is 201346.

Measures of Variability: Stata (Syntax)

This section will cover how to find these measures of variability in Stata using Stata syntax. Basically, you simply use the commands that you saw in the Stata output that I presented in the previous section. To find the variance, standard deviation, range, and interquartile range, you need only type the following into the command window and hit enter:

```
tabstat realrinc, statistics(var sd range iqr)
                  columns(variables)
```

or

```
tabstat realrinc, s(var sd range iqr) c(v)
```

You can see that `tabstat` is the command used and *realrinc* is the variable specified. The statistics that are specified are the variance, standard deviation, range, and interquartile range. The final option, `columns(variables)`, tells Stata to have one column for all the statistics, like this:

```
. tabstat realrinc, statistics( var sd range iqr ) columns(variables)

    stats |   realrinc

 variance |   4.36e+08
       sd |   20871.59
    range |     201346
      iqr |      18382
```

If we had not made this final specification, this would be our result:

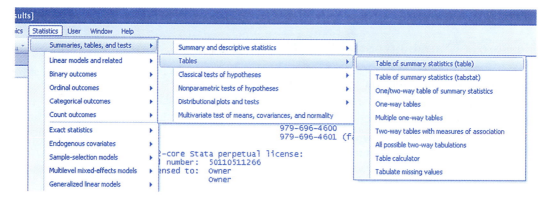

```
. tabstat realrinc, statistics( var sd range iqr )

    variable |  variance        sd       range         iqr
-------------+--------------------------------------------------
     realrinc |  4.36e+08   20871.59      201346       18382
```

Tables: Stata

This section will detail how to make tables within Stata, using both the menu system and Stata syntax. To make a table of *race* using the menu system, click on *Statistics; Summaries, tables, and tests; Tables; and Table of summary statistics (table)*:

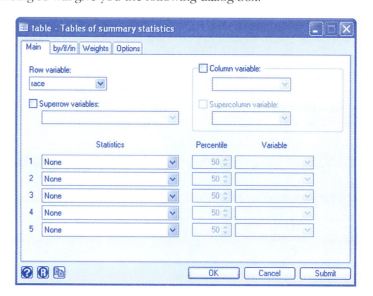

Doing so will give you the following dialog box:

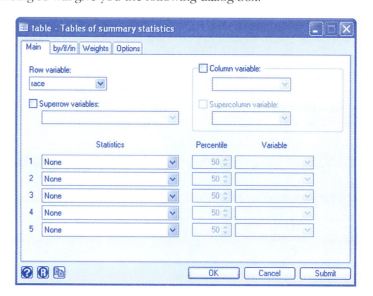

All we need to do here is to type *race* in the *Row variable* box and click *OK*. If you do not have labels for the response categories, you will see the following output:

As you can see, the syntax for creating a table is simply

```
table [variable name]
```

Or this can be simplified as

```
tab [variable name]
```

If you want to print (on the screen) tables for a whole list of variables, this is the format:

```
tab1 [variable 1] [variable 2]
     [variable 3] . . .
```

The only real difference is that "tab" is replaced by "tab1."

Charts and Graphs: Stata

In this section, I will describe how to do the same sorts of graphs and charts presented in the IBM SPSS section but within Stata. Just to reiterate, I will cover bar charts, histograms, pie charts, line graphs (showing both the relationship between two variables and the change in one variable over time), and scatter plots. To make these examples more clear, I will use the same variables as were used in the previous section.

First, I will cover how to do a bar chart in Stata. You may recall from before, bar charts are used for categorical variables, while histograms are used for continuous variables. In Stata, running bar charts is a little confusing. Instead of selecting the "Bar chart" option, you'll select "Histogram" and then specify that the data are either discrete or categorical. To do this, select *Graphics* and *Histogram*:

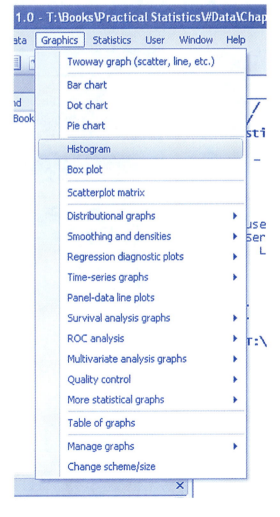

```
. table race
```

race	Freq.
1	38,480
2	6,399
3	1,631

After clicking on this, you will see the following dialog box:

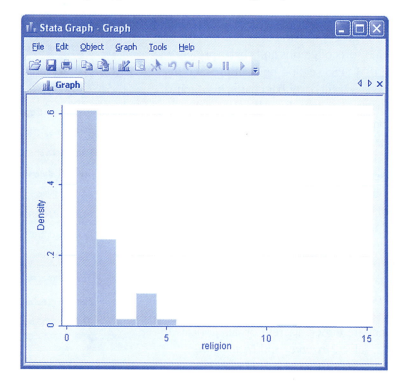

As you can see, I have chosen *relig* as the variable and have specified that it is a discrete (categorical) variable.

After clicking *OK*, you will see the following output:

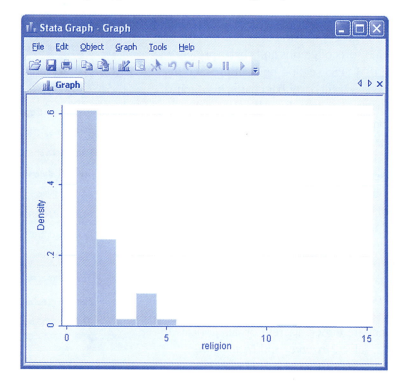

Here, the response categories (Protestant, Catholic, Jewish, etc.) are omitted from the graph, which Stata does by default.

This is the corresponding syntax:

```
histogram relig, discrete
```

To do a histogram within Stata, you'll select the same menu option (*Graphics* and *Histogram*), which will lead you to the same dialog box. However, when doing histograms, we will simply select *Data are continuous*, as shown below:

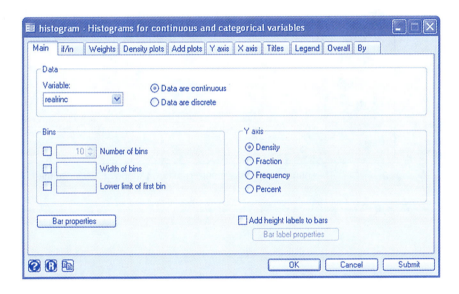

You will see that I've also selected *realrinc* as the variable of choice. Clicking *OK* will give you the following output:

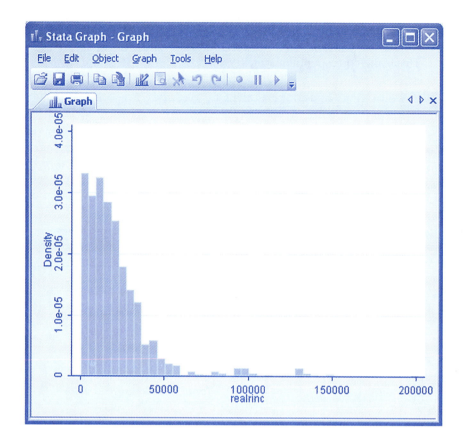

Stata, like IBM SPSS, will automatically come up with a number of discrete categories when running histograms.

This is the corresponding syntax:

```
histogram realrinc
```

As you can see from the previous two examples, by default, Stata will choose "density" as the measure on the *y*-axis. This can be changed to another measure in the *Y axis* box, as shown below:

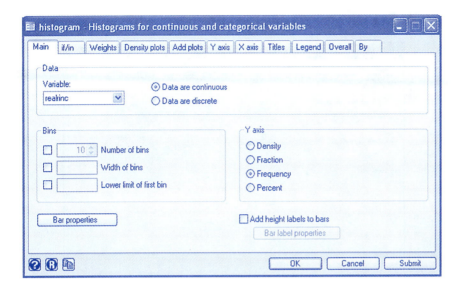

Stata gives you the option of density, fraction, frequency (sum), or percent as the *y*-axis measure. This can also be specified when using Stata syntax. By default (if you do not specify anything), Stata will choose density as the *y*-axis measure. You can change this to fraction, frequency, or percent as shown in the examples below. Simplified versions follow the full versions (e.g., the simplified or shorter version of "fraction" is "frac").

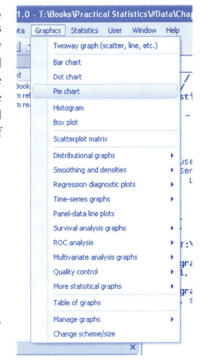

```
histogram realrinc, fraction
hist realrinc, frac
histogram relig, discrete
    frequency
hist relig, d freq
histogram realrinc, percent
```

Now, I will cover how to do pie charts within Stata. Using the menus, navigate to the following selection:

This will open the following dialog box:

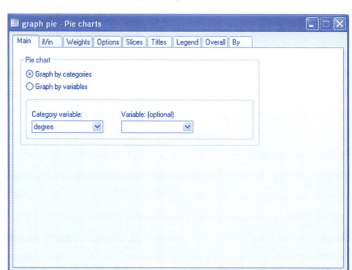

As you can see, I have specified *degree* under the *Category variable* field. Clicking *OK* will give us a pie chart of the *degree* variable, with each section of the pie devoted to a response category, as shown below:

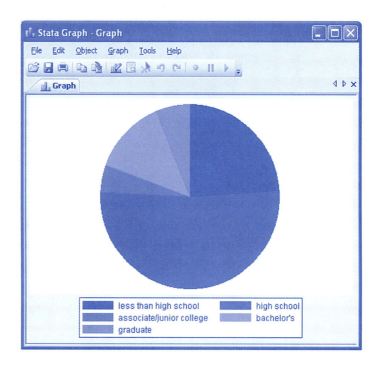

By default, Stata does not include percentages or sums for each slice of the pie. To do this, go back to the dialog box, and then click on the *Slices* tab:

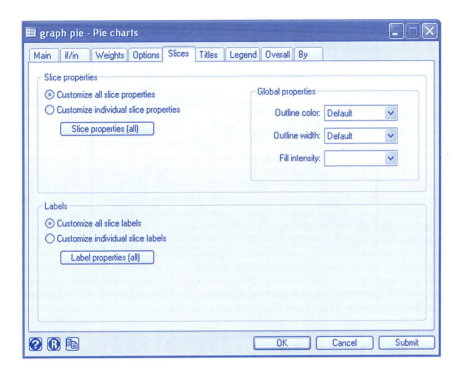

Next, under *Labels*, click on *Label properties (all)*. This will open the following dialog box:

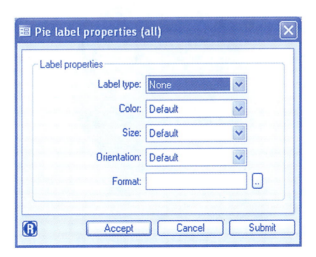

Clicking on the down arrow next to *Label type*, you see that Stata gives you the option of labeling slices by *None*, *Sum*, *Percent*, and *Name*:

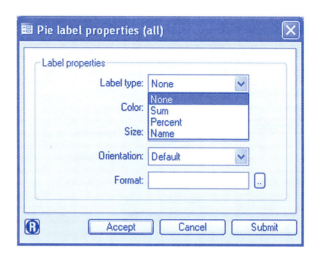

Here, I have selected *Percent* for *Label type* (the default is *None*). After clicking *Accept* and *OK*, I get the following result:

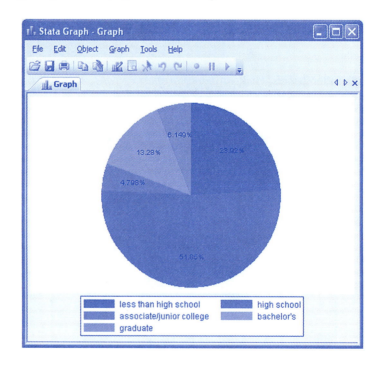

The corresponding syntax for the first pie graph is

```
graph pie, over(degree)
  gr pie, over(degree)
```

And the corresponding syntax for the second pie graph, which includes percents, is

```
graph pie, over(degree) plabel(_all percent)
    gr pie, over(degree) pl(_all per)
```

Now, on to line graphs. This is an area where Stata is deficient. While Stata does a good job at creating line graphs in which the variable on the x-axis maps to one and only one value for the variable on the y-axis, it is not good at creating graphs such as the one presented in the IBM SPSS section, in which education was mapped on the x-axis and income on the y-axis. Therefore, I will recommend using IBM SPSS for those types of graphs and skip ahead to the scatter plot section.

Here, I will use the same example we used in the IBM SPSS section, in which education was mapped on the x-axis, and occupational prestige was mapped on the y-axis. Also, we decided to select only those cases from the year 2004. To do this, first navigate to the following menu selection:

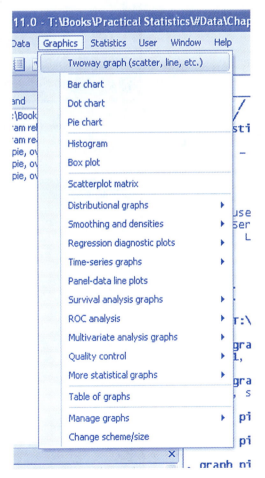

Next, you will see the following dialog box:

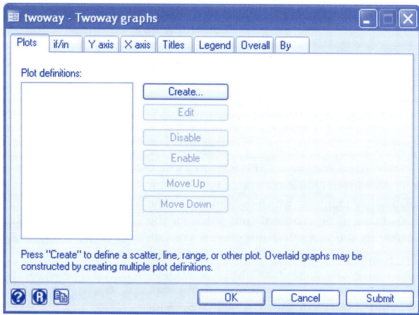

Next, click *Create*. This opens the following dialog box:

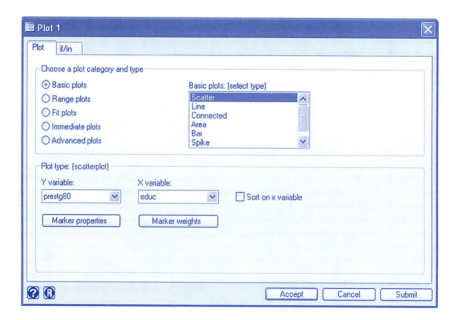

I have selected a scatter plot under *Basic plots: (select type)*, and I have specified *educ* to occupy the *x*-axis and *prestg80* to occupy the *y*-axis, as done previously. Next, we must make sure that only cases from the year 2004 are selected. To do this, click on the "if/in" tab:

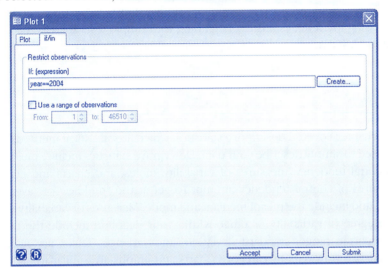

In the "If" field, I have simply written *year==2004,* which specifies that only cases from the year 2004 are included in the scatter plot. Make sure you use two equal signs (this is a Stata particularity). Finally, we click *Accept* and *OK* to get the following result:

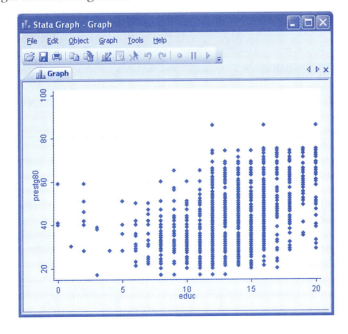

And this is the corresponding syntax:

```
scatter prestg80 educ if year==2004
```

That concludes our section on descriptive statistics. Next, we will begin discussing inferential statistics, beginning with simple tests such as the *t*-test and the ANOVA.

△　Section 4: Summary

This chapter covered descriptive statistics, which are statistical methods that are used to simply describe your data. Descriptive statistics include measures of central tendency, measures of variability, tables, and charts and graphs. Measures of central tendency attempt to get at the "middle," or "average" score and include the mean, median, and mode. Measures of variability show the degree of variability or range within your data and include the range, interquartile range, standard deviation, and variance. Tables are used to summarize your data by category. Charts and graphs are similar to tables in that they are also used to summarize data but are pictorial. After presenting an introduction and theoretical background to descriptive statistics, instructions on how to perform these methods were presented in both IBM SPSS and Stata, using both the menu system as well as syntax.

The following chapter will begin our discussion of inferential statistics, which consist of statistical methods that are used to test hypotheses that relate to relationships between variables. In this next chapter, simple statistical tests are covered. Namely, they are Pearson's correlation coefficient, chi-square, the *t*-test, and the ANOVA.

 ## Resources

You can find more information about IBM SPSS and how to purchase it by navigating to the following Web site: www.spss.com/software/statistics/

You can find more information about Stata and how to purchase it by navigating to the following Web site: www.stata.com

This book's Web site can be found at the following location: www.sage pub.com/kremelstudy

CHAPTER **4**

PEARSON'S *R*, CHI-SQUARE, *T*-TEST, AND ANOVA

OUTLINE OF CHAPTER

△   SECTION 1: INTRODUCTION AND THEORETICAL BACKGROUND

Introduction

Inferential statistics consist of statistical methods that are used to test hypotheses that relate to relationships between variables. For example, you might hypothesize that individuals with greater levels of education tend to have higher incomes. While we can use descriptive statistics such as line plots as outlined in the previous chapter to illustrate the relationship between these two variables, we need to use inferential statistics to more rigorously demonstrate whether or not there is a relationship between these two variables.

With all inferential statistics, which particular statistical test you use will depend on the nature of your data as well as the nature of your hypothesis. In this chapter, Pearson's correlation coefficient (also known as Pearson's r), the chi-square test, the t-test, and the ANOVA will be covered. Pearson's correlation coefficient (r) is used to demonstrate whether two variables are correlated or related to each other. When using Pearson's correlation coefficient, the two variables in question must be continuous, not categorical. So it can be used, for example, to test the relationship between years of education and income, as these are both continuous variables, but not race and highest degree completed, as these are categorical variables. The chi-square statistic is used to show whether or not there is a relationship between two categorical variables. For example, you can use the chi-square statistic to show the relationship between the highest degree completed (e.g., coded as none, high school diploma, bachelors, etc.) and political affiliation (coded as Republican or Democrat). The t-test is used to test whether there is a difference between two groups on a continuous dependent variable. For example, you would select the t-test when testing whether there is a difference in income between males and females. The ANOVA is very similar to the t-test, but it is used to test differences between three or more groups. For example, you would use an ANOVA to test whether there is a difference in income between blacks, whites, and Hispanics. The ANOVA is actually a generalized form of the t-test, and when conducting comparisons on two groups, an ANOVA will give you identical results to a t-test.

Pearson's r: Theory

The purpose of the correlation coefficient is to determine whether there is a significant relationship (i.e., correlation) between two variables. The most commonly used correlation coefficient is the one published by Karl Pearson in 1895, having been developed earlier by Sir Francis Galton. It goes under several names, including Pearson's r, the product-moment correlation coefficient, and Pearson's correlation coefficient. I will typically refer to it as Pearson's r for the sake of brevity.

Pearson's r is used to illustrate the relationship between two continuous variables, such as years of education completed and income. The correlation between any two variables using Pearson's r will always be between –1 and +1. A correlation coefficient of 0 means that there is no relationship, either positive or negative, between these two variables. A correlation coefficient of +1 means that there is a perfect positive correlation, or relationship, between these two variables. In the case of +1, as one variable increases, the second variable increases in exactly the same level or proportion. Likewise, as one variable decreases, the second variable would decrease in exactly the same level or proportion. A correlation coefficient of –1 means that there is a perfect negative correlation, or relationship, between two variables. In this case, as one variable increases, the second variable decreases in exactly the same level or proportion. Also, as one variable decreases, the other would increase in exactly the same level or proportion.

You most likely will never see a correlation between two variables of –1 or +1 in the social sciences as while two variables may be very highly related, the chance of error or random variation is too great to have a perfect correlation. A positive correlation means that generally, as one variable increases, the other will increase, and as one variable decreases, the other will decrease. Also, a negative correlation means that in general, if one variable increases, the other will decrease, and as one variable decreases, the other will increase. Very important here is the notion of significance, which I introduced you to in Chapter 1. When determining Pearson's r, or other correlation coefficients, it is important to be aware of whether your correlation is in fact significant or not at the .05 level.

Let's now compute the Pearson's r for some data. The table below consists of data made up for this example.

Years of Education (x)	Income (in Thousands of $) (y)
8	12
12	15
8	8
14	20
12	18
16	45
20	65
24	85
24	100
24	90

As you may have noticed, I tried to create a positive relationship between years of education and income—I am hoping that this will result in a strong positive correlation coefficient that will be significant.

The equation for Pearson's r is as follows:

$$r = \frac{\sum xy - N\bar{x}\bar{y}}{\sqrt{(\sum x^2 - N\bar{x}^2)(\sum y^2 - N\bar{y}^2)}}$$

This equation requires us to first calculate the sum of the product of all our data pairs, the means of both variables, and the sum of the squared values of both variables.

So first,

$$\sum xy = (8 \times 12) + (12 \times 15) + (8 \times 8) + (14 \times 20) + (12 \times 18) + (16 \times 45)$$
$$+ (20 \times 65) + (24 \times 85) + (24 \times 100) + (24 \times 90)$$

$$= 96 + 180 + 64 + 280 + 216 + 720 + 1{,}300 + 2{,}040 + 2{,}400 + 2{,}160$$

$$= 9{,}456$$

$$\bar{x} = \frac{8 + 12 + 8 + 14 + 12 + 16 + 20 + 24 + 24 + 24}{10} = \frac{162}{10} = 16.2$$

$$\bar{y} = \frac{12 + 15 + 8 + 20 + 18 + 45 + 65 + 85 + 100 + 90}{10} = \frac{458}{10} = 45.8$$

$$\sum x^2 = 8^2 + 12^2 + L + 24^2 = 2{,}996$$

$$\sum y^2 = 12^2 + 15^2 + L + 90^2 = 32{,}732$$

N = Number of cases or data pairs = 10.

Now, plugging these values into our equation, we get the following:

$$r = \frac{\sum xy - N\bar{x}\bar{y}}{\sqrt{(\sum x^2 - N\bar{x}^2)(\sum y^2 - N\bar{y}^2)}}$$

$$= \frac{9456 - 10(16.2)(45.8)}{\sqrt{(2996 - 10(16.2^2))(32732 - 10(45.8^2))}}$$

$$= \frac{9456 - 7419.6}{\sqrt{(2996 - 2624.4)(32732 - 20976.4)}} = \frac{2036.4}{\sqrt{4368380.96}} = 0.9743$$

I will use this same example in the sections on IBM SPSS and Stata—in those sections, you will be able to see that the result for Pearson's r using either of these programs is identical to the value we have calculated by hand.

Now, we can see that our correlation, .9743, is very high as it is very close to +1, the maximum possible value for Pearson's r. But we still need to calculate the p value in order to determine whether this correlation is statistically significant or not.

To determine this, we will first calculate a t ratio using the following equation:

$$t = \frac{r\sqrt{N-2}}{\sqrt{1-r^2}}$$

Now, plugging our values into the equation, we get the following:

$$t = \frac{r\sqrt{N-2}}{\sqrt{1-r^2}} = \frac{.9743\sqrt{10-2}}{\sqrt{1-.9743^2}} = \frac{.9743\sqrt{8}}{\sqrt{.0507}} = \frac{2.7557}{.2251} = 12.2386$$

Also, we will need to know our degrees of freedom (df). This is equal to the number of pairs of data minus 2:

$$df = N - 2 = 10 - 2 = 8$$

Next, we will need to consult a t table to compare our calculated t value with the critical t value in order to determine statistical significance. Looking at a t table, we can see that for 8 degrees of freedom, the critical t value for a p level of .05 (two-tailed) is 2.306. As our calculated t value is greater than the critical t value at the .05 level, we can say that the correlation between education and income is significant at the .05 level. Again referring to our table, we can see that our correlation is even significant at the .001 level, as the critical t value in this case is 5.041, which is still lower than our calculated t value. This means that the probability that the correlation between education and income is simply due to error or chance is less than 0.1%. In this example, I have used the two-tailed critical t value, which is more conservative than a one-tailed test and is generally preferred. If you are not making a **directional hypothesis** (examples of a directional hypothesis: those with greater levels of education will have higher incomes or males have higher incomes than females), then you would use a **two-tailed test**, as it does not make any specification regarding direction. For example, a two-tailed test would be used if you're simply hypothesizing that there will be a correlation between level of education and income, but not specifying the direction of the correlation. However, if you were making a directional hypothesis, for example that those with more education are more likely to have higher incomes, the **one-tailed test** could be used. However, when the direction between your two variables corresponds to the direction stated in your hypothesis, the one-tailed test is less conservative than the two-tailed test and so tends to be used less often.

In the next section, the concept of **R-squared** will be discussed. The R-squared value represents the proportion of variance in the dependent variable (the variable you are trying to predict or explain) that is explained by the independent variable(s) (the variables that you are using to explain or predict the dependent variable). In this example, it would make sense that we would use years of education to predict the respondent's income and not vice versa. What's interesting is that we simply need to square the value we arrived at after calculating Pearson's r to attain the R-squared. Thus,

$$R^2 = r^2 = .9743^2 = .9493$$

Later on, in the Stata section, I will replicate this result. We can interpret this by stating that level of education explains 94.93% of the variance in income. Here, I simply moved the decimal point two places to the right to arrive at this value.

Finally, it is important to state again that Pearson's r is only used for continuous variables. To determine the correlation between variables that are ordered and categorical or dichotomous, there are a number of special options, including Kendall's tau, Spearman's rank correlation coefficient or Spearman's rho, the polyserial correlation, the polychoric correlation, phi, the tetrachoric correlation, and others. Many of these tests require specialized software programs or certain specific add-ons to IBM SPSS or Stata. These additional measures of correlation are described in more detail in Appendix C, Section 4, Part F.

Chi-Square: Theory

The chi-square statistic is used to show whether or not there is a relationship between two categorical variables. It can also be used to test whether or not a number of outcomes are occurring in equal frequencies or not, or conform to a known distribution. For example, when rolling a die, there are six possible outcomes. After rolling a die hundreds of times, you could tabulate the number of times each outcome occurred and use the chi-square statistic to test whether these outcomes were occurring in basically equal frequencies or not (e.g., to test whether the die is weighted). The chi-square statistic was also developed by Karl Pearson.

This is the chi-square equation:

$$\chi^2 = \sum_{i=1}^{n} \frac{(O_i - E_i)^2}{E_i}$$

Here,

χ^2 = the chi-square statistic

O_i = the observed frequency

E_i = the expected frequency

i = the number of the cell (cell 1, cell 2, etc.)

Here, the summation is simple. We simply calculate the square of the difference between the observed and expected frequency and divide that by the expected frequency for each cell. Then, we simply sum all these quotients together. The concept of a "cell" is also easy to understand. If we are testing whether a number of outcomes are occurring in equal frequencies or not, such as in the example of the die, we would count each outcome as a cell. If we were testing a relationship between two variables, say between degree and political affiliation, the data would look like this:

Degree	Political Affiliation	
	Republican	Democrat
None	23	45
HS	17	42
BA	28	35
MA	32	32
Above MA	42	28

And we would have 10 cells all together.

Now, let's use these two examples to calculate the chi-square statistic. Say we roll a die 600 times and get the following results:

Outcome	Frequency
1	95
2	72
3	103
4	105
5	97
6	128

Here, we want to calculate the chi-square statistic to see whether these outcomes are occurring at basically the same frequencies or not. Now, if you remember from previous chapters, simply because the numbers are not exactly the same does not necessarily mean that certain outcomes are occurring more frequently than others in the statistical sense. To find out whether this is true, we need to run a statistical test and find the probability value (p value). To calculate the chi-square value for this particular example, we need to simply plug these numbers into the equation, as shown below. One hundred is chosen as the expected value for all cells, as it would be expected that you would get an equal number of each outcome (100 1s, 100 2s, etc.).

$$\chi^2 = \sum_{i=1}^{n} \frac{(O_i - E_i)^2}{E_i}$$

$$= \frac{(95 - 100)^2}{100} + \frac{(72 - 100)^2}{100} + \frac{(103 - 100)^2}{100} + \frac{(105 - 100)^2}{100}$$

$$+ \frac{(97 - 100)^2}{100} + \frac{(128 - 100)^2}{100}$$

$$= \frac{25}{100} + \frac{784}{100} + \frac{9}{100} + \frac{25}{100} + \frac{9}{100} + \frac{784}{100} = 16.36$$

So 16.36 is our chi-square statistic for this example, but we still do not know whether or not this value is significant (i.e., if the probability level is below .05 or not). To do this next step, you need to calculate the degrees of freedom. In this example, and in all examples in which we are simply looking at the frequencies of the different responses for single variable, degrees of freedom simply equals the number of different responses minus one. So we get,

Degrees of freedom = Number of
response categories – 1 = 6 – 1 = 5

Now that we know both the chi-square value and the degrees of freedom, we simply need to look at a chi-square table to find the critical chi-square value for our degrees of freedom using the .05 probability level.

| | **Probability Level** | | |
Degrees of Freedom	**.05**	**.01**	**.001**
1	3.84	6.64	10.83
2	5.99	9.21	13.82
3	7.82	11.34	16.27
4	9.49	13.28	18.47
5	11.07	15.09	20.52
⋮			

So when looking at this table, we will move down to 5 degrees of freedom, and look at the first column specified by the .05 probability level. Here, we can see that the critical chi-square value for our example is 11.07. We calculated a chi-square value of 16.36. Since the chi-square value that we calculated is greater than the critical chi-square value for the .05 probability level, our results are statistically significant. This means that the die appears to be not being rolled fairly, that some outcomes occur more frequently than others, and that this difference is statistically significant at the .05 level. Looking again at our chi-square table, we can see that our calculated value is also greater than the critical chi-square value at the .01 probability level at 5 degrees of freedom. This means that our results are also significant at the more stringent .01 probability level (meaning that there is a less than 1% chance that these differences between outcomes are not actually significantly different and are instead due to error or chance).

Next, we will calculate the chi-square statistic using the example of political affiliation and the highest degree completed. Here, the equation for the chi-square statistic remains the same. However, degrees of freedom are calculated differently than before. In the case where there are two variables, degrees of freedom are calculated using this equation:

$$\text{Degrees of freedom} = (\text{Rows} - 1)(\text{Columns} - 1)$$

Here is a reproduction of the table from the previous page:

| | Political Affiliation | | |
Degree	Republican	Democrat	Total
None	23	45	68
HS	17	42	59
BA	28	35	63
MA	32	32	64
Above MA	42	28	70
Total	142	182	324

So to calculate the chi-square statistic for this example, we need to do the following.

First, we need to calculate the expected values. In the example with the die, we do not need to formally calculate expected values, since there were six possible outcomes with equal probabilities. We simply divided 600 (the number of times we rolled the die, or the number of cases) by the number of possible outcomes (6) to get 100, the expected value for each possible outcome.

When calculating the chi-square statistic between two variables, we use the following equation to determine the expected value for each cell:

$$E_i = \frac{(\text{Row total})(\text{Column total})}{\text{Grand total}}$$

For example, this is how you would calculate the expected value for the first cell in the top left corner (individuals with no degree who are Republican):

$$E_i = \frac{(\text{Row total})(\text{Column total})}{\text{Grand total}} = \frac{(68)(142)}{324} = \frac{9656}{324} = 29.80$$

So after calculating the expected value for each cell, we would plug all our numbers into the equation for the chi-square statistic:

$$\chi^2 = \sum_{i=1}^{n} \frac{(O_i - E_i)^2}{E_i} = \frac{(23 - 29.80)^2}{29.80} + \frac{(17 - 25.86)^2}{25.86} + \frac{(28 - 27.61)^2}{27.61}$$

$$+ \frac{(32 - 28.05)^2}{28.05} + \frac{(42 - 30.68)^2}{30.68}$$

$$+ \frac{(45 - 38.20)^2}{38.20} + \frac{(42 - 33.14)^2}{33.14} + \frac{(35 - 35.39)^2}{35.39}$$

$$+ \frac{(32 - 35.95)^2}{35.95} + \frac{(27 - 39.32)^2}{39.32}$$

$$= \frac{46.24}{29.80} + \frac{78.50}{25.86} + \frac{0.15}{27.61} + \frac{15.60}{28.05} + \frac{128.14}{30.68} + \frac{46.24}{38.20}$$

$$+ \frac{78.50}{33.14} + \frac{0.15}{35.39} + \frac{15.60}{35.95} + \frac{151.78}{39.32} = 17.20$$

Now, we need to calculate the degrees of freedom. In cases where we are calculating the chi-square statistic between two variables, this is the equation that we use:

$$\text{Degrees of freedom} = (\text{Rows} - 1)(\text{Columns} - 1)$$

So in our example, this would be our degrees of freedom:

$$df = (5 - 1)(2 - 1) = 4$$

So now we know that our chi-square value is 17.20 and our degrees of freedom is 4. Looking at our chi-square table, we see that the critical chi-square value for 4 degrees of freedom at the .05 probability level is 9.49. Since our calculated chi-square value is greater than the critical chi-square value, our results are significant at the .05 probability level. We can also see that our results are also significant at the .01 probability level, but not at the .001 probability level. Therefore, there is a statistically significant relationship between highest degree completed and political affiliation using either .05 or .01 as our standard.

t-Test: Theory

As mentioned in the introduction to this chapter, t-tests are used when you want to test the difference between two groups on some continuous variable. A good example here would be the difference in yearly income between males and females. t-tests can also be used when testing the same group of people at two different times; for example, testing whether there was a significant increase or decrease in the test scores of the same group of students at two different times.

The equation for the t-test depends on whether we are doing an *independent samples* t-test (comparing two different groups) or a **dependent samples** t-test, also called a *paired* t-test (comparing the same group at two different periods of time, or two different groups that have been "matched" on some important variable). There is also a **one-sample** t-test that is used to compare a group of scores with a known population mean. Furthermore, there are separate equations for the *independent samples t-test* depending on whether or not our two groups have equal sample sizes.

This is the equation for a one-sample t-test:

$$t = \frac{\bar{x} - \mu}{s / \sqrt{n}}$$

where

t = the t statistic

$\bar{x}$ = the mean of the sample

μ = the comparison mean

s = the sample standard deviation

n = the sample size

A t-test would be preferred to a z-test in situations where the sample size is less than 30, and the population standard deviation is unknown. If either the sample is greater than 30, *OR* the population standard deviation is known, you would prefer the z-test, which is covered in Appendix C, Section 4, Part A.

Say we had a sample of 10 individuals who had all taken an exam. If we wanted to test whether their scores, all together, are significantly different from the score of 100, we could use a one-sample t-test. First, we would calculate the mean of the sample and the sample standard deviation, both of which were covered in the previous chapter. Say that the mean of scores for these 10 individuals is 107.8, and the standard deviation is 5.35. To calculate the t statistic, we would simply plug these values into the equation:

$$t = \frac{\bar{x} - \mu}{s/\sqrt{n}} = \frac{107.8 - 100}{5.35/\sqrt{10}} = 4.61$$

In this example, we have selected 100 as the value for the comparison mean as we want to test whether the scores in our sample significantly differ from 100. If we wanted to, we could test whether the scores were significantly different from another value, such as 110, by simply plugging this value in for the comparison mean.

Next, we need to calculate the degrees of freedom. Here, the degrees of freedom is simply the sample size minus one. Therefore,

$$\text{Degrees of freedom} = n - 1 = 10 - 1 = 9$$

Now, we will refer to a t table to determine the critical t value for 9 degrees of freedom at the .05 level of significance. Looking at a t table, this value is 2.26 (two-tailed t-test). Since our calculated t value of 4.61 is greater than the critical t value of 2.26, we can say that the scores of our sample of 10 individuals differ significantly from the score of 100. This effect is statistically significant at the .05 probability level. The t value for 9 degrees of freedom at the .01 level of significance is 3.25, while the t value for 9 degrees of freedom at the .001 level of significance is 4.78 (both two-tailed). Since our calculated t statistic of 4.61 is greater than the critical t value for the .01 level of significance, we can say that our result is statistically significant at the .01 probability level. As mentioned previously, when writing up results, you will mention only the most strict level of significance that you're able to obtain, whether .05, .01, or .001. In this case, we would mention only the .01 probability level in our results. For example, we could say the following: Our sample's mean of 107.8 was significantly different from 100 ($t = 4.61$, $df = 9$, $p < .01$).

This is the equation for the independent samples t-test when you have unequal sample sizes:

$$t = \frac{\overline{X}_1 - \overline{X}_2}{\sqrt{\left[\frac{SS_1 + SS_2}{n_1 + n_2 - 2}\right]\left[\frac{1}{n_1} + \frac{1}{n_2}\right]}} = \frac{\overline{X}_1 - \overline{X}_2}{\sqrt{\left[\frac{\sum x_1^2 - \frac{\left(\sum x_1\right)^2}{n_1} + \sum x_2^2 - \frac{\left(\sum x_2\right)^2}{n_2}}{n_1 + n_2 - 2}\right]\left[\frac{1}{n_1} + \frac{1}{n_2}\right]}}$$

Here,

$\overline{X}_1$ and $\overline{X}_2$ are the means of the two different groups

$n_1 = n$ of Group 1

$n_2 = n$ of Group 2

SS = sum of squares

Say we had two classes, one with five students and the other with seven students.

These were their scores:

| | Group | |
Case	1	2
1	78	87
2	82	92
3	87	86
4	65	95
5	75	73
6	82	
7	71	

First we would calculate the means of each group. The mean (average) of Group 1 is 77.14, and the mean for Group 2 is 86.60.

Next, we calculate the sum of squares (SS) for each group. As you can see from the above equation,

$$SS = \sum x^2 - \frac{\left(\sum x\right)^2}{n}$$

So for Group 1,

$$SS_1 = \sum x_1^2 - \frac{\left(\sum x_1\right)^2}{n_1} = \left(78^2 + 82^2 + 87^2 + 65^2 + 75^2 + 82^2 + 71^2\right)$$

$$- \frac{\left(78 + 82 + 87 + 65 + 75 + 82 + 71\right)^2}{7}$$

$$= 41992 - \frac{540^2}{7} = 334.86$$

And, for Group 2,

$$SS_2 = \sum x_2^2 - \frac{\left(\sum x_2\right)^2}{n_2} = \left(87^2 + 92^2 + 86^2 + 95^2 + 73^2\right)$$
$$- \frac{(87 + 92 + 86 + 95 + 73)^2}{5}$$
$$= 37783 - \frac{433^2}{5} = 285.20$$

Finally, plugging all these values into the t-test equation, we get the following:

$$t = \frac{\bar{X}_1 - \bar{X}_2}{\sqrt{\left[\frac{SS_1 + SS_2}{n_1 + n_2 - 2}\right]\left[\frac{1}{n_1} + \frac{1}{n_2}\right]}} = \frac{77.14 - 86.60}{\sqrt{\left[\frac{334.86 + 285.20}{7 + 5 - 2}\right]\left[\frac{1}{7} + \frac{1}{5}\right]}}$$
$$= \frac{-9.46}{\sqrt{\left(\frac{620.06}{10}\right)\left(\frac{12}{35}\right)}} = \frac{-9.46}{\sqrt{21.26}} = -0.44$$

Now, to see whether this is significant or not, we need to do the same thing as we did after calculating the chi-square statistic: Compare this value to the critical t value from a t table. First, we need to get the degrees of freedom. For an independent, or between-subjects, t-test,

$$df = n_1 + n_2 - 2$$

which means, in our example, we have 10 degrees of freedom.
Here is a truncated t table:

df	Two-Tailed t-Test: p Level		
	.05	.01	.001
1	12.706	63.657	636.619
2	4.303	9.925	31.598
3	3.182	5.841	12.924
4	2.776	4.604	8.610
5	2.571	4.032	6.869
6	2.447	3.707	5.959
7	2.365	3.499	5.408
8	2.306	3.355	5.041
9	2.262	3.250	4.781
10	2.228	3.169	4.587

And the top of this table I mention that these critical t scores are for the two-tailed t-test. The two-tailed t-test is used when you are not hypothesizing a direction in the relationship between your two groups and the dependent variable. For example, if you're testing the relationship between gender and religious attendance, and do not have a hypothesis, you would use the critical t scores from a two-tailed t-test table or column. The one-tailed t-test *can* be used if you are hypothesizing a directional relationship, for example, if you are hypothesizing that males will have higher incomes than females or that females will have greater religious attendance than males. However, the two-tailed t-test is a more stringent test and tends to be preferred over the one-tailed t-test, regardless of whether or not you have a directional hypothesis. This is true not only in regard to t-tests specifically but in general.

So in this example, we calculated a t score of -0.44. Before making the comparison with our critical t score table, we can first take the absolute value of this, which is 0.44 (i.e., simply make this number positive if it is a negative number). Now, for the .05 probability level with 10 degrees of freedom, we see from our table that the critical t score is 2.228 for a two-tailed test. Since our calculated t score is lower than the critical t score, our results are not significant at the .05 probability level. So the differences in the means of the scores that we saw between the two groups cannot be statistically attributed to any meaningful difference between these two groups. Here, if we wanted to report this result, we could simply say the following: The differences in test scores between our two groups were not statistically significant at the .05 probability level.

When we are performing an independent samples t-test (between subjects) for two groups having equal sample sizes (n), our equation can be simplified like this:

$$t = \frac{\bar{X}_1 - \bar{X}_2}{\sqrt{\left[\frac{SS_1 + SS_2}{n_1 + n_2 - 2}\right]\left[\frac{1}{n_1} + \frac{1}{n_2}\right]}} = \frac{\bar{X}_1 - \bar{X}_2}{\sqrt{\left[\frac{SS_1 + SS_2}{2n - 2}\right]\left[\frac{2}{n}\right]}} = \frac{\bar{X}_1 - \bar{X}_2}{\sqrt{\frac{2(SS_1 + SS_2)}{2n^2 - 2n}}}$$

$$= \frac{\bar{X}_1 - \bar{X}_2}{\sqrt{\frac{2(SS_1 + SS_2)}{2(n^2 - n)}}} = \frac{\bar{X}_1 - \bar{X}_2}{\sqrt{\frac{SS_1 + SS_2}{n^2 - n}}}$$

where n is the sample size of either group.

For example, say we have the following two groups of scores:

	Group	
Case	1	2
1	63	88
2	57	95
3	48	84
4	52	99
5	38	87
Mean	51.6	90.6

First we would find the sum of squares for each group:

$$SS_1 = \sum x_1^2 - \frac{\left(\sum x_1\right)^2}{n_1} = \left(63^2 + 57^2 + 48^2 + 52^2 + 38^2\right)$$
$$- \frac{(63 + 57 + 48 + 52 + 38)^2}{5}$$
$$= 13670 - \frac{258^2}{5} = 357.20$$

$$SS_2 = \sum x_2^2 - \frac{\left(\sum x_2\right)^2}{n_2} = \left(88^2 + 95^2 + 84^2 + 99^2 + 87^2\right)$$
$$- \frac{(88 + 95 + 84 + 99 + 87)^2}{5}$$
$$= 41195 - \frac{453^2}{5} = 153.20$$

The more complex equation gives us the following:

$$t = \frac{\bar{X}_1 - \bar{X}_2}{\sqrt{\left[\frac{SS_1 + SS_2}{n_1 + n_2 - 2}\right]\left[\frac{1}{n_1} + \frac{1}{n_2}\right]}} = \frac{51.6 - 90.6}{\sqrt{\left[\frac{357.2 + 153.2}{5 + 5 - 2}\right]\left[\frac{1}{5} + \frac{1}{5}\right]}}$$
$$= \frac{-39}{\sqrt{\left(\frac{510.4}{8}\right)\left(\frac{2}{5}\right)}} = \frac{-39}{\sqrt{25.52}} = -7.72$$

And using the simplified equation, we get:

$$t = \frac{\bar{X}_1 - \bar{X}_2}{\sqrt{\frac{SS_1 + SS_2}{n^2 - n}}} = \frac{51.6 - 90.6}{\sqrt{\frac{357.2 + 153.2}{5^2 - 5}}} = \frac{-39}{\sqrt{\frac{510.4}{20}}} = \frac{-39}{\sqrt{25.52}} = -7.72$$

So it works.

Also,

$$df = n_1 + n_2 - 2 = 10 - 2 = 8$$

In this example, we have 8 degrees of freedom, which gives us a critical t score of 2.306 for a two-tailed t-test at the .05 probability level. The absolute value of our calculated t score is 7.72, meaning that the differences between these two groups is significant at the .05 probability level. Furthermore, looking at our critical t score table, we can see that these differences are even significant at the .001 probability level, meaning that there is less than a 0.1% chance that these differences in scores are simply due to error or chance. Here, we could say the following: The difference in scores between our two groups was statistically significant ($t = -7.72$, $df = 8$, $p < .001$).

To calculate a t score for a dependent or within-subjects t-test, we need to use the following equation:

$$t = \sqrt{\frac{n - 1}{\left(\frac{n \sum D^2}{\left(\sum D\right)^2}\right) - 1}}$$

Here,

n = sample size

D = difference in scores for the respondent between Time 1 and Time 2, or between the matched pair

Say we had a class of five students, and they took the SAT (Scholastic Aptitude Test) before and after an extensive training course, and these were their scores:

Case	Score at Time 1	Score at Time 2
1	1250	1375
2	1170	1450
3	890	1250
4	1350	1495
5	750	1220

First, we would need to calculate the difference and the difference squared for each pair of scores:

Case	Score at Time 1	Score at Time 2	Difference	Difference Squared
1	1250	1375	−125	15625
2	1170	1450	−280	78400
3	890	1250	−360	129600
4	1350	1495	−145	21025
5	750	1220	−470	220900
Sum	—	—	−1380	465550

Plugging these values into our equation, we get the following:

$$t = \sqrt{\frac{n-1}{\left(\frac{n \sum D^2}{\left(\sum D\right)^2}\right) - 1}} = \sqrt{\frac{5-1}{\left(\frac{5 \times 465550}{1380^2}\right) - 1}} = \sqrt{\frac{4}{\left(\frac{2327750}{1904400}\right) - 1}}$$

$$= \sqrt{\frac{4}{0.22}} = \sqrt{17.99} = 4.24$$

For dependent samples t-tests,

$$df = n - 1$$

where n = the number of matched cases or pairs.

So for this example, we have 4 degrees of freedom. Using the .05 probability level, our critical t score is 2.776 for a two-tailed t-test. Since our calculated t score of 4.24 is greater than the critical t score of 2.776, the differences in scores from Time 1 to Time 2 are significant at the .05 probability level (i.e., the increase in scores was statistically significant at the .05 level). However, our calculated t score is not greater than the critical t value at the .01 probability level, 4.604. Here, we could say the following: The increase in SAT scores for our sample of five individuals from Time 1 to Time 2 was statistically significant ($t = 4.24, df = 4, p < .05$).

ANOVA: Theory

The ANOVA, which stands for analysis of variance, is like a generalized version of the t-test that can be used to test the difference in a continuous dependent variable between three or more groups or to test the level of a continuous dependent variable in a single group of respondents who were tested at three or more points in time. The t-test was published by William Sealy Gosset in 1908 under the pen name *Student*, which is why the t-test is sometimes referred to as the Student's t-test. The ANOVA was developed several decades later by Sir Ronald Fisher, which is why the ANOVA is sometimes called Fisher's ANOVA.

While the t-test relies on the t statistic, the ANOVA uses what is called the F statistic or F-test. When comparing two groups, either the t-test or the ANOVA may be used as they will both give you the same results. For example, below are the results from Stata for both the t-test and an ANOVA on years of education by gender for cases from the year 2004. You can see that the probability levels for both analyses are the same.

```
. ttest educ if year==2004, by(sex)

Two-sample t test with equal variances

---------------------------------------------------------------------
  Group |    Obs      Mean    Std. Err.   Std. Dev.  [95% Conf. Interval]
---------+-----------------------------------------------------------
      1 |   1279   13.81939   .0842611   3.013439   13.65408    13.9847
      2 |   1531    13.597    .0710005   2.778106   13.45773   13.73626
---------+-----------------------------------------------------------
combined |   2810  13.69822   .0545035   2.889202   13.59135   13.80509
---------+-----------------------------------------------------------
   diff |           .2223947   .1093871              .0079075   .4368819
---------------------------------------------------------------------
    diff = mean(1) - mean(2)                                  t =   2.0331
Ho: diff = 0                              degrees of freedom =     2808

   Ha: diff < 0               Ha: diff != 0                Ha: diff > 0
 Pr(T < t) = 0.9789       Pr(|T| > |t|) = 0.0421       Pr(T > t) = 0.0211
```

```
. oneway educ sex if year==2004

                         Analysis of Variance
     Source           SS        df       MS            F     Prob > F
-------------------------------------------------------------------------
Between groups    34.4657999     1    34.4657999      4.13     0.0421
Within groups     23413.6253   2808   8.33818565
-------------------------------------------------------------------------
    Total         23448.0911   2809   8.34748704


Bartlett's test for equal variances:  chi2(1) =    9.2396  Prob>chi2 = 0.002
```

Calculating an ANOVA is slightly more complicated than calculating a t-test. Say we gave a survey to 10 whites, 10 blacks, and 10 Hispanics asking about their highest year of education completed, and we got the following data:

Whites	Blacks	Hispanics
14	12	14
12	14	16
16	12	10
20	12	10
12	12	14
12	10	12
16	8	12
16	10	12
14	12	8
20	20	8

First, we will calculate the following values for each group:

Σx: a sum of all the scores of that group

$\overline{X}$: the mean of that group's scores

$\Sigma(x^2)$: a sum of the square of the group's scores

Next, we will calculate these values for the entire set of cases:

$\Sigma(\Sigma x)$: summing the three values for Σx that we computed previously

$\Sigma[\Sigma(x^2)]$: summing the three values for $\Sigma(x^2)$ that we computed previously

For example, we would get these values for whites:

$$\sum x = 14 + 12 + 16 + 20 + 12 + 12 + 16 + 16 + 14 + 20 = 152$$

$$\bar{x} = \frac{152}{10} = 15.2$$

$$\sum (x^2) = 14^2 + 12^2 + 16^2 + 20^2 + 12^2 + 12^2 + 16^2 + 16^2 + 14^2 + 20^2 = 2392$$

Doing the same computations for the other two groups would give you the following values:

Stat.	Whites	Blacks	Hispanics
Σx	152.0	122.0	116.0
$\overline{x}$	15.2	12.2	11.6
$\Sigma(x^2)$	2392.0	1580.0	1408.0

Then,

$$\sum\left(\sum x\right) = 152 + 122 + 116 = 390$$

$$\sum\left(\sum\left(x^2\right)\right) = 2392 + 1580 + 1408 = 5380$$

Now, we need to calculate three different sum of squares values: the sum of squares total, the sum of squares between, and the sum of squares within. Then, we will compute the mean squares for between groups and within groups. Finally, we will compute the F statistic by dividing the mean squares between by the mean squares within.

So to begin,

$$SS\,\text{total} = \sum\left(\sum\left(x^2\right)\right) - \frac{\left[\sum\left(\sum x\right)\right]^2}{N} = 5380 - \frac{390^2}{30}$$

$$= 5380 - \frac{152100}{30} = 5380 - 5070 = 310$$

$$SS\,\text{between} = \sum\frac{\left(\sum x\right)^2}{n} - \frac{\left[\sum\left(\sum x\right)\right]^2}{N} = \left(\frac{152^2}{10} + \frac{122^2}{10} + \frac{116^2}{10}\right)$$

$$- \left(\frac{390^2}{30}\right) = 5144.4 - 5070 = 74.4$$

$$SS\,\text{within} = SS\,\text{total} - SS\,\text{between} = 310 - 74.4 = 235.6$$

As a check,

$$SS\,\text{within} = SS\,\text{total for Group 1} + SS\,\text{total for Group 2}$$
$$+ SS\,\text{total for Group 3}$$

$$= \left(\sum\left(x^2\right) - \frac{\left(\sum x\right)^2}{N}\right) + \left(\sum\left(x^2\right) - \frac{\left(\sum x\right)^2}{N}\right)$$

$$+ \left(\sum\left(x^2\right) - \frac{\left(\sum x\right)^2}{N}\right)$$

$$= \left(2392 - \frac{152^2}{10}\right) + \left(1580 - \frac{122^2}{10}\right) + \left(1408 - \frac{116^2}{10}\right)$$

$$= 81.6 + 91.6 + 62.4 = 235.6$$

Next,

$$MS\,\text{between} = \frac{SS\,\text{between}}{df\,\text{between}} = \frac{74.4}{n(\text{groups}) - 1} = \frac{74.4}{3 - 1} = \frac{74.4}{2} = 37.2$$

$$MS\ \text{within} = \frac{SS\ \text{within}}{df\ \text{within}} = \frac{235.6}{N - n(\text{groups})} = \frac{235.6}{30 - 3} = \frac{235.6}{27} = 8.726$$

Finally,

$$F = \frac{MS\ \text{between}}{MS\ \text{within}} = \frac{37.2}{8.726} = 4.263$$

Done.

Now, we need to consult an F table containing critical F values to see whether our results are significant or not. In our example, we had 2 degrees of freedom in the numerator (MS between) and 27 degrees of freedom in the denominator (MS within). Looking at an F table, this would give us a critical F value of approximately 3.38 at the .05 probability level. As you can see, our results were significant at the .05 probability level as our calculated F value, 4.263, was greater than the critical F value for the .05 probability level, 3.38. Here, we could say the following: There is a significant difference in the level of education between whites, blacks, and Hispanics ($F(2, 27) = 4.26, p < .05$). The first value for our degrees of freedom, 2, is equal to the number of groups minus one. The second value, 27, is equal to the total sample size or number of respondents, 30, minus the number of groups, 3.

If you wanted to combine all these steps into one, you would get the following equation for the F statistic:

$$F = \frac{MS\ \text{between}}{MS\ \text{within}} = \frac{\frac{SS\ \text{between}}{df\ \text{between}}}{\frac{SS\ \text{within}}{df\ \text{within}}} = \frac{\frac{SS\ \text{between}}{df\ \text{between}}}{\frac{SS\ \text{total} - SS\ \text{between}}{df\ \text{within}}}$$

$$= \frac{\left(\frac{\sum \frac{\left(\sum x\right)^2}{n} - \frac{\left[\sum\left(\sum x\right)\right]^2}{N}}{n(\text{groups}) - 1} \right)}{\left(\frac{\left[\sum\left(\sum (x^2)\right) - \frac{\left[\sum\left(\sum x\right)\right]^2}{N} \right] - \left[\sum \frac{\left(\sum x\right)^2}{n} - \frac{\left[\sum\left(\sum x\right)\right]^2}{N} \right]}{N - n(\text{groups})} \right)}$$

There are several versions of the ANOVA that will be covered in the SPSS and Stata sections of this chapter. The first, which was just presented, is called a **one-way ANOVA**. A one-way ANOVA is used when you have only one categorical independent or **predictor variable**. A **factorial ANOVA** is used when you have two or more categorical independent or predictor variables. Finally, a **repeated measures ANOVA** is used when you are looking at scores on a dependent variable across two or more points in time.

SECTION 2: IBM SPSS   △

Pearson's *r*: IBM SPSS

In this section, I will use the example from the previous section on Pearson's *r*, which determined the correlation coefficient between years of education and income. First, we will create two new variables in IBM SPSS, one called *educ* and another called *inc*, like the following:

Next, we will enter the data, reproduced below, into IBM SPSS:

Years of Education	Income (in Thousands of $)
8	12
12	15
8	8
14	20
12	18
16	45
20	65
24	85
24	100
24	90

When you are finished, the *Data View* of IBM SPSS should look like this:

Next, make the following menu selection:

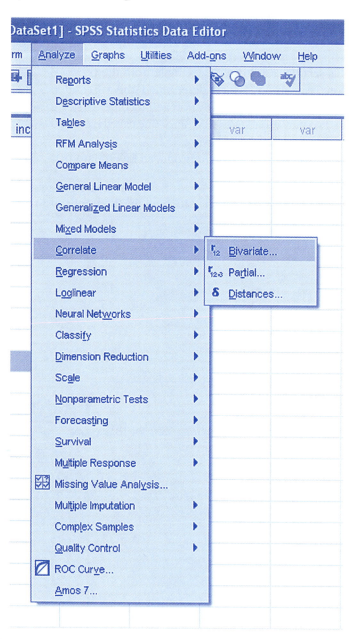

This will reveal the following dialog box:

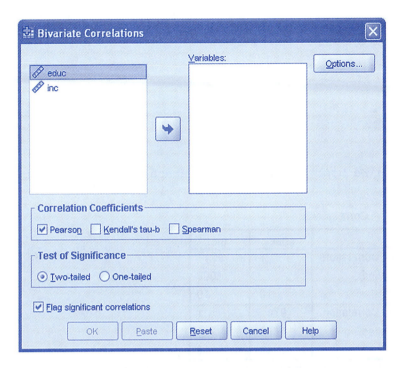

Next, we will move our two variables over to the *Variables* box, like so:

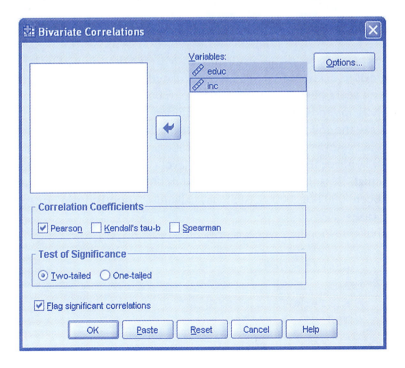

We can leave all the other options as they are. Finally, clicking the *OK* button will give us the following results:

➡ **Correlations**

```
[DataSet1] T:\Md book\#Data\Chapter 4\stata 9 - educ and inc.sav
```

Correlations

		educ	inc
educ	Pearson Correlation	1	.974**
	Sig. (2-tailed)		.000
	N	10	10
inc	Pearson Correlation	.974**	1
	Sig. (2-tailed)	.000	
	N	10	10

**. Correlation is significant at the 0.01 level (2-tailed).

As you can see, these results match what we determined by hand in the previous section. IBM SPSS has calculated the correlation coefficient between years of education and income to be 0.974 with a p level of less than .001 (as indicated by the ".000" under "Sig. (2-tailed)"). Here, we could say the following: There is a statistically significant positive correlation between years of education and income ($r = .97$, $p < .001$). As a note, whenever IBM SPSS gives your p level ("Sig.") as ".000," this means it is actually less than .001 but not equal to 0. For example, here, it might have been .0002 or .00005. SPSS basically just "rounds down" to zero in these cases.

The corresponding syntax is presented below:

```
CORRELATIONS
/VARIABLES=educ inc
/PRINT=TWOTAIL NOSIG
/MISSING=PAIRWISE.
```

Chi-Square: IBM SPSS

Calculating the chi-square statistic in IBM SPSS is very quick and easy, and it is obviously preferred to calculating it by hand. In our examples here, we will look at the relationship between highest degree completed and political affiliation, using actual data from the General Social Survey (GSS).

First, navigate to the following menu selection:

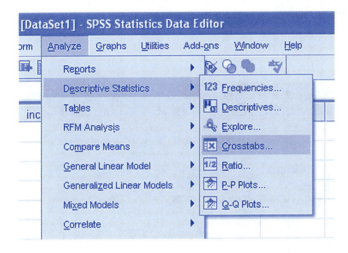

This will bring up the following dialog box:

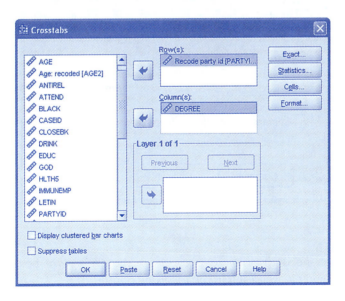

Here, I have selected a recoded version of *partyid* (political party affiliation) under *Row*, and *degree* (highest degree completed) under *Column*. In case you are following along yourself, I recoded respondents who answered 0 through 2 (strong Democrat, not very strong Democrat, or independent close to Democrat) as "1," those who responded 3 (independent) as "2," and those responded 4 through 6 (independent close to Republican, not very strong Republican, strong Republican) as "3." Those who responded 7 (other party or refused), or were missing (8 or 9), I recoded as missing.

Next, you will want to click on *Statistics*. This will bring up the following dialog box:

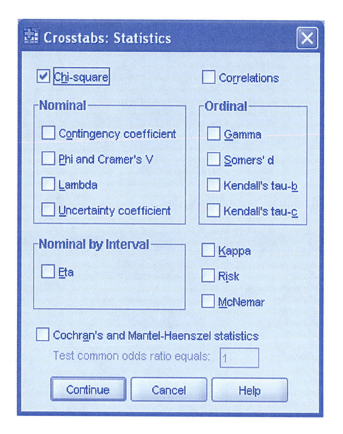

All you need to do here is to check the *Chi-square* box. Clicking *Continue* and *OK* will result in the following output:

→ **Crosstabs**

[DataSet2] T:\Md book\#Data\Chapter 3 GSS data\data.sav

Case Processing Summary

	Cases					
	Valid		Missing		Total	
	N	Percent	N	Percent	N	Percent
Recode party id * DEGREE	45462	97.7%	1048	2.3%	46510	100.0%

Recode party id * DEGREE Crosstabulation

Count

		DEGREE					Total
		Less than high school	High school	Associate/Jun ior College	Bachelor's	Graduate	
Recode party id	Democrat	6334	11563	1045	2618	1431	22991
	Independent	1698	3529	303	601	286	6417
	Republican	2832	8513	825	2812	1072	16054
Total		10864	23605	2173	6031	2789	45462

Chi-Square Tests

	Value	df	Asymp. Sig. (2-sided)
Pearson Chi-Square	834.007[a]	8	.000
Likelihood Ratio	847.994	8	.000
Linear-by-Linear Association	388.345	1	.000
N of Valid Cases	45462		

a. 0 cells (.0%) have expected count less than 5. The minimum expected count is 306.72.

The calculated chi-square value in this example was 834.007. We had 8 degrees of freedom $((3 - 1) \times (5 - 1))$. IBM SPSS tells us that this was significant at the .001 probability level. Here, we could say the following: There was a statistically significant relationship between highest degree completed and political party affiliation ($\chi^2 = 834.0, df = 8, p < .001$).

This is the corresponding syntax for this example:

```
DATASET ACTIVATE DataSet2.
CROSSTABS
/TABLES=PARTYIDR BY DEGREE
```

```
/FORMAT=AVALUE TABLES
/STATISTICS=CHISQ
/CELLS=COUNT
/COUNT ROUND CELL.
```

And if you wanted to omit the crosstabulation table, you would use this syntax:

```
CROSSTABS
/TABLES=PARTYIDR BY DEGREE
/FORMAT=NOTABLES
/STATISTICS=CHISQ
/COUNT ROUND CELL.
```

t-Test: IBM SPSS

To run an independent samples *t*-test within IBM SPSS, we will choose the following menu selection:

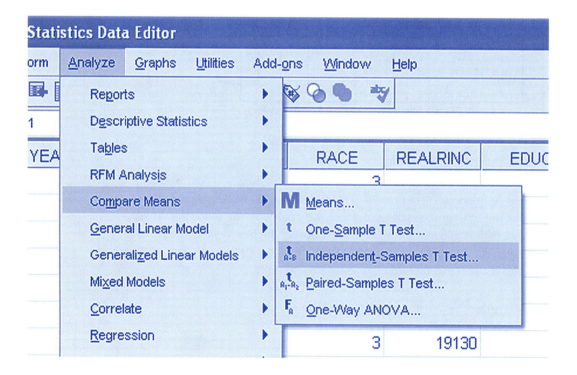

This will open the following dialog box:

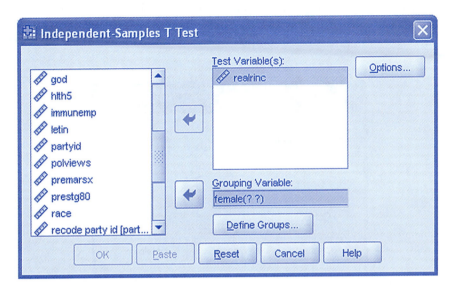

As you can see, I have taken the liberty of adding the respondents' yearly income, *realrinc*, into the *Test Variable(s)* box, and adding *female* (a constructed **dummy variable**, where *female* = 1 and *male* = 0) into the *Grouping Variable* box. Right now, inside the parentheses next to the sex variable, there are two question marks. Before we can run the *t*-test within IBM SPSS, we click on the *Define Groups* button. Clicking on the button will reveal this dialog box:

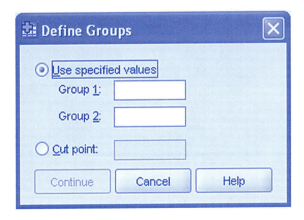

Here, we specify the values for the two different groups (males and females). Since females are coded 1 and males are coded 0, I simply specified Group 1 as equal to 1 (*females*), and Group 2 as equal to 0 (*males*), like this:

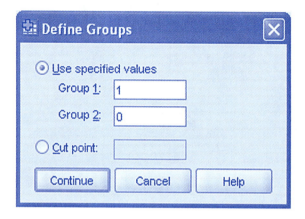

Now, you can see that our two groups are defined correctly:

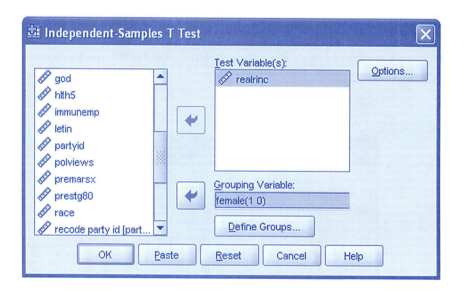

Clicking *OK* will result in the following output:

→ **T-Test**

[DataSet1] T:\Md book\#Data\Chapter 3 GSS data\gss data.sav

Group Statistics

	female	N	Mean	Std. Deviation	Std. Error Mean
realrinc	1	13301	14811.22	14022.518	121.586
	0	13862	26983.16	24339.702	206.729

Independent Samples Test

		Levene's Test for Equality of Variances		t-test for Equality of Means					95% Confidence Interval of the Difference	
		F	Sig.	t	df	Sig. (2-tailed)	Mean Difference	Std. Error Difference	Lower	Upper
realrinc	Equal variances assumed	1318.087	.000	-50.228	27161	.000	-12171.943	242.331	-12646.925	-11696.962
	Equal variances not assumed			-50.752	22324.904	.000	-12171.943	239.834	-12642.034	-11701.852

First, we see that Levene's test for equality of variances was significant at the .05 probability level. This means that the variances between groups are significantly different, and therefore when looking up the *t* values and significance, we should use the second row labeled "Equal variances not assumed." Here, we see that we obtained a *t* score of –50.752 with 22324.9 degrees of freedom, which was significant at the .001 probability level. In IBM SPSS, if the probability level or level of significance is ever listed as ".000," this means that it is less than .001—this is an IBM SPSS bug. The results also show us the mean for the two different groups: the mean income for males is approximately $26,983 per year, while the mean income for females is approximately $14,811 per year. These results could be stated as follows: Males were found to have a significantly higher income as compared with female respondents ($t = -50.75, df = 22324.90, p < .001$). Keep in mind that this analysis includes all data, starting in the year 1972. If we include only cases from the year 2004, we get the following results:

→ **T-Test**

[DataSet1] T:\Md book\#Data\Chapter 3 GSS data\gss data.sav

Group Statistics

	female	N	Mean	Std. Deviation	Std. Error Mean
realrinc	1	833	19191.23	21500.991	744.965
	0	855	31380.56	32430.227	1109.090

Independent Samples Test

		Levene's Test for Equality of Variances		t-test for Equality of Means					95% Confidence Interval of the Difference	
		F	Sig.	t	df	Sig. (2-tailed)	Mean Difference	Std. Error Difference	Lower	Upper
realrinc	Equal variances assumed	68.334	.000	-9.077	1686	.000	-12189.334	1342.860	-14823.182	-9555.487
	Equal variances not assumed			-9.123	1487.614	.000	-12189.334	1336.059	-14810.095	-9568.574

And this is the corresponding syntax:

```
T-TEST GROUPS=female(1 0)
/MISSING=ANALYSIS
/VARIABLES=realrinc
/CRITERIA=CI(.95).
```

Now, let's use IBM SPSS to run a dependent samples *t*-test. Because the GSS does not contain any variables that would be appropriate to use in a dependent samples *t*-test, I simply created a new file within IBM SPSS and created two new variables: *test1* and *test2*. Then, I typed in the following data as an example:

	test1	test2
1	78.00	95.00
2	72.00	78.00
3	75.00	71.00
4	83.00	95.00
5	92.00	98.00
6	65.00	85.00
7	85.00	98.00
8	74.00	89.00
9	85.00	87.00
10	65.00	85.00

Simply input the same data values if you want to follow along in IBM SPSS. Next, you will navigate to the following menu selection:

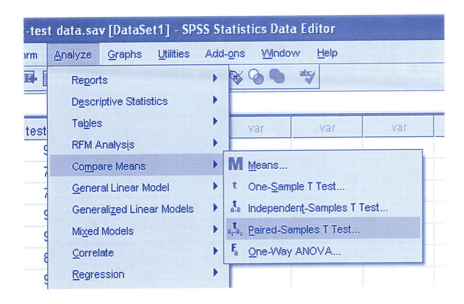

Next, the following dialog box will appear:

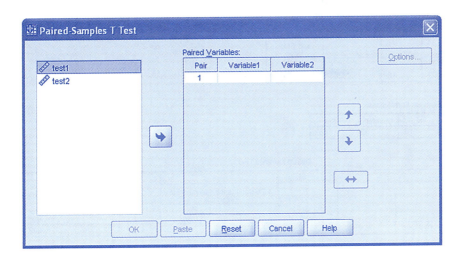

In this dialog box, I've simply selected the variables *test1* and *test2* and moved them to the *Paired Variables* box on the right, like this:

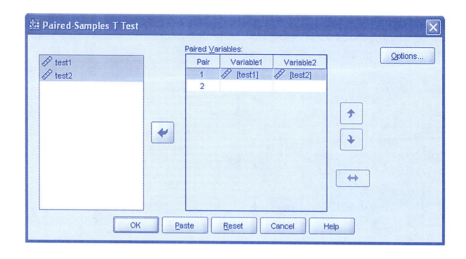

After clicking *OK*, we get the following output:

→ T-Test

[DataSet1] T:\Md book\#Data\Chapter 4\chapter 4- paired samples t-test data.sav

Paired Samples Statistics

		Mean	N	Std. Deviation	Std. Error Mean
Pair 1	test1	77.4000	10	8.90942	2.81741
	test2	88.1000	10	8.86253	2.80258

Paired Samples Correlations

		N	Correlation	Sig.
Pair 1	test1 & test2	10	.596	.069

Paired Samples Test

		Paired Differences							
					95% Confidence Interval of the Difference				
		Mean	Std. Deviation	Std. Error Mean	Lower	Upper	t	df	Sig. (2-tailed)
Pair 1	test1 - test2	-10.70000	7.98679	2.52565	-16.41341	-4.98659	-4.237	9	.002

IBM SPSS calculated the *t* score in this example to be –4.237. With 9 degrees of freedom, our results are significant at the .002 probability level (2-tailed). When writing up these results, you would simply say that it was significant at the $p < .01$ level: you will only use .05, .01, or .001 as standards. For example, you could report this result in the following way: Scores on Test 2 were found to be significantly higher as compared with scores on Test 1 ($t = -4.24$, $df = 9$, $p < .01$).

This is the corresponding syntax:

```
T-TEST PAIRS=test1 WITH test2 (PAIRED)
/CRITERIA=CI(.9500)
/MISSING=ANALYSIS.
```

One-Way ANOVA: IBM SPSS

Let's try running an ANOVA on differences in years of education based on race, similar to the race example that was presented in the theoretical section. In this example, race is coded as three categories: blacks, whites, and those of other race. These data are derived from the GSS, a large national survey of American adults.

First, navigate to the following menu selection:

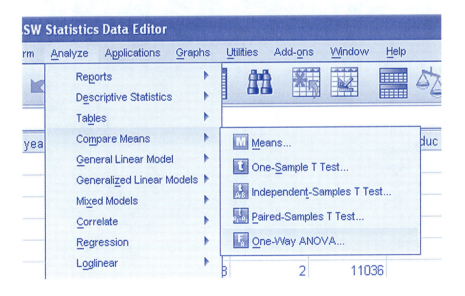

This will open the following dialog box:

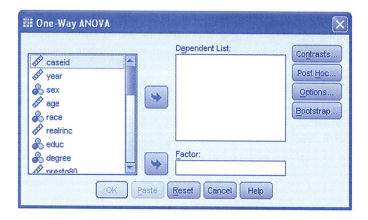

Here, I will simply add the dependent variable *educ*, representing the highest year of education completed, in the *Dependent List* and *race* into the *Factor* box, like this:

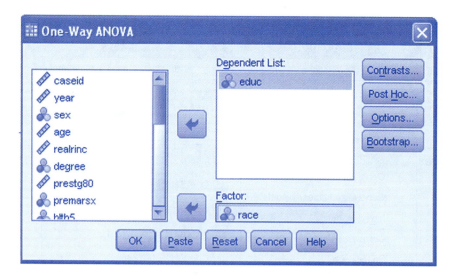

Next, you'll want to click on the *Post Hoc* button. This dialog box will pop up:

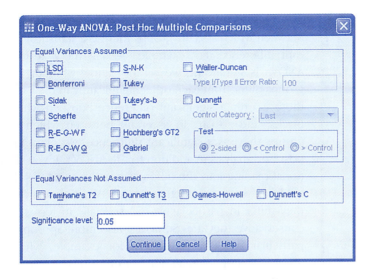

In this window, I will simply select two post hoc tests, the LSD (least significant difference) and the Games-Howell post hoc tests:

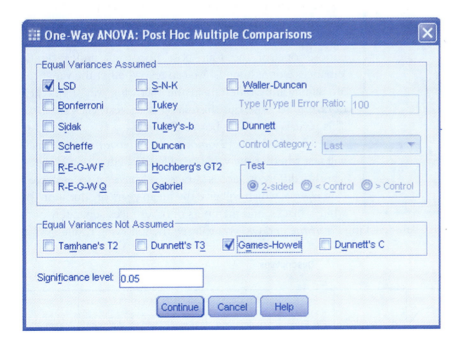

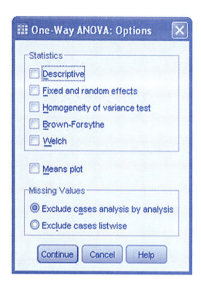

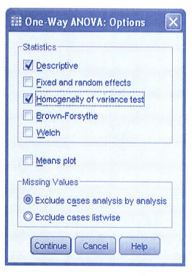

If you do not run a post hoc test, you will not know between which specific groups there is a statistically significant difference. For example, even if the F test for the ANOVA is significant, we will not know whether all three groups differ from each other significantly in their scores, if there is only a significant difference between whites and blacks, and so on. To ascertain between which specific groups there is a significant difference, we need to run a post hoc analysis in addition to the ANOVA. If you do additional reading into the different post hoc analyses that are available when conducting an ANOVA, you will find that they differ in particular ways, especially in terms of how conservative they are. Some are also more appropriate for particular types of situations: for example, when your ANOVA includes a small number of groups or a large number of groups.

The LSD post hoc test is less conservative, while the Games-Howell post hoc test is more conservative. As you can see, SPSS includes two categories, a large set of tests under "Equal Variances Assumed," and a smaller set under "Equal Variances Not Assumed." In our example, if the variance in years of education is significantly different between whites, blacks, and members of other races, we should choose one of the four post hoc tests under "Equal Variances Not Assumed." We can test whether the variances are significantly different in the following way: first, click *Continue* to close out this dialog box. Next, click *Options*. This reveals the dialog box to the left.

Here, I will select *Homogeneity of variance test*, which will test whether the variance of level of education is significantly different across race. I have also selected *Descriptive*, which will give the mean years of education for whites, blacks, and members of other races separately.

After clicking *Continue* and *OK*, you will see the following results:

Descriptives

educ

	N	Mean	Std. Deviation	Std. Error	95% Confidence Interval for Mean		Minimum	Maximum
					Lower Bound	Upper Bound		
White	38383	12.76	3.095	.016	12.72	12.79	0	20
Black	6360	11.64	3.311	.042	11.56	11.72	0	20
Other	1626	12.90	3.562	.088	12.73	13.08	0	20
Total	46369	12.61	3.167	.015	12.58	12.64	0	20

Test of Homogeneity of Variances

educ

Levene Statistic	df1	df2	Sig.
23.817	2	46366	.000

ANOVA

educ

	Sum of Squares	df	Mean Square	F	Sig.
Between Groups	6898.374	2	3449.187	349.095	.000
Within Groups	458112.554	46366	9.880		
Total	465010.928	46368			

Post Hoc Tests

Multiple Comparisons

Dependent Variable: educ

	(I) race	(J) race	Mean Difference (I-J)	Std. Error	Sig.	95% Confidence Interval	
						Lower Bound	Upper Bound
LSD	White	Black	1.112[*]	.043	.000	1.03	1.20
		Other	-.147	.080	.064	-.30	.01
	Black	White	-1.112[*]	.043	.000	-1.20	-1.03
		Other	-1.260[*]	.087	.000	-1.43	-1.09
	Other	White	.147	.080	.064	.00	.30
		Black	1.260[*]	.087	.000	1.09	1.43
Games-Howell	White	Black	1.112[*]	.044	.000	1.01	1.22
		Other	-.147	.090	.229	-.36	.06
	Black	White	-1.112[*]	.044	.000	-1.22	-1.01
		Other	-1.260[*]	.098	.000	-1.49	-1.03
	Other	White	.147	.090	.229	-.06	.36
		Black	1.260[*]	.098	.000	1.03	1.49

[*]. The mean difference is significant at the 0.05 level.

In the first table, labeled "Descriptives," we see the mean of years of education for whites, blacks, members of other races, and all groups combined. While the differences are not huge, it does appear that whites and members of other races tend to have more education as compared with blacks.

The second table, labeled "Test of Homogeneity of Variances," reports Levene's test for the equality of variances. Our probability level, which is circled, was found to be less than .05, which means that the variances in the level of education are significantly different across race. This also means that we will select as a post hoc test an option that does not assume equal variances. In this example, I selected the Games-Howell post hoc test, which does not assume equal variances.

Before moving to the results of the post hoc test, let's first discuss the results of the ANOVA itself. We see that the F statistic was calculated by IBM SPSS to be 349.095, with 2 degrees of freedom between groups and 46366 degrees of freedom within groups. This was significant at the $p < .001$ level. As the F test in this ANOVA was found to be significant, this means that level of education differs significantly based on race. However, to ascertain between which groups specifically there is a significant difference in education, we need to look at the results of our post hoc test. In regard to the degrees of freedom, which will be reported when writing up the results of an ANOVA, the between-groups degrees of freedom, calculated here to be 2, is simply the total number of groups minus one. In this example, we had three categories of race, so the between-groups degrees of freedom is simply 3 minus 1. The within-groups degrees of freedom is calculated as the total sample size minus the number of groups. The total sample size for this ANOVA, reported in the final row of the "Descriptives" table under N, was 46369. As we had three groups, the within-groups degrees of freedom is simply 46369 minus 3.

Finally, let's look at the results of our post hoc analysis, which are displayed under the "Post Hoc Tests" table. As you may notice, the results of our two post hoc analyses are quite similar, despite the fact that the LSD test assumes the equality of variances, while the Games-Howell test does not. This is not rare, as different tests commonly result in similar or identical results.

However, let's focus on the results of the Games-Howell test, as we found that the variances of level of education based on race significantly vary. Here, two results that were significant at the .05 probability level, denoted by asterisks, were found. First, whites were found to have significantly higher levels of education as compared with blacks. Specifically, whites were found, on average, to have 1.112 greater years of education as compared with blacks. Looking under the *Sig.* column, we can see that this was significant at the $p < .001$ level. As you may notice, the results of each comparison are actually reported twice in this table. Moving down two rows, the opposite comparison, blacks as compared with whites, is displayed. If you preferred, you could instead report this result, stating that blacks were found, on average, to have 1.112 fewer years of education as compared with whites. Just make sure to choose only one of these two results to report so you are not in effect reporting the same result twice.

Finally, we can see in the final row of the table that members of other races were found, on average, to have 1.260 greater years of education as compared with blacks. Looking under the *Sig.* column, we can see that this was significant at the $p < .001$ level. Our results highlight the importance of running a post hoc test whenever we are conducting an ANOVA on more than two groups: While a significant difference was found between whites and blacks and between members of other races and blacks, no significant difference was found between whites and members of other races in regard to years of education.

Our results can be stated in the following way: A significant difference in years of education between whites, blacks, and members of other races was found, $F(2, 46366) = 349.10$, $p < .001$. Specifically, a Games-Howell post hoc test found the mean level of education for both whites and members of other races to be significantly greater than that of blacks, $p < .001$.

Factorial ANOVA: IBM SPSS

While one-way ANOVAs only include one categorical independent or predictor variable, factorial ANOVAs include more than one. In the example presented in the previous section, a one-way ANOVA was used as there was only one independent or predictor variable, race of the respondent. In this example, I will incorporate both race of the respondent as well as the respondent's gender in a factorial ANOVA that includes the respondent's income as the dependent variable. This example will also use data from the GSS.

To begin, first make the following menu selection:

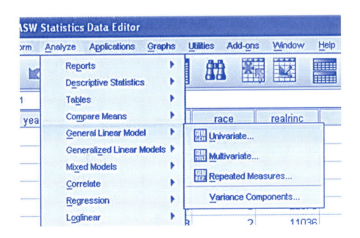

Next, the following dialog box will appear:

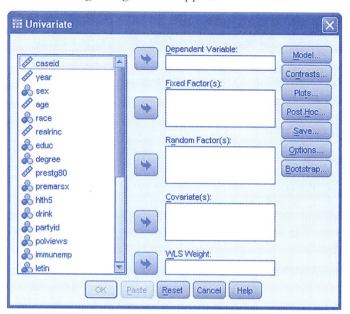

While this selection allows us to run a number of different tests, in this example, it will be used to run a factorial ANOVA. Next, I will move income, *realrinc*, into the *Dependent Variable* box and will move race and sex into the *Fixed Factor(s)* box, which is used for categorical independent variables. When completed, the dialog box will look as shown below.

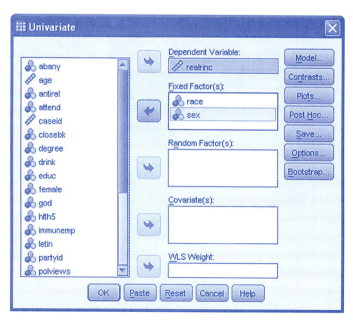

Next, click *Post Hoc*. This will open the following dialog box:

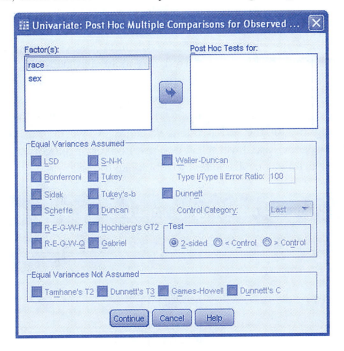

Here, I will move one of our independent variables, *race*, into the "Post Hoc Tests for" box:

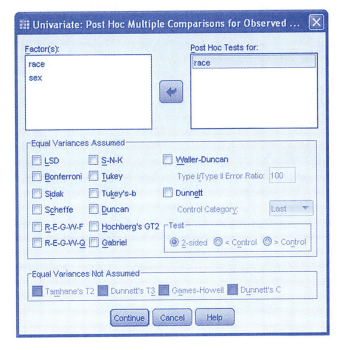

As there are only two categories for sex, male and female, a post hoc test is not necessary. As in the previous example, I will select both the LSD as well as the Games-Howell post hoc tests. The LSD post hoc test is less conservative, while the Games-Howell post hoc test is more conservative. More conservative tests are sometimes preferred, as you are less likely to get a "false positive," or a significant result, in situations where there actually is no real difference. As explained in the previous section, most post hoc tests assume that the variances in the dependent variable are not significantly different across categories of the independent variables. As we do not yet know whether this is the case, I will select one test from each category. After making these selections, our dialog box will look like the following:

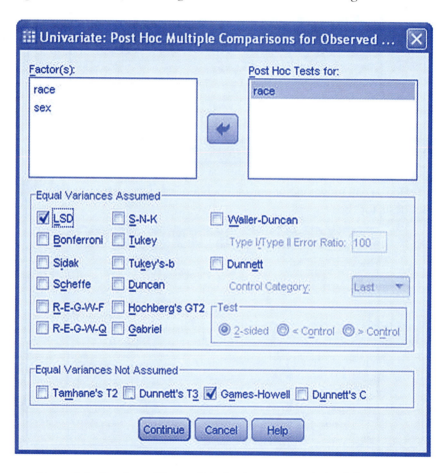

Next, click *Continue*. Then, click *Options* to reveal the following dialog box:

Here, we will simply select "Homogeneity tests" to test whether the variance in income is significantly different across race and sex. This is important in determining which post hoc test we will use and report in this analysis. I'll also select "Descriptive statistics," which will give us the mean score on respondent's income by race and sex. After making the selections, our dialog box will look like the following:

Finally, click *Continue* and *OK* to run the analysis.

As the results of this analysis are rather lengthy, I'll go through them step by step as opposed to presenting the entire set of results all at once. The first two tables are presented on the following page.

Between-Subjects Factors

		Value Label	N
race	1	White	22507
	2	Black	3563
	3	Other	1093
sex	1	Male	13862
	2	Female	13301

Descriptive Statistics

Dependent Variable:realrinc

race	sex	Mean	Std. Deviation	N
White	Male	28176.87	25095.351	11766
	Female	15094.84	14427.765	10741
	Total	21933.74	21708.267	22507
Black	Male	19068.24	15621.340	1527
	Female	13284.99	11596.369	2036
	Total	15763.53	13768.218	3563
Other	Male	23540.04	23387.082	569
	Female	14927.64	13846.850	524
	Total	19411.13	19870.964	1093
Total	Male	26983.16	24339.702	13862
	Female	14811.22	14022.518	13301
	Total	21022.88	20871.594	27163

The first table, titled "Between-Subjects Factors," gives us the sample size, or number of respondents, for each category of our independent variables. For example, in the first row, we see that there are 22,507 white respondents included in this analysis. In the final row of this table, we see that there are 13,301 female respondents included in the analysis.

The second table, titled "Descriptive Statistics," gives us the mean for every possible combination of our independent variables. For example, in the first row, we see that the mean income for white males included in this analysis is $28176.87. If we wanted to find the mean income for females of other races, we simply find the *Other* category for race, which is the third one down, and then find female, which is the second row. Here, we see that the mean income for females of other races is $14927.64.

Next, I will present the tables for Levene's test of the equality of variances and the table presenting the main results of the ANOVA.

Levene's Test of Equality of Error Variances[a]

Dependent Variable:realrinc

F	df1	df2	Sig.
303.008	5	27157	.000

Tests the null hypothesis that the error variance of the dependent variable is equal across groups.

a. Design: Intercept + race + sex + race * sex

Tests of Between-Subjects Effects

Dependent Variable:realrinc

Source	Type III Sum of Squares	df	Mean Square	F	Sig.
Corrected Model	1.130E12	5	2.261E11	573.719	.000
Intercept	2.609E12	1	2.609E12	6619.628	.000
race	9.294E10	2	4.647E10	117.926	.000
sex	1.513E11	1	1.513E11	383.954	.000
race * sex	4.342E10	2	2.171E10	55.086	.000
Error	1.070E13	27157	3.941E8		
Total	2.384E13	27163			
Corrected Total	1.183E13	27162			

a. R Squared = .096 (Adjusted R Squared = .095)

The first table here gives us the results of Levene's test of the equality of variances. This result was found to be significant at the $p < .001$ level, which means that the variance in income significantly varies across the categories of our independent variables and also means that we will select a post hoc test that does not assume equal variances.

The second table, titled "Tests of Between-Subjects Effects," presents the main results of the ANOVA. The first row, titled *Corrected Model*, gives us the results of the F test for the overall model. Here, the calculated F statistic was 573.719 and was significant at the $p < .001$ level. The three other results that are circled in this table give us the effects of race on income, sex on income, and the interaction between race and sex on income. First, the F statistic for race was 117.926. This was significant at the $p < .001$ level, which means that respondent's income was found to significantly vary based on race. Next, the F statistic for sex was 383.954. This result was also significant at the $p < .001$ level, meaning that respondent's income significantly varies based on sex. Finally, the interaction between race and sex, denoted as *race * sex*, had a calculated F statistic of 55.086 and was also significant at the $p < .001$ level. This means that the effect of race on income significantly varies by sex. Alternatively, you could state that the effect of sex on income varies significantly by race. For example, this would be the case if race were an important predictor of income for males but not for females. Likewise, this would be the case if males have higher incomes than females for whites but if females had higher incomes than males for blacks. In essence, the significant interaction effect in this example means that the effect of one of the independent variables on the dependent variable varies significantly depending on the level of the second independent variable. Interaction effects can clearly be trickier to deal with and can take some additional time to fully understand. The degrees of freedom, which you will report, come from the df column in the table just presented. For example, the F test for the full model would be reported as the following: $F(5, 27157) = 573.72$. The first value, 5, comes from the first row, while the second value, 27157, comes from the *Error* row. As you can see in the results write-up presented at the end of this section, this second value will always be equal to the value presented in the *Error* row.

Finally, I'll present the table which included the results of the post hoc tests we conducted.

Post Hoc Tests

race

Multiple Comparisons

Dependent Variable:realrinc

	(I) race	(J) race	Mean Difference (I-J)	Std. Error	Sig.	95% Confidence Interval	
						Lower Bound	Upper Bound
LSD	White	Black	6170.21*	357.927	.000	5468.66	6871.77
		Other	2522.61*	614.862	.000	1317.45	3727.77
	Black	White	-6170.21*	357.927	.000	-6871.77	-5468.66
		Other	-3647.60*	686.403	.000	-4992.98	-2302.21
	Other	White	-2522.61*	614.862	.000	-3727.77	-1317.45
		Black	3647.60*	686.403	.000	2302.21	4992.98
Games-Howell	White	Black	6170.21*	272.289	.000	5531.91	6808.52
		Other	2522.61*	618.220	.000	1071.92	3973.31
	Black	White	-6170.21*	272.289	.000	-6808.52	-5531.91
		Other	-3647.60*	643.787	.000	-5158.02	-2137.18
	Other	White	-2522.61*	618.220	.000	-3973.31	-1071.92
		Black	3647.60*	643.787	.000	2137.18	5158.02

Based on observed means.
The error term is Mean Square(Error) = 394077231.261.

*. The mean difference is significant at the .05 level.

As mentioned previously, a post hoc test for sex was not necessary as there are only two groups, males and females. The results of the ANOVA, presented previously, found that respondent's income varied significantly based on sex. Looking at the "Descriptive Statistics" table, presented previously, we see that the average income for males is $26983.16, while the average income for females is $14811.22. Using this information, we can state that the average income for males is significantly higher than that of females.

Now, to look at the results presented in this table. First, as the variance in income was found to significantly differ across categories of our independent variables, we will focus only on the second post hoc test presented in this table, the Games-Howell post hoc test, as it does not assume equal variances, while the LSD test does. As you may notice, the results for these two tests are similar. However, we should focus on and report the results from the Games-Howell test as it does not assume equal variances. In this post hoc test, three significant comparisons were found, which means that there are significant differences in income between all three of our racial categories. As mentioned in the previous section, all comparisons are made twice, so all results are repeated. For example, the white versus black comparison had a mean difference of 6170.21, while the black versus white comparison had a mean difference of –6170.21. In essence, this is the same result, simply flipped, so when looking at this table, we can simply focus on positive mean differences, which are circled.

The first circled mean difference, which looks at the mean difference between whites and blacks, is 6170.21. This means that the average income for whites is $6170.21 greater than the average income for blacks. This result was significant at the $p < .001$ level. Next, the difference in income between whites and those of other race was found to be significant at the $p < .001$ level. Here, the mean income for whites was, on average, $2522.61 greater than that of members of other races. Finally, the difference in income between members of other races and blacks was found to be significant at the $p < .001$ level. In this case, the mean income for members of other races was, on average, $3647.60 greater than the average income for blacks.

Our results can be stated in the following way: A factorial ANOVA found a significant difference in income based on both race and gender, $F(5, 27157) = 573.72$, $p < .001$. Specifically, males were found to have significantly higher incomes than females, $F(1, 27157) = 383.95$, $p < .001$. Also, income was found to vary significantly based on race, $F(2, 27157) = 117.93$, $p < .001$. A Games-Howell post hoc test found that income for whites was significantly higher than that of blacks and those of other race, while the mean income for members of other races was significantly greater than the average income for blacks. Finally, a significant interaction between race and gender was found, $F(2, 27157) = 55.09$, $p < .001$.

Repeated Measures ANOVA: IBM SPSS

Repeated measures ANOVAs are used when your dependent variable consists of a measure that was recorded or measured at several points in time. For example, if you had a set of two or more exam grades for a set of respondents, these data, along with one or more independent predictor variables, could be analyzed using a repeated measures ANOVA. This is the example that I'll be using in this section. A repeated measures ANOVA could also be used in other situations, for example, if you had a measure for respondents that was taken before and after some medical treatment. Using a repeated measures ANOVA, you can also include predictor variables such as sex and age.

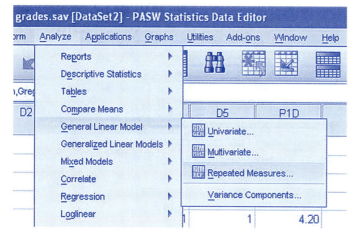

To run a repeated measures ANOVA, first make the following menu selection:

This will open the following dialog box:

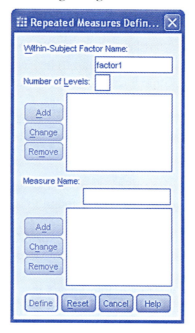

The data that I am using in this example consist of three exam scores in a sample of 37 students. The dependent variable consists of the three exam scores, while I will include year in college, categorized as Freshman, Sophomore, Junior, and Senior, as the independent variable. In the dialog box just presented, I will rename the *Within-Subject Factor Name* as simply *time*. Next, I will specify it as having three levels, as we have three separate exam scores. Finally, I will click *Add* under *Number of Levels*. When finished, the dialog box will look as follows:

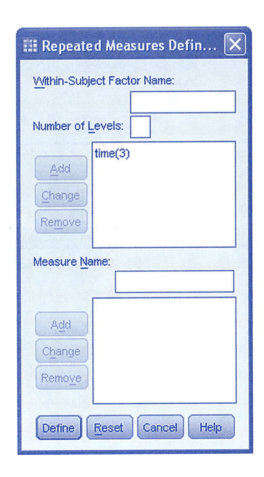

Next, we can click *Define*. This will reveal the following dialog box:

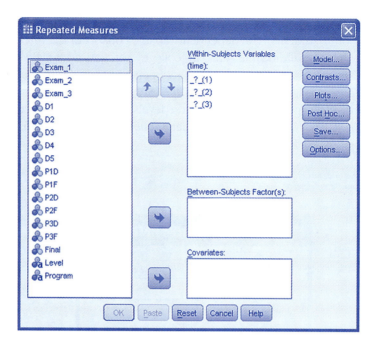

Here, we will begin by selecting the three exam scores, named *Exam_1*, *Exam_2*, and *Exam_3* and move them to the *Within-Subjects Variables (time)* box. After this step, the dialog box will look as follows:

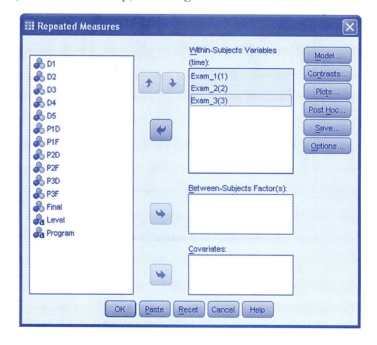

Next, we will specify our independent predictor variable, year at college. Any categorical predictor variables included in the repeated measures ANOVA will be included in the *Between-Subjects Factor(s)* box. In this example, we only have year at college as a categorical predictor variable, which is named *level* in this data set. After selecting this variable and moving it into the appropriate box, our dialog box will look as follows:

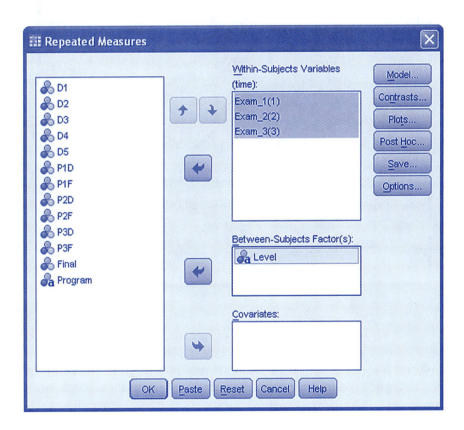

Next, let's click on the *Post Hoc* option, so we can specify post hoc tests for this ANOVA. This will allow us to see whether there are differences in exam scores between each category of year at college. For example, it will tell us whether Seniors have higher exam scores compared with Freshman. A post hoc test is needed here as the ANOVA will only tell you whether there are significant differences overall. The initial dialog box that you'll see when you first select this option is presented here:

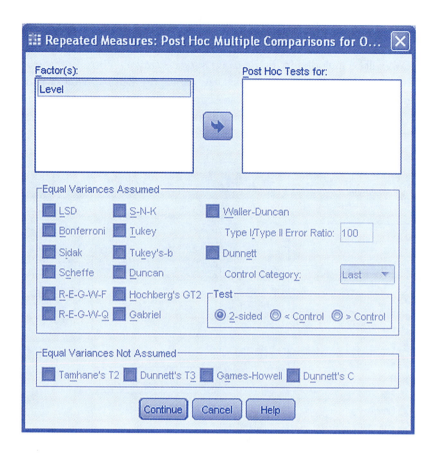

Next, we will simply select our *level* variable and move it to the right. Then, we will select the post hoc tests desired. Here, I will select both the LSD post hoc test as well as the Games-Howell post hoc test. The LSD post hoc test is less conservative while the Games-Howell post hoc test is more conservative. With more conservative tests, you are less likely to find a significant result, while their stricter standards mean that you're less likely to find a "false positive," or a result that is reported to be significant by SPSS, which in actuality is not. The LSD test incorporates the assumption that the variance in your dependent variable is approximately equal across the different categories of your independent variable, while the Games-Howell test does not. In this example, it would be assumed that variances in test scores are relatively the same regardless of the respondent's year of college. We will be testing this assumption which will determine which of these two post hoc tests we end up using in our analysis. After making our selections, our dialog box will appear as follows:

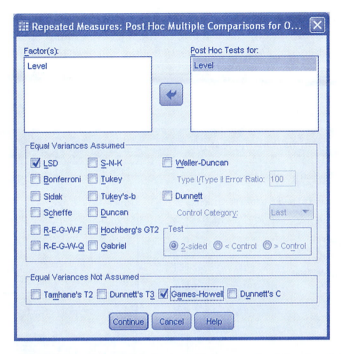

Next, click *Continue*. Then click *Options*. This opens the following dialog box:

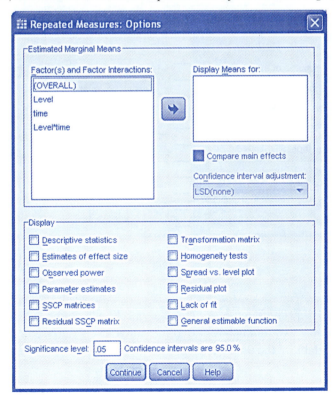

Here, I will select *Descriptive statistics* and *Homogeneity tests*. The *Descriptive statistics* option will give us the mean of exam scores by year at college, while the *Homogeneity tests* option will test the assumption of equal variances. After making these selections, your dialog box should look as follows:

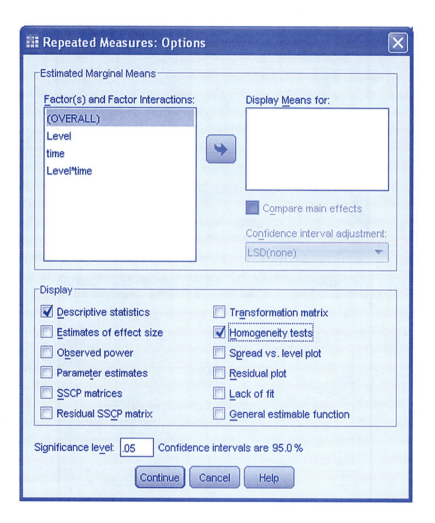

Finally, we can click *Continue* and *OK* to run the analysis.

Instead of presenting the results all at once, I will go through the tables a few at a time as running a repeated measures ANOVA in SPSS results in a large set of tables. The first three tables of the output are presented here:

Within-Subjects Factors

Measure:MEASURE_1

time	Dependent Variable
1	Exam_1
2	Exam_2
3	Exam_3

Between-Subjects Factors

		N
Level	Freshman	2
	Junior	8
	Senior	7
	Sophomore	20

Descriptive Statistics

	Level	Mean	Std. Deviation	N
Exam_1	Freshman	70.00	14.142	2
	Junior	91.75	5.258	8
	Senior	83.71	12.842	7
	Sophomore	83.10	12.226	20
	Total	84.38	11.910	37
Exam_2	Freshman	81.50	7.778	2
	Junior	93.00	3.780	8
	Senior	87.29	10.781	7
	Sophomore	84.10	13.242	20
	Total	86.49	11.423	37
Exam_3	Freshman	70.00	2.828	2
	Junior	84.50	6.568	8
	Senior	82.29	4.536	7
	Sophomore	70.40	25.111	20
	Total	75.68	19.695	37

The first table, "Within-Subjects Factors," simply presents the different measures of the dependent variable that we had specified. Here, you can see that we have simply specified the three different exam scores as the dependent variable in this repeated measures ANOVA. Next, the "Between-Subjects Factors" table presents the number of respondents for each category of our independent variable. The third table, titled "Descriptive Statistics," presents mean scores for each exam separately by year at college. For example, the first row presents the mean score on Exam 1 for freshmen, which is 70.00. The final row presents the mean score on Exam 3 for all respondents, which is 75.68.

Here are the next two tables of the output:

Box's Test of Equality of Covariance Matrices[a]

Box's M	46.536
F	3.151
df1	12.000
df2	1470.214
Sig.	.000

Tests the null hypothesis that the observed covariance matrices of the dependent variables are equal across groups.

a. Design: Intercept + Level Within Subjects Design: time

Multivariate Tests[c]

Effect		Value	F	Hypothesis df	Error df	Sig.
time	Pillai's Trace	.108	1.941[a]	2.000	32.000	.160
	Wilks' Lambda	.892	1.941[a]	2.000	32.000	.160
	Hotelling's Trace	.121	1.941[a]	2.000	32.000	.160
	Roy's Largest Root	.121	1.941[a]	2.000	32.000	.160
time * Level	Pillai's Trace	.107	.625	6.000	66.000	.710
	Wilks' Lambda	.894	.615[a]	6.000	64.000	.717
	Hotelling's Trace	.117	.605	6.000	62.000	.725
	Roy's Largest Root	.102	1.123[b]	3.000	33.000	.354

a. Exact statistic

b. The statistic is an upper bound on F that yields a lower bound on the significance level.

c. Design: Intercept + Level
Within Subjects Design: time

The first table presented here, titled "Box's Test of Equality of Covariance Matrices" includes a calculation of Box's M statistic and its significance. The statistic is used to test the assumptions of the multivariate model, which will be explained shortly. If the significance of the statistic is less than .05, it means that the assumptions of the multivariate model have been violated, and therefore, the multivariate model should not be used. Here, you can see that the probability level is less than .001, which means that the assumptions of the multivariate model have been violated.

The next table, titled "Multivariate Tests," presents the results of the repeated measures ANOVA. In short, "multivariate" means that you are incorporating more than one predictor variable, while "univariate" means that you are incorporating only one predictor. In this example, both *level* (year at college) and *time* are included, making this a multivariate model. You can see that for each variable or interaction effect included, SPSS gives you four different versions of the F test. Wilks's Lambda is very commonly used, so I'll focus on that version here. As mentioned in the previous paragraph, as the assumptions of the multivariate model have been violated, you would prefer not to focus on the multivariate model. However, I will explain the results for your understanding. We can see that the Wilks's Lambda F test calculated an F statistic for *time* of 1.941 with a p value of .160. This means that in this multivariate model, test scores were not found to significantly vary based on time. In regard to the time * level interaction effect, the calculated F statistic using the Wilks's Lambda F test was .615 with a p level of .717. This means that in this multivariate model, the effect of year at college on test scores did not vary significantly based on time. Alternatively, you could state that the effect of time on test scores did not vary significantly based on year at college.

The next two tables are presented here:

Mauchly's Test of Sphericity[b]

Measure:MEASURE 1

Within Subject...	Mauchly's W	Approx. Chi-Square	df	Sig.	Epsilon[a]		
					Greenhouse-Geisser	Huynh-Feldt	Lower-bound
time	.600	16.323	2	.000	.715	.806	.500

Tests the null hypothesis that the error covariance matrix of the orthonormalized transformed dependent variables is proportional to an identity matrix.

a. May be used to adjust the degrees of freedom for the averaged tests of significance. Corrected tests are displayed in the Tests of Within-Subjects Effects table.

b. Design: Intercept + Level Within Subjects Design: time

Tests of Within-Subjects Effects

Measure:MEASURE 1

Source		Type III Sum of Squares	df	Mean Square	F	Sig.
time	Sphericity Assumed	918.973	2	459.486	2.658	.078
	Greenhouse-Geisser	918.973	1.429	643.082	2.658	.097
	Huynh-Feldt	918.973	1.611	570.295	2.658	.090
	Lower-bound	918.973	1.000	918.973	2.658	.113
time * Level	Sphericity Assumed	509.048	6	84.841	.491	.813
	Greenhouse-Geisser	509.048	4.287	118.741	.491	.755
	Huynh-Feldt	509.048	4.834	105.301	.491	.776
	Lower-bound	509.048	3.000	169.683	.491	.691
Error(time)	Sphericity Assumed	11407.943	66	172.848		
	Greenhouse-Geisser	11407.943	47.157	241.912		
	Huynh-Feldt	11407.943	53.176	214.531		
	Lower-bound	11407.943	33.000	345.695		

The first table, titled "Mauchly's Test of Sphericity" presents a test of the assumptions of the univariate model, the results of which are presented in the second table. The probability level, which is circled, is below .05, which means that the assumption of sphericity has been violated. However, this does not prevent us from using the results of the univariate model. The final three columns of the table present three corrections to the calculated F statistic. The Huynh-Feldt correction is somewhat less conservative than the others and is what I will focus on here.

The second table, titled "Tests of Within-Subjects Effects," presents the effect of time on test scores. As discussed in the previous paragraph, the Huynh-Feldt correction will be used here. The effect of time on test scores was not found to be significant, having an F value of 2.658 with a probability level of .090. The interaction between time and year at college (*level*) was also not found to be significant, having an F value of .491 with a probability level of .776. I will skip the next table of the output, titled "Tests of Within-Subjects Contrasts," as it is not commonly used.

The next two tables are presented here:

Levene's Test of Equality of Error Variances[a]

	F	df1	df2	Sig.
Exam_1	2.076	3	33	.122
Exam_2	1.532	3	33	.225
Exam_3	1.628	3	33	.202

Tests the null hypothesis that the error variance of the dependent variable is equal across groups.

a. Design: Intercept + Level
Within Subjects Design: time

Tests of Between-Subjects Effects

Measure:MEASURE_1
Transformed Variable:Average

Source	Type III Sum of Squares	df	Mean Square	F	Sig.
Intercept	392737.160	1	392737.160	1376.014	.000
Level	2432.320	3	810.773	2.841	.053
Error	9418.743	33	285.416		

The first table, titled "Levene's Test of Equality of Error Variances," tests the assumption that the variances in test scores are equal across the categories of the independent variable, which is year at college in this example. This is important for the post hoc test that will be presented shortly, as a number of post hoc tests assume that these variances are equal. As you can see, the probability levels, which are circled, are not significant at the .05 level, which means that this assumption has not been violated and that we can use post hoc tests that assume the equality of variances.

The second table, titled "Tests of Between-Subjects Effects," tests the effect of our independent variable, *level* or year at college, on exam scores. As you can see, this effect approaches significance with an F value of 2.841 and a probability level of .053.

The final table, presenting the results of our post hoc tests, is presented here:

Post Hoc Tests

Level

Multiple Comparisons

Measure:MEASURE_1

	(I) Level	(J) Level	Mean Difference (I-J)	Std. Error	Sig.	95% Confidence Interval Lower Bound	95% Confidence Interval Upper Bound
LSD	Freshman	Junior	-15.92*	7.711	.047	-31.61	-.23
		Senior	-10.60	7.821	.185	-26.51	5.32
		Sophomore	-5.37	7.234	.463	-20.08	9.35
	Junior	Freshman	15.92	7.711	.047	.23	31.61
		Senior	5.32	5.048	.299	-4.95	15.59
		Sophomore	10.55	4.080	.014	2.25	18.85
	Senior	Freshman	10.60	7.821	.185	-5.32	26.51
		Junior	-5.32	5.048	.299	-15.59	4.95
		Sophomore	5.23	4.283	.231	-3.49	13.94
	Sophomore	Freshman	5.37	7.234	.463	-9.35	20.08
		Junior	-10.55*	4.080	.014	-18.85	-2.25
		Senior	-5.23	4.283	.231	-13.94	3.49
Games-Howell	Freshman	Junior	-15.92	2.316	.113	-46.04	14.21
		Senior	-10.60	2.870	.107	-25.11	3.92
		Sophomore	-5.37	3.527	.480	-17.49	6.75
	Junior	Freshman	15.92	2.316	.113	-14.21	46.04
		Senior	5.32	2.053	.116	-1.21	11.85
		Sophomore	10.55*	2.901	.007	2.49	18.61
	Senior	Freshman	10.60	2.870	.107	-3.92	25.11
		Junior	-5.32	2.053	.116	-11.85	1.21
		Sophomore	5.23	3.360	.421	-4.03	14.49
	Sophomore	Freshman	5.37	3.527	.480	-6.75	17.49
		Junior	-10.55*	2.901	.007	-18.61	-2.49
		Senior	-5.23	3.360	.421	-14.49	4.03

Based on observed means.
The error term is Mean Square(Error) = 95.139.

*. The mean difference is significant at the .05 level.

As mentioned earlier, Levene's test of the equality of variances found that the assumption that the variances are equal was not violated. This means that we can use a post hoc test that assumes equal variances. The LSD post hoc test, presented in this table, assumes equal variances and will be used in this analysis. As mentioned earlier in this chapter, as every possible group comparison is included in the table of the post hoc test results, all comparisons will appear twice. For example, the "Junior versus Freshman" comparison, with a mean difference of 15.92 (circled), is also presented in the first row of the table as the "Freshman versus Junior" comparison, with a mean difference of –15.92. A good way to make sure that you do not report the same comparison twice is to simply focus only on significant comparisons that have a positive mean difference.

The first significant comparison was that of Junior and Freshman. Juniors were found to have test scores that were, on average, 15.92 points higher than that of Freshman. This effect was found to be significant, having a probability level of below .05. The second significant comparison, also circled, was between Junior and Sophomore. Juniors were found to have test scores that were, on average, 10.55 points higher than that of Sophomore. This effect was found to be significant, also having a probability level of below .05.

Our results can be stated in the following way:

A repeated measures ANOVA was conducted on a series of three exam grades with year at college (Freshman, Sophomore, Junior, and Senior) as the independent predictor. The multivariate model will not be used as Box's M test found significant variability in the observed covariance matrices of the dependent variables across groups. Mauchly's test of sphericity was found to be significant at the .05 alpha level; hence, the Huynh-Feldt adjustment will be used in the univariate model. Neither the effects of time nor the interaction between time and year at college were found to significantly predict exam grades. However, the effect of year at college approached significance, $F(3, 33) = 2.84$, $p = .053$.

An LSD post hoc test was used to analyze the differences in exam grades based on year at college. Significant differences in exam scores were found between Junior and Freshman and between Junior and Sophomore. Juniors were found to have test scores that were, on average, 15.92 points higher than that of Freshman, $p < .05$. Juniors were also found to have test scores that were, on average, 10.55 points higher than that of Sophomores, $p < .05$.

ANOVA Syntax Summary

One-Way ANOVA

```
ONEWAY educ BY race
/STATISTICS DESCRIPTIVES HOMOGENEITY
/MISSING ANALYSIS
/POSTHOC=LSD GH ALPHA(.05).
```

The general format being as follows:

```
ONEWAY [Dependent variable] BY [Independent
variable]
/STATISTICS [Options]
/MISSING ANALYSIS
```

```
/POSTHOC=[Post hoc tests]  ALPHA([Alpha or
   probability level]).
```

Factorial ANOVA

```
UNIANOVA realrinc BY race sex
/METHOD=SSTYPE(3)
/INTERCEPT=INCLUDE
/POSTHOC=race(LSD GH)
/PRINT=HOMOGENEITY DESCRIPTIVE
/CRITERIA=ALPHA(.05)
/DESIGN=race sex race*sex.
```

The general format being as follows:

```
UNIANOVA [Dependent variable] BY [List of
   independent variables]
/METHOD=SSTYPE(3)
/INTERCEPT=INCLUDE
/POSTHOC=[Independent variables to include in
the post hoc test] ([Post hoc tests])
/PRINT=[Options]
/CRITERIA=ALPHA([Alpha or probability level])
/DESIGN=[Design of model].
```

Repeated Measures ANOVA

```
GLM Exam_1 Exam_2 Exam_3 BY Level
/WSFACTOR=time 3 Polynomial
/METHOD=SSTYPE(3)
/POSTHOC=Level(LSD GH)
/PRINT=DESCRIPTIVE HOMOGENEITY
/CRITERIA=ALPHA(.05)
/WSDESIGN=time
/DESIGN=Level.
```

The general format being as follows:

```
GLM [Dependent measures] BY [Independent
   variable]
/WSFACTOR=[Repeated measures "factor" name (can
   specify any name)] [Number of times the
   measure is repeated] Polynomial
```

```
/METHOD=SSTYPE(3)
/POSTHOC=[Independent variables to include in
   the post hoc test]  ([ Post hoc tests])
/PRINT=[Options]
/CRITERIA=ALPHA([Alpha or probability level])
/WSDESIGN=[Repeated measures "factor" name]
/DESIGN=[Design of model] .
```

◭ SECTION 3: STATA

Pearson's *r*: Stata

Calculating Pearson's *r* in Stata is quite simple. In this section, I will use the same data as were presented in the first section on Pearson's *r*. First, I will create two new variables, one for income and one for education, by entering the following commands:

```
gen inc=.
gen educ=.
```

Next, I will enter the data displayed in the table below using the data editor by entering the command ed, which stands for edit.

Years of Education (x)	Income (in Thousands of $) (y)
8	12
12	15
8	8
14	20
12	18
16	45
20	65
24	85
24	100
24	90

When you have finished entering data, your data editor should look like this:

After closing the editor, we can make the following menu selection:

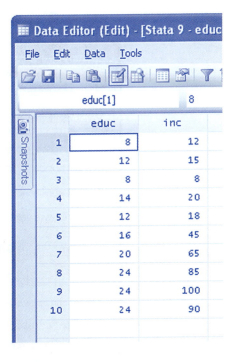

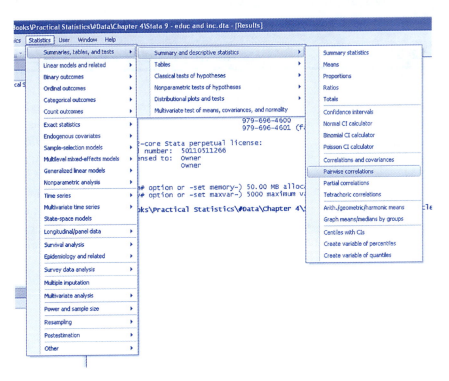

This will open the following dialog box:

```
. pwcorr inc educ, sig

               inc       educ

      inc    1.0000

     educ    0.9743    1.0000
             0.0000
```

As you can see, I have listed the income and education variables under the *Variables* entry. Also, I have selected the *Print significance level for each entry* option so that the *p* level is included in our results. Clicking *OK* will give us this result:

Comparing this result from the one we obtained in the initial section on Pearson's *r*, we can see that the calculated correlation coefficient is identical.

Secondly, we have generated the syntax that is used to determine the correlation coefficient between two variables in Stata:

```
pwcorr inc educ, sig
```

Specifying the sig option tells Stata to include the significance level of the correlation coefficient in the results. Here, our *p* level is listed as "0.0000," which simply means that our true *p* level is less than .0001. Stata incorrectly rounded our *p* level down to zero, while it can never be zero in actuality. Here, we could say the following: There is a statistically significant positive correlation between years of education and income ($r = .97, p < .001$).

Chi-Square: Stata

To calculate a chi-square statistic in Stata, first navigate to the following menu selection:

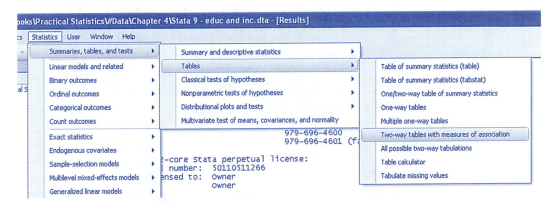

This will open the following dialog box:

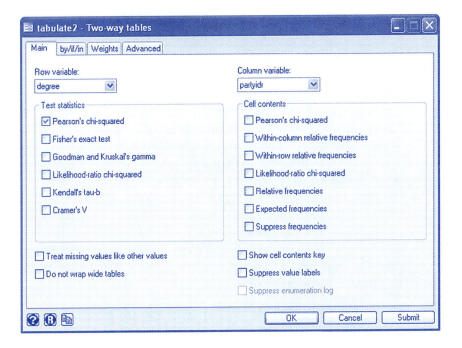

Using the same example from the IBM SPSS section, I have selected *degree* under *Row variable* and the recoded *partyid* variable, which I have renamed *partyidr*, under *Column variable*. Clicking *OK* will give you the following output:

```
. tabulate degree partyidr, chi2

                        recode party id
         degree   democrat  independe  republica  |   Total
less than high school      6,334      1,698      2,832  |  10,864
          high school     11,563      3,529      8,513  |  23,605
associate/junior coll      1,045        303        825  |   2,173
           bachelor's      2,618        601      2,812  |   6,031
             graduate      1,431        286      1,072  |   2,789
                Total     22,991      6,417     16,054  |  45,462

        Pearson chi2(8) = 834.0072   Pr = 0.000
```

As you can see, both IBM SPSS and Stata calculated a Pearson chi-square value of 834.007 in this particular example. As you may notice, Stata puts the degrees of freedom on the last line right next to chi2, in parentheses. As you may remember, in this example, the degrees of freedom was 8. Stata also calculates the probability level as being less than .001. Here, we could say the following: There was a statistically significant relationship between highest degree completed and political party affiliation ($\chi^2 = 834.01$, $df = 8$, $p < .001$).

Finally, this is the corresponding Stata syntax for this particular example:

```
tabulate degree partyidr, chi2
```

t-Test: Stata

To run an independent samples *t*-test within Stata, we must first test whether our dependent variable has equal variances across groups. We will do this using Levene's test for the equality of variances as was reported in the previous section on running *t*-tests within IBM SPSS. In this example, we are testing differences in respondents' income based on sex. To test whether the variances in scores are equal across sex, we will use the following syntax command:

```
robvar realrinc, by(sex)
```

Typing this command into the command window and hitting enter would give you the following results:

Look at the first line, under "w0." As you can see, the calculated *F* statistic for Levene's test for the equality of variances here in Stata is identical to the score calculated previously in IBM SPSS. Also, looking at the $Pr > F =$ entry for *w0*, you notice that this test is significant at the .05 level.

Next, we will run the actual *t*-test. First, choose the following menu selection:

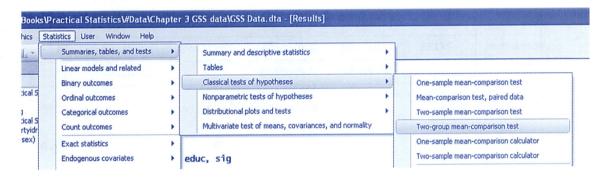

This will load the following dialog box:

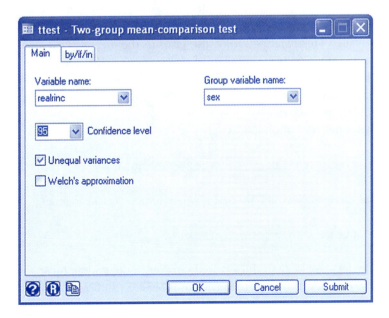

As you can see, I have specified *sex* under *Group variable name* (which will always contain the variable that you have two groups of) and *realrinc* under *Variable name* (the dependent, continuous variable). Because we know that the variances between groups are significantly different, I have also specified *Unequal variances* in this dialog box. Clicking *OK* will give us the following output:

```
. ttest realrinc, by(sex) unequal

Two-sample t test with unequal variances
```

Group	Obs	Mean	Std. Err.	Std. Dev.	[95% Conf. Interval]	
1	13862	26983.16	206.7294	24339.7	26577.94	27388.38
2	13301	14811.22	121.5861	14022.52	14572.89	15049.54
combined	27163	21022.88	126.6388	20871.59	20774.66	21271.1
diff		12171.94	239.8338		11701.85	12642.03

```
    diff = mean(1) - mean(2)                                   t =   50.7516
Ho: diff = 0                         Satterthwaite's degrees of freedom =   22324.9

    Ha: diff < 0                     Ha: diff != 0                      Ha: diff > 0
 Pr(T < t) = 1.0000        Pr(|T| > |t|) = 0.0000             Pr(T > t) = 0.0000
```

We can see that the calculated *t* score is 50.7516 with 22324.9 degrees of freedom. For the probability level, we can look at the second entry at the bottom. Here, we can see that our results are significant at the $p < .0001$ probability level under the "Pr($|T| > |t|$)" entry, which represents the *p* level for the two-tailed *t*-test. Stata's output also gives us the means of the two different groups, along with the number of observations and several other statistics. These results could be stated as follows: Males were found to have a significantly higher income as compared with female respondents ($t = 50.75$, $df = 22324.9$, $p < .001$).

This is the corresponding syntax:

```
ttest realrinc, by(sex) unequal
```

And this syntax would be used if you assumed equal variances:

```
ttest realrinc, by(sex)
```

Now, let's use Stata to run a paired samples or dependent *t*-test. I will use the same example as used in the previous IBM SPSS example in which we had

10 respondents who took an exam at two different periods of time. I will also use the identical values that were used previously. First, navigate to the following menu selection:

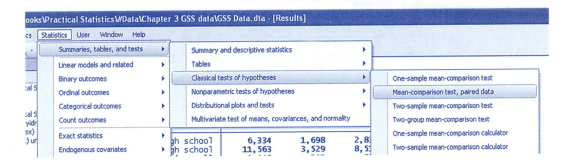

This will reveal the following dialog box:

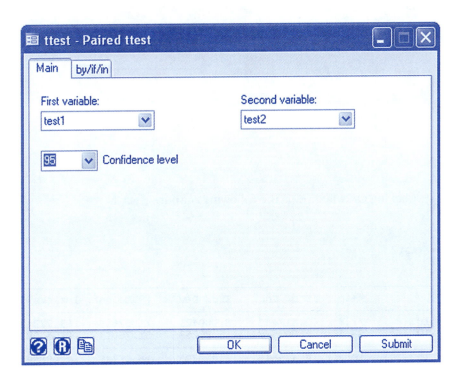

Here, I have simply specified *test1* and *test2* as the two variables to be included in this paired *t*-test. These are the data I am using in this example:

Data Editor (Edit) - [chapter 4- p

File   Edit   Data   Tools

test1[1]   78

	test1	test2
1	78	95
2	72	78
3	75	71
4	83	95
5	92	98
6	65	85
7	85	98
8	74	89
9	85	87
10	65	85

Clicking *OK* will give us the following output:

```
. ttest test1 == test2

Paired t test
```

Variable	Obs	Mean	Std. Err.	Std. Dev.	[95% Conf. Interval]	
test1	10	77.4	2.817406	8.909421	71.02658	83.77342
test2	10	88.1	2.802578	8.86253	81.76013	94.43987
diff	10	−10.7	2.525646	7.986795	−16.41341	−4.986591

```
    mean(diff) = mean(test1 - test2)                          t =  -4.2365
Ho: mean(diff) = 0                           degrees of freedom =         9

Ha: mean(diff) < 0          Ha: mean(diff) != 0          Ha: mean(diff) > 0
Pr(T < t) = 0.0011       Pr(|T| > |t|) = 0.0022       Pr(T > t) = 0.9989
```

Here, we see that for this **paired samples *t*-test**, Stata has calculated a *t* value of –4.2365 with 9 degrees of freedom. By again looking at the middle entry at the bottom of the output, which is used for a two-tailed *t*-test, we see that this is significant at the .0022 probability level. You could report this result in the following way: "Scores on Test 2 were found to be significantly different from scores on Test 1 (*t* = –4.24, *df* = 9, *p* < .01). Specifically, the mean of Test 2 scores was 10.7 points higher than the mean of Test 1 scores." This second sentence is constructed using the values under the *Mean* column as well as the value under the *diff* row, which represents the difference between our two variables (*test1* and *test2*).

Finally, the equivalent syntax is simply this:

```
ttest test1 == test2
```

One-Way ANOVA: Stata

To run an ANOVA within Stata, first navigate to the following menu selection:

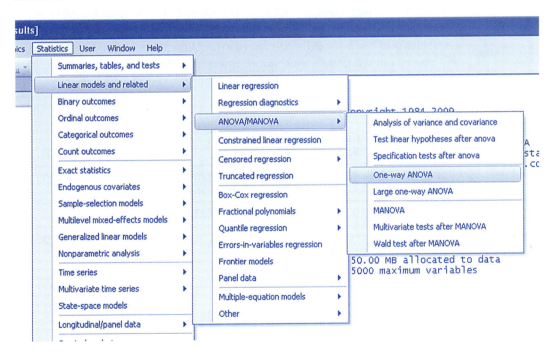

This will bring up the following dialog box:

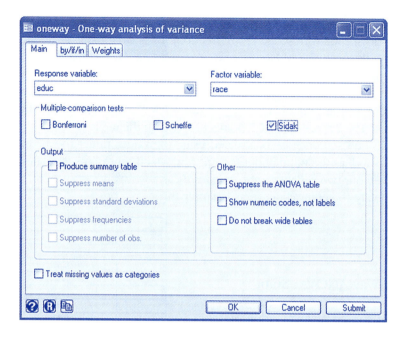

Using the same example as used previously, I have specified *educ* as the *Response variable* and *race* as the *Factor variable*. I also specified that the Sidak post hoc analysis (here referred to as "Multiple-comparison tests") be run. As you can see, Stata is much more limited than SPSS in regard to the number of post hoc tests it supports. Clicking *OK* will give you the following results:

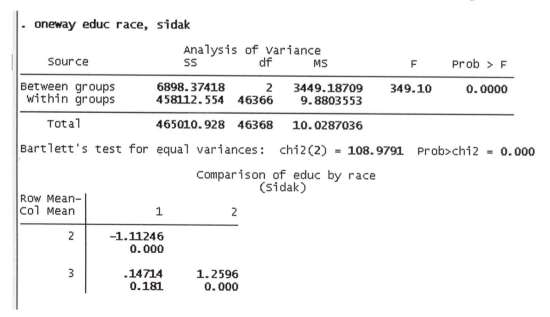

As you can see, Stata has calculated the F statistic to be 349.10 with the degrees of freedom of 2 and 46,366, significant at the $p < .001$ probability level. In the Sidak post hoc table shown below the ANOVA results, we see that only Groups 1 and 2 and Groups 2 and 3 are significantly different from each other at the .05 probability level, just as we found within IBM SPSS. We can tell this from the significance levels. Here, there are only two comparisons in which the probability level is below .05: the comparison between Groups 1 and 2 (whites and blacks, respectively) and between Groups 2 and 3 (blacks and those of other race, respectively). Our results can be stated in the following way:

> A significant difference in the level of education between whites, blacks, and those of other races was found ($F(2, 46366) = 349.10$, $p < .001$). Specifically, a Sidak post hoc test found the mean income for whites to be significantly different from that of blacks, with whites having greater incomes, on average, than blacks. Also, the mean income for blacks was found to significantly differ from those of other races, with members of other races having higher incomes as compared with blacks.

Our value of –1.11 at the top of the table represents the mean of blacks' education (coded 2) minus the mean of whites' education (coded 1), where education was coded in years. This value of –1.11 means that the mean of years of education for blacks is less than that of whites, as it is negative. The value of 1.2596 in the lower right-hand cell of the table represents the mean of education for those of other race (coded 3) minus the mean of blacks' education (coded 2). The values will always represent the mean for the row (in this case, 3) minus the mean for the column (in this case, 2).

We could check this using the following syntax:

```
. tabstat educ, by(race)

Summary for variables: educ
    by categories of: race

    race |       mean
---------+----------
       1 |   12.75507
       2 |   11.64261
       3 |   12.90221
---------+----------
   Total |   12.60765
-------------------
```

Here, we see that the mean years of education for blacks, coded 2, is less than that of whites, coded 1.

This is the corresponding syntax for the ANOVA:

```
oneway educ race, sidak
```

Factorial ANOVA: Stata

While one-way ANOVAs only include one categorical independent or predictor variable, factorial ANOVAs include more than one. In the example presented in the previous section, a one-way ANOVA was used as there was only one independent or predictor variable, race of the respondent. In this example, I will incorporate both race of the respondent as well as the respondent's gender in a factorial ANOVA that includes the respondent's income as the dependent variable. This example will also use data from the GSS.

To begin, first make the following menu selection:

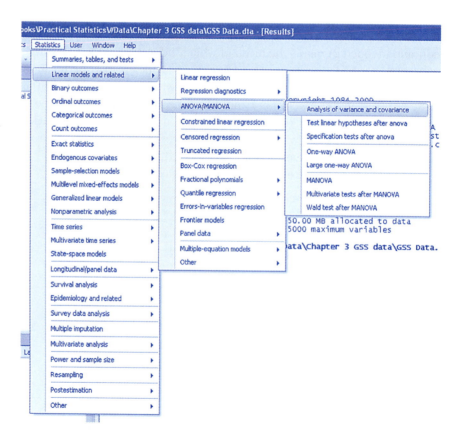

This will open the following dialog box:

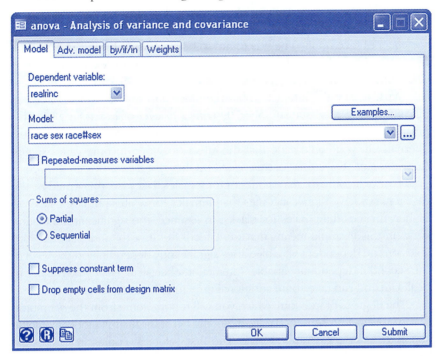

As you can see, I have specified the variable *realrinc*, a measure of the respondent's annual income, as the dependent variable. I have also specified the model to include two independent variables, the respondents' race and sex. Also, I have included as a term *race#sex*, which is the interaction between these two variables. It is possible that the effect of race on income varies by gender or likewise that the effect of gender on income varies by race. The inclusion of this interaction effect will test whether this is the case. After clicking *OK*, you will see the following results:

```
. anova realrinc race sex race#sex

                      Number of obs =    27163      R-squared     =  0.0955
                      Root MSE      = 19851.4      Adj R-squared =  0.0954

        Source |  Partial SS     df        MS            F       Prob > F
    -----------+----------------------------------------------------------
         Model |  1.1304e+12      5   2.2609e+11       573.72     0.0000
    -----------+----------------------------------------------------------
          race |  9.2944e+10      2   4.6472e+10       117.93     0.0000
           sex |  1.5131e+11      1   1.5131e+11       383.95     0.0000
      race#sex |  4.3417e+10      2   2.1708e+10        55.09     0.0000
    -----------+----------------------------------------------------------
      Residual |  1.0702e+13  27157    394077231
    -----------+----------------------------------------------------------
         Total |  1.1832e+13  27162    435623423
```

As you can see under the "Model" row, this ANOVA had a calculated F statistic of 573.72, with a probability level of less than .001. The effect of race, sex, and the interaction between race and sex were all found to be significant. First, the effect of race on income was found to be significant, having an F statistic of 117.93 with a p level of less than .001. Next, the effect of sex on income was also found to be significant, having an F statistic of 383.95 with a p level of less than .001. Finally, the interaction between race and sex was found to be significant, having an F statistic of 55.09 with a p level of less than .001. This means that the effect of race on income significantly varies by sex. Alternatively, you could state that the effect of sex on income varies significantly by race. For example, this would be the case if race was an important predictor of income for males but not for females. Likewise, this would be the case if males have higher incomes than females for whites but if females had higher incomes than males for blacks. In essence, the significant interaction effect in this example means that the effect of one of the independent variables on the dependent variable varies significantly depending on the level of the second independent variable. Interaction effects can clearly be trickier to deal with and can take some additional time to fully understand.

The degrees of freedom, which you will report, come from the df column in the table just presented. For example, the F test for the full model would be reported as $F(5, 27157) = 573.72$. The first value, 5, comes from the first "Model" row, while the second value, 27157, comes from the "Residual" row.

Our results can be stated in the following way: A factorial ANOVA found a significant difference in income based on both race and gender, $F(5, 27157) = 573.72$, $p < .001$. Specifically, males were found to have significantly higher incomes than females, $F(1, 27157) = 383.95$, $p < .001$. Also, income was found to vary significantly based on race, $F(2, 27157) = 117.93$, $p < .001$. Finally, a significant interaction between race and gender was found, $F(2, 27157) = 55.09$, $p < .001$.

Repeated Measures ANOVA: Stata

Repeated measures ANOVAs are used when your dependent variable consists of a measure that was recorded or measured at several points in time. For example, if you had a set of two or more exam grades for a set of respondents, these data, along with one or more independent predictor variables, could be analyzed using a repeated measures ANOVA. This is the example that I'll be using in this section. A repeated measures ANOVA could also be used in other situations; for example, if you had a measure for respondents that was taken before and after some medical treatment. Using a repeated measures ANOVA, you can also include predictor variables such as sex and age.

To run a repeated measures ANOVA in Stata, we will first need to "reshape" the data. Currently, the data are in this format:

Data Editor (Edit) - [repeated measures anova - grades

File   Edit   Data   Tools

exam_1[1]   60

	exam_1	exam_2	exam_3	level
1	60	89	88	Senior
2	87	91	96	Junior
3	90	87	84	Sophomore
4	97	86	84	Sophomore
5	94	98	76	Junior
6	94	90	88	Junior

where each respondent has his or her own single row. We need to get the data into this format:

Data Editor (Edit) - [Untitled]

File   Edit   Data   Tools

case[1]   1

	case	exnum	exam_	level
1	1	1	60	Senior
2	1	2	89	Senior
3	1	3	88	Senior
4	2	1	87	Junior
5	2	2	91	Junior
6	2	3	96	Junior

Where each respondent has three rows, one for each exam score. To do this, we need to first create a new variable to identify respondents by number, such as *case*. Here, I have simply used "1" for the first respondent and have continued from there:

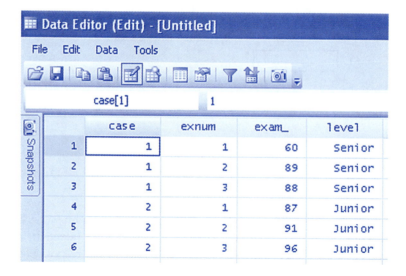

In Stata, you can simply use the command:

```
gen case=.
```

And then enter the values for *case* by typing ed.

Next, use the following syntax command:

```
reshape long exam_, i(case) j(exnum)
```

This transforms the data into the necessary "long" format using the *exam* variable. The variable *case* will identify the respondent, and *exnum* will identify the exam number. The new exam variable will be simply *exam_*.

This will transform the data into the necessary format:

Next, to run a repeated measures ANOVA, make the following menu selection:

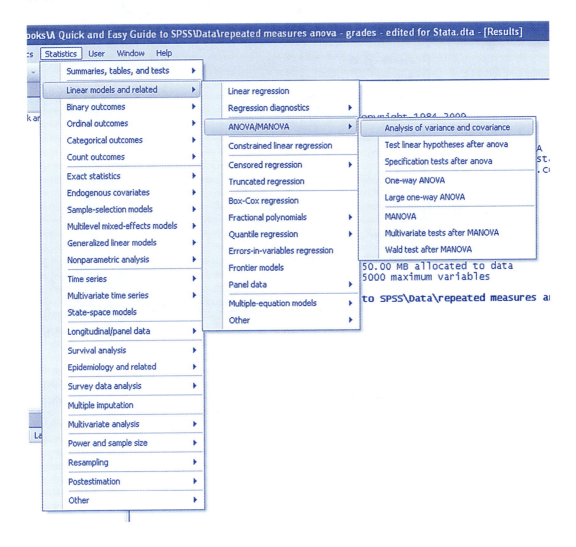

This will open the following dialog box:

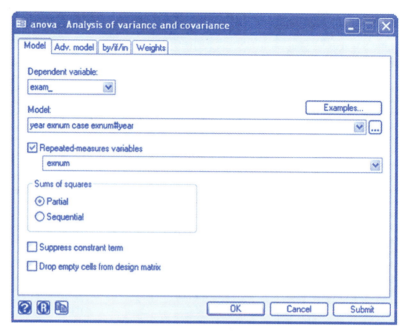

As you can see, I have specified the new exam grade variable, *exam_*, as the dependent variable in this model. I have included *year* (year at college), *exnum* (exam number), and *case* (respondent number) as independent variables in this model. I have also included *exnum#year*, which is the interaction between exam number and year at college. This tests whether the effect of time (exam number) on exam scores varies significantly by year at college. Also, I have specified that *exnum* is the repeated measures variable. Next, I will click on the *Adv. model* tab:

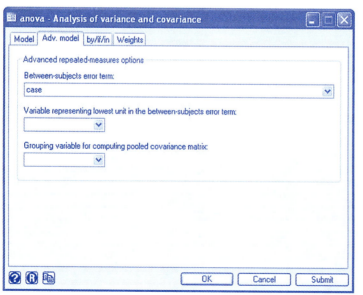

Here, I will need to specify *case*, the respondent number, as the between-subjects error term. Clicking *OK* results in the following output:

```
. anova exam_ year exnum case exnum#year, repeated(exnum) bse(case)
```

| | Number of obs = | 111 | R-squared | = | 0.5646 |
| | Root MSE = | 13.1472 | Adj R-squared = | | 0.2743 |

Source	Partial SS	df	MS	F	Prob > F
Model	14790.4535	44	336.146671	1.94	0.0070
year	1608.91667	3	536.305556	3.10	0.0325
exnum	918.972718	2	459.486359	2.66	0.0776
case	9418.74286	33	285.41645	1.65	0.0421
exnum#year	509.048134	6	84.8413556	0.49	0.8129
Residual	11407.9429	66	172.847619		
Total	26198.3964	110	238.16724		

```
Between-subjects error term:  case
                     Levels:  37          (33 df)
        Lowest b.s.e. variable:  case

Repeated variable: exnum
```

		Huynh-Feldt epsilon	=	0.8152
		Greenhouse-Geisser epsilon =		0.7223
		Box's conservative epsilon =		0.5000

| | | | | Prob > F | | |
Source	df	F	Regular	H-F	G-G	Box
exnum	2	2.66	0.0776	0.0895	0.0960	0.1125
exnum#year	6	0.49	0.8129	0.7778	0.7566	0.6910
Residual	66					

Here, the model was found to be significant, having an *F* statistic of 1.94, with $p < .01$. Year at college was found to be a significant predictor of exam scores, having an *F* statistic of 3.10, with $p < .05$. Next, the exam number was not found to have a significant effect on exam scores. The interaction between exam number and year at college was also not found to be significant at the $p < .05$ level.

The syntax command, shown in the output, is as follows:

```
anova exam_ year exnum case exnum#year,
     repeated(exnum) bse(case)
```

△   SECTION 4: SUMMARY

This chapter covered Pearson's r, chi-square, the t-test, and the ANOVA. Pearson's r, a correlation coefficient, is used to determine the strength and direction of the relationship between two continuous variables. Chi-square is used to show whether or not there is a relationship between two categorical variables. It can also be used to test whether or not a number of outcomes are occurring in equal frequencies or not, or conform to a certain distribution. Both the t-test and the ANOVA are used to test differences in scores between groups. While the t-test can only be used to test the differences between two groups on some continuous variable, the ANOVA can be used to test the differences between two or more groups on a continuous variable. When conducting an ANOVA on more than two groups, it is necessary to select a post hoc comparison test in order to determine between which specific groups there is a significant difference. A one-way ANOVA includes only one independent, predictor variable, while factorial ANOVAs include two or more. Also, repeated measures ANOVAs are used to look at a dependent variable that is measured at multiple points in time. The next chapter will cover linear regression, which is a particular form of regression that is used when your dependent variable is continuous. Regression is a powerful statistical tool as it allows you to determine the effect of one independent variable on your dependent variable while holding any number of other independent variables constant. Starting with the following chapter, we will begin constructing and analyzing models that include more than one independent variable, moving on from bivariate (two variables) statistics and beginning our journey into what is called multivariate statistics.

RESOURCES

You can find more information about IBM SPSS and how to purchase it by navigating to the following Web site: www.spss.com/software/statistics/

You can find more information about Stata and how to purchase it by navigating to the following Web site: www.stata.com

This book's Web site can be found at the following location: www.sage pub.com/kremelstudy

CHAPTER 5

LINEAR REGRESSION

SECTION 1: INTRODUCTION AND THEORETICAL BACKGROUND △

Introduction

You will find linear regression, as well as other forms of regression, to be much more powerful than the statistical methods that were presented in the previous chapters. This is due to the fact that in regression, you are able to determine the effect of one independent variable on a dependent variable while holding constant any number of other independent variables or controls. So, for example, using the methods presented in the previous chapter, you can determine whether there is a relationship between gender and income, for example, using a *t*-test. Additionally, you can determine the directionality of this relationship. For example, you may find that males have higher incomes than females and that this difference is statistically significant at the .05 probability level. However, it may be the case that it is not in fact sex that is causing differences in income but instead differences in levels of education between males and females. So it could be the case that females on average have a lower level of education than males and that this difference between groups is driving the difference between males and females in regard to income, and not sex itself. This type of situation lends itself to the use of regression, since when conducting a regression analysis, you could easily include both sex and level of education as independent variables in a model predicting income. The results of this analysis would tell you, among other things, the effect of sex on income holding the level of education constant as well as the effect of level of education on income while holding the effect of sex constant. In other words, it would show you the impact of sex on income while controlling for level of education as well as the effect of level of education on income while controlling for the effect of sex. While this example only includes two independent variables, you are able to include as many independent variables as you desire in a regression model.

In this chapter, linear regression is covered. There are several different types of regression, each of which is appropriate for specific types of dependent variables. **Linear regression** is used when your dependent variable is continuous. Examples of dependent variables in which you would conduct a linear regression include income, socioeconomic status, and occupational prestige. **Logistic regression** is used when your dependent variable is binary (only two possible response categories, usually coded as zero or one). **Ordered logistic regression** is appropriate when your dependent variable is categorical and ordered. **Multinomial logistic regression** is appropriate when your dependent variable is categorical and unordered. **Negative binomial regression** or **Poisson regression** (which are two distinct but similar methods) are used when your dependent variable is a count variable. These distinctions are summarized in the following table. Linear regression is the focus of this chapter, while these other forms of regression will be covered in the following chapter.

Type of Regression	Nature of Dependent Variable
Linear regression	Continuous
Logistic regression	Binary
Ordered logistic regression	Ordinal (categorical and ordered)
Multinomial logistic regression	Nominal (categorical and unordered)
Negative binomial regression	Count
Poisson regression	Count

Two terms you will most likely come across in other books on statistics or quantitative methods are simple linear regression and multiple linear regression. **Simple linear regression** refers to regression models that contain only a single independent variable, while **multiple linear regression** refers to regression models that contain two or more independent variables. This distinction is mostly arbitrary, in the sense that you will conduct a regression in exactly the same manner in both IBM SPSS and Stata regardless of the number of independent variables that your model contains. However, as you increase the number of independent variables over one, the calculations for the regression model quickly become very involved and lengthy. In this theoretical section, I will present the equations for a regression model with a single independent variable and for a regression model with two independent variables. The calculations for a simple linear regression for a small data set are not particularly extensive; however, a computer is needed to analyze most regression models that you will run.

A simple linear regression equation will take the form

$$y = \alpha + \beta x$$

where

y = the value of your dependent variable

α = the y-intercept

β = the beta coefficient

x = your independent variable

For example, say you were running a regression with income (in thousands of dollars) as your dependent variable and years of education as your independent variable. The results of your regression might be similar to the following equation:

$$y = 12 + 2.2x$$

In some statistics textbooks, you might see y represented as $\hat{y}$, which stands for the predicted or estimated value for y, our independent variable. Here, I will simply represent it as y.

In this example, our y-intercept is 12. The **y-intercept** can be interpreted as the predicted value for your dependent variable when your independent variable(s) are all zero. In this example, an individual's predicted income when years of education is zero is $12,000. The **beta coefficient** in this example is 2.2. This means that for every additional year of education, a respondent's predicted income is expected to increase by $2,200. The figure below presents this relationship pictorially.

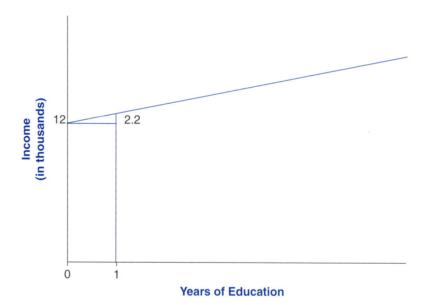

Years of Education

Here, we have our x- and y-axes, with education being plotted on the x-axis and income being plotted on the y-axis. At the point where years of education is 0, income is $12,000 (our y-intercept). For each additional year of education, income increases by $2,200. Linear regression always models the relationship as a line, just as in the example just presented. If, for example, you believe the relationship is not linear, you can sometimes include certain terms in your regression equation to account for this, such as the square of your independent variable.

Continuing with our example, say that, for example, we have an individual with 20 years of education. To calculate their predicted income, we simply need to plug this number into the equation presented earlier. So we get,

$$y = 12 + 2.2x = 12 + 2.2(20) = 12 + 44 = 56$$

Based on the results of our regression, an individual with 20 years of education would have a predicted income of $56,000.

A multiple linear regression equation would take the following form:

$$y = \alpha + \beta_1 x_1 + \beta_2 x_2 + \cdots + \beta_k x_k$$

where

y = the value of your dependent variable

α = the y-intercept

β_1 = the beta coefficient for your first independent variable

x_1 = your first independent variable

k = the number of independent variables in your model

As you can see, this equation is quite similar to the equation presented for simple linear regression, with the exception that in this equation, we have multiple independent variables and, hence, multiple beta coefficients. So to calculate a predicted value for your dependent variable, you will add your y-intercept to the product of the value of your first independent variable with its corresponding beta coefficient and continue to add to this sum the product of your remaining independent variables with their corresponding beta coefficients. If this is confusing, do not worry, as I will present an example shortly.

Now, to expand on the example presented in the previous section that predicted income from an individual's years of education, I will present a hypothetical example of a multiple linear regression equation in which income is predicted on the basis of years of education, race, and sex.

At this point, I need to introduce you to the concept of dummy variables. Dummy variables are variables that are binary, or more specifically, consist of only zeros and ones as data points. If we want to enter categorical variables into a regression equation as independent variables, they need to be coded as dummy variables. For variables that are already **binary variables**, such as sex, this is simple. In a case like this, we simply need to make sure that one category is coded as 0 and that the other category is coded as 1. So let's say that we have coded males as 0 and females as 1.

A variable that contains multiple categories is slightly more involved, as you need to create a dummy variable for each response category with the exception of what is termed the comparison category. To explain the concept of the comparison category, let me simply continue with my example of race. Say that our race variable contains three response categories: white, black, and Hispanic. We would first need to select one of these three response categories as the **comparison category**: the category that we will use as a standard, which we will compare the other two categories against. So, selecting whites as the comparison category, we do not need to create a dummy variable for whites, as they will not be included in the analysis as they are the comparison category (the comparison category is always omitted from the analysis). To create dummy variables for blacks and Hispanics, we need to create two new variables. The black dummy variable will equal 1 if the respondent is black and will equal 0 if the respondent is not black. The Hispanic dummy variable will equal 1 if the respondent is Hispanic and will equal 0 if the respondent is not Hispanic. Dummy variables are always constructed in this manner. In our regression, we will include these two new dummy variables to account for race, the black dummy variable and the Hispanic dummy variable.

Our regression equation in which income is predicted using years of education, sex, and race would take the following form:

$$y = \alpha + \beta_1 x_1 + \beta_2 x_2 + \beta_3 x_3 + \beta_4 x_4$$

Or, more specifically,

$$\text{Income} = \alpha + \beta_1(\text{Years of education}) + \beta_2(\text{Sex}) + \beta_3(\text{Black dummy}) + \beta_4(\text{Hispanic dummy})$$

If we had run this regression, the resulting equation might look similar to this:

$$\text{Income} = 11 + 2(\text{Years of education}) + -3.5(\text{Sex}) + -2(\text{Black dummy}) + -1(\text{Hispanic dummy})$$

To interpret the y-intercept, if the values for all our independent variables were 0, the respondents' predicted income would be $11,000. Here, we have hypothetically coded income in thousands of dollars (i.e., if a respondent had a "7" for income, this would mean that their income was $7,000), so the *y*-intercept as well as all beta coefficients are in units of $1,000. So if all independent variables had the value of 0, the respondent would have 0 years of education, be male, and have values of 0 for both the black and the Hispanic dummy variables, which means that he would be white. To interpret the beta coefficients, for each additional year of education, the respondent's predicted income increases by $2,000. In regard to sex, females are predicted to have an income that is, on average, $3,500 less than that of males. In regard to race, black respondents are predicted to have incomes $2,000 lower than those of whites, while Hispanics are predicted to have incomes $1,000 lower than those of whites. As you can see, both of the races that were included in the regression were compared with that of white, which was selected as the comparison category. In regard to the sex variable, males can be considered to be the comparison category, as females were coded 1 and males coded 0.

Now, for example, say that we have an individual with 16 years of education who is a Hispanic female. We would simply plug in these values to the previous equation to determine their predicted income:

$$\begin{aligned} \text{Income} &= 11 + 2(\text{Years of education}) + -3.5(\text{Sex}) + -2(\text{Black dummy}) \\ &\quad + -1(\text{Hispanic dummy}) \\ &= 11 + 2(16) + -3.5(1) + -2(0) + -1(1) \\ &= 11 + 32 + -3.5 + 0 + -1 = 38.5 \end{aligned}$$

We start off knowing that this respondent has 16 years of education. We have previously specified that in terms of the sex variable, males will be coded as 0 and females will be coded as 1, so she has a 1 for this variable. As the respondent is Hispanic, she is not black, which means she has a 0 for the black dummy variable. Because she is Hispanic, she has a 1 for the Hispanic dummy variable. After plugging all these numbers into the equation and computing the sum, we arrive at the value of 38.5, which means that the predicted income for this respondent is $38,500.

Equations

Simple Linear Regression

In this section, I will present the equations for a simple linear regression and calculate an example. The equations are presented here:

$$\alpha = \bar{y} - \beta\bar{x}$$

$$\beta = \frac{n(\sum xy) - (\sum x)(\sum y)}{n(\sum x^2) - (\sum x)^2}$$

You may find these equations to be different in other statistics or quantitative methods textbooks. There are several versions of these equations; however, this one tends to be easier to calculate by hand. Other versions of these equations should give you identical results.

Let's use these hypothetical data in our example:

Test Score (y)	IQ (x)
56	78
58	83
62	89
75	115
98	145

In this example, we want to use the respondents' IQs to predict their test scores (i.e., test score being the dependent variable and IQ being the independent variable). As the equation for our alpha value requires the beta value in the equations that we are using, we will first need to calculate the beta value. To calculate the beta value, we'll first have to calculate its components:

$$\sum xy = (78 \times 56) + (83 \times 58) + (89 \times 62) + (115 \times 75) + (145 \times 98)$$
$$= 4368 + 4814 + 5518 + 8625 + 14210 = 37{,}535$$

$$\sum x = 78 + 83 + 89 + 115 + 145 = 510$$

$$\sum y = 56 + 58 + 62 + 75 + 98 = 349$$

$$n = 5$$

$$\sum x^2 = 78^2 + 83^2 + 89^2 + 115^2 + 145^2 = 55144$$

$$(\sum x)^2 = 510^2 = 260{,}100$$

Plugging these values into our equation for beta,

$$\beta = \frac{n(\sum xy) - (\sum x)(\sum y)}{n(\sum x^2) - (\sum x)^2} = \frac{5(37535) - (510)(349)}{5(55144) - (260100)}$$
$$= \frac{187675 - 177990}{15620} = \frac{9685}{15620} = 0.6200$$

Now, to calculate our alpha, or y-intercept,

$$\alpha = \bar{y} - \beta\bar{x}$$

First we'll need the means of x and y:

$$\bar{y} = \frac{\sum y}{n} = \frac{349}{5} = 69.8$$

$$\bar{x} = \frac{\sum x}{n} = \frac{510}{5} = 102$$

Next, plugging these values into our equation,

$$\alpha = \bar{y} - \beta\bar{x} = 69.8 - (0.62)(102) = 6.56$$

Finally, the full regression equation could be represented in this way:

$$\text{Test score} = 6.56 + 0.62(\text{IQ})$$

In short, an individual's predicted test score is equal to 6.56 plus 0.62 multiplied by their IQ score.

In putting the data presented for this problem into Stata and running a linear regression, we get the following results:

```
. regress score iq

      Source |       SS       df       MS              Number of obs =       5
-------------+------------------------------           F(  1,      3) =  305.72
       Model |  1201.0144      1   1201.0144           Prob > F      =  0.0004
    Residual |  11.7855954     3   3.9285318           R-squared     =  0.9903
-------------+------------------------------           Adj R-squared =  0.9870
       Total |     1212.8      4      303.2            Root MSE      =  1.9821

------------------------------------------------------------------------------
       score |      Coef.   Std. Err.      t    P>|t|     [95% Conf. Interval]
-------------+----------------------------------------------------------------
          iq |   .6200384   .0354617    17.48   0.000     .5071834    .7328934
       _cons |   6.556082   3.724121     1.76   0.177    -5.295732     18.4079
------------------------------------------------------------------------------
```

Looking at the coefficients presented by Stata, we can see that our calculations for the alpha and beta coefficients for this simple linear regression were correct. Just as we have calculated by hand, Stata has calculated the beta coefficient for IQ to be 0.62 and has calculated the *y*-intercept, or constant, as approximately 6.556.

Now, let's interpret our results. The *y*-intercept in this regression is 6.56. While not significant here, as we had a *p* level of .177, the *y*-intercept, or constant, will nearly always be significant. Our nonsignificant result for the constant was most likely due to the extremely small data set we used. We could interpret the *y*-intercept by stating that the predicted test score for an individual with an IQ of 0 is 6.56. As you can see, sometimes the interpretation of the *y*-intercept is not particularly useful. The beta coefficient for IQ, 0.62, is significant at the $p < .001$ level. We can interpret this coefficient in the following way: Each additional IQ point is expected to increase a respondent's predicted test score by 0.62 points.

Next, to calculate our *R*-squared, or the percent variation in our dependent variable explained by our independent variable,

$$R^2 = 1 - \frac{SS_{\text{error}}}{SS_{\text{total}}} = 1 - \frac{\sum (y - \hat{y})^2}{\sum (y - \bar{y})^2}$$

As you can see, the value for *R*-squared is equal to 1 minus the sum of squared errors divided by the total sum of squares. To calculate the sum of squared errors, we first need to calculate the predicted score on the independent variable for each respondent or case based on the results of our regression analysis. Then, for each respondent, we find the difference between their actual score (y) and their predicted score ($\hat{y}$). Squaring these differences and then summing all these squared products together, we will arrive at the sum of squared errors.

To calculate the total sum of squares, we would first calculate the mean for our dependent variable. Then, we would calculate the difference between the respondent's score on the dependent variable and the mean of the dependent variable for each respondent. Squaring all these differences and then summing all these squared products together would lead us to the total sum of squares.

This is how we would calculate *R*-squared for the regression example just presented, in which test score was predicted using IQ:

Test Score (y)	IQ (x)
56	78
58	83
62	89
75	115
98	145

These are our original data. This is the regression equation that we calculated:

$$\text{Test score} = 6.56 + 0.62(\text{IQ})$$

First, we need to calculate predicted values for the respondents' test scores on the basis of our regression equation. So for the five respondents in our data set, the calculations are as follows:

Respondent 1: Predicted test score = $6.56 + 0.62(78) = 54.9191$

Respondent 2: Predicted test score = $6.56 + 0.62(83) = 58.0193$

Respondent 3: Predicted test score = $6.56 + 0.62(89) = 61.7395$

Respondent 4: Predicted test score = $6.56 + 0.62(115) = 77.8605$

Respondent 5: Predicted test score = $6.56 + 0.62(145) = 96.4616$

Let's add this to the table:

Test Score (y)	IQ (x)	Predicted Test Score (ŷ)
56	78	54.9191
58	83	58.0193
62	89	61.7395
75	115	77.8605
98	145	96.4616

Next, we simply need to find the sum of squared differences between actual or observed test scores and predicted test scores to calculate our sum of squared errors. This would be calculated in the following way:

$$
\begin{aligned}
SS_{\text{error}} &= \sum (y - \hat{y})^2 = (56 - 54.9191)^2 + (58 - 58.0193)^2 \\
&\quad + (62 - 61.7395)^2 + (75 + 77.8605)^2 + (98 - 96.4616)^2 \\
&= 1.1684 + 0.0004 + 0.0679 + 8.1824 + 2.3665 = 11.7855
\end{aligned}
$$

Next, we would need to calculate the mean of our dependent variable. We calculated this previously as 69.8. Now, we can calculate our total sum of squares:

$$
\begin{aligned}
SS_{\text{total}} &= \sum (y - \bar{y})^2 = (56 - 69.8)^2 + (58 - 69.8)^2 + (62 - 69.8)^2 \\
&\quad + (75 - 69.8)^2 + (98 - 69.8)^2 \\
&= 190.44 + 139.24 + 60.84 + 27.04 + 795.24 = 1212.8
\end{aligned}
$$

Finally, we can calculate our R-squared:

$$R^2 = 1 - \frac{SS_{\text{error}}}{SS_{\text{total}}} = 1 - \frac{11.7855}{1212.8} = 1 - 0.00972 = 0.9903$$

One issue with R-squared is that it tends to be inflated when running a regression with a large number of independent variables. This led to the development of the **adjusted R-squared**, which is a modification of the original R-squared value to help protect against this artificial inflation. The equation for the adjusted R-squared is presented here:

$$\text{Adjusted } R^2 = 1 - \left(1 - R^2\right)\left[\frac{n-1}{n-k-1}\right]$$

where

R^2 = your original, or nonadjusted, R^2 value

n = sample size

k = number of independent variables

In our model, we only had one independent variable, and the adjusted R-squared would be calculated in this way:

$$\text{Adjusted } R^2 = 1 - \left(1 - 0.9903\right)\left[\frac{5-1}{5-1-1}\right] = 1 - (.0097)\left[\frac{4}{3}\right] = 0.9870$$

Looking at the Stata output presented earlier, we can see that our calculated values for R-squared and adjusted R-squared for this model are correct. In this example, our adjusted R-squared is less than but very close to our original (nonadjusted) R-squared value, as we only had a single independent variable in this model. We would likely notice a much more substantial difference between the R-squared and adjusted R-squared values in models with a large number of independent variables. Say, for example, we ran a regression model that gave us an R-squared value of 0.4, contained 40 independent variables, and was run on a data set with 500 cases. We would calculate the adjusted R-squared to be:

$$\text{Adjusted } R^2 = 1 - \left(1 - 0.4\right)\left[\frac{500-1}{500-40-1}\right] = 1 - (0.6)\left[\frac{499}{459}\right] = 0.3477$$

In this example, we see a much more substantial difference between our R-squared and adjusted R-squared values.

Multiple Linear Regression

Now, let's compute a multiple linear regression with two independent variables. These are the equations you can use:

For

$$y = \alpha + \beta_1 x_1 + \beta_2 x_2$$

$$\alpha = \bar{y} - \beta_1 \bar{x}_1 - \beta_2 \bar{x}_2$$

$$\beta_1 = \left[\frac{r_{x_1 y} - (r_{x_2 y})(r_{x_1 x_2})}{1 - (r_{x_1 x_2})^2} \right] \times \left[\frac{s_y}{s_{x_1}} \right]$$

$$\beta_2 = \left[\frac{r_{x_2 y} - (r_{x_1 y})(r_{x_1 x_2})}{1 - (r_{x_1 x_2})^2} \right] \times \left[\frac{s_y}{s_{x_2}} \right]$$

Say we had the following data:

Prejudice Score (y)	Age (x_1)	Education (x_2)
2	23	24
3	24	20
6	35	20
7	54	12
9	76	14

Now normally, we would want a greater sample size, but just to present an example of a hand calculation of a multiple linear regression, I will only use these five cases.

First, we need to calculate Pearson's r between x_1 and x_2, x_1 and y, and x_2 and y, along with the standard deviations of x_1, x_2, and y:

The correlation between x_1 and y:

$$\Sigma x_1 y = (23 \times 2) + (24 \times 3) + (35 \times 6) + (54 \times 7) + (76 \times 9) = 1390$$

$$\bar{x}_1 = \frac{23 + 24 + 35 + 54 + 76}{5} = 42.4$$

$$\bar{y} = \frac{2 + 3 + 6 + 7 + 9}{5} = 5.4$$

$$\sum x_1^2 = 23^2 + 24^2 + 35^2 + 54^2 + 76^2 = 11022$$

$$\sum y^2 = 2^2 + 3^2 + 6^2 + 7^2 + 9^2 = 179$$

$$r_{xy} = \frac{\sum xy - N\bar{x}_1\bar{y}}{\sqrt{(\sum x_1^2 - N\bar{x}_1^2)(\sum y^2 - N\bar{y}^2)}}$$

$$= \frac{1390 - 5(42.4)(5.4)}{\sqrt{(11022 - 5(42.4^2))(179 - 5(5.4^2))}}$$

$$= \frac{245.2}{\sqrt{(2033.2)(33.2)}} = \frac{245.2}{259.8119} = 0.9438$$

Now, for the correlation between x_2 and y:

$$\sum x_2 y = (24 \times 2) + (20 \times 3) + (20 \times 6) + (12 \times 7) + (14 \times 9) = 438$$

$$\bar{x}_2 = \frac{24 + 20 + 20 + 12 + 14}{5} = 18$$

$$\sum x_2^2 = 24^2 + 20^2 + 20^2 + 12^2 + 14^2 = 1716$$

$$r_{x_2 y} = \frac{\sum x_2 y - N\bar{x}_2\bar{y}}{\sqrt{(\sum x_2^2 - N\bar{x}_2^2)(\sum y^2 - N\bar{y}^2)}}$$

$$= \frac{438 - 5(18)(5.4)}{\sqrt{(1716 - 5(18^2))(179 - 5(5.4^2))}}$$

$$= \frac{-48}{\sqrt{(96)(33.2)}} = \frac{-48}{56.4553} = -0.8502$$

Finally, the correlation between x_1 and x_2:

$$\sum x_1 x_2 = (23 \times 24) + (24 \times 20) + (35 \times 20) + (54 \times 12) + (76 \times 14) = 3444$$

$$r_{x_1 x_2} = \frac{\sum x_1 x_2 - N\bar{x}_1\bar{x}_2}{\sqrt{(\sum x_1^2 - N\bar{x}_1^2)(\sum \bar{x}_2^2 - N\bar{x}_2^2)}}$$

$$= \frac{3444 - 5(42.4)(18)}{\sqrt{(11022 - 5(42.4^2))(1716 - 5(18^2))}}$$

$$= \frac{-372}{\sqrt{2033.2(96)}} = \frac{-372}{441.8} = -0.8420$$

And the standard deviations of our variables:

$$s_{x_1} = \sqrt{\frac{\sum (x_1 - \bar{x}_1)^2}{n - 1}}$$

$$= \sqrt{\frac{(23 - 42.4)^2 + (24 - 42.4)^2 + (35 - 42.4)^2 + (54 - 42.4)^2 + (76 - 42.4)^2}{5 - 1}}$$

$$= \sqrt{\frac{2033.2}{4}} = 22.5455$$

$$s_{x_2} = \sqrt{\frac{\sum (x_2 - \bar{x}_2)^2}{n - 1}}$$

$$= \sqrt{\frac{(24 - 18)^2 + (20 - 18)^2 + (20 - 18)^2 + (12 - 18)^2 + (14 - 18)^2}{5 - 1}}$$

$$= \sqrt{\frac{96}{4}} = 4.8990$$

$$s_y = \sqrt{\frac{\sum (y - \bar{y})^2}{n - 1}}$$

$$= \sqrt{\frac{(2 - 5.4)^2 + (3 - 5.4)^2 + (6 - 5.4)^2 + (7 - 5.4)^2 + (9 - 5.4)^2}{5 - 1}}$$

$$= \sqrt{\frac{33.2}{4}} = 2.8810$$

Next, plugging these values into our beta equations,

$$\beta_1 = \left[\frac{r_{x_1y} - (r_{x_2y})(r_{x_1x_2})}{1 - (r_{x_1x_2})^2} \right] \times \left[\frac{s_y}{s_{x_1}} \right] = \left[\frac{0.9438 - (-0.8502)(-0.8420)}{1 - (-0.8420)^2} \right]$$

$$\times \left[\frac{2.8810}{22.5455} \right] = \left[\frac{.2279}{.2910} \right] \times \left[\frac{2.8810}{22.5455} \right] = .7832 \times .1278 = 0.1001$$

$$\beta_2 = \left[\frac{r_{x_2y} - (r_{x_1y})(r_{x_1x_2})}{1 - (r_{x_1x_2})^2} \right] \times \left[\frac{s_y}{s_{x_2}} \right] = \left[\frac{-0.8502 - (0.9438)(-0.8420)}{1 - (-0.8420)^2} \right]$$

$$\times \left[\frac{2.8810}{4.8990} \right] = \left[\frac{-0.0555}{.2910} \right] \times \left[\frac{2.8810}{4.8990} \right] = -0.1908 \times .5881 = -0.1122$$

$$\alpha = \bar{y} - \beta_1 \bar{x}_1 - \beta_2 \bar{x}_2 = 5.4 - (0.1001)(42.2) - (-0.1122)(18)$$
$$= 5.4 - 4.2442 - (-2.0196) = 3.17$$

Now, I will simply verify these results in Stata:

```
. regress prej age educ

      Source |       SS       df       MS              Number of obs =       5
-------------+------------------------------           F(  2,     2) =    9.13
       Model | 29.9230015        2  14.9615008         Prob > F      =  0.0987
    Residual | 3.27699848        2  1.63849924         R-squared     =  0.9013
-------------+------------------------------           Adj R-squared =  0.8026
       Total |      33.2         4         8.3         Root MSE      =    1.28

------------------------------------------------------------------------------
        prej |      Coef.   Std. Err.      t    P>|t|     [95% Conf. Interval]
-------------+----------------------------------------------------------------
         age |   .1000507   .0526226     1.90   0.198    -.1263661    .3264675
        educ |  -.1123035   .2421736    -0.46   0.688    -1.154292    .9296853
       _cons |   3.179314   6.378622     0.50   0.668    -24.26568    30.62431
------------------------------------------------------------------------------
```

As you can see, our results match.

◭ SECTION 2: IBM SPSS

Conducting regressions in both IBM SPSS and Stata is quite simple. In this section, as well as the following section on Stata, I'll use the same data set from the General Social Survey that was used in previous chapters. In this section, I will run a multiple linear regression in which the respondents' income is predicted using their level of education, occupational prestige score, sex, and race. This is a somewhat more involved regression but serves as a better introduction to performing regressions in IBM SPSS and Stata than one that is overly simple.

Before we run the actual regression, we first need to create dummy variables for sex and race. Currently, the values for sex are 1 and 2, while the values for race are 1, 2, and 3. In our sex variable, males are coded 1 and females are coded 2. I will recode this variable so that males are coded 0 and females are coded 1, creating a dummy variable for females. In regard to the race variable, whites are coded 1, blacks are coded 2, and individuals of other races are coded 3. For this variable, I will create two dummy variables, one dummy variable for blacks, and one dummy variable for individuals of other races. Whites will be selected as the comparison category.

Recoding variables was covered in Chapter 2; however, I will briefly discuss how to recode the *sex* variable and create the dummy variables before presenting the instructions on running the regression. The other two variables in this model are education and occupational prestige. The education variable measures years of education completed, while the occupational prestige score variable is a measure of how prestigious the respondent's occupation is. Both of these variables are continuous and do not need to be recoded or modified.

I will begin by recoding the sex variable. First, I will make the following menu selection:

Then, in the following dialog box, I will select the sex variable, renaming it as *female*:

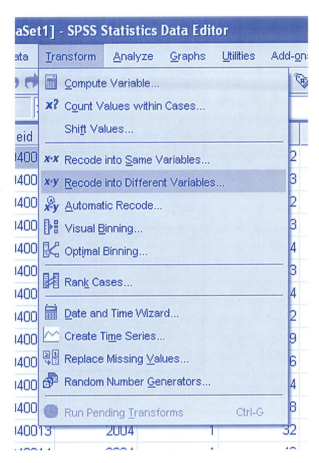

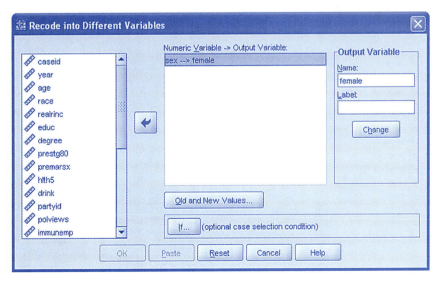

Then clicking *Old and New Values*, I will specify that the coding for males be changed from 1 to 0 and the coding for females be changed from 2 to 1:

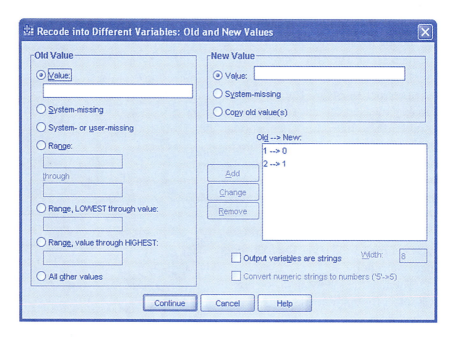

I'll then make the same menu selection to create the two dummy variables for race. First, I will create the black dummy variable:

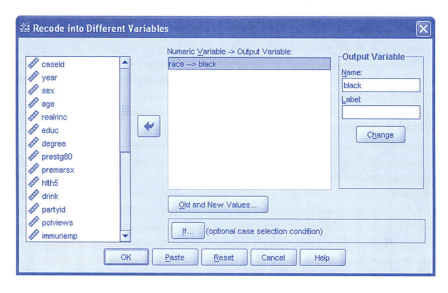

I will recode the data so that individuals who are black will be recoded as 1, while both individuals who are white and individuals who are members of other races will be recoded as 0:

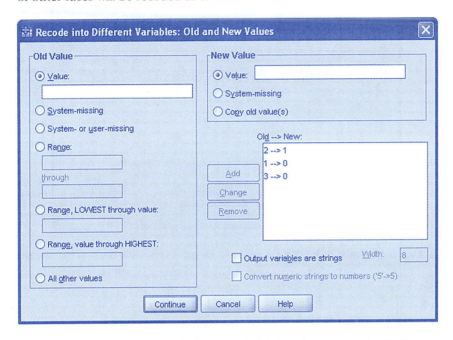

Originally, blacks were coded as 2, and this is being recoded to 1. Whites were coded as 1, which is being recoded to 0. Individuals of other races were coded as 3, and this is also being recoded to 0. After creating this variable, we need to create another dummy variable for members of other races. First, I will once again navigate to the initial dialog box:

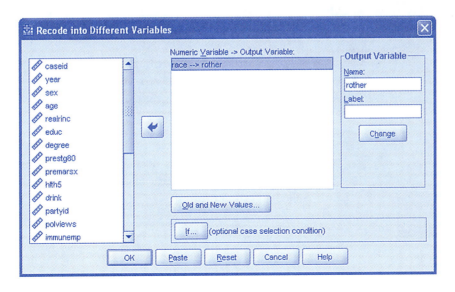

Next, I'll specify that this variable be recoded in the following way:

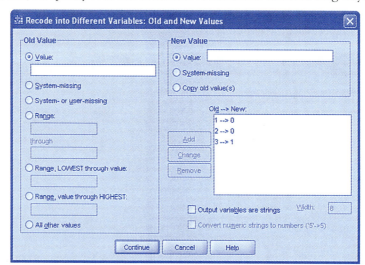

Here, I specify that both whites (1) and blacks (2) will be recoded to 0. Members of other races (3) will be recoded as 1.

The equivalent syntax for these variable recodes is presented here:

```
RECODE sex (1=0) (2=1)
INTO female.
EXECUTE.
RECODE race (1=0)
  (2=1) (3=0) INTO
  black.
EXECUTE.
RECODE race (1=0)
  (2=0) (3=1) INTO
  rother.
EXECUTE.
```

Finally, we can begin our regression analysis. First, we will make the following menu selection:

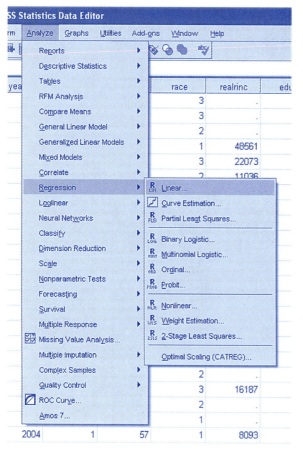

This will open the following dialog box:

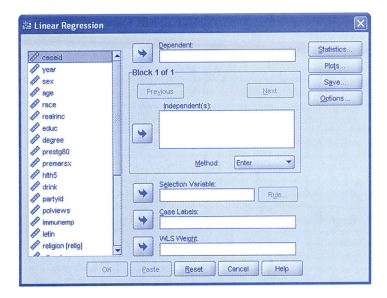

Here, we will specify the respondent's income (*realrinc*) as the dependent variable. Next, we will specify *educ* (years of education completed), *prestg80* (occupational prestige score), *female* (our recoded sex variable), *black* (our black dummy variable), and *rother* (our dummy variable for members of other races) as our independent variables. When we have finished, our dialog box should look something like this:

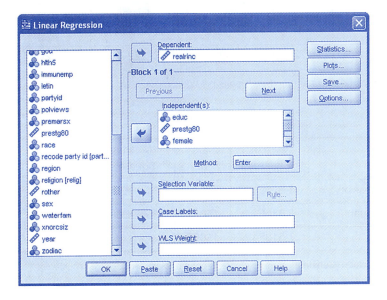

Here, the *realrinc* variable is in the *Dependent* box, and the variables *educ*, *prestg80*, *sex*, *black*, and *rother* are all in the *Independent(s)* box. Next, we can simply click *OK* to run this regression. The results obtained are shown below:

```
REGRESSION
/MISSING LISTWISE
/STATISTICS COEFF OUTS R ANOVA
/CRITERIA=PIN(.05) POUT(.10)
/NOORIGIN
/DEPENDENT realrinc
/METHOD=ENTER educ prestg80 female black rother.
```

Regression

[DataSet1] T:\Md book\#Data\Chapter 5\gss data.sav

Variables Entered/Removed

Model	Variables Entered	Variables Removed	Method
1	rother, female, prestg80, black, educ[a]	.	Enter

a. All requested variables entered.

Model Summary

Model	R	R Square	Adjusted R Square	Std. Error of the Estimate
1	.472[a]	.222	.222	19293.455

a. Predictors: (Constant), rother, female, prestg80, black, educ

ANOVA[b]

Model	Sum of Squares	df	Mean Square	F	Sig.
Regression	1.670E12	5	3.340E11	897.198	.000[a]
Residual	5.840E12	15688	3.722E8		
Total	7.510E12	15693			

a. Predictors: (Constant), rother, female, prestg80, black, educ

b. Dependent Variable: realrinc

Coefficients[a]

Model	Unstandardized Coefficients		Standardized Coefficients	t	Sig.
	B	Std. Error	Beta		
(Constant)	−12547.059	821.687		−15.270	.000
educ	1746.323	66.072	.219	26.430	.000
prestg80	367.684	13.165	.231	27.928	.000
female	−10953.201	308.819	−.250	−35.468	.000
black	−2269.182	466.448	−.035	−4.865	.000
rother	−2245.328	665.354	−.024	−3.375	.001

a. Dependent Variable: realrinc

The actual results of the regression are presented in the final "Coefficients" table. Our beta coefficients are presented in the second column of this table under *B*, which is under the *Unstandardized Coefficients* heading. The probability levels for our independent variables and *y*-intercept are presented in the rightmost column, under *Sig.* As we can see, all our independent variables are significant at the .01 level, with all but one being significant at the $p < .001$ level.

Now, let's interpret all our beta coefficients. The first beta coefficient is for the constant, or *y*-intercept. Here, IBM SPSS calculated the beta coefficient to be −12547.1. So for male individuals with 0 years of education, an occupational prestige score of 0, who are not black or a member of another race (i.e., are white), predicted income would be −$12547.10 (here, income was coded in dollars, not thousands of dollars as in my previous example). Obviously, this does not make sense, in that it is impossible to have a negative income, but this is simply part of the model's equation.

Next, we have a beta coefficient for years of education of 1746.32. This means that for every additional year of education, the respondent's predicted income is expected to increase by $1746.32. In regard to occupational prestige score, IBM SPSS has calculated a beta coefficient of 367.68. This means that for each additional occupational prestige score point, the respondent's predicted income is expected to increase by $367.68.

Our beta coefficients for our race dummy variables were both negative. Keep in mind that as we have chosen whites as the comparison category, the results for both of these variables are compared with those of whites. The beta coefficient for our black dummy variable is −2269.18. This means that on average, being black, as compared with being white, reduces your income by

$2269.18. The calculated beta coefficient for members of other races was −2245.33. This can be stated as, on average, being a member of another race, as compared with being white, reduces your income by $2245.33. Finally, the beta coefficient for sex was −10953.2. As in this variable, females were coded as 1 and males were coded as 0, this can be seen as a dummy variable for females, with males as the comparison category. Specifically, it can be said that on average, females make $10953.20 less than males do.

The regression, as a whole, can be represented by the following equation:

$$Income = -12547.06 + 1746.32(educ) + 367.68(prestg80) + -10953.20(female) + -2269.18(black) + -2245.33(rother)$$

This was obtained simply by plugging the calculated unstandardized beta coefficients into our regression equation.

Another important element of our regression output is our R-squared value. The concept of R-squared was introduced in the previous chapter in the section on Pearson's correlation coefficient. R-squared measures the amount of variation in one variable that is explained by one or more other variables. In terms of regression, R-squared measures the amount of variation in your dependent variable that is explained by your independent variable(s). Our R-squared value is given in the second table of our output, which is reproduced below:

Model Summary

Model	R	R Square	Adjusted R Square	Std. Error of the Estimate
1	.472[a]	.222	.222	19293.455

a. Predictors: (Constant), rother, female, prestg80, black, educ

Here, our R-squared value was calculated to be .222. To convert this to a percentage, you will simply move the decimal point two places to the right, arriving at the value of 22.2%. We can interpret our R-squared value in this way: Years of education completed, occupational prestige score, sex, and race collectively explain 22.2% of the variation in income. As you can see in the table, IBM SPSS has also calculated an adjusted R-squared. The equation for R-squared is such that adding an additional independent variable will typically increase our *R*-squared value even if it is not in fact actually predictive of the dependent variable. So in models with a large number of independent variables, the *R*-squared value may become artificially inflated. The adjusted *R*-squared accounts for this possibility by lowering the calculated value as the number of independent variables in the model increases.

Finally, the equivalent syntax for this regression is the following:

```
REGRESSION
/MISSING LISTWISE
/STATISTICS COEFF OUTS R ANOVA
/CRITERIA=PIN(.05) POUT(.10)
/NOORIGIN
/DEPENDENT realrinc
/METHOD=ENTER educ prestg80 female black rother.
```

SECTION 3: STATA △

This section will outline how to conduct a linear regression within Stata, using the same data set from the General Social Survey that has been used in previous chapters. In this section, I will perform the same multiple linear regression that was presented in the previous section, in which the respondent's income is predicted using their level of education, occupational prestige score, sex, and race.

Before we run the actual regression, we first need to create dummy variables for sex and race. Currently, the values for sex are 1 and 2, while the values for race are 1, 2, and 3. Currently, for the sex variable, males are coded 1 and females are coded 2. I will recode this variable so that males are coded 0 and females are coded 1. In regard to the race variable, whites are coded 1, blacks are coded 2, and individuals of other races are coded 3. For this variable, I will create two dummy variables, one dummy variable for blacks and one dummy variable for individuals of other races. Whites will be selected as the comparison category.

Recoding variables was covered in Chapter 2; however, I will briefly discuss how to recode the sex variable and create the dummy variables for race before I present instructions on running the regression. The other two variables in this model are education and occupational prestige. The education variable measures years of education completed, while the occupational prestige score variable is a measure of how prestigious the respondent's occupation is. Both of these variables are continuous and do not need to be recoded or modified.

The following syntax commands will recode our sex and race variables, creating a dummy variable for females and a dummy variable for blacks and those of other races:

```
gen female=sex==2
gen black=race==2
gen otherr=race==3
```

The syntax above creates new variables for the sex as well as the race variables, which is a method I prefer over recoding the original variables themselves. The first line of syntax creates a new variable called *female*, which we set to equal 1 in cases where the original *sex* variable is equal to 2. This command also sets all other values for *sex* (in this example, the only other value is 1) equal to 0. Therefore, females, originally coded 2, are now coded 1, and males, who were coded 1, are now coded 0. This type of command is very useful for creating dummy variables, as it only requires a single line. The second line of syntax creates a new variable called *black*. What this command does is set *black* equal to 1 if the *race* variable is equal to 2, which was the coding representing blacks. If the respondents had a value other than 2 for the *race* variable, they will be coded as 0 in the *black* variable. This is very similar to how we created the dummy variable for *female*. The final line of syntax creates a new variable called *otherr*, which is set equal to 1 if the respondent had a value of 3 on *race*, and set equal to 0 if the respondent had a value other than 3 on the *race* variable. These latter two syntax commands make it very easy to create dummy variables for inclusion in regression analyses as well as other types of analyses.

To conduct a linear regression using the menus, we can make the following menu selection:

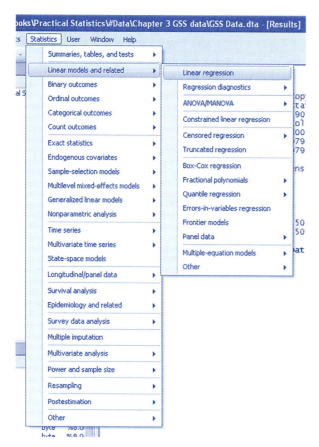

This will open the following dialog box:

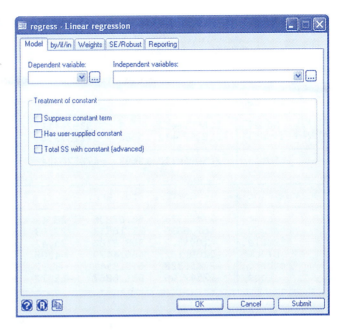

Here, we will specify income as the dependent variable and specify the level of education, occupational prestige score, sex, and race as our independent variables, using our variable names. Here, I have created a female dummy variable (=1 for females, =0 for males), and a dummy variable for blacks and a dummy variable for those of other races. When completed, the dialog box should look as shown here:

Next, click *OK* to run the regression. This same regression could also be run using the following syntax, which you may find to be more efficient. Here, after typing the `regress` command, you simply list your dependent variable followed by your independent variable(s).

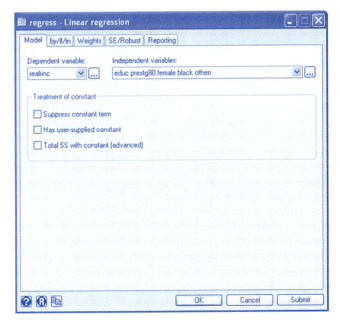

```
regress realrinc educ
prestg80 female black
otherr
```

By running the regression using either method, Stata gives us the following results:

```
. regress realrinc educ prestg80 female black otherr
```

Source	SS	df	MS		
Model	1.6699e+12	5	3.3397e+11		
Residual	5.8397e+12	15688	372237396		
Total	7.5095e+12	15693	478526324		

Number of obs = 15694
F(5, 15688) = 897.20
Prob > F   = 0.0000
R-squared   = 0.2224
Adj R-squared = 0.2221
Root MSE   = 19293

realrinc	Coef.	Std. Err.	t	P>|t|	[95% Conf. Interval]	
educ	1746.323	66.07236	26.43	0.000	1616.813	1875.832
prestg80	367.6839	13.16533	27.93	0.000	341.8783	393.4895
female	−10953.2	308.8186	−35.47	0.000	−11558.52	−10347.88
black	−2269.182	466.4479	−4.86	0.000	−3183.473	−1354.89
otherr	−2245.328	665.3541	−3.37	0.001	−3549.499	−941.1576
_cons	−12547.06	821.6867	−15.27	0.000	−14157.66	−10936.46

As we can see, these results matched those obtained in the previous section on IBM SPSS. In the table just presented, we can see that all our independent variables are significant at the $p < .01$ level, and all except one are significant at the $p < .001$ level. Now, I will interpret all the beta coefficients. The first beta coefficient is for the constant, or y-intercept. Here, Stata has calculated the y-intercept to be −12547.1. So for male individuals with 0 years of education, an occupational prestige score of 0, and who are not black or members of another race (i.e., are white), predicted income would be −$12547.1. Obviously, this does not make sense, in that it is impossible to have a negative income, but this is simply part of the model's equation.

Next, we have a beta coefficient for years of education of 1746.32. This means that for every additional year of education, the respondent's predicted income is expected to increase by $1746.32. In regard to occupational prestige score, Stata has calculated a beta coefficient of 367.68. This means that for each additional occupational prestige score point, the respondent's predicted income is expected to increase by $367.68.

Our beta coefficients for our race dummy variables were both negative. Keep in mind that as whites were chosen as the comparison category, the results for both of these variables are compared with those of whites. The beta coefficient for our black dummy variable is −2269.18. This means that on average, being black, as compared with being white, reduces your income by $2269.18. The calculated beta coefficient for members of other races was −2245.33. This can be stated as, on average, being a member of another race, as compared with being white, reduces your income by $2245.33. Finally, the beta coefficient for sex was −10,953.2. As in this variable, females were coded as 1 and males were coded as 0, this can be seen as a dummy variable for females, with males as the comparison category. Specifically, it can be said that on average, females make $10,953.20 less than males do.

The regression, as a whole, can be represented by the following equation:

$$Income = -12547.06 + 1746.32(educ) + 367.68(prestg80) +$$
$$-10953.20(female) + -2269.18(black) + -2245.33(otherr)$$

This was obtained simply by plugging the calculated beta coefficients from our results into our regression equation.

Next, we can see that Stata calculated an R-squared value of .2224 and an adjusted R-squared value of .2221. We can interpret the R-squared value in the following way: Years of education, race, sex, and occupational prestige score collectively explain slightly over 22% of the variation in income. The value of 22% was arrived at by simply moving the decimal point from the R-squared value two points to the right. As discussed previously, the adjusted R-squared is a modification of the original R-squared value, taking into account the number of independent variables in your model. As the number of independent variables in a regression model increases, R-squared has a tendency to be artificially inflated. The adjusted R-squared helps to control for this phenomenon. In our regression, we can see that both the original and adjusted R-squared values are almost identical, largely owing to the small number of independent variables we included in our model.

SECTION 4: SUMMARY △

This chapter covered linear regression, which is a particular form of regression that is used when your dependent variable is continuous. Simple linear regression refers to a linear regression in which there is only one independent variable, while multiple linear regression refers to a linear regression in which there are two or more independent variables. While the calculations for linear regression with one or two independent variables can be done by hand, the mathematics become considerably more complicated in cases with three or more independent variables. When including categorical variables in a regression model as independent variables, you must first construct one or a series of dummy variables that you will include in your model. The results of a regression will include a y-intercept, or constant, along with beta coefficients for every independent variable included in your model. These values can be used to construct an equation in which you can predict an individual's response or value on your dependent variable based on his or her responses or values on your independent variables. The results of a regression analysis will also include a *R*-squared value, which is a measure of the proportion of variation in the dependent variable that is explained by your independent variable(s). The second and third sections of this chapter provided instructions on how to conduct a regression analysis in both IBM SPSS and Stata, using both menus and syntax.

The following chapter will discuss logistic, ordered, multinomial, negative binomial, and Poisson regression. Logistic regression is used when your dependent variable is binary (coded as 0 or 1). Ordered logistic regression is used when your dependent variable is categorical and ordered. Multinomial logistic regression is used in situations where your dependent variable is categorical but cannot be ordered in any meaningful way. Finally, both negative binomial and Poisson regression are used when your dependent variable is a count variable. From the following chapter onward, less emphasis will be placed on the mathematical foundations of statistical methods, and I will focus more strongly on the practical use of these more advanced methods.

 ## RESOURCES

You can find more information about IBM SPSS and how to purchase it by navigating to the following Web site: www.spss.com/software/statistics/

You can find more information about Stata and how to purchase it by navigating to the following Web site: www.stata.com

This book's Web site can be found at the following location: www.sage pub.com/kremelstudy

CHAPTER 6

LOGISTIC, ORDERED, MULTINOMIAL, NEGATIVE BINOMIAL, AND POISSON REGRESSION

OUTLINE OF CHAPTER

◬   SECTION 1: INTRODUCTION

While the previous chapter covered linear regression, which is used when your dependent variable is continuous, this chapter covers other forms of regression that are used when your dependent variable takes another form. Logistic regression is used when your dependent variable is binary, or only has two outcomes, and can be coded as simply 0 or 1. Ordered logistic regression is used when your dependent variable is a categorical variable that can be ordered (i.e., ordinal). Some examples include highest degree completed or socioeconomic status, if it was categorized as low, medium, or high. Multinomial logistic regression is used when your dependent variable is categorical but cannot be ordered (i.e., nominal). Some examples include college major, region of residence, and occupation. Negative binomial and Poisson regression are two distinct but similar methods that are used when your dependent variable is a count variable. Some examples include the number of times the respondent saw a doctor in the past year or the number of jobs a person has held in the past decade. In these examples, it might be possible to consider these variables to be continuous and simply conduct a linear regression. Poisson regression would be preferred in situations where nonzero cases are rare (e.g., if one were using accidents per year as the dependent variable, where most years saw zero accidents). Negative binomial would be preferred to Poisson regression in situations where there is **overdispersion**, which is defined as a situation where your data have greater variance than expected. If we find that our dependent variable has a variance that is greater than its mean, we can choose negative binomial regression over Poisson regression. It is common in cases of overdispersion that your count variable will have a very large proportion of zero cases.

It is important, when conducting a regression, to select the appropriate test based on the nature of your dependent variable. The differences between these types of regression are summarized in the table presented here:

Type of Regression	Nature of Dependent Variable
Linear regression	Continuous
Logistic regression	Binary
Ordered logistic regression	Ordinal (categorical and ordered)
Multinomial logistic regression	Nominal (categorical and unordered)
Negative binomial regression	Count
Poisson regression	Count

While you might initially find that conducting these new forms of regression in IBM SPSS or Stata and interpreting the results can be slightly more involved than in linear regression, with practice this will become second nature.

SECTION 2: IBM SPSS △

Introduction to the Data

To conduct these other forms of regression in IBM SPSS, you will need to have one of the newer versions of the program. To perform most of the regression analyses presented in this section, you will also need the "Regression Models" add-on. This is one of the reasons why I strongly prefer Stata for regression analysis in general, as you simply need the program itself to run everything IBM SPSS can with the add-on. Stata also can run certain regression analyses and tests that cannot be done in IBM SPSS.

In this section, I will use data from the General Social Survey for the examples presented. As an example of a binary variable, which will be used in a logistic regression, I will select a variable that asks whether the respondents have gone through any specialized training in school to obtain a vocational certificate, diploma, degree, or license for their occupation. The frequency table for this variable is shown as follows:

IF THE RESPONDENT IS A TEACHER, ENGINEER, SCIENTIST, MEDICAL PRACTITIONER, LAWYER, ACCOUNTANT, PLEASE ENTER OPTION 1 (YES) FOR THE RESPONDENT WITHOUT ACTUALLY ASKING Q.695A.

695.   A.   Have you gone through any specialized training in school to obtain a vocational certificate, diploma, degree, or license for this occupation?

[VAR: OCCTRAIN]

RESPONSE	PUNCH	1972-82	1982B	1983-87	1987B	1988-91	1993-96	1998	2000	2002	2004	2006	ALL
						YEAR						COL. 2902	
Yes	1	0	0	0	0	0	0	504	0	0	0	0	504
No (SKIP TO Q.696)	2	0	0	0	0	0	0	739	0	0	0	0	739
Don't know	8	0	0	0	0	0	0	0	0	0	0	0	0
No answer	9	0	0	0	0	0	0	134	0	0	0	0	134
Not applicable (Form 2 and Col. 9 not 1-2)	BK	13626	354	7542	353	5907	7502	1455	2817	2765	2812	4510	49643

As an example of an ordinal variable, which will be used in an ordinal logistic regression, I will select highest degree completed. As an example of a nominal variable, which will be used in a multinomial logistic regression,

I will select political party affiliation. Finally, for examples of count variables, I will select the following two variables: the number of times the respondent was injured on the job in the past 12 months, and the number of days the respondent felt overjoyed about something in the past week. Frequency tables for these last two variables are presented here:

912.   In the past 12 months, how many times have you been injured on the job?

[VAR: HURTATWK]

RESPONSE	PUNCH	YEAR										COL. 3789	
		1972-82	1982B	1983-87	1987B	1988-91	1993-96	1998	2000	2002	2004	2006	ALL
None	0	0	0	0	0	0	0	0	0	1577	0	1526	3103
1	1	0	0	0	0	0	0	0	0	128	0	123	251
2	2	0	0	0	0	0	0	0	0	25	0	40	65
3	3	0	0	0	0	0	0	0	0	17	0	8	25
4	4	0	0	0	0	0	0	0	0	4	0	7	11
5	5	0	0	0	0	0	0	0	0	6	0	7	13
6	6	0	0	0	0	0	0	0	0	6	0	4	10
7 or more	7+	0	0	0	0	0	0	0	0	8	0	7	15
Don't know	8	0	0	0	0	0	0	0	0	8	0	1	9
No answer	9	0	0	0	0	0	0	0	0	17	0	11	28
Not applicable	BK	13626	354	7542	353	5907	7502	2832	2817	969	2812	2776	47490

J.   Felt overjoyed about something?

[VAR: OVRJOYED]

RESPONSE	PUNCH	YEAR										COL. 2238	
		1972-82	1982B	1983-87	1987B	1988-91	1993-96	1998	2000	2002	2004	2006	ALL
0 days	0	0	0	0	0	0	584	0	0	0	0	0	584
1 day	1	0	0	0	0	0	264	0	0	0	0	0	264
2 days	2	0	0	0	0	0	185	0	0	0	0	0	185
3 days	3	0	0	0	0	0	145	0	0	0	0	0	145
4 days	4	0	0	0	0	0	73	0	0	0	0	0	73
5 days	5	0	0	0	0	0	56	0	0	0	0	0	56
6 days	6	0	0	0	0	0	30	0	0	0	0	0	30
7 days	7	0	0	0	0	0	107	0	0	0	0	0	107
Don't know	8	0	0	0	0	0	12	0	0	0	0	0	12
No answer	9	0	0	0	0	0	4	0	0	0	0	0	4
Not applicable	BK	13626	354	7542	353	5907	6042	2832	2817	2765	2812	4510	45050

I will use the same set of independent variables in most of the models in this section. Here, I'll simply use a small set of variables: the respondent's sex, age, years of education, and income. To download the data set that I'll be using in the analyses presented in this section, simply go to the following Web site: http://sda.berkeley.edu/cgi-bin/hsda?harcsda+gss04

Select *Download* and *Customized Subset*

And choose to select the following variables: *sex age educ realrinc occtrain degree partyid hurtatwk ovrjoyed*

Before we begin our analyses, I will first recode some of the variables. I will first create a new variable called *female* that will act as a dummy variable for females, with female respondents coded 1 and male respondents coded 0. I will recode *realrinc* by dividing its value by 1,000, so our results will be in units of $1,000. Party identification I will recode in the following way: Respondents who replied "strong Democrat" and "not strong Democrat" I will recode as "Democrat." Those who replied "independent, near Democrat," "independent," and "independent, near Republican," I will recode as "independent." Those who replied "not strong Republican" and "strong Republican" I will recode as "Republican." Finally, those who replied "other party" I will recode as "other." Our final four categories of our recoded party identification variable consist of Democrat, Independent, Republican, and other party affiliation. The variable *occtrain* was also recoded so that 0 represents "no" and 1 represents "yes." Finally, I'll make sure all respondents who replied with "not applicable," "don't know," and so on, for any of these questions will be recoded as missing for that question.

Logistic Regression

In the logistic regression presented in this section, the variable *occtrain* will be selected as our dependent variable. This variable asks whether the respondents have gone through any specialized training in school to obtain a vocational certificate, diploma, degree, or license for their occupation. Our independent variables in this analysis will consist of sex, age, years of education, and the respondent's income. After loading our data file into IBM SPSS, we will need to make the following menu selection:

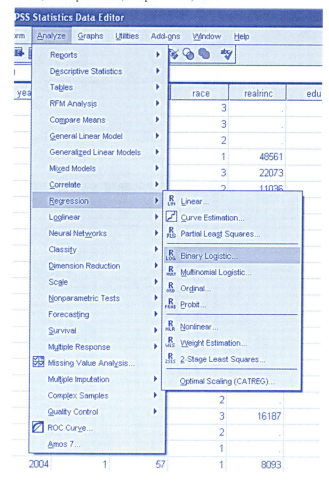

After selecting *Binary Logistic*, the following dialog box will appear:

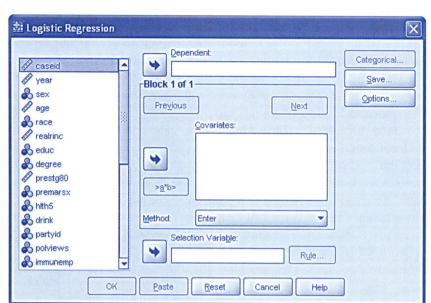

Next, we will specify *occtrain* as our dependent variable and *female*, *age*, *educ*, and *realrinc* as our independent variables. In this dialog box, we can move these to the *Covariates* entry, as shown here:

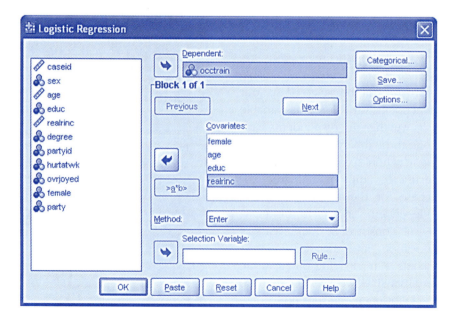

Next, clicking *OK* will give us the following results:

```
DATASET ACTIVATE DataSet2. LOGISTIC REGRESSION
VARIABLES occtrain /METHOD=ENTER female age
educ realrinc /CRITERIA=PIN(.05) POUT(.10)
ITERATE(20) CUT(.5).
```

Logistic Regression

[DataSet2] T:\Md book\#Data\Chapter 6\data 2—variables recoded.sav

Case Processing Summary

Unweighted Cases[a]		N	Per cent
Selected Cases	Included in Analysis	109 6	2.4
	Missing Cases	454 14	97. 6
	Total	465 10	100 .0
Unselected Cases		0	.0
Total		465 10	100 .0

a. If weight is in effect, see classification table for the total number of cases.

Dependent Variable Encoding

Original Value	Internal Value
No	0
Yes	1

Block 0: Beginning Block

Classification Table[a,b]

			Predicted		
			occtrain		
Observed			No	Yes	Percentage Correc
Step 0	occtrain	No	643	0	100.0
		Yes	453	0	.0
	Overall Percentage				58.7

a. Constant is included in the model.
b. The cut value is .500

Variables in the Equation

	B	S.E.	Wald	df	Sig.	Exp(B)
Step 0	-.350	.06	32.	1	.00	.70
Constant		1	603		0	5

Variables not in the Equation

			Score	df	Sig.
Step 0	Variables	female	.499	1	.480
		age	.424	1	.515
		educ	139.733	1	.000
		realrinc	28.647	1	.000
	Overall Statistics		142.805	4	.000

Block 1: Method = Enter

Omnibus Tests of Model Coefficients

		Chi-square	df	Sig.
Step 1	Step	154.891	4	.000
	Block	154.891	4	.000
	Model	154.891	4	.000

Model Summary

Step	-2 Log likelihood	Cox & Snell R Square	Nagelkerke R Square
1	1331.382[a]	.132	.178

a. Estimation terminated at iteration number 4 because parameter estimates changed by less than .001.

Classification Table[a]

			Predicted		
			occtrain		
	Observed		No	Yes	Percentage Correct
Step 1	occtrain	No	500	143	77.8
		Yes	228	225	49.7
	Overall Percentage				66.1

a. The cut value is .500

Variables in the Equation

		B	S.E.	Wald	df	Sig.	Exp(B)
Step 1	a female	.139	.136	1.035	1	.309	1.149
	age	-.003	.006	.279	1	.597	.997
	educ	.311	.031	102.607	1	.000	1.365
	realrinc	.005	.003	2.494	1	.114	1.005
	Constant	-4.791	.478	100.296	1	.000	.008

a. Variable(s) entered on step 1: female, age, educ, realrinc.

In the results just presented, the table of greatest interest to us is the final one, "Variables in the Equation." Here, both the unstandardized ("B") and standardized ("Exp(B)") coefficients are presented. In our recoded *occtrain* variable, 0 represented "no" and 1 represented "yes." Of the four independent variables included in this analysis, only years of education was predictive of specialized training at the .05 probability level. In this case, a higher level of education was associated with a higher probability of having specialized training for the respondent's occupation. This is evident from the fact that our beta value (B) is greater than 0, signifying a **positive** or **direct relationship**. Here, a value of 0 would indicate no relationship, while a negative value would indicate a **negative** or **inverse relationship**. To be able to interpret the coefficient for the logistic regression, we will use the **odds ratios** ("Exp(B)" in our table) for our independent variables, which are much easier to interpret than the **unstandardized coefficients** ("B").

Looking at our odds ratio for education, we see that it is 1.36. This can be interpreted in the following way: One additional year of education increases the odds of having had specialized training by a factor of 1.36. In the case of unstandardized coefficients in logistic regression, a positive value would indicate a positive or direct relationship between the independent variable and the dependent variable, while a negative value would indicate a negative or inverse relationship between the two variables. However, in the case of odds ratios in logistic regression, a value greater than 1 would indicate a positive or direct relationship between the independent and dependent variables, while a value less than 1 would indicate a negative or inverse relationship between these two variables. In regard to odds ratios, a value of exactly 1 would have the same meaning as an unstandardized coefficient of exactly 0, which would be in the case where an independent variable has no positive or negative effect on the dependent variable. To briefly review, in a positive or direct relationship, as the value of the independent variable increases, so does the value of the dependent variable. Likewise, if the value of the independent variable decreases, so does the value of the dependent variable. On the other hand, in the case of a negative or inverse relationship, as the value of the independent variable increases, the value of the dependent variable decreases accordingly. Also, as the value of the independent variable decreases, the value of the dependent variable would increase accordingly.

Three of the independent variables included in our analysis—age, education, and income—are continuous. However, our female variable is a binary variable. If this had been statistically significant, we could interpret its effect in the following way: The odds of having had specialized training for females is 1.15 times as large as for males. When interpreting odds ratios for dummy variables, you simply need to take note of the comparison category, realizing that the odds ratio presented relates to the dummy variable itself as compared with the comparison category that you have selected.

In logistic regression, there is no direct equivalent of the R-squared value that we discussed in the previous chapter on linear regression. However, there are a number of what are called **Pseudo R-squared** formulas that can be seen as providing an estimate of the linear regression R-squared value. These Pseudo R-squared formulas do not directly calculate the percent variance in the dependent variable explained by our independent variables and should not be interpreted as such. The Pseudo R-squared measures given to us by IBM SPSS in this analysis are presented in the table below:

Model Summary

Step	-2 Log likelihood	Cox & Snell R Square	Nagelkerke R Square
1	1331.382[a]	.132	.178

a. Estimation terminated at iteration number 4 because parameter estimates changed by less than .001.

Here, we are given two Pseudo R-squared calculations: Cox and Snell's R-squared and Nagelkerke's R-squared. The one used by Stata is McFadden's R-squared. There are a number of other Pseudo R-squared calculations, while probably the one most commonly used is Nagelkerke's R-squared.

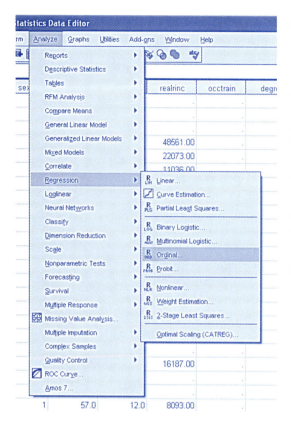

Ordered Logistic Regression

The ordered logistic regression presented here will use highest degree completed as the dependent variable. As discussed previously, this variable consists of the following response categories: less than high school, high school, junior college, bachelor's degree, and graduate degree. Our independent variables include the respondent's sex and age. Years of education and income will be omitted from this analysis, as I felt that these are not appropriate predictor variables of highest degree completed. To perform the ordered logistic regression, we will first make the following menu selection:

This will reveal the following dialog box:

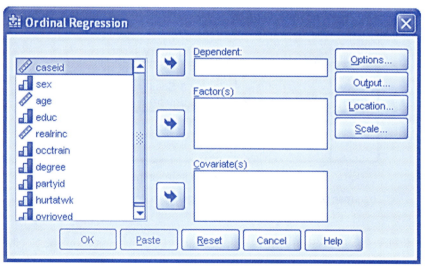

Next, we will move *degree* into the *Dependent* box and move the variables *female* and *age* into the *Covariate(s)* box, as shown here:

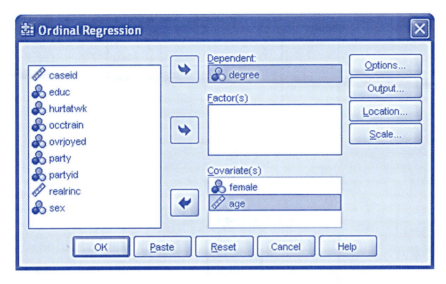

Next, clicking *OK* will give us the following output:

[DataSet2]   T: \Md book \#Data \Chapter 6 \data 2 —variables recoded.sav

Warnings

There are 27 (3.8%) cells (i.e., dependent variable levels by combinations of predictor variable values) with zero frequencies.

PLUM   — Ordinal Regression

Case Processing Summary

		N	Marginal Percentage
degree	LT High School	11046	23.9%
	High School	23961	51.9%
	Junior College	2215	4.8%
	Bachelor	6133	13.3%
	Graduate	2841	6.1%
Valid		46196	100.0%
Missing		314	
Total		46510	

Model Fitting Information

Model	-2 Log Likelihood	Chi-Square	df	Sig.
Intercept Only	9945.319			
Final	8049.905	1895.415	2	.000

Link function: Logit.

Goodness-of-Fit

	Chi-Square	df	Sig.
Pearson	5013.666	570	.000
Deviance	5406.397	570	.000

Link function: Logit.

Pseudo R-Square

Cox and Snell	.040
Nagelkerke	.044
McFadden	.016

Link function: Logit.

Parameter Estimates

		Estimate	Std. Error	Wald	df	Sig.	95% Confidence Interval	
							Lower Bound	Upper Bound
Threshold	[degree = 0]	-2.245	.029	6166.492	1	.000	-2.301	-2.189
	[degree = 1]	.137	.026	27.358	1	.000	.085	.188
	[degree = 2]	.422	.026	255.748	1	.000	.370	.473
	[degree = 3]	1.728	.030	3287.322	1	.000	1.669	1.787
Location	Female	-.132	.018	55.338	1	.000	-.167	-.097
	Age	-.022	.001	1796.517	1	.000	-.023	-.021

Link function: Logit.

Again, the table of greatest interest to us is the final one presented. Here, the coefficients for our independent variables are presented. Unfortunately, no odds ratios are presented here. However, Stata can easily calculate odds ratios when conducting an ordered logistic regression. If we wanted to strictly use IBM SPSS, we could calculate them by hand by raising the mathematical constant e, which is equal to approximately 2.71828, to the power of the unstandardized coefficient. For example:

$$\text{Odds ratio for female} = e^{-.132} = 2.71828^{-.132} = 0.876$$

The calculated odds ratio for our female variable is 0.876, and our odds ratio for our age variable would be calculated to be 0.978. Both of these independent variables are significant at the $p < .001$ probability level. To interpret our *female* variable, we could say the following: Being female decreases the odds of having the next more advanced degree by a factor of 0.876. As you can see, stating it in this way is somewhat awkward. What ordered logistic regression does is assume that the effect of your independent variables on your dependent variable is constant. Using the regression just presented as an example, in regard to our female variable, you could say the following: Being female decreases the odds of having a high school diploma as compared with having less than a high school diploma by a factor of 0.876. You could also say this: Being female decreases the odds of having a junior college degree as compared with a high school diploma by a factor of 0.876. As you can see, the odds ratio does not change for any comparison between one level of the dependent variable and its next highest level. If you did not assume that this effect would be constant, or if you did not assume that the "distances" between the different levels of your dependent variable were constant, you could instead perform a multinomial logistic regression instead of an ordered logistic regression. This method will be covered in the next section. Another option would be a generalized ordered logistic regression (gologit in Stata, but it needs to be installed first). Generalized ordered logistic regression is not as commonly used as multinomial logistic regression.

Finally, let's interpret our odds ratio for age. We could say the following: for each additional year of age, the odds of having the next more advanced degree decreases by a factor of 0.978. Again, more specifically, we could say that each additional year of age decreases the odds of having a high school diploma as compared with having less than a high school diploma by a factor of 0.978. Likewise, we can make the same statement comparing any level of our dependent variable with its next highest level.

Multinomial Logistic Regression

Multinomial logistic regression is used when your dependent variable is nominal (i.e., categorical and unordered) and consists of more than two categories. In the example presented in this section, political party affiliation will be chosen as our dependent variable. This variable consists of the following response categories: Democrat, Republican, Independent, and other party affiliation. Our independent variables in this model consist of the respondents' sex, age, income, and years of education completed. To conduct this multinomial logistic regression, we would first make the following menu selection:

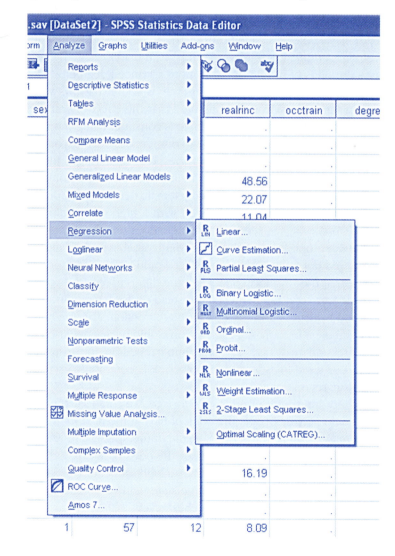

This will open the following dialog box:

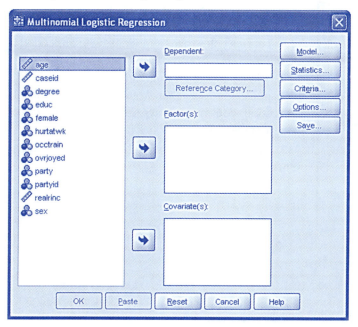

Now, we will move *party* into our *Dependent* field, and move our independent variables, *female*, *age*, *educ*, and *realrinc,* into our *Covariate(s)* field, as shown here:

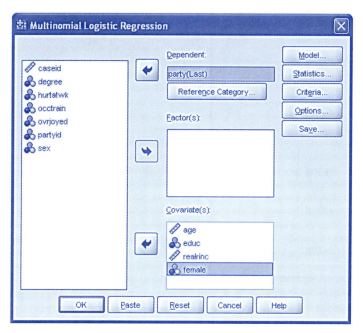

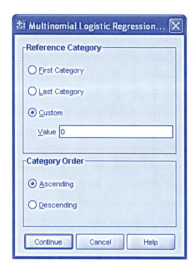

Next, we will click the *Reference Category* option, revealing the following dialog box:

Here, I have selected *Custom* and have specified a value of 0. This specifies that Democrats, who are coded as 0, will be the reference or comparison category in this analysis. This issue will be explained in greater detail later in this section, but suffice it to say that when using multinomial logistic regression, you must always select one of the categories of your dependent variable to be the comparison category. Next, click *Continue* and *OK*. This will give us the following output:

Nominal Regression

[DataSet2] T:\Md book\#Data\Chapter 6\data 2—variables recoded.sav

Case Processing Summary

		N	Marginal Percentage
party	Democrat	9701	35.9%
	Independent	9927	36.8%
	Republican	7023	26.0%
	Other	350	1.3%
Valid		27001	100.0%
Missing		19509	
Total		46510	
Subpopulation		24386[a]	

a. The dependent variable has only one value observed in 22814 (93.6%) subpopulations.

Model Fitting Information

Model	Model Fitting Criteria -2Log Likelihood	Likelihood Ratio Tests Chi-Square	df	Sig.
Intercept Only	5.913E4			
Final	5.826E4	872.785	12	.000

Pseudo R-Square

Cox and Snell	.032
Nagelkerke	.035
McFadden	.014

Likelihood Ratio Tests

Effect	Model Fitting Criteria -2 Log Likelihood of Reduced Model	Likelihood Ratio Tests Chi-Square	df	Sig.
Intercept	5.882E4	558.881	3	.000
age	5.858E4	316.546	3	.000
educ	5.840E4	143.162	3	.000
realrinc	5.834E4	80.640	3	.000
female	5.841E4	147.783	3	.000

The chi-square statistic is the difference in -2 log-likelihoods between the final model and a reduced model. The reduced model is formed by omitting an effect from the final model. The null hypothesis is that all parameters of that effect are 0.

party[a]	B	Std. Error	Wald	df	Sig.	Exp(B)	95% Confidence Interval for Exp(B)	
							Lower Bound	Upper Bound
Independent Intercept	.841	.087	92.748	1	.000			
age	-.018	.001	265.498	1	.000	.982	.980	.984
educ	.005	.005	.760	1	.383	1.005	.994	1.016
realrinc	.001	.001	2.093	1	.148	1.001	1.000	1.003
female	-.348	.030	131.207	1	.000	.706	.665	.749
Republican Intercept	-1.110	.096	132.771	1	.000			
age	-.002	.001	1.607	1	.205	.998	.996	1.001
educ	.062	.006	110.696	1	.000	1.064	1.052	1.077
realrinc	.007	.001	63.716	1	.000	1.007	1.005	1.008
female	-.261	.033	61.465	1	.000	.770	.721	.822
Other Intercept	-3.718	.331	126.111	1	.000			
age	-.011	.004	6.003	1	.014	.989	.981	.998
educ	.088	.021	18.063	1	.000	1.092	1.049	1.137
realrinc	-.005	.003	2.570	1	.109	.995	.988	1.001
female	-.516	.115	20.120	1	.000	.597	.476	.748

a. The reference category is: Democrat.

First, look at our coefficient for *female* in the *Independent* category in the final table presented. Its value here is −.348. To interpret our coefficient, we could say that being female decreases the likelihood of being an independent as compared with being a Democrat. In this analysis, I have specified Democrat to be the reference or comparison category of our dependent variable. That's why in all our results, one of the other three categories is being compared with that of Democrat.

To include the actual values of our coefficients in our interpretation, we need to first determine the **relative risk ratios**. Relative risk ratios, which are used in multinomial logistic regression, are similar to the odds ratios that we used in logistic and ordered logistic regression. The relative risk ratios are included in the output just presented under the *Exp(B)* column. They are calculated just as odds ratios are, by raising the mathematical constant *e* to the power of the unstandardized coefficient. For example,

$$\text{Relative risk ratio for female}$$
$$\text{for Independents} = e^{-.348} = 2.71828^{-.348} = 0.706$$

We could interpret our calculated relative risk ratio in the following way: The likelihood (or "risk") of being an independent as compared with being a Democrat is 0.706 times as high for females as for males. If we were to calculate the relative risk ratio for education under the "Other" category, we would obtain a relative risk ratio of 1.092. We could interpret this in the following way: Each additional year of education increases the likelihood of having an alternative political party affiliation as compared with being a Democrat by a factor of 1.092.

Negative Binomial and Poisson Regression

As mentioned previously, negative binomial and Poisson regression are two distinct but similar methods that are used when your dependent variable is a count variable. Some examples of count variables include the number of times the respondent saw a doctor in the past year or the number of jobs a person has held in the past decade. In these two examples, it might be possible to consider these variables to be continuous variables and simply conduct a linear regression. Poisson regression would be preferred in situations where nonzero cases are rare (e.g., if one were using accidents per year as the dependent variable, where most years saw zero accidents). Negative binomial would be preferred over Poisson regression in situations where there is overdispersion, which is defined as a situation where your data has greater variance than expected. If we find that our dependent variable has a variance that is greater than its mean, we can choose negative binomial regression over Poisson regression. It is common in cases of overdispersion that your count variable will have a very large proportion of zero cases. The two variables that will be used as dependent variables in this section are *hurtatwk* and *ovrjoyed*. *Hurtatwk* measures the number of times the respondent was injured on the job in the past 12 months, while *ovrjoyed* measures the number of days the respondent felt overjoyed about something in the past week. Frequency tables for both of these variables are listed here:

Frequency Table

hurtatwk

		Frequency	Percent	Valid Percent	Cumulative Percent
Valid	0	1577	3.4	89.0	89.0
	1	128	.3	7.2	96.3
	2	25	.1	1.4	97.7
	3	17	.0	1.0	98.6
	4	4	.0	.2	98.9
	5	6	.0	.3	99.2
	6	6	.0	.3	99.5
	7	8	.0	.5	100.0
	Total	1771	3.8	100.0	
Missing	System	44739	96.2		
	Total	46510	100.0		

ovrjoyed

		Frequency	Percent	Valid Percent	Cumulative Percent
Valid	0	584	1.3	40.4	40.4
	1	264	.6	18.3	58.7
	2	185	.4	12.8	71.5
	3	145	.3	10.0	81.6
	4	73	.2	5.1	86.6
	5	56	.1	3.9	90.5
	6	30	.1	2.1	92.6
	7	107	.2	7.4	100.0
	Total	1444	3.1	100.0	
Missing	System	45066	96.9		
Total		46510	100.0		

Also, the means and variances for these two variables are displayed here:

Statistics

		hurtatwk	ovrjoyed
N	Valid	1771	1444
	Missing	44739	45066
	Mean	.21	1.78
	Variance	.637	4.592

As you can see, the mean for our *hurtatwk* variable is .21, while the variance is .637. Our *ovrjoyed* variable has a mean of 1.78 and a variance of 4.592. Technically, you would prefer to use negative binomial regression for both of these variables, as they are both overdispersed, having variances that are

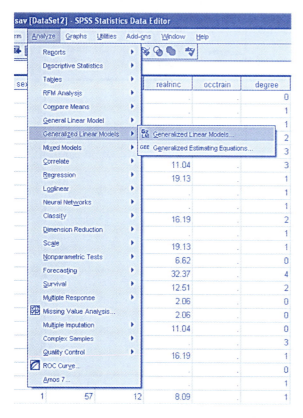

greater than their means. However, *ovrjoyed* will be analyzed in this section using Poisson regression simply to present an example of a Poisson regression. To conduct a Poisson regression with *ovrjoyed* as our dependent variable and *female*, *age*, *educ*, and *realrinc* as our independent variables, first navigate to the following menu selection in IBM SPSS:

This will open the following dialog box:

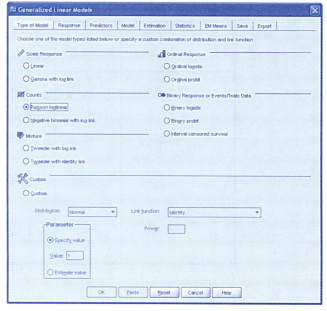

Here, we want to make sure that *Poisson loglinear* is selected under the *Counts* entry. Next, we can navigate to our *Response* tab and identify *ovrjoyed* as our dependent variable, as shown here:

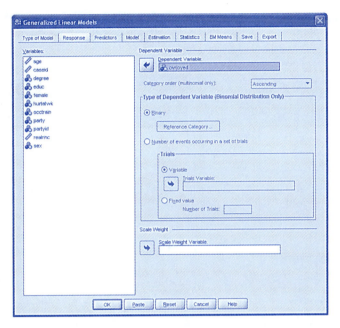

Next, we can navigate to our *Predictors* tab:

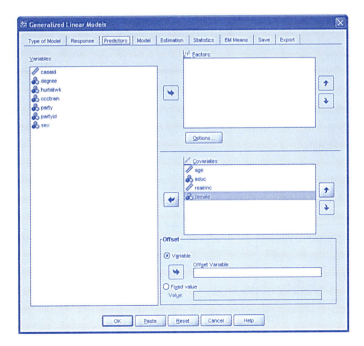

Here, I have specified *age*, *educ*, *realrinc*, and *female* as independent variables, placing them into the *Covariates* field. Next, I will navigate to the *Model* tab, as shown here:

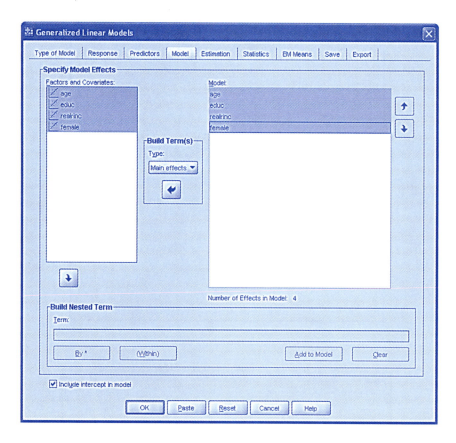

Here, I've specified our four independent variables as main effects in our model. Now, we can simply click *OK* to run the model. This produces the following output:

Generalized Linear Models

[DataSet2] T:\Md book\#Data\Chapter 6\data 2—variables recoded.sav

Model Information

Dependent Variable	ovrjoyed
Probability Distribution	Poisson
Link Function	Log

Case Processing Summary

	N	Percent
Included	985	2.1%
Excluded	45525	97.9%
Total	46510	100.0%

Continuous Variable Information

		N	Minimum	Maximum	Mean	Std.Deviation
Dependent Variable	ovrjoyed	985	0	7	1.79	2.114
Covariate	age	985	19	83	40.17	12.681
	educ	985	5	20	13.86	2.709
	realrinc	985	.36	92.69	21.3103	20.15144
	female	985	0	1	.50	.500

Goodness of Fit[b]

	Value	df	Value/df
Deviance	2465.053	980	2.515
Scaled Deviance	2465.053	980	
Pearson Chi-Square	2439.380	980	2.489
Scaled Pearson Chi-Square	2439.380	980	
Log Likelihood [a]	-2067.554		
Akaike's Information Criterion (AIC)	4145.108		
Finite Sample Corrected AIC (AICC)	4145.170		
Bayesian Information Criterion (BIC)	4169.572		
Consistent AIC (CAIC)	4174.572		

Dependent Variable: ovrjoyed

Model: (Intercept), age, educ, realrinc, female

a. The full log likelihood function is displayed and used in computing information criteria.

b. Information criteria are in small-is-better form.

Omnibus Test[a]

Likelihood Ratio Chi-Square	df	Sig.
28.615	4	.000

Dependent Variable: ovrjoyed
Model: (Intercept), age, educ, realrinc, female
a. Compares the fitted model against the intercept-only model.

Tests of Model Effects

	Type III		
Source	Wald Chi-Square	df	Sig.
(Intercept)	33.977	1	.000
age	16.577	1	.000
educ	.982	1	.322
realrinc	1.314	1	.252
female	8.795	1	.003

Dependent Variable: ovrjoyed
Model: (Intercept), age, educ, realrinc, female

Parameter Estimates

Parameter	B	Std. Error	95% Wald Confidence Interval		Hypothesis Test		Sig.
			Lower	Upper	Wald Chi-Square	df	
(Intercept)	.874	.1499	.580	1.167	33.977	1	.000
age	-.008	.0020	-.012	-.004	16.577	1	.000
educ	.010	.0096	-.009	.028	.982	1	.322
rearincl	-.002	.0014	-.004	.001	1.314	1	.252
female	-.147	.0497	-.245	-.050	8.795	1	.003
(Scale)	1[a]						

Dependent Variable: ovrjoyed
Model: (Intercept), age, educ, realrinc, female

a. Fixed at the displayed value.

Again, our table of greatest interest is the final one presented in our output. As we can see, both age and sex were significant at the $p < .05$ level. Specifically, being older and being female were both associated with fewer days per week in which the respondent felt overjoyed about something. To be able to incorporate the coefficients themselves into our interpretation, we need to obtain what are called the **incidence rate ratios** for our independent variables, which are similar to the odds ratios and relative risk ratios discussed previously. While Stata provides a simple syntax command that will determine the incidence rate ratios, if you were to use only IBM SPSS, you would need to calculate them by hand. To do this, we simply raise the mathematical constant e to the power of the unstandardized coefficient. For example, in the case of female,

$$\text{Incidence rate ratio for female} =$$
$$e^{-.147} = 2.71828^{-.147} = 0.863$$

Our incidence rate ratio for female could be interpreted as follows: The average number of days per week that one feels overjoyed about something for females is 0.863 times that of males. In regard to age, which has an incidence rate ratio of 0.992, you could say the following: With each additional year of age, the average number of days per week one feels overjoyed about something decreases by a factor of 0.992.

To run a negative binomial regression in which *hurtatwk* is the dependent variable and *female*, *age*, *educ*, and *realrinc* are our independent variables, we would first make the following menu selection:

In the following dialog box, we will select *Negative binomial with log link* under the *Counts* option, as shown here:

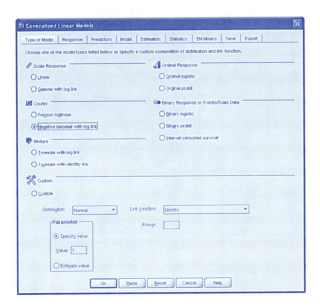

Next, under the *Response* tab, you will identify *hurtatwk* as our dependent variable, as shown here:

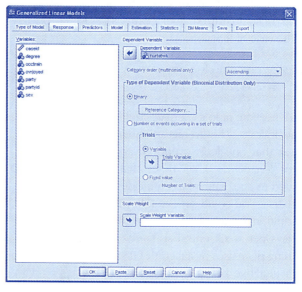

Next, we will select the *Predictors* tab, identifying *female*, *age*, *educ*, and *realrinc* as our independent variables, and placing them under the *Covariates* category:

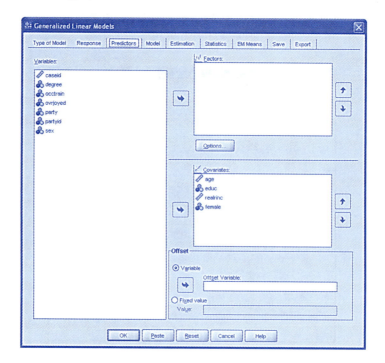

Finally, under the *Model* tab, you will identify our four independent variables as main effects, as shown here:

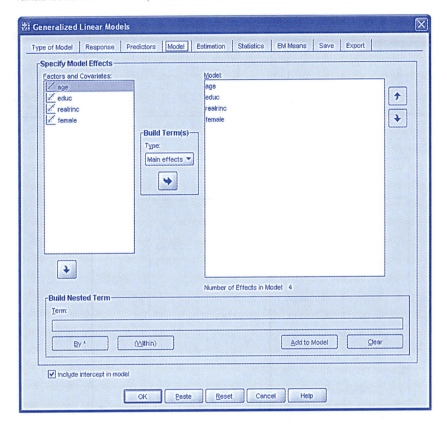

Finally, clicking *OK* will give us the following output:

Generalized Linear Models

```
[ DataSet2]  T:\Md book\ #Data\ Chapter 6\ data 2—variables recoded.sav
```

Model Information

Dependent Variable	hurtatwk
Probability Distribution	Negative binomial (1)
Link Function	Log

Case Processing Summary

	N	Percent
Included	1538	3.3%
Excluded	44972	96.7%
Total	46510	100.0%

Continuous Variable Information

		N	Minimum	Maximum	Mean	Std. Deviation
Dependent Variable	hurtatwk	1538	0	7	.20	.782
Covariate	age	1538	18	86	41.38	12.754
	educ	1538	0	20	13.81	.7862
	rearincl	1538	.31	132.33	24.4354	25.86995
	female	1538	0	1	.51	.500

Goodness of Fit[b]

	Value	df	Value/df
Deviance	1071.171	1533	.699
Scaled Deviance	1071.171	1533	
Pearson Chi-Square	3774.071	1533	2.462
Scaled Pearson Chi-Square	3774.071	1533	
Log Likelihood[a]	-823.629		
Akaike's Information Criterion (AIC)	1657.258		
Finite Sample Corrected AIC (AICC)	1657.297		
Bayesian Information Criterion (BIC)	1683.949		
Consistent AIC (CAIC)	1688.949		

Dependent Variable: hurtatwk

Model: (Intercept), age, educ, realrinc, female

a. The full log likelihood function is displayed and used in computing information criteria.

b. Information criteria are in small-is-better form.

Omnibus Test[a]

Likelihood Ratio Chi-Square	df	Sig.
42.225	4	.000

Dependent Variable: hurtatwk

Model: (Intercept), age, educ, realrinc, female

a. Compares the fitted model against the intercept-only model.

Tests of Model Effects

Source	Type III		
	Wald Chi-Square	df	Sig.
(Intercept)	.112	1	.738
age	14.387	1	.000
educ	.704	1	.401
realrinc	4.362	1	.037
female	17.680	1	.000

Dependent Variable: hurtatwk

Model: (Intercept), age, educ, realrinc, female

Parameter Estimates

Parameter	B	Std. Error	95% Wald Confidence Interval		Hypothesis Test		
			Lower	Upper	Wald Chi-Square	df	Sig.
(Intercept)	-.123	.3685	-.846	.599	.112	1	.738
age	-.020	.0052	-.030	-.010	14.387	1	.000
educ	-.020	.0241	-.067	.027	.704	1	.401
realrinc	-.007	.0034	-.014	.000	4.362	1	.037
female	-.549	.1305	-.805	-.293	17.680	1	.000
(Scale)	1[a]						
(Negative binomial)	1						

Dependent Variable: hurtatwk

Model: (Intercept), age, educ, realrinc, female

a. Fixed at the displayed value.

As we can see, our female, age, and income independent variables are significant at the $p < .05$ level. The incident rate ratios can be calculated and interpreted in the same way as with Poisson regression. For example,

$$\text{Incidence rate ratio for female} = e^{-.549} = 2.71828^{-.549} = 0.578$$

For example, the effect of our female variable can be interpreted in the following way: The average number of times that one is hurt on the job for females is 0.578 times that of males. In regard to age, an increase in age by one year decreases the number of accidents per year by a factor of 0.980.

SECTION 3: STATA

Introduction to the Data

Conducting these new forms of regression in Stata is quite straightforward. In this section, I will focus exclusively on the use of syntax in running these new forms of regression, as this is much more efficient and much less time consuming than using the menus. As in the previous section on IBM SPSS, I will use data from the General Social Survey, which contains items on a number of sociological and social psychological variables. As an example of a binary variable, which will be used in a logistic regression, I will select a variable that asks whether the respondent has gone through any specialized training in school to obtain a vocational certificate, diploma, degree, or license for their occupation. The frequency table for this variable is shown here:

IF THE RESPONDENT IS A TEACHER, ENGINEER, SCIENTIST, MEDICAL PRACTITIONER, LAWYER, ACCOUNTANT, PLEASE ENTER OPTION 1 (YES) FOR THE RESPONDENT WITHOUT ACTUALLY ASKING Q.695A.

695. A. Have you gone through any specialized training in school to obtain a vocational certificate, diploma, degree, or license for this occupation?

[VAR: OCCTRAIN]

RESPONSE	PUNCH	YEAR											COL. 2902
		1972-82	1982B	1983-87	1987B	1988-91	1993-96	1998	2000	2002	2004	2006	ALL
Yes	1	0	0	0	0	0	0	504	0	0	0	0	504
No (SKIP TO Q.696)	2	0	0	0	0	0	0	739	0	0	0	0	739
Don't know	8	0	0	0	0	0	0	0	0	0	0	0	0
No answer	9	0	0	0	0	0	0	134	0	0	0	0	134
Not applicable (Form 2 and Col. 9 not 1-2)	BK	13626	354	7542	353	5907	7502	1455	2817	2765	2812	4510	49643

As an example of an ordinal variable, which will be used in an ordinal logistic regression, I will select highest degree completed. As an example of a nominal variable, which will be used in a multinomial logistic regression, I will select political party affiliation. Finally, for examples of count variables, I will select the following two variables: the number of times the respondent was injured on the job in the past 12 months and the number of days the respondent felt overjoyed about something in the past week. Frequency tables for these two variables are presented here:

912. In the past 12 months, how many times have you been injured on the job?

[VAR: HURTATWK]

RESPONSE	PUNCH	YEAR											COL. 3789
		1972-82	1982B	1983-87	1987B	1988-91	1993-95	1998	2000	2002	2004	2006	ALL
None	0	0	0	0	0	0	0	0	0	1577	0	1526	3103
1	1	0	0	0	0	0	0	0	0	128	0	123	251
2	2	0	0	0	0	0	0	0	0	25	0	40	65
3	3	0	0	0	0	0	0	0	0	17	0	8	25
4	4	0	0	0	0	0	0	0	0	4	0	7	11
5	5	0	0	0	0	0	0	0	0	6	0	7	13
6	6	0	0	0	0	0	0	0	0	6	0	4	10
7 or more	7+	0	0	0	0	0	0	0	0	8	0	7	15
Don't know	8	0	0	0	0	0	0	0	0	8	0	1	9
No answer	9	0	0	0	0	0	0	0	0	17	0	11	28
Not applicable	BK	13626	354	7542	353	5907	7502	2832	2817	969	2812	2776	47490

J. Felt overjoyed about something?

[VAR: OVRJOYED]

RESPONSE	PUNCH	YEAR											COL. 2238
		1972-82	1982B	1983-87	1987B	1988-91	1993-95	1998	2000	2002	2004	2006	ALL
0 days	0	0	0	0	0	0	584	0	0	0	0	0	584
1 day	1	0	0	0	0	0	264	0	0	0	0	0	264
2 days	2	0	0	0	0	0	185	0	0	0	0	0	185
3 days	3	0	0	0	0	0	145	0	0	0	0	0	145
4 days	4	0	0	0	0	0	73	0	0	0	0	0	73
5 days	5	0	0	0	0	0	56	0	0	0	0	0	56
6 days	6	0	0	0	0	0	30	0	0	0	0	0	30
7 days	7	0	0	0	0	0	107	0	0	0	0	0	107
Don't know	8	0	0	0	0	0	12	0	0	0	0	0	12
No answer	9	0	0	0	0	0	4	0	0	0	0	0	4
Not applicable	BK	13626	354	7542	353	5907	6042	2832	2817	2765	2812	4510	45050

I will use the same set of independent variables in all the models in this section. Here, I'll simply use a small set of variables: the respondent's sex, age, years of education, and income. To download the data set that I'll be using in the analyses presented in this section, simply go to the following Web site: http://sda.berkeley.edu/cgi-bin/hsda?harcsda+gss04

Select *Download* and *Customized Subset*

And choose to select the following variables: *sex age educ realrinc occtrain degree partyid hurtatwk ovrjoyed*

Before we begin our analyses, I will first recode some of the variables. I will first create a new variable called *female* that will act as a dummy variable for females, with female respondents coded 1 and male respondents coded 0. I will recode *realrinc* by dividing its value by 1,000, so our results will be in units of $1,000. Party identification I will recode in the following way: Respondents who replied "strong Democrat" and "not strong Democrat" I will recode as "Democrat." Those who replied "independent, near Democrat," "independent," and "independent, near Republican," I will recode as "independent." Those who replied "not strong Republican" and "strong Republican" I will recode as "Republican." Finally, those who replied "other party" I will recode as "other." Our final four categories of our recoded party identification variable consist of Democrat, Independent, Republican, and other party affiliation. The variable *occtrain* was also recoded so that 0 represented "no" and 1 represented "yes." Finally, I'll make sure all respondents who replied with "not applicable," "don't know," and so on, for any of these questions will be recoded as missing for that question.

Logistic Regression

In our logistic regression, *occtrain*, which asks whether the respondent has gone through any specialized training in school to obtain a vocational certificate, diploma, degree, or license for his or her occupation, will be chosen as the dependent variable. As previously mentioned, our independent variables will consist of sex, age, years of education, and the respondent's income. To conduct this logistic regression, we simply need to type the following syntax into Stata:

```
logit occtrain female age educ realrinc
```

Here, we have first specified the `logit` command, which will run a logistic regression. Then, we specified our dependent variable, followed by our four independent variables. Hitting *Enter* will run the regression and present us with the following results:

```
Iteration 0:   log likelihood = -743.13683
Iteration 1:   log likelihood = -667.31647
Iteration 2:   log likelihood = -665.69519
Iteration 3:   log likelihood = -665.69124

Logistic regression                              Number of obs   =       1096
                                                 LR chi2(4)      =     154.89
                                                 Prob > chi2     =     0.0000
Log likelihood = -665.69124                      Pseudo R2       =     0.1042
```

occtrain	Coef.	Std. Err.	z	P>|z|	[95% Conf. Interval]	
female	.1386484	.1363121	1.02	0.309	-.1285185	.4058152
age	-.0031103	.0058882	-0.53	0.597	-.014651	.0084303
educ	.310888	.0306911	10.13	0.000	.2507346	.3710414
realrinc	.0048808	.0030907	1.58	0.114	-.0011769	.0109385
_cons	-4.791458	.4784359	-10.01	0.000	-5.729175	-3.853741

In the table presented above, we can see whether each of our independent variables is predictive of whether the respondent has had specialized training for their occupation. As you remember, in our recoded *occtrain* variable, 0 represented "no" and 1 represented "yes." Of our four independent variables, only years of education was predictive of specialized training at the .05 probability level. In this case, higher levels of education were associated with a higher probability of having specialized training for the respondent's occupation. To be able to interpret the coefficient for the logistic regression, we will first need to obtain the odds ratios for our independent variables, which are much easier to interpret than the unstandardized coefficients listed in the previous table.

To obtain the odds ratios, we simply type the same command, adding `, or` to the end, like so:

```
logit occtrain female age educ realrinc, or
```

```
Iteration 0:   log likelihood = -743.13683
Iteration 1:   log likelihood = -667.31647
Iteration 2:   log likelihood = -665.69519
Iteration 3:   log likelihood = -665.69124

Logistic regression                              Number of obs   =       1096
                                                 LR chi2(4)      =     154.89
                                                 Prob > chi2     =     0.0000
Log likelihood = -665.69124                      Pseudo R2       =     0.1042

------------------------------------------------------------------------------
   occtrain | Odds Ratio   Std. Err.      z    P>|z|     [95% Conf. Interval]
------------+-----------------------------------------------------------------
     female |   1.14872    .1565844     1.02   0.309     .8793973    1.500525
        age |   .9968945   .0058699    -0.53   0.597     .9854558    1.008466
       educ |   1.364636   .0418821    10.13   0.000     1.284969    1.449243
   realrinc |   1.004893   .0031058     1.58   0.114     .9988238    1.010999
------------------------------------------------------------------------------
```

Looking again at our one significant independent variable, education, we see that its odds ratio is 1.36. This can be interpreted in the following way: One additional year of education increases the odds of having had specialized training by a factor of 1.36. In the case of unstandardized coefficients in logistic regression, a positive value would indicate a positive or direct relationship between the independent variable and the dependent variable, while a negative value would indicate a negative or inverse relationship between the two variables. However, in the case of odds ratios in logistic regression, a value greater than 1 would indicate a positive or direct relationship between the independent and dependent variable, while a value less than 1 would indicate a negative or inverse relationship between these two variables. In regard to odds ratios, a value of exactly 1 would have the same meaning as an unstandardized coefficient of exactly 0, which would be in the case where an independent variable has no positive or negative effect on the dependent variable. To briefly review, in a positive or direct relationship, as the value of the independent variable increases, so does the value of the dependent variable. Likewise, if the value of the independent variable decreases, so does the value of the dependent variable. On the other hand, in the case of a negative or inverse relationship, as the value of the independent variable increases, the value of the dependent variable decreases accordingly. Also, as the value of the independent variable decreases, the value of the dependent variable would increase accordingly.

Three of our independent variables, age, education, and income, are continuous. However, our female variable is a binary variable. If this had been significant, we could interpret it in the following way: The odds of having had specialized training for females is 1.15 times as large as for males. When interpreting odds ratios for dummy variables, you simply need to take note of your comparison category, realizing that the odds ratio presented relates to the dummy variable as compared with the comparison category.

In logistic regression, there is no direct equivalent of the R-squared value that we discussed in the previous chapter on linear regression. However, there are a number of what are called Pseudo R-squared formulas that can be seen as an estimate of the linear R-squared value. These Pseudo R-squared formulas do not directly calculate the percent variance in the dependent variable explained by our independent variables and should not be interpreted as such.

In the output presented above, we arrived at a Pseudo R-squared value of .10. There are a number of different Pseudo R-squared formulas. The one used by Stata and presented here is McFadden's R-squared. Some others include Cox and Snell's R-squared, Nagelkerke's R-squared, and others. Probably the one most commonly used is Nagelkerke's R-squared, which is reported in the output of logistic regressions conducted in IBM SPSS.

Ordered Logistic Regression

The ordered logistic regression presented in this section will use highest degree completed as our dependent variable. As mentioned previously, this variable consists of the following response categories: less than high school, high school, Junior College, bachelor, and graduate degree. Our independent variables include the respondent's sex and age. Years of education and income will be omitted from this analysis as I feel that these are not appropriate predictor variables of highest degree completed. To perform the ordered logistic regression, we simply type the following syntax into Stata:

```
ologit degree female age
```

This gives us the following output:

```
Iteration 0:   log likelihood = -58569.452
Iteration 1:   log likelihood = -57626.939
Iteration 2:   log likelihood = -57621.746
Iteration 3:   log likelihood = -57621.745

Ordered logistic regression               Number of obs   =      46196
                                          LR chi2(2)      =    1895.41
                                          Prob > chi2     =     0.0000
Log likelihood = -57621.745               Pseudo R2       =     0.0162

------------------------------------------------------------------------------
   degree |      Coef.   Std. Err.      z    P>|z|     [95% Conf. Interval]
----------+-------------------------------------------------------------------
   female |  -.1321119   .0178058    -7.42   0.000    -.1670107   -.0972131
      age |  -.0218738   .0005198   -42.09   0.000    -.0228925   -.0208551
----------+-------------------------------------------------------------------
    /cut1 |  -2.245064   .0284655                     -2.300855   -2.189273
    /cut2 |   .1366721   .0258665                      .0859746    .1873695
    /cut3 |   .4216216   .0261694                      .3703305    .4729127
    /cut4 |   1.728243   .0302023                      1.669047    1.787438
------------------------------------------------------------------------------
```

Here, we can see that both sex and age are predictive of highest degree completed. First, being female is associated with having a less advanced degree. Also, being older is also associated with having a less advanced degree as your highest degree. To incorporate the coefficients themselves into an interpretation, we would first want to obtain the odds ratios for our independent variables, which are the same as the odds ratios discussed in the previous section on logistic regression. To do this, we simply add `,or` to the end of our syntax, just as we did to obtain the odds ratios when conducting a logistic regression, like so:

```
ologit degree female age,or
```

This will give us the following output:

```
Iteration 0:    log likelihood = -58569.452
Iteration 1:    log likelihood = -57626.939
Iteration 2:    log likelihood = -57621.746
Iteration 3:    log likelihood = -57621.745
```

```
Ordered logistic regression                      Number of obs   =      46196
                                                 LR chi2(2)      =    1895.41
                                                 Prob > chi2     =     0.0000
Log likelihood = -57621.745                      Pseudo R2       =     0.0162
```

degree	Odds Ratio	Std. Err.	z	P>|z|	[95% Conf. Interval]	
female	.8762429	.0156022	-7.42	0.000	.8461905	.9073626
age	.9783637	.0005085	-42.09	0.000	.9773675	.9793608
/cut1	-2.245064	.0284655			-2.300855	-2.189273
/cut2	.1366721	.0258665			.0859746	.1873695
/cut3	.4216216	.0261694			.3703305	.4729127
/cut4	1.728243	.0302023			1.669047	1.787438

Here, we can see that the odds ratio for our female variable is 0.876 and our odds ratio for our age variable is 0.978. Both of these independent variables are significant at the $p < .001$ level. To interpret our female variable, we could say the following: Being female decreases the odds of having the next more advanced degree by a factor of 0.876. As you can see, stating it in this way is somewhat awkward. What ordered logistic regression does is assume that the effect of your independent variables on your dependent variable is constant. Using the regression just presented as an example, in regard to our female variable, you could say the following: Being female decreases the odds of having a high school diploma as compared with having less than a high school diploma by a factor of 0.876. You could also say this: Being female decreases the odds of having a junior college degree as compared with a high school diploma by a factor of 0.876. As you can see, the odds ratio does not change for any comparison between one level of the dependent variable and its next highest level. If you did not assume that this effect would be constant, or if you did not assume that the "distances" between the different levels of your dependent variable were constant, you could perform a multinomial logistic regression instead of an ordered logistic regression. This method will be covered in the next section. Another option would be a generalized ordered logistic regression (gologit in Stata, but it needs to be installed first). Generalized ordered logistic regression is not as commonly used as multinomial logistic regression.

Finally, let's interpret our odds ratio for age. We could say the following: For each additional year of age, the odds of having the next more advanced degree decreases by a factor of 0.978. Again, more specifically, we could say that each additional year of age decreases the odds of having a high school diploma as compared with having less than a high school diploma by a factor of 0.978. Likewise, we can make the same statement comparing any level of our dependent variable with its next highest level.

Multinomial Logistic Regression

Multinomial logistic regression is used when your dependent variable is nominal (i.e., categorical and unordered). In the example presented in this section, political party affiliation will be used as your dependent variable. This variable consists of the following response categories: Democrat, Republican, Independent, and other party affiliation. Our independent variables in this model consist of the respondent's sex, age, income, and years of education completed. To conduct this multinomial logistic regression, we simply enter the following syntax into Stata:

```
mlogit party female age realrinc educ
```

This gives us the following output:

```
Iteration 0:    log likelihood = -30842.242
Iteration 1:    log likelihood = -30407.384
Iteration 2:    log likelihood = -30405.849
Iteration 3:    log likelihood = -30405.849

Multinomial logistic regression                Number of obs   =       27001
                                                LR chi2(12)     =      872.79
                                                Prob > chi2     =      0.0000
Log likelihood = -30405.849                     Pseudo R2       =      0.0141
```

party	Coef.	Std. Err.	z	P>|z|	[95% Conf. Interval]	
Democrat						
female	.3482172	.0303999	11.45	0.000	.2886345	.4077999
age	.0184599	.0011329	16.29	0.000	.0162394	.0206804
realrinc	-.0012372	.0008551	-1.45	0.148	-.0029132	.0004389
educ	-.0047675	.0054693	-0.87	0.383	-.0154872	.0059522
_cons	-.8406432	.0872888	-9.63	0.000	-1.011726	-.6695603
Republican						
female	.0868297	.0331857	2.62	0.009	.0217868	.1518726
age	.016919	.0012505	13.53	0.000	.014468	.0193699
realrinc	.0054266	.000816	6.65	0.000	.0038272	.0070259
educ	.0575379	.0059364	9.69	0.000	.0459029	.069173
_cons	-1.950265	.0960502	-20.30	0.000	-2.13852	-1.76201
Other						
female	-.1679238	.1149642	-1.46	0.144	-.3932495	.057402
age	.0078603	.0043341	1.81	0.070	-.0006343	.0163549
realrinc	-.0067194	.0034153	-1.97	0.049	-.0134132	-.0000255
educ	.0832396	.0207006	4.02	0.000	.0426672	.123812
_cons	-4.559106	.3308663	-13.78	0.000	-5.207592	-3.91062

(party==Independent is the base outcome)

If you remember our discussion of dummy variables, when we create a set of dummy variables for a variable such as political party identification, we would select one category as a comparison category and create dummy variables for the remaining categories. In our analysis, the coefficients that we obtained would tell us, for example, the effect of being Republican as compared with being Democrat (if we had selected "Democrat" as our comparison category) on some dependent variable. This is similar to the results that you obtain when conducting a multinomial logistic regression. In this example, as mentioned, political party identification can be Democrat, Republican, Independent, or other. If you look at the final line in the output presented above, you can see that "Independent" has been selected as the "base outcome" or comparison category in this analysis. To explain this, let's look at some of our results. Look at the first of the three sets of results, which are for Democrats, in the table just presented. Under female, our coefficient is 0.348 and has a probability level of less than .001. This could be interpreted in the following way: Being female increases the likelihood of being a Democrat as compared with being an independent. Now, let's look at our effect for education under the final set of results for those of other party affiliation. Our coefficient here for our education variable is 0.083 and has a probability level of less than .001. This effect could be interpreted in the following way: Higher levels of education increase the likelihood of having an alternative political party affiliation as compared with being independent. In the analysis just performed, as we did not specify which category of our dependent variable to select as the comparison category or base outcome, Stata simply selected one for us. Say, for example, we wanted to choose Democrats as our comparison category in our regression. To do this, we first need to check our coding for Democrats. Here, I have coded Democrats as "0." Now, to choose Democrats as our base outcome, we can simply enter the following syntax into Stata:

```
mlogit party female age realrinc educ,b(0)
```

This gives us the following output:

```
Iteration 0:   log likelihood = -30842.242
Iteration 1:   log likelihood = -30407.384
Iteration 2:   log likelihood = -30405.849
Iteration 3:   log likelihood = -30405.849

Multinomial logistic regression              Number of obs   =        27001
                                             LR chi2(12)     =       872.79
                                             Prob > chi2     =       0.0000
Log likelihood = -30405.849                  Pseudo R2       =       0.0141

-----------------------------------------------------------------------------
       party |     Coef.   Std. Err.      z    P>|z|     [95% Conf. Interval]
-------------+---------------------------------------------------------------
Independent  |
      female | -.3482172   .0303999   -11.45   0.000    -.4077999   -.2886345
         age | -.0184599   .0011329   -16.29   0.000    -.0206804   -.0162394
    realrinc |  .0012372   .0008551     1.45   0.148    -.0004389    .0029132
        educ |  .0047675   .0054693     0.87   0.383    -.0059522    .0154872
       _cons |  .8406432   .0872888     9.63   0.000     .6695603    1.011726
-------------+---------------------------------------------------------------
Republican   |
      female | -.2613875   .0333405    -7.84   0.000    -.3267337   -.1960413
         age |  -.001541   .0012157    -1.27   0.205    -.0039238    .0008419
    realrinc |  .0066637   .0008348     7.98   0.000     .0050275    .0082999
        educ |  .0623054   .0059219    10.52   0.000     .0506988    .0739121
       _cons | -1.109622   .0962992   -11.52   0.000    -1.298365   -.9208791
-------------+---------------------------------------------------------------
Other        |
      female |  -.516141   .1150687    -4.49   0.000    -.7416714   -.2906106
         age | -.0105996   .0043261    -2.45   0.014    -.0190787   -.0021206
    realrinc | -.0054822     .00342    -1.60   0.109    -.0121853    .0012209
        educ |  .0880071    .020707     4.25   0.000     .0474221    .1285921
       _cons | -3.718463   .3311213   -11.23   0.000    -4.367449   -3.069477
-----------------------------------------------------------------------------
(party==Democrat is the base outcome)
```

First, look at our coefficient for female under the independent category. Its value here is −0.348. Looking at our first table of results, we see that our coefficient for our female variable under Democrat is 0.348. This makes sense; as in our first set of results, our coefficient is comparing Democrats with independents (the base outcome), while in our second analysis, this coefficient is comparing independents with Democrats (our specified base outcome). To interpret our new coefficient of −0.348, we could say that being female decreases the likelihood of being an independent as compared with being a Democrat.

To include the actual values of our coefficients in our interpretation, we need to first determine the relative risk ratios. Relative risk ratios, which are used in multinomial logistic regression, are similar to the odds ratios that we used in logistic and ordered logistic regression. To obtain these values, we simply add rrr to our syntax, as shown here:

```
mlogit party female age realrinc educ,b(0) rrr
```

As you can see, I have still specified Democrats to be the base outcome or comparison category of our dependent variable. The results of this regression are shown here:

```
Iteration 0:   log likelihood = -30842.242
Iteration 1:   log likelihood = -30407.384
Iteration 2:   log likelihood = -30405.849
Iteration 3:   log likelihood = -30405.849

Multinomial logistic regression                Number of obs   =      27001
                                                LR chi2(12)     =     872.79
                                                Prob > chi2     =     0.0000
Log likelihood = -30405.849                     Pseudo R2       =     0.0141

------------------------------------------------------------------------------
       party |       RRR   Std. Err.      z    P>|z|     [95% Conf. Interval]
-------------+----------------------------------------------------------------
Independent  |
      female |   .7059455   .0214607   -11.45   0.000     .6651119    .749286
         age |   .9817094   .0011122   -16.29   0.000      .979532   .9838917
     realrinc|   1.001238   .0008562     1.45   0.148     .9995612   1.002917
        educ |   1.004779   .0054955     0.87   0.383     .9940655   1.015608
-------------+----------------------------------------------------------------
Republican   |
      female |   .7699825   .0256716    -7.84   0.000     .7212758   .8219782
         age |   .9984602   .0012139    -1.27   0.205     .9960839   1.000842
     realrinc|   1.006686   .0008404     7.98   0.000      1.00504   1.008334
        educ |   1.064287   .0063026    10.52   0.000     1.052006   1.076712
-------------+----------------------------------------------------------------
Other        |
      female |   .5968192   .0686752    -4.49   0.000     .4763171   .7478068
         age |   .9894564   .0042805    -2.45   0.014     .9811022   .9978817
     realrinc|   .9945328   .0034013    -1.60   0.109     .9878887   1.001222
        educ |   1.091996    .022612     4.25   0.000     1.048564   1.137226
------------------------------------------------------------------------------
(party==Democrat is the base outcome)
```

Let's look at our relative risk ratio for female under the independent category. The relative risk ratio here is 0.706 and is significant at the $p <$ .001 level. We could interpret this ratio in the following way: The likelihood (or "risk") of being an independent as compared with being a Democrat is 0.706 times as high for females as for males. Now, let's look at the relative risk ratio for education under the "Other" category. Here, this relative risk ratio is 1.092. We could interpret it in the following way: Each additional year of education increases the likelihood of having an alternative political party affiliation, as compared with being a Democrat, by a factor of 1.092.

Negative Binomial and Poisson Regression

As mentioned previously, negative binomial and Poisson regression are two distinct but similar methods that are used when your dependent variable is a count variable. Some examples of count variables include the number of times the respondent saw a doctor in the past year or the number of jobs a person has held in the past decade. In these examples, it might be possible to consider these variables to be continuous variables and simply conduct a linear regression. Poisson regression would be preferred in situations where nonzero cases are rare (e.g., if one were using accidents per year as the dependent variable, where most years saw zero accidents). Negative binomial would be preferred over Poisson regression in situations where there is overdispersion, which is defined as a situation where your data have greater variance than expected. If we find that our dependent variable has a variance that is greater than its mean, we can choose negative binomial regression over Poisson regression. It is common in cases of overdispersion that your count variable will have a very large proportion of zero cases. The two variables that will be used as dependent variables in this section are *hurtatwk* and *ovrjoyed*. *Hurtatwk* measures the number of times the respondent was injured on the job in the past 12 months, while *ovrjoyed* measures the number of days the respondent felt overjoyed about something in the past week. Frequency tables for both of these variables are listed here:

```
. tab1 hurtatwk ovrjoyed

-> tabulation of hurtatwk
```

hurtatwk	Freq.	Percent	Cum.
0	1,577	89.05	89.05
1	128	7.23	96.27
2	25	1.41	97.68
3	17	0.96	98.64
4	4	0.23	98.87
5	6	0.34	99.21
6	6	0.34	99.55
7	8	0.45	100.00
Total	1,771	100.00	

```
-> tabulation of ovrjoyed
```

ovrjoyed	Freq.	Percent	Cum.
0	584	40.44	40.44
1	264	18.28	58.73
2	185	12.81	71.54
3	145	10.04	81.58
4	73	5.06	86.63
5	56	3.88	90.51
6	30	2.08	92.59
7	107	7.41	100.00
Total	1,444	100.00	

Also, the means and variances for these two variables are displayed here:

```
. sum hurtatwk ovrjoyed,det
```

```
                            hurtatwk
-------------------------------------------------------------
      Percentiles    Smallest
 1%        0              0
 5%        0              0
10%        0              0         Obs                1771
25%        0              0         Sum of Wgt.        1771

50%        0                        Mean           .2072276
                       Largest      Std. Dev.      .7979308
75%        0              7
90%        1              7         Variance       .6366935
95%        1              7         Skewness       5.691651
99%        5              7         Kurtosis        40.6185
```

```
                                    ovrjoyed
        -----------------------------------------------------------------
               Percentiles      Smallest
        1%            0               0
        5%            0               0
        10%           0               0         Obs                    1444
        25%           0               0         Sum of Wgt.            1444

        50%           1                         Mean               1.779778
                                   Largest      Std. Dev.          2.142849
        75%           3               7
        90%           5               7         Variance           4.591801
        95%           7               7         Skewness           1.197233
        99%           7               7         Kurtosis            3.38933
```

As you can see, the mean for our *hurtatwk* variable is 0.207, while the variance is 0.637. Our *ovrjoyed* variable has a mean of 1.780 and a variance of 4.592. Technically, you would prefer to use negative binomial regression for both of these variables, as they are both overdispersed, having variances that are greater than their means. However, *ovrjoyed* will be analyzed in this section using Poisson regression simply to present an example of a Poisson regression. To conduct a Poisson regression with *ovrjoyed* as our dependent variable and *female*, *age*, *educ*, and *realrinc* as our independent variables, we simply type the following command into Stata:

```
poisson ovrjoyed female age educ realrinc
```

This will give us the following output:

```
Iteration 0:   log likelihood = -2067.5542
Iteration 1:   log likelihood = -2067.5542

Poisson regression                              Number of obs    =         985
                                                LR chi2(4)       =       28.62
                                                Prob > chi2      =      0.0000
Log likelihood = -2067.5542                     Pseudo R2        =      0.0069

------------------------------------------------------------------------------
   ovrjoyed |     Coef.   Std. Err.      z    P>|z|    [95% Conf. Interval]
------------+-----------------------------------------------------------------
     female |  -.1473907   .0496997    -2.97   0.003   -.2448003   -.0499811
        age |  -.0080952   .0019882    -4.07   0.000   -.0119921   -.0041983
       educ |   .0095327   .0096221     0.99   0.322   -.0093262    .0283916
   realrinc |  -.0016031   .0013984    -1.15   0.252   -.0043439    .0011376
      _cons |   .8736485   .1498803     5.83   0.000    .5798886    1.167408
------------------------------------------------------------------------------
```

As we can see, both sex and age are significant predictors of feeling overjoyed about something. Specifically, females and older individuals are less likely to have felt overjoyed about something in the past week. To be able to incorporate our coefficients into our interpretations, we need to obtain the incidence rate ratios for our independent variables. These are similar to both the odds ratios and the relative risk ratios that we have discussed previously. To obtain the incidence rate ratios, we simply add `,irr` to the end of our syntax command, as shown here:

```
poisson ovrjoyed female age educ realrinc,irr
```

This gives us the following output:

```
Iteration 0:   log likelihood = -2067.5542
Iteration 1:   log likelihood = -2067.5542

Poisson regression                              Number of obs   =         985
                                                LR chi2(4)      =       28.62
                                                Prob > chi2     =      0.0000
Log likelihood = -2067.5542                     Pseudo R2       =      0.0069

------------------------------------------------------------------------------
   ovrjoyed |       IRR   Std. Err.      z    P>|z|     [95% Conf. Interval]
------------+-----------------------------------------------------------------
     female |  .8629568   .0428887    -2.97   0.003     .7828608    .9512474
        age |  .9919374   .0019722    -4.07   0.000     .9880795    .9958105
       educ |  1.009578   .0097142     0.99   0.322     .9907171    1.028798
   realrinc |  .9983982   .0013961    -1.15   0.252     .9956656    1.001138
------------------------------------------------------------------------------
```

Here, we can see that our incidence rate ratio for female is 0.863. This could be interpreted as follows: The average number of days per week that one feels overjoyed about something for females is 0.863 times that of males. In regard to age, with each additional year of age, the average number of days per week one feels overjoyed about something decreases by a factor of 0.992.

To run a negative binomial regression in which *hurtatwk* is the dependent variable and *female*, *age*, *educ*, and *realrinc* are our independent variables, we would simply type the following command into Stata:

```
nbreg hurtatwk female age educ realrinc
```

This gives us the following output:

```
Fitting Poisson model:

Iteration 0:   log likelihood = -952.91961
Iteration 1:   log likelihood = -952.91934
Iteration 2:   log likelihood = -952.91934

Fitting constant-only model:

Iteration 0:   log likelihood =  -844.7413  (not concave)
Iteration 1:   log likelihood = -745.32203
Iteration 2:   log likelihood = -744.77101
Iteration 3:   log likelihood = -744.77086
Iteration 4:   log likelihood = -744.77086

Fitting full model:

Iteration 0:   log likelihood =  -735.9562
Iteration 1:   log likelihood = -735.27284
Iteration 2:   log likelihood = -735.26966
Iteration 3:   log likelihood = -735.26966

Negative binomial regression              Number of obs   =       1538
                                          LR chi2(4)      =      19.00
Dispersion     = mean                     Prob > chi2     =     0.0008
Log likelihood = -735.26966               Pseudo R2       =     0.0128

------------------------------------------------------------------------------
    hurtatwk |      Coef.   Std. Err.      z    P>|z|     [95% Conf. Interval]
-------------+----------------------------------------------------------------
      female |  -.5582381   .1925797    -2.90   0.004    -.9356874   -.1807888
         age |  -.0197095   .0076764    -2.57   0.010    -.0347549    -.004664
        educ |  -.0177806   .0353039    -0.50   0.615    -.0869749    .0514138
     realrinc |  -.0075415   .0047484    -1.59   0.112    -.0168483    .0017652
       _cons |  -.1436971   .5452047    -0.26   0.792    -1.212279    .9248845
-------------+----------------------------------------------------------------
     /lnalpha |   2.089433   .1326436                       1.829457    2.34941
-------------+----------------------------------------------------------------
       alpha |   8.080335   1.071805                         6.2305   10.47939
------------------------------------------------------------------------------
Likelihood-ratio test of alpha=0:  chibar2(01) =  435.30 Prob>=chibar2 = 0.000
```

To obtain our incident rate ratios, we simply type `,irr`, as with Poisson regression:

```
nbreg hurtatwk female age educ realrinc,irr
```

This gives us the following output:

```
Fitting Poisson model:

Iteration 0:   log likelihood = -952.91961
Iteration 1:   log likelihood = -952.91934
Iteration 2:   log likelihood = -952.91934

Fitting constant-only model:

Iteration 0:   log likelihood =  -844.7413   (not concave)
Iteration 1:   log likelihood = -745.32203
Iteration 2:   log likelihood = -744.77101
Iteration 3:   log likelihood = -744.77086
Iteration 4:   log likelihood = -744.77086

Fitting full model:

Iteration 0:   log likelihood =  -735.9562
Iteration 1:   log likelihood = -735.27284
Iteration 2:   log likelihood = -735.26966
Iteration 3:   log likelihood = -735.26966
```

```
Negative binomial regression                    Number of obs   =       1538
                                                LR chi2(4)      =      19.00
Dispersion     = mean                           Prob > chi2     =     0.0008
Log likelihood = -735.26966                     Pseudo R2       =     0.0128

------------------------------------------------------------------------------
    hurtatwk |      IRR    Std. Err.      z    P>|z|     [95% Conf. Interval]
-------------+----------------------------------------------------------------
      female |  .5722164   .1101973    -2.90   0.004     .3923161    .8346116
         age |  .9804835   .0075266    -2.57   0.010     .9658421    .9953468
        educ |  .9823766   .0346817    -0.50   0.615     .9167001   1.052758
    realrinc |  .9924869   .0047128    -1.59   0.112     .9832929   1.001767
-------------+----------------------------------------------------------------
    /lnalpha |  2.089433   .1326436                      1.829457    2.34941
-------------+----------------------------------------------------------------
       alpha |  8.080335   1.071805                        6.2305   10.47939
------------------------------------------------------------------------------
Likelihood-ratio test of alpha=0:  chibar2(01) =  435.30 Prob>=chibar2 = 0.000
```

As we can see, both our female and age independent variables are significant at the $p < .05$ level. The incident rate ratios can be interpreted in the same way as with Poisson regression. For example, the effect of our female variable can be interpreted in the following way: The average number of times that one is hurt on the job for females is 0.572 times that of males. In regard to *age*, an increase in age by one year decreases the number of accidents per year by a factor of 0.98.

△   SECTION 4: SUMMARY

This chapter covered logistic, ordered logistic, multinomial logistic, Poisson, and negative binomial regression. Logistic regression is used when your dependent variable is a binary variable, having only two outcomes, and can be coded as simply 0 or 1. Ordered logistic regression is used when your dependent variable is a categorical variable that can be ordered (i.e., ordinal). Multinomial logistic regression is used when your dependent variable is categorical but cannot be ordered (i.e., nominal). Negative binomial and Poisson regression are two distinct but similar methods that are used when your dependent variable is a count variable. Poisson regression is preferred over linear regression in situations where nonzero cases are rare (e.g., if one were using accidents per year as the dependent variable, where most years saw zero accidents). Negative binomial would be preferred over Poisson regression in situations where there is overdispersion, which is defined as a situation where your data has greater variance than expected. If we find that our dependent variable has a variance that is greater than its mean, we can choose negative binomial regression over Poisson regression. It is common in cases of overdispersion that your count variable will have a very large proportion of zero cases. It is important, when conducting a regression, to select the appropriate test based on the nature of your dependent variable. How to conduct each of these types of regression in both IBM SPSS and Stata was covered in this chapter.

RESOURCES

You can find more information about IBM SPSS and how to purchase it by navigating to the following Web site: www.spss.com/software/statistics/

You can find more information about Stata and how to purchase it by navigating to the following Web site: www.stata.com

This book's Web site can be found at the following location: www.sagepub.com/kremelstudy

FACTOR ANALYSIS

SECTION 1: INTRODUCTION

This chapter covers **factor analysis**, which is a method that is used to determine whether a larger number of variables can be reduced to a smaller number of factors. For example, say that you are a psychologist studying the nature of human intelligence. You develop an intelligence test that contains 200 distinct questions. After running a factor analysis, you might find, for example, that these 200 questions can be reduced to seven distinct factors, each with a different conceptual meaning. One factor might contain 15 questions and be focused on mathematical intelligence. Another factor might consist of 29 questions and be focused on verbal skills. In this example, as a result of running a factor analysis, you realize that instead of measuring 200 different components of intelligence you are really only measuring seven different components or facets of intelligence. Factor analysis is very useful in that the factors that are obtained after running a factor analysis can themselves be used as dependent variables in methods such as regression analysis, as opposed to using the potentially much larger number of dependent variables that we started out with. In this example, instead of using the 200 separate questions in our survey as dependent variables in regression analyses, we can instead construct factor scores for the seven factors that we arrived at and use these new seven variables as dependent variables in regression analyses.

There are two main forms of factor analysis. One form of factor analysis, which tends to be more common, is called **exploratory factor analysis**. In exploratory factor analysis, you do not predetermine the number of factors or predefine which variables will load on which factors. In **confirmatory factor analysis**, you predetermine the final number of factors. Also, the variables that are associated with each factor are also typically predetermined in confirmatory factor analysis. As exploratory factor analysis is more commonly used than confirmatory factor analysis, it will be the focus of this chapter. Confirmatory factor analysis is commonly conducted using structural equation modeling, which is covered in Chapter 10. Also, there are various methods of **factor extraction** that can be used in factor analysis. The two most popular methods are **principal factor analysis** and **principal components analysis**. When conducting exploratory factor analysis, you would typically use principal components analysis, while principal factor analysis is more popular when conducting confirmatory factor analysis. As exploratory factor analysis is the focus of this chapter, principal components analysis is the method of factor extraction that will be used.

When conducting an exploratory factor analysis, there is a series of steps that you must take. The first is conducting one or a series of factor analyses in IBM SPSS or Stata. If you ran a series of factor analyses, which would typically use different methods of **rotation**, the second step would be to select which one of these analyses you will keep as your final analysis. The third step is determining the number of factors that you will keep. There are a number of methods that are used, and this topic will be covered later in this section. The fourth step consists of deciding which variables load on which factors (i.e., which variables are associated with which factors). Finally, you will create new variables for these factors that you will use in later analyses. This final step is optional but is typically done.

When conducting an exploratory factor analysis, there are a number of methods of rotation that can be used. While it is not required to use a method of rotation when conducting a factor analysis (in this case, your factors would be unrotated), it may make your factors easier to interpret. Also, using rotation may give you stronger results in the sense that you may end up with a greater number of factors, or have factors with higher **eigen-values** (this term will be discussed shortly), or have higher **factor loadings** of your indicators on your factors. The most popular method of rotation is called **varimax rotation**, which commonly makes small factor loadings smaller and large ones larger, making it easier to associate specific variables with the factor that they load on. Another method that is used is called the **direct oblimin rotation**, which is a method of oblique rotation. **Oblique rotation** is a method of rotation in which the factors are allowed to correlate with each other. When there is no rotation or when varimax or other methods of rotation that are not oblique are used, the factors are not allowed to correlate with each other, and each variable will typically load on only one factor. When an oblique rotation is used, this is generally not the case, and you may have variables that load on two or more factors. This may end up making the interpretation of your factors more difficult but may be the preferred method of rotation in cases where theory suggests that your factors should be related in some way. Some other methods of rotation that are less commonly used include equimax rotation, quartimax rotation, and promax rotation.

So let's now cover the steps of a factor analysis in more detail. If we wanted to be more thorough in our factor analysis, we could run it using the following methods: no rotation, varimax rotation, and the direct oblimin rotation. Next, we could compare our results. In a factor analysis, each factor will have what is called an eigenvalue. As a general rule of thumb, factors with eigenvalues of 1 or higher can be kept, while factors with eigenvalues less than 1 can be discarded. This method is called the **Kaiser criterion**. Another method of determining how many factors we will keep in our analysis is by using what is called a **scree plot**. This is simply a plot of your eigenvalues. An example of this is presented in Figure 7.1.

In a scree plot, your factors are plotted on the *x*-axis, with their corresponding eigenvalues plotted on the *y*-axis. To determine the number of factors, you will find the "elbow" of the curve, or the point at which the curve begins to level off. This determination would equal the number of factors you would keep. In this example, I would judge this point to be at two factors (where the case number equals 2), suggesting we only keep the first two factors. This method is known as the **Cattell scree test**.

Finally, it is also important to consider the meaning of each of the factors generated and not simply use strictly quantitative methods in your determination of the number of factors to keep. For example, if quantitative methods suggested that you keep either two or three factors (i.e., the two methods

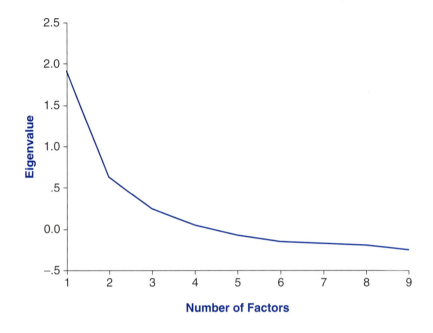

Figure 7.1   Eigenvalues Versus Number of Factors

discussed give you different determinations), but the third factor does not have any clear conceptual meaning, it would be best to drop it.

Also, for each factor, the factor loadings will be specified between each variable and that factor. There are several different standards that can be used, but generally, a variable will only be assigned to a factor if it has a factor loading for that factor of at least 0.5 or 0.6. In some cases, you may have variables that are reversed. For example, if you gave a survey on depression where in 8 out of the 10 questions a higher score meant greater levels of depression and in 2 of the questions a higher score meant lower levels of depression, those 2 questions could be considered to be reversed. In these cases, if you left all these variables in their original state in a factor analysis, the factor loadings for the two reversed variables would be expected to be negative. Here, as long as the absolute value of their factor loading is at least 0.5 or 0.6, they would be assigned to that factor in question. Comparing both of these sets of results, the eigenvalues and the factor loadings, will help decide which of our three factor analyses (in this example, unrotated, varimax, and direct oblimin) to keep as our final analysis. Also, we will want to study which variables load on which factors in order to determine the meaning of each factor. The concept of each factor may differ depending on which method of rotation, if any, we use. Also, it may be more difficult to interpret the meaning of factors using one method of rotation versus another. Taking into consideration both these quantitative as well as more conceptual methods of judgment, we would determine which of the three factor analyses to keep as our final analysis. Next, we would use the same methods just discussed to determine how many factors to keep as well as to determine which variables will be associated with which factors. Finally, assuming we will use these new factors as dependent variables in other analyses, we will want to create a new variable for each of these factors. These steps will be covered in the next two sections on IBM SPSS and Stata.

SECTION 2: IBM SPSS   △

While IBM SPSS and Stata are both very good programs for factor analysis, I have a slight preference for IBM SPSS as it seems slightly more user-friendly when conducting factor analyses. In both the IBM SPSS and Stata sections presented in this chapter, nine variables measuring anti-Semitic attitudes will be used in our examples of factor analyses. These data come from the General Social Survey, and the particular data set used in this chapter can be downloaded from http://sda.berkeley.edu/cgi-bin/hsda?harcsda+gss04.

Select *Download* and *Customized* Subset

And choose to select the following variables: *farejews workjews influjew intljews patrjews violjews wlthjews livejews marjew*

Farejews asks respondents whether Jews tend to prefer to be self-supporting or live off welfare. *Workjews* asks respondents whether Jews tend to be hard-working or lazy. The variable *influjew* asks whether people feel Jews have too much influence in American life and politics, just about the right amount of influence, or too little influence. *Intljews* asks the respondent whether Jews tend to be unintelligent or intelligent. The variable *patrjews* asks people whether they feel Jews tend to be patriotic or unpatriotic. *Violjews* asks respondents whether Jews tend to be prone to violence or not. *Wlthjews* asks respondents whether they feel Jews are rich, poor, or somewhere in between. The variable *livejews* asks people whether they would favor or oppose living in a neighborhood where half of their neighbors were Jews. Finally, *marjew* asks respondents whether they would favor or oppose

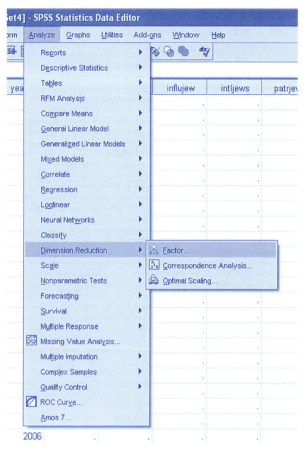

having a close relative marry a Jewish person. Both the variables *livejews* and *marjew* are 5-point Likert scales. *Influjew* is a 3-point Likert scale. The remainder of the variables are 7-point Likert scales.

After recoding the variables so that the respondents who replied "don't know," "not applicable," and so on are recoded as missing, we can open IBM SPSS and begin our factor analysis. To begin, make the following menu selection:

This will open the following dialog box:

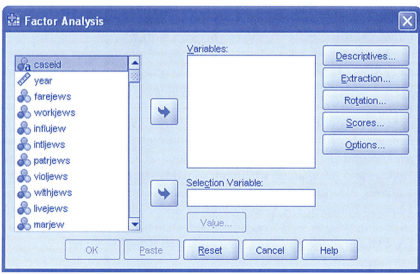

My data set contains additional variables that will not be used in this chapter on factor analysis. The next step you'll take, if you're following along, is to simply select the nine variables previously specified and move them into the *Variables* box on the right:

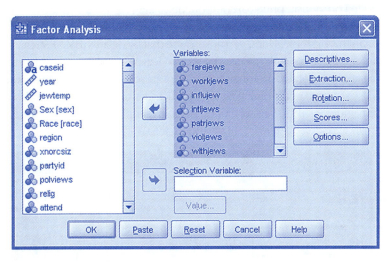

Next, we can click on the *Extraction* option, which will bring up the following dialog box:

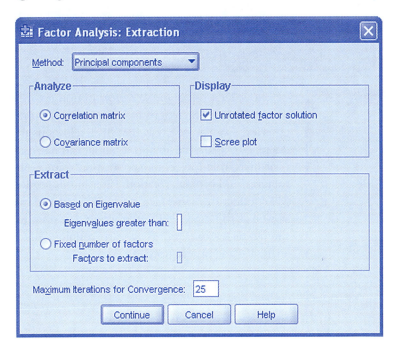

If you click on the down arrow next to the *Method* entry, you'll see that IBM SPSS allows you to choose among the following methods of factor extraction: principal components, unweighted least squares, generalized least squares, maximum likelihood, principal axis factoring, alpha factoring, and image factoring. As mentioned previously, principal components analysis is the extraction method of choice when conducting an exploratory factor analysis and will be the method chosen in this example. Here, we can also see that by default IBM SPSS calculates an unrotated factor solution. For now, we can leave this option alone, beginning with a simple unrotated factor solution. We can select the *Scree plot* option as this will assist us in determining how many factors we should keep. We can leave the remainder of the options alone. So after simply selecting the *Scree plot* option and clicking *Continue*, we will be back to our main screen:

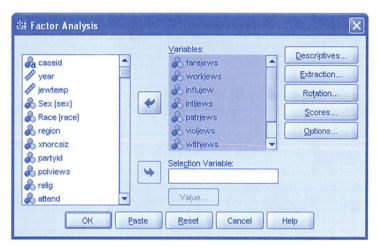

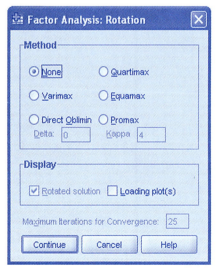

Now, let's select the *Rotation* option to see what options IBM SPSS gives us for rotating our factors:

Here, we can see that IBM SPSS allows us to conduct factor analysis using no rotation, varimax rotation, quartimax rotation, equimax rotation, direct oblimin rotation, and promax rotation. Later in this section, we will conduct this same factor analysis using the varimax as well as the direct oblimin rotation. For now, we can simply click *Continue* as we are running this initial analysis using no rotation.

After going back to our main screen, let's click on *Scores*:

Here, IBM SPSS gives us the option of saving the factors generated by the factor analysis as new variables in our data set, which can be used as variables in later analysis. Here, we can check this option and select the default method of *Regression* as shown below:

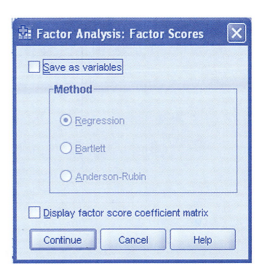

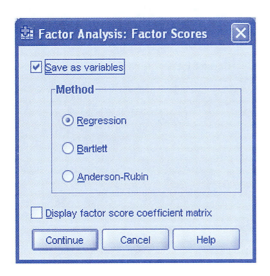

After clicking *Continue*, click *OK* to run the analysis. This is our output:

Factor Analysis

[DataSet4] T:\anti-Semitism dissertation\#Data\Ch 3 and 4\spss_data_final.sav

Communalities

	Initial	Extraction
farejews	1.000	.590
workjews	1.000	.567
influjew	1.000	.626
intljews	1.000	.515
patrjews	1.000	.402
violjews	1.000	.518
wlthjews	1.000	.591
livejews	1.000	.718
marjew	1.000	.692

Extraction Method: Principal Component Analysis.

Total Variance Explained

Component	Initial Eigenvalues			Extraction Sums of Squared Loadings		
	Total	% of Variance	Cumulative %	Total	% of Variance	Cumulative %
1	2.631	29.236	29.236	2.631	29.236	29.236
2	1.500	16.668	45.904	1.500	16.668	45.904
3	1.086	12.068	57.972	1.086	12.068	57.972
4	.870	9.667	67.639			
5	.703	7.816	75.455			
6	.630	7.001	82.456			
7	.551	6.123	88.579			
8	.540	6.004	94.584			
9	.487	5.416	100.000			

Extraction Method: Principal Component Analysis.

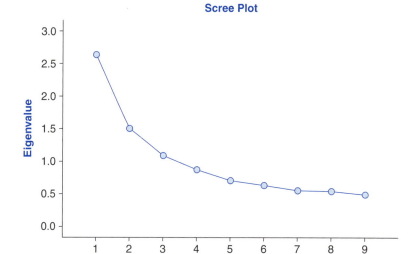

Scree Plot

Component Matrix [a]

	Component		
	1	2	3
farejews	.766	-.021	.056
workjews	.750	-.029	.052
influjew	.313	-.282	.669
intljews	-.629	.064	.339
patrjews	.566	.204	-.201
violjews	-.484	.093	.524
wlthjews	.631	-.177	.401
livejews	.170	.817	.146
marjew	.085	.816	.139

Extraction Method: Principal Component Analysis.

a. 3 components extracted.

First, let's look at our second table, titled "Total Variance Explained":

Total Variance Explained

Component	Initial Eigenvalues			Extraction Sums of Squared Loadings		
	Total	% of Variance	Cumulative %	Total	% of Variance	Cumulative %
1	2.631	29.236	29.236	2.631	29.236	29.236
2	1.500	16.668	45.904	1.500	16.668	45.904
3	1.086	12.068	57.972	1.086	12.068	57.972
4	.870	9.667	67.639			
5	.703	7.816	75.455			
6	.630	7.001	82.456			
7	.551	6.123	88.579			
8	.540	6.004	94.584			
9	.487	5.416	100.000			

Extraction Method: Principal Component Analysis.

The first *Component* column in the final table presented lists of all our possible factors. The second column lists each factor's corresponding eigenvalue. As you can see, we have three factors with eigenvalues more than 1, with our first factor having an eigenvalue of 2.631, our second factor having an eigenvalue of 1.5, and our third factor having an eigenvalue of 1.086. Next, let's look at our scree plot:

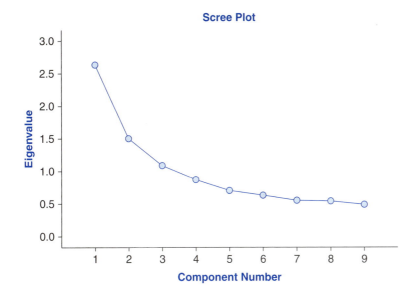

In this scree plot, it is difficult to find the "elbow" of the curve as it is a rather smooth curve. I would judge the point at which the curve begins to level off to be at either two or three factors.

Next, let's look at our factor loadings, which are presented in the final table of our output:

Component Matrix[a]

	Component		
	1	2	3
farejews	.766	-.021	.056
workjews	.750	-.029	.052
influjew	.313	-.282	.669
intljews	-.629	.064	.339
patrjews	.566	.204	-.201
violjews	-.484	.093	.524
wlthjews	.631	-.177	.401
livejews	.170	.817	.146
marjew	.085	.816	.139

Extraction Method: Principal Component Analysis.

a. 3 components extracted.

Looking at the factor loadings, I feel that the third factor, which only includes the variables regarding the influence of Jews and the violence of Jews, does not really have a clear meaning. Based on this information and the information presented above, my final decision is to keep the first two factors only. As this change will not alter the factor loadings for the first two factors, we do not need to rerun our analysis specifying only two factors. Looking at our table just presented and using 0.5 as our standard, the first factor contains the following variables: Jews and welfare, Jews and work, the intelligence of Jews, the patriotism of Jews, and the wealth of Jews. As you can see, the intelligence of Jews has a negative loading on this factor, and this variable would have to be reversed if you were to construct these factor scores by hand. Our second factor contains the following variables: living in a Jewish neighborhood and having a relative marry a Jew.

If we go back to the *Data View* of IBM SPSS and scroll down to *caseid*'s that begins with "1990," also scrolling over to the right, we will see the following:

These are the new scores that IBM SPSS calculated in our analysis for Factors 1, 2, and 3. IBM SPSS has included three factors simply because there were three factors that had eigenvalues over the value of 1. Here, as we are only using the first two factors, we can go to the *Variable View* and delete the third new variable if we wish. By default, IBM SPSS uses listwise deletion, which means that respondents who were

	FAC1_1	FAC2_1	FAC3_1
38814	-0.62591	-0.90973	-0.58946
38815	-0.01761	-0.99179	-1.38990
38816	-0.64754	0.23932	1.16053
38817	-1.70569	0.12036	-0.00712
38818	0.26359	-0.89490	-0.91051
38819	.	.	.
38820	.	.	.
38821	.	.	.
38822	.	.	.
38823	1.53199	-0.94670	0.81473
38824	-0.13142	-0.54287	-0.19018
38825	-0.86901	0.08234	0.27486
38826	.	.	.
38827	.	.	.
38828	.	.	.
38829	-0.87583	0.77781	-1.70423
38830	.	.	.
38831	.	.	.
38832	0.92873	-0.72751	-0.10517
38833	.	.	.
38834	-0.46958	1.72209	0.66586
38835	-0.86774	-1.67718	-0.61296

missing data on one or more of our nine original variables were removed from the analysis. This is why we see a number of cases with missing data for our newly generated factor variables.

At this point, we will run both the varimax and the direct oblimin rotations, seeing how they compare with our initial analysis, which was unrotated.

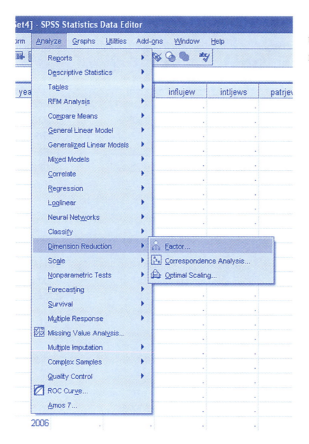

To conduct the factor analysis using the varimax rotation, first make the initial menu selection:

This will open the dialog box:

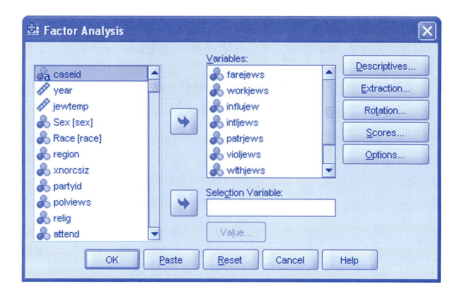

Next, select *Rotation*:

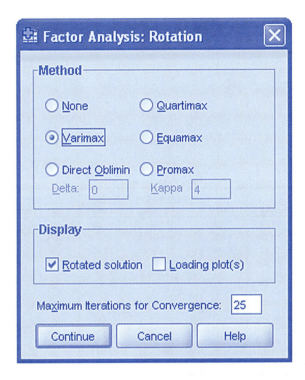

Here, you can see that I have selected *Varimax* as my rotation method of choice. Then I click *Continue* and *Scores* to open the following dialog box:

Here, I have deselected *Save as variables* as I don't want IBM SPSS to create any more new variables at this point. Clicking *Continue* and *OK* will give us the following results:

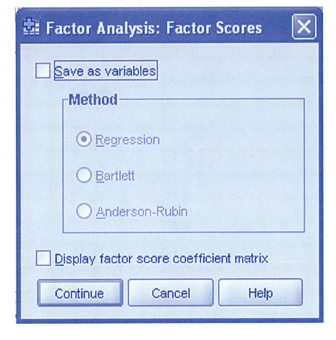

Factor Analysis

[DataSet4] T:\anti-Semitism dissertation\#Data\Ch 3 and 4\spss_data_final.sav

Communalities

	Initial	Extraction
farejews	1.000	.590
workjews	1.000	.567
influjew	1.000	.626
intljews	1.000	.515
patrjews	1.000	.402
violjews	1.000	.518
wlthjews	1.000	.591
livejews	1.000	.718
marjew	1.000	.692

Extraction Method: Principal Component Analysis.

Total Variance Explained

Component	Initial Eigenvalues			Extraction Sums of Squared Loadings			Rotation Sums of Squared Loadings		
	Total	% of Variance	Cumulative %	Total	% of Variance	Cumulative %	Total	% of Variance	Cumulative %
1	2.631	29.236	29.236	2.631	29.236	29.236	2.126	23.617	23.617
2	1.500	16.668	45.904	1.500	16.668	45.904	1.587	17.629	41.246
3	1.086	12.068	57.972	1.086	12.068	57.972	1.505	16.726	57.972
4	.870	9.667	67.639						
5	.703	7.816	75.455						
6	.630	7.001	82.456						
7	.551	6.123	88.579						
8	.540	6.004	94.584						
9	.487	5.416	100.000						

Extraction Method: Principal Component Analysis.

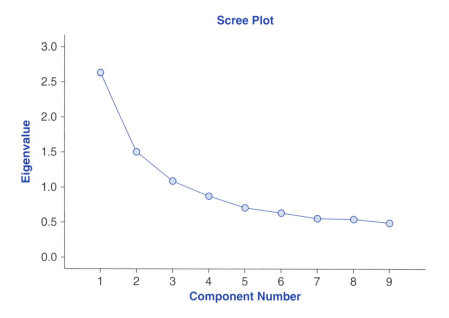

Scree Plot

Component Matrix [a]

	Component		
	1	2	3
farejews	.766	-.021	.056
workjews	.750	-.029	.052
influjew	.313	-.282	.669
intljews	-.629	.064	.339
patrjews	.566	.204	-.201
violjews	-.484	.093	.524
wlthjews	.631	-.177	.401
livejews	.170	.817	.146
marjew	.085	.816	.139

Extraction Method: Principal Component Analysis.

a. 3 components extracted.

Rotated Component Matrix [a]

	Component		
	1	2	3
farejews	.596	.474	.101
workjews	.586	.464	.090
influjew	-.127	.776	-.089
intljews	-.710	-.096	.043
patrjews	.579	.102	.237
violjews	-.697	.124	.130
wlthjews	.288	.713	.003
livejews	.057	.003	.846
marjew	-.009	-.049	.830

Extraction Method: Principal Component Analysis.

Rotation Method: Varimax with Kaiser Normalization.

a. Rotation converged in 5 iterations.

Component Transformation Matrix

Component	1	2	3
1	.820	.554	.143
2	.002	-.253	.967
3	-.572	.793	.209

Extraction Method: Principal Component Analysis.

Rotation Method: Varimax with Kaiser Normalization.

As you can see, the eigenvalues presented here for our factors are different from the ones that we arrived at when we did not use rotation. Our new eigenvalues appear under the *Rotation Sum of Squared Loadings* column in the "Total Variance Explained" table. As you may notice, another important difference between our unrotated results and the rotated results presented here is the differences in the factor loadings. The table titled "Component Matrix" reproduces the factor loadings that were presented earlier. These are simply the factor loadings with no rotation. The next table, titled "Rotated Component Matrix," presents the factor loadings using varimax rotation. Compare these two tables and see how these factors differ. Looking at Factor 1, you'll notice that varimax rotation adds the violence of Jews as an indicator but removes the wealth of Jews. The second factor in the **unrotated solution** corresponds to the third factor in the varimax rotation and vice versa. Both the second factor in the unrotated solution and the third factor in the varimax rotation include only living in a Jewish neighborhood and having a relative marry a Jew as indicators. The third factor in the unrotated solution includes the influence of Jews and the violence of Jews as factors. The second factor in the rotated solution includes the influence of Jews and the wealth of Jews as factors. This factor makes much more sense to me conceptually as compared with one that includes only the influence of Jews and violence of Jews, which is one of the major reasons why I prefer the varimax rotation to the unrotated solution. I also prefer having three conceptually distinct factors as compared with two, which is another reason why I prefer the varimax rotation in this example.

Before we get ahead of ourselves, I will first run the same factor analysis using the direct oblimin rotation—an oblique rotation. First, make the initial menu selection:

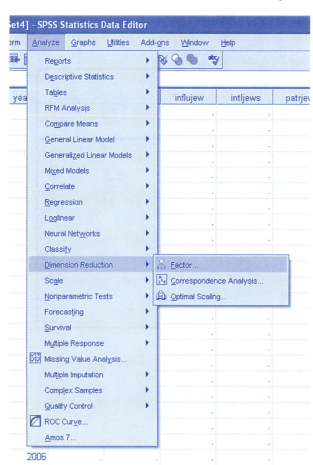

In the following dialog box, select *Rotation*:

Here, you can see that I've selected the *Direct Oblimin* option. The Delta option here has a default value of 0, which would give us the "most oblique" solution. We can simply leave the default value as it is and click *Continue*. Next, clicking *OK* will give us the following output:

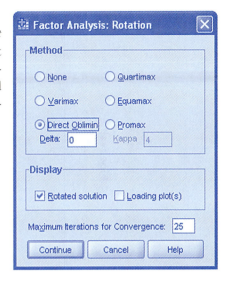

Factor Analysis

[DataSet4] T:\anti-Semitism dissertation\#Data\Ch 3 and 4\spss_data_final.sav

Communalities

	Initial	Extraction
farejews	1.000	.590
workjews	1.000	.567
influjew	1.000	.626
intljews	1.000	.515
patrjews	1.000	.402
violjews	1.000	.518
wlthjews	1.000	.591
livejews	1.000	.718
marjew	1.000	.692

Extraction Method: Principal Component Analysis.

Total Variance Explained

Component	Initial Eigenvalues			Extraction Sums of Squared Loadings			Rotation Sums of Squared Loadings[a]
	Total	% of Variance	Cumulative %	Total	% of Variance	Cumulative %	Total
1	2.631	29.236	29.236	2.631	29.236	29.236	2.295
2	1.500	16.668	45.904	1.500	16.668	45.904	1.535
3	1.086	12.068	57.972	1.086	12.068	57.972	1.737
4	.870	9.667	67.639				
5	.703	7.816	75.455				
6	.630	7.001	82.456				
7	.551	6.123	88579				
8	.540	6.004	94.584				
9	.487	5.416	100.000				

Extraction Method: Principal Component Analysis.

a. When components are correlated, sums of squared loadings cannot be added to obtain a total variance.

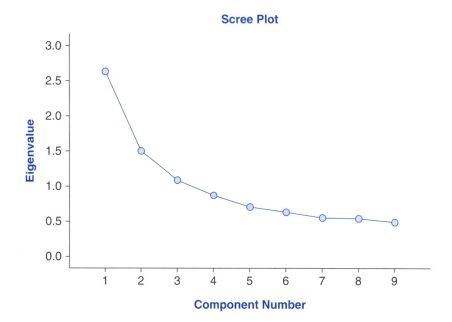

Component Matrix [a]

	Component		
	1	2	3
farejews	.766	-.021	.056
workjews	.750	-.029	.052
influjew	.313	-.282	.669
intljews	-.629	.064	.339
patrjews	.566	.204	-.201
violjews	-.484	.093	.524
wlthjews	.631	-.177	.401
livejews	.170	.817	.146
marjew	.085	.816	.139

Extraction Method: Principal Component Analysis.

a. 3 components extracted.

Pattern Matrix[a]

	Component		
	1	2	3
farejews	.553	.081	.407
workjews	.544	.071	.399
influjew	-.206	-.089	.808
intljews	-.719	.064	-.012
patrjews	.567	.220	.028
violjews	-.733	.151	.208
wlthjews	.219	-.009	.690
livejews	.006	.848	-.025
marjew	-.055	.835	-.070

Extraction Method: Principal Component Analysis.

Rotation Method: Oblimin with Kairs Normalization.

a. Rotation converged in 11 iterations.

Structure Matrix

	Component		
	1	2	3
farejews	.651	.154	.533
workjews	.639	.143	.522
influjew	-.036	-.071	.758
intljews	-.715	-.006	-.168
patrjews	.594	.277	.163
violjews	-.673	.089	.053
wlthjews	.371	.045	.738
livejews	.082	.847	.016
marjew	.010	.826	-.043

Extraction Method: Principal Component Analysis.

Rotation Method: Oblimin with Kaiser Normalization.

Component Correlation Matrix

Component	1	2	3
1	1.000	.097	.221
2	.097	1.000	.047
3	.221	.047	1.000

Extraction Method: Principal Component Analysis.

Rotation Method: Oblimin with Kaiser Normalization.

The factor loadings for the direct oblimin rotation are presented in the table titled "Structure Matrix." Again using 0.5 as our standard, the first factor includes Jews and welfare, Jews and work, the intelligence of Jews, the patriotism of Jews, and the violence of Jews. The second factor includes living in a Jewish neighborhood and having a relative marry a Jew. The third factor includes Jews and welfare, Jews and work, the influence of Jews, and the wealth of Jews. You'll notice here the effects of allowing the factors to correlate as is done when conducting a factor analysis using an oblique rotation. Looking at the first two variables, for example, that of Jews and welfare and Jews and work, you can see that they load strongly both on the first and the third factor. You would not expect to see this when conducting a factor analysis using no rotation or using an orthogonal (nonoblique) rotation, such as that of varimax rotation. The factors here are fairly similar to the factors we obtained using the varimax rotation, with the exception of the addition of the Jews and welfare and Jews and work variables to the factors that originally contained only the influence and wealth of Jews, if we use the more liberal 0.5 cutoff as opposed to 0.6. I feel that the factors that were produced using the varimax rotation had the most clear and obvious conceptual meaning. Because of this, I prefer the varimax rotation over both the unrotated solution and the direct oblimin rotation.

◬ SECTION 3: STATA

Factor analysis in Stata is quite simple. In this section, I will simply present the syntax to run factor analyses in Stata, as this is much more efficient and much less time-consuming than using the menus. First, I will provide an introduction to the data set, which is the same one that was used in the previous section on IBM SPSS.

Our factor analysis will use nine variables measuring anti-Semitic attitudes. These data come from the General Social Survey, and the particular data set used in this chapter can be downloaded from: http://sda.berkeley.edu/cgi-bin/hsda?harcsda+gss04

Select *Download* and *Customized Subset*

And choose to select the following variables: *farejews workjews influjew intljews patrjews violjews wlthjews livejews marjew*

Farejews asks respondents whether Jews tend to prefer to be self-supporting or live off welfare. *Workjews* asks respondents whether Jews tend to be hard-working or lazy. The variable *influjew* asks whether people feel Jews have too much influence in American life and politics, just about the right amount of influence, or too little influence. *Intljews* asks the respondent whether Jews tend to be unintelligent or intelligent. The variable *patrjews* asks people whether they feel Jews tend to be patriotic or unpatriotic. *Violjews* asks respondents whether Jews tend to be prone to violence or not. *Wlthjews* asks respondents whether they feel Jews are rich, poor, or somewhere in between. The variable *livejews* asks people whether they would favor or oppose living in a neighborhood where half of their neighbors were Jews. Finally, *marjew* asks respondents whether they would favor or oppose having a close relative marry a Jewish person. Both the variables *livejews* and *marjew* are 5-point Likert scales. *Influjew* is a 3-point Likert scale. The remainder of the variables are 7-point Likert scales.

After recoding the variables so that the respondents who replied "don't know," "not applicable," and so on are recoded as missing, we can open Stata and begin our factor analysis. First, to run a factor analysis using principal components analysis, the method of choice for exploratory factor analysis, we can enter the following syntax:

```
factor farejews workjews influjew intljews
patrjews violjews wlthjews livejews marjew, pcf
```

After typing the factor command, we simply list all the variables that we will include in the factor analysis. After this, we use the command pcf to specify that principal components analysis will be the method of extraction to be used. This is our output:

```
(obs=1074)
```

Factor analysis/correlation		Number of obs	=	1074
Method: principal-component factors		Retained factors	=	3
Rotation: (unrotated)		Number of params	=	24

Factor	Eigenvalue	Difference	Proportion	Cumulative
Factor1	2.63128	1.13116	0.2924	0.2924
Factor2	1.50012	0.41402	0.1667	0.4590
Factor3	1.08610	0.21611	0.1207	0.5797
Factor4	0.86999	0.16652	0.0967	0.6764
Factor5	0.70347	0.07337	0.0782	0.7546
Factor6	0.63010	0.07904	0.0700	0.8246
Factor7	0.55106	0.01067	0.0612	0.8858
Factor8	0.54040	0.05292	0.0600	0.9458
Factor9	0.48748	.	0.0542	1.0000

LR test: independent vs.saturated: chi2(36) = 1527.27 Prob>chi2 = 0.0000

Factor loadings (pattern matrix) and unique variances

```
-------------------------------------------------------------
    Variable |  Factor1    Factor2    Factor3  |  Uniqueness
-------------+----------------------------------+-------------
    farejews |   0.7656    -0.0212     0.0557   |    0.4103
    workjews |   0.7503    -0.0289     0.0517   |    0.4335
    influjew |   0.3128    -0.2825     0.6694   |    0.3742
    intljews |  -0.6294     0.0643     0.3394   |    0.4846
    patrjews |   0.5656     0.2043    -0.2007   |    0.5980
    violjews |  -0.4839     0.0931     0.5242   |    0.4824
    wlthjews |   0.6310    -0.1766     0.4014   |    0.4095
    livejews |   0.1697     0.8174     0.1460   |    0.2818
     marjew  |   0.0845     0.8156     0.1394   |    0.3082
-------------------------------------------------------------
```

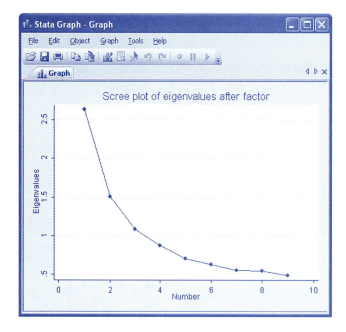

As you can see, both the eigenvalues and the factor loadings match those that were obtained when conducting the initial unrotated factor analysis within IBM SPSS. Now, after running the factor analysis, to obtain a scree plot, simply type the following command:

```
scree
```

This will give you the following output:

Now, to run the same factor analysis using varimax rotation, we can simply type the following command after running the initial factor analysis:

```
rotate
```

This will, by default, rerun the factor analysis using varimax rotation. This is our output:

```
Factor analysis/correlation                       Number of obs    =     1074
    Method: principal-component factors           Retained factors =        3
    Rotation: orthogonal varimax (Horst off)      Number of params =       24
```

Factor	Variance	Difference	Proportion	Cumulative
Factor1	2.15514	0.60259	0.2395	0.2395
Factor2	1.55255	0.04275	0.1725	0.4120
Factor3	1.50980	.	0.1678	0.5797

```
    LR test: independent vs. saturated:  chi2(36) = 1527.27 Prob>chi2 = 0.0000
```

Rotated factor loadings (pattern matrix) and unique variances

Variable	Factor1	Factor2	Factor3	Uniqueness
farejews	0.6062	0.4591	0.1071	0.4103
workjews	0.5958	0.4497	0.0964	0.4335
influjew	-0.1067	0.7784	-0.0923	0.3742
intljews	-0.7128	-0.0780	0.0342	0.4846
patrjews	0.5785	0.0888	0.2438	0.5980
violjews	-0.6949	0.1417	0.1212	0.4824
wlthjews	0.3050	0.7053	0.0051	0.4095
livejews	0.0468	0.0039	0.8462	0.2818
marjew	-0.0203	-0.0465	0.8302	0.3082

Factor rotation matrix

	Factor1	Factor2	Factor3
Factor1	0.8317	0.5339	0.1521
Factor2	-0.0163	-0.2503	0.9680
Factor3	-0.5549	0.8076	0.1995

As you may notice, the eigenvalues and factor loadings using varimax rotation as presented here differ from the values obtained when no method of rotation was used. Looking at Factor 1, you'll notice that varimax rotation adds the violence of Jews as an indicator but removes the wealth of Jews. The second factor in the unrotated solution corresponds to the third factor in the varimax rotation and vice versa. Both the second factor in the unrotated solution and the third factor in the varimax rotation include only living in a Jewish neighborhood and having a relative marry a Jew as indicators. The third factor in the unrotated solution includes the influence of Jews and the violence of Jews as factors. The second factor in the rotated solution includes the influence of Jews and the wealth of Jews as factors. This factor makes much more sense to me conceptually as compared with the one that includes only the influence of Jews and violence of Jews, which is one of the major reasons why I prefer the varimax rotation to the unrotated solution. I also prefer having three conceptually distinct factors as compared with two, which is another reason why I prefer the varimax rotation in this example.

Finally, let us run this same factor analysis using the direct oblimin rotation. To do this, we simply need to enter the following syntax after running the initial factor analysis:

```
rotate, oblimin oblique
```

This will give us the following output:

```
Factor analysis/correlation                   Number of obs     =     1074
    Method: principal-component factors       Retained factors =        3
    Rotation: oblique oblimin (Horst off)     Number of params =       24


    -----------------------------------------------------------------------
        Factor |    Variance   Proportion    Rotated factors are correlated
    -------------+---------------------------------------------------------
       Factor1  |    2.35470      0.2616
       Factor2  |    1.65269      0.1836
       Factor3  |    1.52622      0.1696
    -----------------------------------------------------------------------
    LR test: independent vs. saturated:  chi2(36) = 1527.27 Prob>chi2 = 0.0000
```

Rotated factor loadings (pattern matrix) and unique variances

```
    -----------------------------------------------------------------
    Variable |  Factor1   Factor2   Factor3 |   Uniqueness
    -------------+-----------------------------------+--------------
    farejews |   0.5832    0.3722    0.0893 |     0.4103
    workjews |   0.5738    0.3643    0.0789 |     0.4335
    influjew |  -0.1625    0.8059   -0.0861 |     0.3742
    intljews |  -0.7253    0.0285    0.0572 |     0.4846
    patrjews |   0.5769   -0.0004    0.2258 |     0.5980
    violjews |  -0.7261    0.2475    0.1445 |     0.4824
    wlthjews |   0.2607    0.6684   -0.0021 |     0.4095
    livejews |   0.0168   -0.0125    0.8463 |     0.2818
     marjew  |  -0.0477   -0.0532    0.8323 |     0.3082
    -----------------------------------------------------------------
```

Factor rotation matrix

```
    -------------------------------------------
             | Factor1   Factor2   Factor3
    -------------+-----------------------------
    Factor1  |  0.9060    0.5913    0.1913
    Factor2  | -0.4226    0.7660    0.1922
    Factor3  | -0.0227   -0.2522    0.9625
    -------------------------------------------
```

Notice that Stata presents only a pattern matrix and not a structure matrix when running an oblique rotation, whereas IBM SPSS presents both matrices. While it is debated which matrix is better to use in determining which factors to associate with which factors, I have suggested using the structure matrix. Here, as we are given only a pattern matrix, we would need to rely solely on that. For this reason, I would prefer the use of IBM SPSS when conducting factor analyses with oblique rotations.

Using 0.5 as our standard, our first factor includes Jews and welfare, Jews and work, the intelligence of Jews, the patriotism of Jews, and the violence of Jews. The second factor includes the influence and wealth of Jews. The third factor includes living in a Jewish neighborhood and having a relative marry a Jew. If we were making these judgments on the basis of the structure matrix, the interpretation of our factors would have been less clear. Overall, I feel that the factors that are produced using the varimax rotation had the most clear and obvious conceptual meaning. Because of this, I will prefer the varimax rotation over both the unrotated solution and the direct oblimin rotation.

When running other factor analyses, keep in mind that you must first run the initial factor analysis using the factor command before you can run these rotate commands. To have Stata calculate the factor scores for these three factors after running the varimax rotation (our rotation method of choice), you would simply type the following command:

```
predict f1 f2 f3
```

where *f1*, *f2*, and *f3* are the variable names of our three new factors. Here, we would simply enter as many new variables names as we want factors. Entering ed to view our data set and scrolling to the right and downward, we see the following:

Here, you can see our three new variables and their calculated values. Their values have been calculated using regression.

Data Editor (Edit) - [spss_data_final.dta]

File   Edit   Data   Tools

caseid[1]   2006 1

	f1	f2	f3
38690	-.9724773	-.48791	.169257
38691	.	.	.
38692	.2124902	-.9414566	.5108313
38693	-1.580214	-.6854857	.9716286
38694	.0447792	-1.097088	-1.14939
38695	-.3680169	-.2699325	.1161151
38696	-.3128834	-.5642353	-.3701501
38697	-.8992418	.2619763	.7885723
38698	-1.638397	.0006351	.1803781
38699	.	.	.
38700	.4130345	.4974029	-.0553339
38701	.1224688	-.1224507	1.444034
38702	-.384691	-1.123309	1.460403
38703	.	.	.
38704	.3868693	.2989219	.1699441
38705	-.5782479	-.6740175	-2.170408
38706	1.068491	-.1221857	-.1682069
38707	-.6727625	.3586451	2.433679
38708	.0286178	-1.208567	-3.206433
38709	.7578381	.5354531	.1784421
38710	.3883848	1.064837	.2430045
38711	.7861382	1.958721	-.6803265
38712	.	.	.

△   SECTION 4: SUMMARY

This chapter covered factor analysis, which is a method that is used to determine whether a larger number of variables can be reduced to a smaller number of factors. It is most especially useful in developing new dependent variables for use in later analyses. There are two types of factor analysis, exploratory factor analysis and confirmatory factor analysis. In exploratory factor analysis, you do not predefine the number of factors or predetermine which variables are associated with which factors. In confirmatory factor analysis, you do predefine the number of factors and, typically, also predetermine which variables are associated with which factors. Exploratory factor analysis is more common in social science and was the focus of this chapter. When conducting an exploratory factor analysis, there are several possible methods of factor extraction that can be used, the most common of which is principal components analysis. Also, when conducting a factor analysis, there are several methods of rotation that are available that may give you more easily interpretable factors or stronger factors as compared with an unrotated solution. There are several methods for determining how many factors to keep after conducting a factor analysis, as well as a simple method of determining which variables are associated with which factors. Both IBM SPSS and Stata are quite adept at factor analysis, and both programs incorporate the different methods of factor analysis I have just discussed. The following chapter will cover **time-series analysis**, which is a set of methods that is used to model changes that occur over time.

 RESOURCES

You can find more information about IBM SPSS and how to purchase it by navigating to the following Web site: www.spss.com/software/statistics/

You can find more information about Stata and how to purchase it by navigating to the following Web site: www.stata.com

This book's Web site can be found at the following location: www.sage pub.com/kremelstudy

CHAPTER **8**

TIME-SERIES ANALYSIS

OUTLINE OF CHAPTER

SECTION 1: INTRODUCTION

Time-series analysis consists of a number of methods that are used to model data that are collected over time. These methods can be used simply to model the nature of the change in data over time or to predict future values based on previous levels or trends. This chapter will serve as an introduction to time-series analysis and will include instructions on how to perform expo-nential smoothing, ARIMA models, and curve fitting. **Exponential smoothing** is used for very short-term predictions or forecasting, specifically being focused on the forecasting of the very next value in your series of data. **ARIMA (auto-regressive integrated moving average) models** are used to model changes over time as well as predict the future values of a variable. Finally, **curve fitting** uses regression methods to determine how well a series of different curves, which are specified by equations, "fit" your data. In this chapter, all three of these methods will be covered in IBM SPSS, while only exponential smoothing and ARIMA models will be covered in Stata, as Stata is not as adept at curve fitting as IBM SPSS.

△ SECTION 2: IBM SPSS

Exponential Smoothing

To run most of the more advanced versions of time-series analysis in IBM SPSS, you will need a newer version of the program, along with the time-series add-on for the program. The data used for both the exponential smoothing and ARIMA models are the daily close price of the Dow Jones Industrial Index from January 2 through February 20, 2009. This data set can be accessed from the following Web site: http://finance.yahoo.com/q/hp?s=^DJI.

After opening this file in IBM SPSS, I simply created a new variable called *case* that is coded 1 for the earliest date, January 2, and is incremented by one for each following date, ending with a value of 34 for February 20. Next, I will sort the cases by this new *case* variable so that they are ordered from 1 to 34, as the data from Yahoo finance begin with the most recent date and end with the earliest date. We'll need to reverse this to run the time-series analysis. To do this, click on *Data* and *Sort Cases*. Next, select the new *case* variable and select *Ascending* under *Sort Order*. Finally, click *OK*, and your data will now be sorted in the correct order.

In this example, I will use exponential smoothing to arrive at a predicted value for the close of the Dow Jones Industrial Index for the following day, February 23. To do this, we will first make the following menu selection:

This will open the following dialog box:

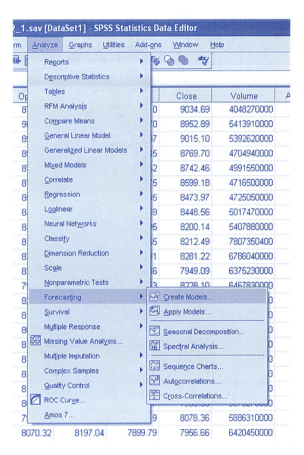

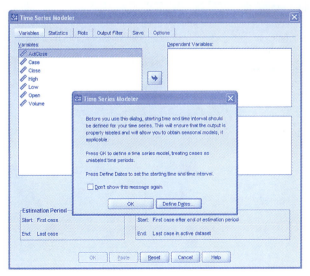

Here, I will simply click *OK*, which reveals the following dialog box:

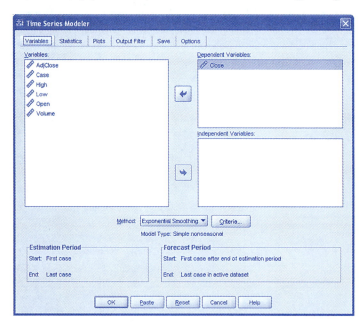

Here, you can see that I have moved our *Close* variable into the *Dependent Variables* field and have selected *Exponential Smoothing* under our *Method* option. Next, I will click on the *Criteria* button. This will open the following dialog box:

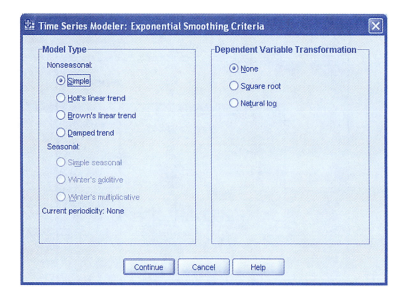

Here, you can see that IBM SPSS provides us with four different model type options for nonseasonal data and three model type options for seasonal data. A **seasonal model** would be used if we saw a pattern, like a spike, appear at regular time intervals, for example, quarterly or annually. Graphing our data, we can see the following:

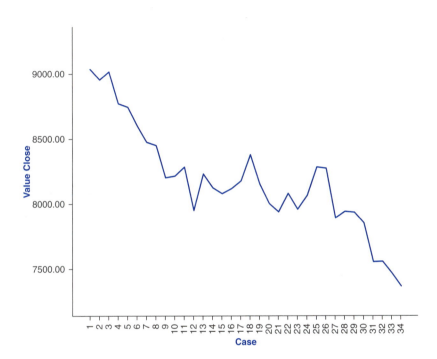

In the graph presented above, no seasonal effects are apparent. This leaves us with four **nonseasonal model** types: simple, Holt's linear trend, Brown's linear trend, and damped trend. The **simple model** is used when there are no seasonal effects and there is no apparent trend in the data. **Holt's linear trend** and **Brown's linear trend** are both used when there are no seasonal effects, but there does appear to be a linear trend in the data. Finally, **damped trend** is used when there is no seasonality and when there is a linear trend that is decreasing in magnitude. Looking at the graph presented above, there is a clear linear downward trend, and I will select Holt's linear trend. Either Holt's linear trend or Brown's linear trend could be used in this case, but I will prefer Holt's linear trend as it is a more general model than Brown's linear trend. We will now make this selection and click *Continue*:

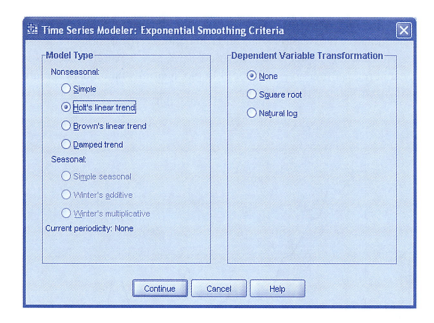

Next, click on the *Options* tab:

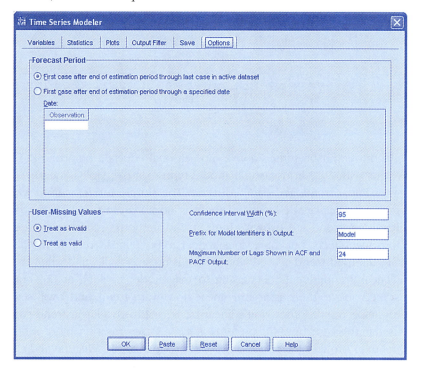

Here, we will make the second selection under the *Forecast Period* field: "First case after end of estimation period through a specified date." In our data set, our final case has a value of 34. We will set the *Date* field equal to 35 so that IBM SPSS will give us a prediction for the close of the Dow Jones Industrial Index for the following day, February 23:

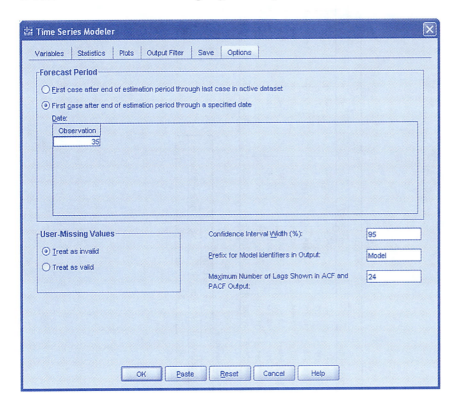

Then, click *OK*. This will give us the following output:

Time Series Modeler

[DataSet1] T:\Md book\#Data\Chapter 8\Dow Jones I—Jan 1—Fe

Model Description

			Model Type
Model ID	Close	Model_1	Holt

Model Summary

Model Fit

Fit Statistic	Mean	SE	Minimum	Maximum	Percentile						
					5	10	25	50	75	90	95
Stationary R-squared	.627	.	.627	.627	.627	.627	.627	.627	.627	.627	.627
R-squared	.872	.	.872	.872	.872	.872	.872	.872	.872	.872	.872
RMSE	918149.	.	149.918	149.918	149.918	149.918	149.918	149.918	149.918	149.918	149.918
MAPE	1.381	.	1.381	1.381	1.381	1.381	1.381	1.381	1.381	1.381	1.381
MaxAPE	3.945	.	3.945	3.945	3.945	3.945	3.945	3.945	3.945	3.945	3.945
MAE	112.349	.	112.349	112.349	112.349	12.3491	112.349	112.349	112.349	112.349	112.349
MaxAE	311.251	.	311.251	311.251	311.251	311.251	311.251	311.251	311.251	311.251	311.251
Normalized BIC	10.228	.	10.228	10.228	10.228	10.228	10.228	10.228	10.228	10.228	10.228

Model Statistics

Model	Number of Predictors	Model Fit statistics Stationary R-squared	Ljung-Box Q(18) Statistics	Ljung-Box Q(18) DF	Ljung-Box Q(18) Sig.	Number of Outliers
Close-Model_1	0	.627	18.257	16	.309	0

322

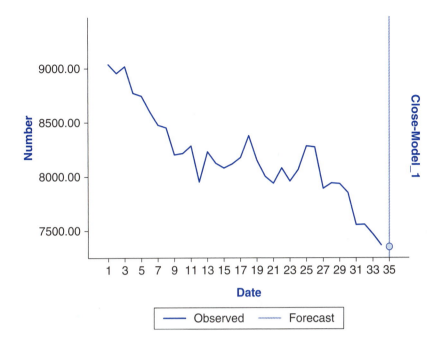

The final graph shows us our prediction for tomorrow's close. According to our results, the Dow Jones Industrial Index is expected to close at a lower point tomorrow than it did today. To determine this exact predicted value, we could navigate to the following screen:

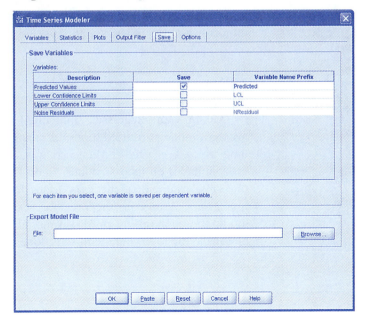

Under the *Save* tab, I have simply specified that the predicted values be saved by checking that box. Running this analysis again, we see a new variable in our data set:

		Volume	AdjClose	Case	Predicted_Close_Model_1	var
	24	6624030000	8063.07	24	7927.94	
	25	6484100000	8280.59	25	7984.99	
	26	5574370000	8270.87	26	8156.61	
	27	6770169600	7888.88	27	8200.13	
	28	5926460000	7939.53	28	7941.30	
	29	6476460000	7932.76	29	7901.67	
	30	5296650000	7850.41	30	7885.42	
	31	5907820000	7552.60	31	7822.24	
	32	5740710000	7555.63	32	7592.04	
	33	5746940000	7465.95	33	7526.93	
	34	8210590400	7365.67	34	7444.23	
	35		.	.	7348.83	
	36					

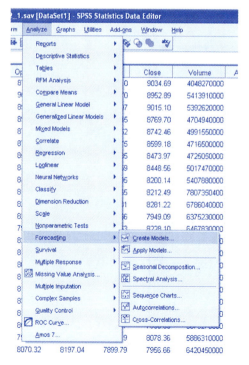

The final variable, *Predicted_Close_Model_1*, is the predicted value of the close of the Dow Jones Industrial Index. We can see the predicted value for tomorrow's close under case 35: 7348.83.

ARIMA Models

ARIMA (Auto-Regressive Integrated Moving Average) models are used to model changes over time as well as predict the current value of a variable based on its past values. Here, I will use the same example of the Dow Jones Industrial Index data as used in the previous section. To model these data using an ARIMA model, we will first make the following menu selection:

This will open our main dialog box, where I have specified *Close* as our dependent variable:

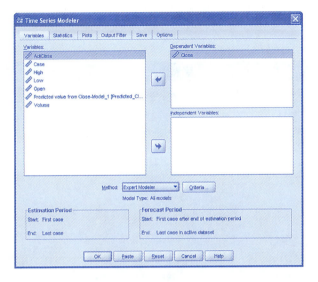

Here, you can see that under *Method*, I have simply selected the *Expert Modeler* option. In an ARIMA model, there are three parameters that need to be specified: p, d, and q. If we wanted to define these values ourselves, we could select "ARIMA" under *Method*. Then, clicking *Criteria* would open the following dialog box:

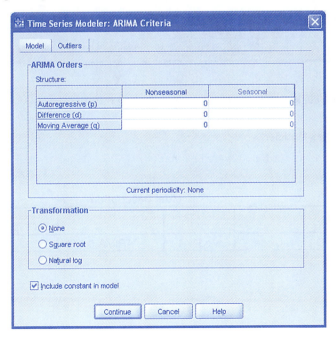

But here, I have simply selected the "Expert Modeler" option, which will allow IBM SPSS to select the best values for these parameters automatically. Back in our main dialog box, I will now select the *Options* tab. Here, I will specify IBM SPSS to calculate future values for cases 35 through 40:

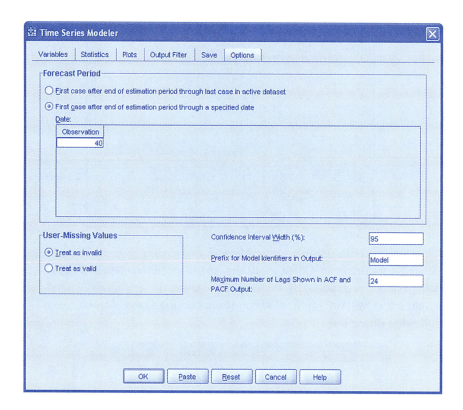

Now, clicking *OK* will give us the following output:

Time Series Modeler

[DataSet1] T:\Md book\#Data\Chapter 8\Dow Jones I—Jan 1—Feb 22

Model Description

			Model Type
Model ID	Close	Model_1	ARIMA(0,1,0)

Model Summary

Model Fit

Fit Statistic	Mean	SE	Minimum	Maximum	Percentile						
					5	10	25	50	75	90	95
Stationary R-squared	3.178E-15	.	3.178E-15	3.178E-15	3.178E-15	3.178E-15	3.178E-15	3.178E-15	3.178E-15	3.178E-15	3.178E-15
Rsquared	.841	.	.841	.841	.841	.841	.841	.841	.841	.841	.841
RMSE	155.127	.	155.127	155.127	155.127	155.127	155.127	155.127	155.127	155.127	155.127
MAPE	1.479	.	1.479	1.479	1.479	1.479	1.479	1.479	1.479	1.479	1.479
MaxAPE	4.201	.	4.201	4.201	4.201	4.201	4.201	4.201	4.201	4.201	4.201
MAE	120.288	.	120.288	120.288	120.288	120.288	120.288	120.288	120.288	120.288	120.288
MaxAE	331.414	.	331.414	331.414	331.414	331.414	331.414	331.414	331.414	331.414	331.414
Normalized BIC	10.194	.	10.194	10.194	10.194	10.194	10.194	10.194	10.194	10.194	10.194

Model Statistics

Model	Number of Predictors	Model Fit statistics	Ljung-Box Q(18)			Number of Outliers
		Stationary R-squared	Statistics	DF	Sig.	
Close-Model_1	0	3.178E-15	.20322	18	.223	0

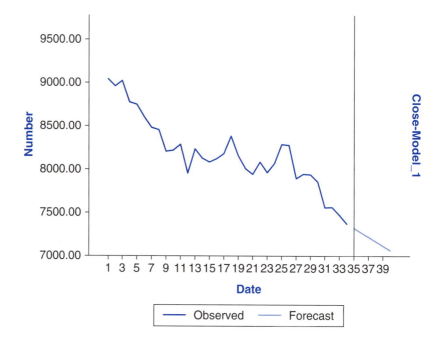

In our "Model Description" table:

Model Description

				Model Type
Model ID	Close	Model_1		ARIMA(0,1,0)

We can see that IBM SPSS has specified a model type of ARIMA (0, 1, 0). This means IBM SPSS has assigned values of 0 for p, 1 for d, and 0 for q. The final graph, presented above, illustrates the predictions this model makes on future values of the close of the Dow Jones Industrial Index.

As the option to save the predicted values as new variables is still selected, we can see that SPSS has generated values for the predicted close of the Dow Jones Industrial Index for the next 5 days:

Curve Fitting

Curve fitting uses regression methods to determine how well a series of different curves, which are specified by equations, "fit" your data. For this example, I will use historical estimates of the world's population, which come from the United Nations:

www.un.org/esa/population/publications/sixbillion/sixbilpart1.pdf

www.census.gov/ipc/www/worldhis.html

This is the actual data set that I will be using in this section:

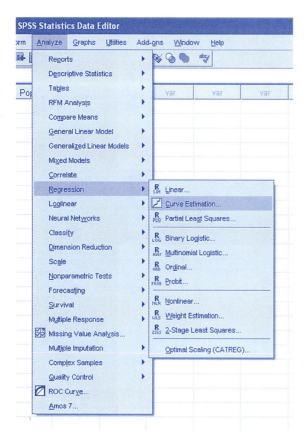

Here, population is coded in millions of persons. To perform curve fitting models, I will first make the following menu selection:

This will open the following dialog box:

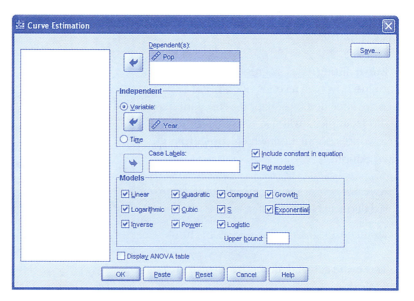

Here, I have specified population as our dependent variable and year as our independent variable. Also, I have selected all the possibilities under the *Models* heading. Clicking *OK* will give us the following results:

Curve Fit

```
[DataSet2] T: \Md book \#Data \Chapter 8 \Population.sav
```

Warnings

The Cubic model could not be fitted due to near-collinearity among model terms.

Model Description

	Model Name		MOD_1
Dependent Variable		1	Pop
	Equation	1	Linear
		2	Logarithmic
		3	Inverse
		4	Quadratic
		5	Cubic
		6	Compound[a]
		7	Power[a]
		8	S[a]
		9	Growth[a]
		10	Exponential[a]
		11	Logistic[a]
	Independent Variable		Year
	Constant		Included
	Variable Whose Values Label Observations in Plots		Unspecified
	Tolerance for Entering Terms in Equations		.0001

a. The model requires all nonmissing values to be positive.

Case Processing Summary

	N
Total Cases	14
Excluded Cases[a]	0
Forecasted Cases	0
Newly Created Cases	0

a. Cases with a missing value in any
variable are excluded from the analysis.

Variable Processing Summary

		Variables	
		Dependent	Independent
		Pop	Year
Number of Positive Values		14	14
Number of Zeros		0	0
Number of Negative Values		0	0
Number of Missing Values	User-Missing	0	0
	System-Missing	0	0

Model Summary and Parameter Estimates

Dependent Variable:Pop

Equation	Model Summary					Parameter Estimates			
	R Square	F	df1	df2	Sig.	Constant	b1	b2	b3
Linear	.675	24.867	1	12	.000	-32266.275	18.227		
Logarithmic	.658	23.110	1	12	.000	-252803.909	33803.302		
Inverse	.642	21.506	1	12	.001	35363.163	-6.257E7		
Quadratic	.937	81.394	2	11	.000	517205.186	-567.433	.156	
Cubic	.942	89.306	2	11	.000	163976.259	.000	-.148	5.405E-5
Compound	.894	101.570	1	12	.000	.001	1.008		
Power	.883	90.615	1	12	.000	7.506E-46	14.770		
S	.871	81.247	1	12	.000	22.090	-27501.834		
Growth	.894	101.570	1	12	.000	-7.454	.008		
Exponential	.894	101.570	1	12	.000	.001	.008		
Logistic	.894	101.570	1	12	.000	1727.483	.992		

The independent variable is Year.

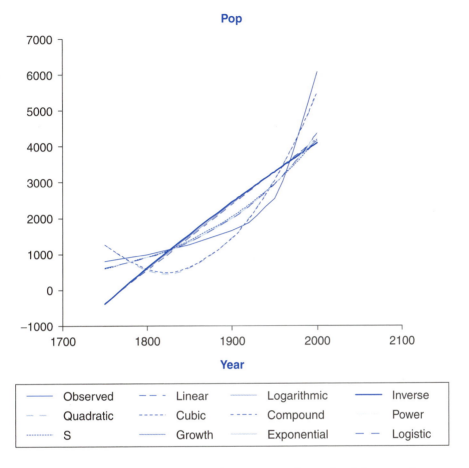

In the final table, SPSS gives us the estimates for each of the equations that we have specified, along with their *R*-squared values. The *R*-squared values tell us how much of the variation in our dependent variable, population, is explained by the corresponding equation that incorporates our independent variable, year. For example, the quadratic equation has an *R*-squared value of 0.937, explaining 93.7% of the variation in world population. Its equation would take this form

$$Y = \beta_0 + (\beta_1 x) + (\beta_2 x^2)$$

In our example,

$$Y = \beta_0 + (\beta_1 x) + (\beta_2 x^2) = 517205.186 - 567.433x + .156x^2$$

The predicted population for the year 2050 based on this model would be

$$Y = \beta_0 + (\beta_1 x) + (\beta_2 x^2) = 517205.186 - 567.433x + .156x^2$$
$$= 517205.186 - 567.433(2050) + .156(2050^2) = 9557.536$$

Or 9,557,536,000, as population in our data set was coded in millions.

If we wanted to predict when the world's population would reach 10 billion based on the quadratic model, we could solve this equation for x:

$$517205.186 - 567.433x + .156x^2 = 10,000$$

Again, with 10,000 representing 10,000 million, or 10 billion, this would give us a value of 2056.0519 or January 18, 2056.

These are the forms of all the equations supplied to us by IBM SPSS:

Linear: $Y = \beta_0 + (\beta_1 x)$

Logarithmic: $Y = \beta_0 + \beta_1 (e^x)$

Inverse: $Y = \beta_0 + \left(\dfrac{\beta_1}{x} \right)$

Quadratic: $Y = \beta_0 + (\beta_1 x) + (\beta_2 x^2)$

Cubic: $Y = \beta_0 + (\beta_1 x) + (\beta_2 x^2) + (\beta_3 x^3)$

Compound: $Y = (\beta_0)(\beta_1{}^x)$

Power: $Y = \beta_0 + x^{\beta_1}$

S: $Y = e^{\left[\beta_0 + \left(\frac{\beta_1}{x} \right) \right]}$

Growth: $Y = e^{[\beta_0 + \beta_1(x)]}$

Exponential: $Y = \beta_0 + e^{[(\beta_1)(x)]}$

Logistic: $Y = \dfrac{1}{\left(\frac{1}{u} \right) + (\beta_0)(\beta_1{}^x)}$

where u is the upper-boundary value.

When running curve fitting models, you may prefer an older version of IBM SPSS as you may find their colored charts somewhat easier to read.

Exponential Smoothing

The data used for both the exponential smoothing and ARIMA models in these sections are the daily close price of the Dow Jones Industrial Index from January 2 through February 20, 2009. This data set can be accessed from the following Web site: http://finance.yahoo.com/q/hp?s=^DJI.

After converting and opening this file in Stata, I simply created a new variable called *case* that begins with one for the earliest date, January 2, and is incremented by one for each following date, ending with a value of 34 for February 20. Next, I will sort the cases by this new *case* variable so that they are ordered from 1 to 34, as the data from Yahoo finance begin with the most recent date and end with the earliest date. We'll need to reverse this to run the time-series analysis. To do this, simply enter the following command:

```
sort case
```

This will sort your data in ascending order by the new *case* variable.

In this example, I will use exponential smoothing to arrive at a predicted value for the close of the Dow Jones Industrial Index for the following market day, Monday, February 23. To do this, we will type the following two commands into Stata:

```
tsset case
tssmooth e closef1=close, forecast(1)
```

The first command, `tsset case`, sets our "time" variable to be the new *case* variable that we have created. The second command is our exponential smoothing command. We are telling Stata to create a new variable, called *closef1*, based on our *close* variable. Also, we are requesting an estimate of the next close price using the `forecast(1)` option.

The output of our commands are:

```
. tsset case
    time variable: case, 1 to 34
. tssmooth e closef1=close, forecast(1)
```

```
computing optimal exponential coefficient (0,1)
optimal exponential coefficient = 0.8693
sum-of-squared residuals = 1192239.7
root mean squared error = 187.25884
```

And if we type ed, opening our data set, we see our predicted value for the close of the Dow Jones Industrial Index for the next market day, February 23, 2009: 7380.3906. This is under case 35 of the new variable created by the second syntax command, *closef1*. In our syntax, we have specified that the new variable that is created will be called *closef1*, and we have also specified that we would like to see a prediction, or forecast, of the close price for one unit of time (day) in the future.

ARIMA Models

ARIMA models are used to model changes over time as well as to predict the future values of a variable. Here, I will use the same example of the Dow Jones Industrial Index data as was used in the previous section. Stata incorporates ARIMA models as does IBM SPSS, although SPSS incorporates an automatic method for determining your p, d, and q values, which are three parameters that need to be specified when running an ARIMA model. When we ran this in IBM SPSS, p, d, and q values of 0, 1, and 0, respectively, were identified as the optimal values to use. To run this in Stata, we would first type

```
tsset case
```

if we haven't run this command previously, in order to identify *case* as our "time" variable. Next, to run the ARIMA model, we would type

```
arima close, arima(0,1,0)
```

Here, we are specifying that we are using the *close* variable for this ARIMA model, and we are specifying p, d, and q values of 0, 1, and 0, respectively. The way in which these three parameters are determined is more complex and is not covered in this book.

Running this ARIMA model gives us the following output:

```
(setting optimization to BHHH)
Iteration 0:   log likelihood = -212.77736
Iteration 1:   log likelihood = -212.77736

ARIMA regression

Sample:  2 - 34                          Number of obs    =        33
                                         Wald chi2(.)     =         .
Log likelihood = -212.7774               Prob > chi2      =         .

------------------------------------------------------------------------------
             |                 OPG
     D.close |     Coef.   Std. Err.      z    P>|z|     [95% Conf. Interval]
-------------+----------------------------------------------------------------
close        |
       _cons |  -50.57638   26.63254    -1.90   0.058    -102.7752    1.622448
-------------+----------------------------------------------------------------
      /sigma |   152.7588   19.98459     7.64   0.000     113.5897    191.9279
------------------------------------------------------------------------------
```

If you then type the command, predict close_ar, a new variable called *close_ar* will be created, which contains the forecasting data as predicted by the ARIMA model we just ran. If we type ed, we see that our ARIMA model predicts a change in closing price by –50.576 points for the following day. This type of ARIMA model, notated as ARIMA (0, 1, 0), predicts only a constant linear trend, while other ARIMA models, such as ARIMA (1, 1, 0), do not. This chapter is meant only to provide an introduction to time-series modeling, so these more complex issues are not covered here.

SECTION 4: SUMMARY ▲

This section was meant to provide you with an introduction to time-series modeling, which consists of a number of methods that are used to model data that are collected over time. These methods can be used simply to model the nature of the change in data over time or to predict future values based on previous levels or trends. This chapter included instructions on how to perform exponential smoothing, ARIMA models, and curve fitting. Exponential smoothing is used for very short-term prediction or forecasting, specifically being focused on the forecasting of the very next value in your series of data. ARIMA (Auto-Regressive Integrated Moving Average) models are used to model changes over time as well as predict the future values of a variable. Finally, curve fitting uses regression methods to determine how well a series of different curves, which are specified by equations, "fit" your data. In this chapter, all three of these methods were covered in IBM SPSS, while only exponential smoothing and ARIMA models were covered in Stata, as Stata is not as adept at curve fitting as IBM SPSS. The next chapter will cover HLM, or Hierarchical Linear Modeling. This is a specialized statistical method that is used to model data that are **nested**; for example, modeling scores of students who are "nested" inside classrooms, which are "nested" inside schools.

RESOURCES

You can find more information about IBM SPSS and how to purchase it by navigating to the following Web site: www.spss.com/software/statistics/

You can find more information about Stata and how to purchase it by navigating to the following Web site: www.stata.com

This book's Web site can be found at the following location: www .sagepub.com/kremelstudy

HIERARCHICAL LINEAR MODELING

SECTION 1: INTRODUCTION △

Hierarchical linear modeling (HLM) is a method that is used to analyze data that are "nested." It is not simply used to analyze all nested data but is commonly used when the focus of the analysis or research question is strongly dependent on the "nested" nature of the data. "Nested" data refer to a situation in which cases can be clustered into higher-order groups, with the assumption that cases that belong to the same group are more similar than cases that belong to different groups. A common example of these sort of data, which are also commonly analyzed using HLM, are student data. In these examples, generally, you see students nested inside classrooms, which themselves are nested inside schools. Here, you would expect students who are in the same classroom to be more similar (e.g., in terms of test scores) than students from two different classrooms. Likewise, you would expect two students from the same school to be more similar than two students from different schools, on average. HLM is well suited to analyzing this type of data while taking into consideration their nested nature.

◬   SECTION 2: HIERARCHICAL LINEAR MODELING

Hierarchical linear modeling is commonly abbreviated as simply HLM. Interestingly, the most popular program used in hierarchical linear modeling has that same name: HLM. You can find more information about the HLM software program and how to purchase it by navigating to the following Web site: www.ssicentral.com/hlm/index.html.

When you first open the program, you will see the following screen:

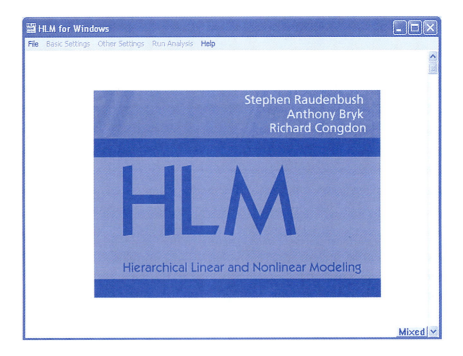

In this section, the example presented will use a data set that is supplied along with the free student edition of HLM. This particular data set resides in the "Chapter2" folder that will be installed during the installation of the student edition of the HLM program. The particular file that you can use is called "HSB.MDMT." The HLM program uses what are called MDMT files for data analysis. Here, we already have our MDMT file, so we could simply import this file into HLM, specify our model, and begin our analysis. However, before I outline this process, I will first run you through how to import data provided in IBM SPSS format into the HLM program. As the HLM program supplies us not only with HSB.MDMT but also the original IBM SPSS files, I will use this as the example here. To import data in IBM SPSS format into HLM, you would first need to create two separate files, one in which each case represents an individual and another in which each case represents the higher-order category. For example, in the case of school data, you might have one data file in which each case represents an individual student and a second data file in which each case represents a classroom. The first data file might contain variables such as the students' socioeconomic status, race, and so on. The second data file may contain variables such as the mean socioeconomic status of the class. Finally, you would also need a variable linking the cases in the student file to the cases in the class file. For example, you could create an *ID* variable, with the first class coded 1, and all students from the first class, in their data file, also coded 1. To begin the process of importing the data into HLM, we would first make the following menu selection:

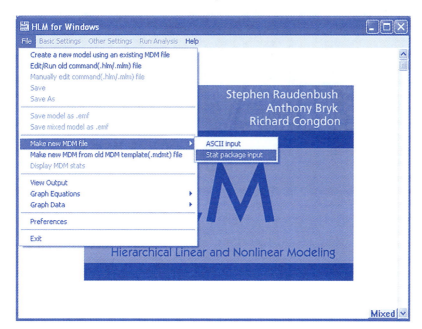

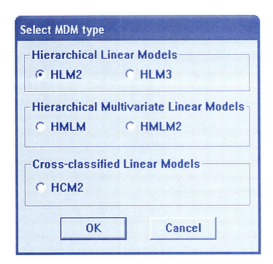

This will open the following dialog box:

Here, as our data only has data on two levels (students and classrooms), we can simply click *OK*. Doing so will reveal the following dialog box:

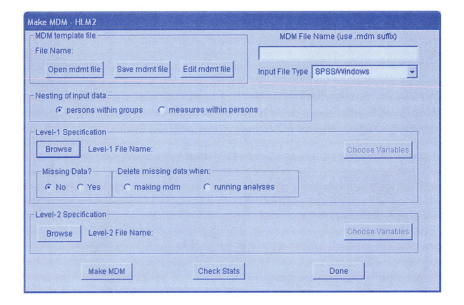

First, we can specify our Level 1 file by clicking *Browse* under *Level-1 Specification*. The Level 1 file refers to our data file that contains individuals as individual cases. Here, I will browse to the *Chapter2* directory and select the appropriate file, as shown below:

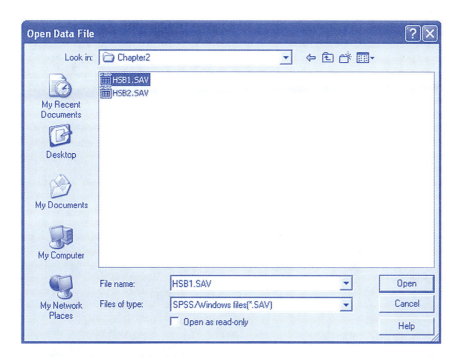

After clicking open, I will now click *Browse* under *Level-2 Specification*. Here, I will now simply select the second data file, like so:

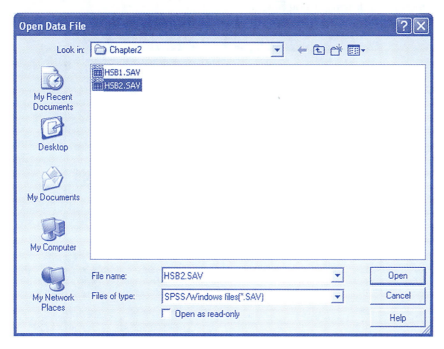

Next, after opening this file, I need to specify the variables in each of the two data sets to be included in our MDM file. Now, back at our main screen:

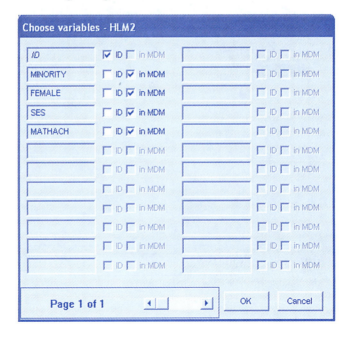

I will first click *Choose Variables* under *Level-1 Specification*. This will open the following dialog box:

Here, I have selected *ID* as the identification variable (the variable linking each individual to a classroom) and selected all the remaining variables to be included in the MDM file that will be created by the HLM program shortly. After clicking *OK*, I will click *Choose variables* under *Level-2 Specification*. This will open the following dialog box:

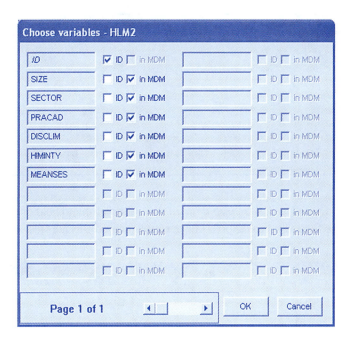

As you can see, I have again selected *ID* as the identification variable and selected the remaining variables as variables to include in the MDM file created by the HLM program. After clicking *OK* and returning to our main screen, I have specified that our new file be named *test.mdm*, as shown here:

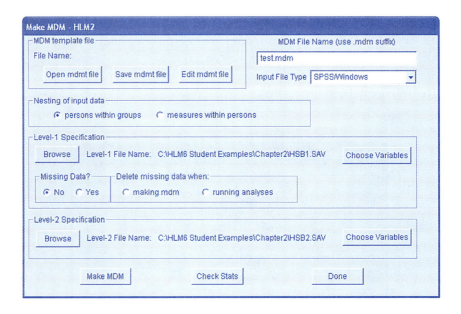

Next, we will click *Save mdmt file in* the upper-left-hand field of this dialog box. In the following dialog box, I have simply named this file "test.mdmt":

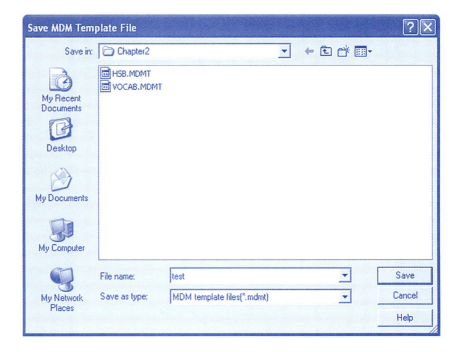

Finally, after clicking *Save*, we can click *Make MDM* to create our MDM file, which is the file format used by the HLM program. A DOS window quickly appears:

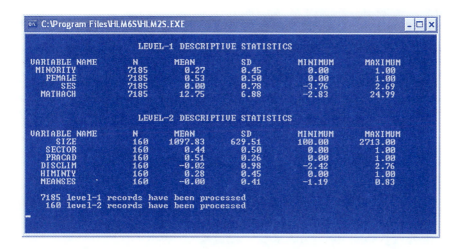

And then we are back at our main "Make MDM" window. If we click *Check Stats*, we see the following:

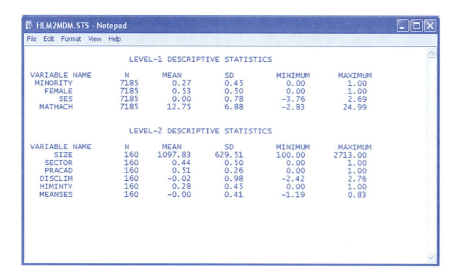

We can close this out, and finally, click *Done* in our main "Make MDM" window, in the lower-right-hand corner:

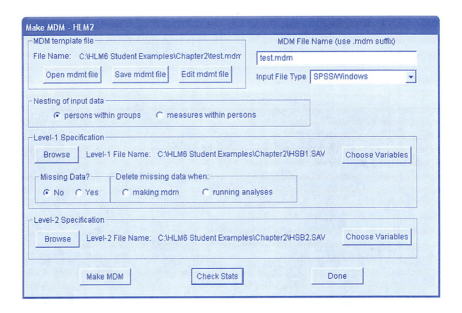

Now, we can see that our new MDM file has automatically been loaded into the HLM program, as we see our variables in the left-hand column:

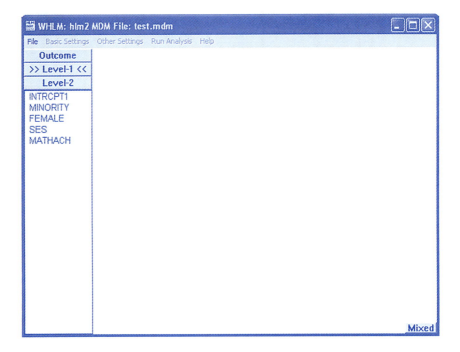

And we can begin our analysis. In this example, I will be using math achievement as the dependent variable. For the independent variables on *Level-1*, I will select gender (*FEMALE*), socioeconomic status (*SES*), and minority status (*MINORITY*). As independent variables on *Level-2*, I will select mean SES score (*meanses*) and location (*sector*).

First, we need to specify our outcome variable, or dependent variable. To do this, we simply click on our variable of choice, *MATHACH*, and choose *Outcome variable*, as shown here:

After clicking this, we see the following:

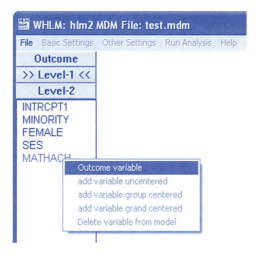

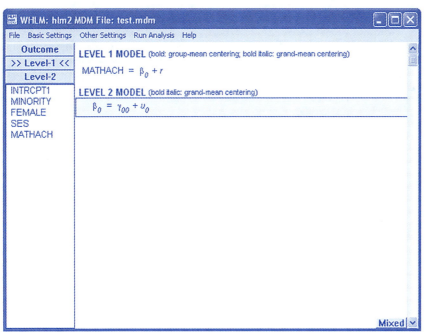

Here, we can see that the HLM program has begun building our model. Next, we can select our independent variables on *Level-1*. Again, these are *MINORITY*, *FEMALE*, and *SES*. To select *MINORITY*, we simply click on it and choose to add the variable. Here, the HLM program gives us three options:

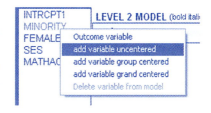

Here, we can either choose to add the variable **uncentered**, **group centered**, or **grand centered**. If data are uncentered, it is unmodified. If data are centered, the mean of scores is subtracted from each individual score so that the new mean of scores is equal to 0. In the case of group centering, the group mean is subtracted from each individual score to create a new value that is used in the analysis. In the case of grand centering, the grand or total mean is subtracted from each individual score to create a new variable that is used in the analysis. In our example of school data, group centering the variable would mean subtracting the mean of the school from each individual score. Also, grand centering the variable would refer to subtracting the mean of all students from each individual score. How a variable would be centered is generally made on a theoretical basis. In this example, I will not center *MINORITY* or *FEMALE* but will center *SES*, which I am group centering. When completed, your model should match the one shown here:

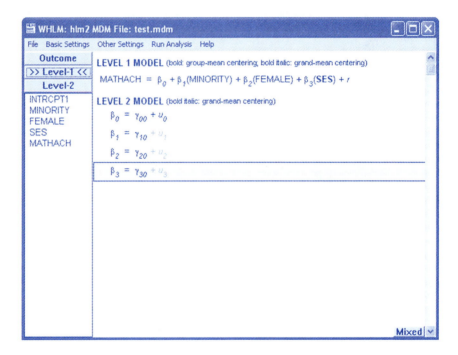

Here, you can see that our error terms, u_1, u_2, and u_3, are grayed out. This means that the slopes for these variables are fixed, or not allowed to vary between groups. To allow them to vary, we can simply click on them so that they become black. For example, if we wanted to allow the effect of minority on math achievement scores to vary between schools, we could click the error term, u_1, turning it black and allowing it to vary. You may consider letting them vary in models that you run, but for the purposes of this example, I will simply keep them constant. Now, I will click on *Level-2* to add our Level 2 predictors:

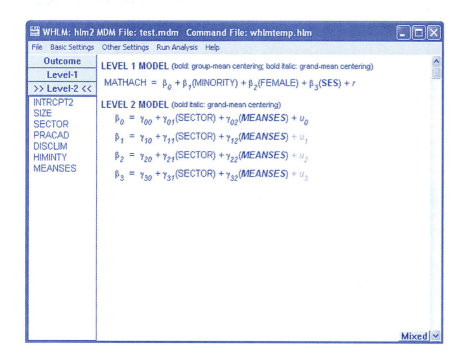

Here, I have added the sector and meanses variables as predictors for all our betas: our intercepts as well as our slopes for our *MINORITY, FEMALE*, and *SES* Level 1 independent variables. To explain, adding the variables *SECTOR* and *MEANSES* to the β_0 equation, which is the intercept for math achievement, means that we are going to estimate the effect of *SECTOR* and *MEANSES* on math achievement scores. Adding *SECTOR* to the equation for β_1 and the beta coefficient for *MINORITY* means that we are going to estimate the effect of sector on the effect of minority on math achievement. It sounds confusing, but basically we're going to see whether the location of the school has any influence on the effect of being a minority on math achievement scores. Let us say, for example, that location is a binary variable (i.e., there are only two neighborhoods or locations): the Seaside neighborhood, which is very affluent, and the Buxton neighborhood, which is middle class. Now, say that in the Seaside neighborhood, people tend to be very affluent regardless of race. However, in the Buxton neighborhood, Whites tend to be upper middle class, while the minorities tend to be lower middle class or lower class. In this example, you definitely want to include sector in the equation for β_1. This is because in one sector, the Seaside neighborhood, we would expect being a member of a minority to have little or no effect on math achievement scores because as everyone is affluent all schools receive much funding. However, in the Buxton neighborhood, schools that are predominantly white would receive more funding than schools that are primarily made up of minority students, so we would expect being a member of a minority to have a large impact on math achievement scores. Hopefully by now this makes sense: In this example, we would expect the effect of minority status on math achievement scores to vary greatly depending on sector, hence the reason for including the sector in the equation for β_1, the beta coefficient for minority.

To add our Level 2 variables, you would first click on one of the betas, like the following:

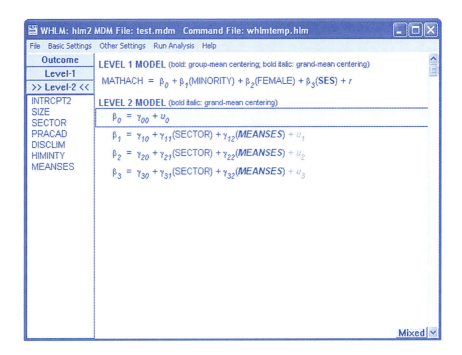

Then, click on *SECTOR*:

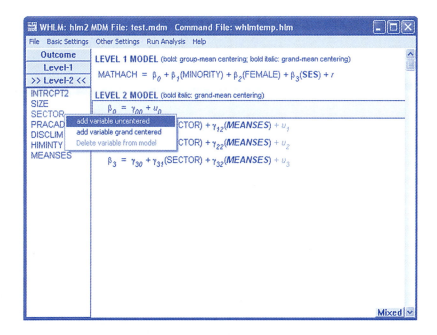

And select *add variable uncentered*. Here, I am adding *SECTOR* uncentered and *MEANSES* grand centered. As you can see, I have done this for all four betas, β_0 through to β_3. Finally, we can run our model. Select the *Run Analysis* menu option from the menu bar. Then click *File* and *View Output*:

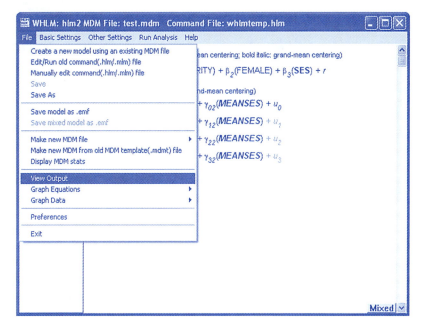

This is the output generated:

```
Program:              HLM 6 Hierarchical Linear and Nonlinear Modeling
Authors:              Stephen Raudenbush, Tony Bryk, & Richard Congdon
Publisher:            Scientific Software International, Inc. (c) 2000
                                            techsupport@ssicentral.com
                                                    www.ssicentral.com
--------------------------------------------------------------------------
Module:    HLM2S.EXE (6.06.2857.2)
Date:      24 February 2009, Tuesday
Time:         3:16: 2
--------------------------------------------------------------------------


SPECIFICATIONS FOR THIS HLM2 RUN


 Problem Title: no title

 The data source for this run  = C:\HLM6 Student Examples\Chapter2\test.mdm
 The command file for this run = whlmtemp.hlm
 Output file name             = C:\HLM6 Student Examples\Chapter2\hlm2.txt
 The maximum number of level-1 units = 7185
 The maximum number of level-2 units = 160
 The maximum number of iterations = 100
 Method of estimation: restricted maximum likelihood

Weighting Specification
-----------------------
                         Weight
                         Variable
           Weighting?    Name        Normalized?
Level 1       no
Level 2       no
Precision     no

 The outcome variable is  MATHACH

 The model specified for the fixed effects was:
 ----------------------------------------------------


  Level-1                 Level-2
  Coefficients            Predictors
 ---------------------    ---------------

          INTRCPT1, B0    INTRCPT2, G00
                          SECTOR, G01
$                         MEANSES, G02
#  MINORITY slope, B1     INTRCPT2, G10
                          SECTOR, G11
$                         MEANSES, G12
#    FEMALE slope, B2     INTRCPT2, G20
                          SECTOR, G21
$                         MEANSES, G22
#*      SES slope, B3     INTRCPT2, G30
                          SECTOR, G31
$                         MEANSES, G32

'#' - The residual parameter variance for this level-1 coefficient has been set
      to zero.
'*' - This level-1 predictor has been centered around its group mean.
'$' - This level-2 predictor has been centered around its grand mean.

The model specified for the covariance components was:
  --------------------------------------------------------


          Sigma squared (constant across level    -2 units )

          Tau dimensions
                INTRCPT1


 Summary of the model specified (in equation format)
 --------------------------------------------------


Level -1 Model

Y = B0 + B1*(MINORITY) + B2*(FEMALE) + B3*(SES) + R

Level -2 Model
B0 = G00 + G01 *(SECTOR) + G02*(MEANSES) + U0
B1 = G10 + G11 *(SECTOR) + G12*(MEANSES)
B2 = G20 + G21 *(SECTOR) + G22*(MEANSES)
B3 = G30 + G31 *(SECTOR) + G32*(MEANSES)


Iterations stopped due to small change in likelihood function
```

```
******* ITERATION 6 *******

 Sigma_squared =     35.61167

 Tau
 INTRCPT1,B0     1.86780


Tau (as correlations)
 INTRCPT1,B0  1.000

 ----------------------------------------------------
  Random level-1 coefficient   Reliability estimate
 ----------------------------------------------------
   INTRCPT1, B0                        0.690
 ----------------------------------------------------

The value of the likelihood function at iteration 6 = -2.312380E+004


The outcome variable is  MATHACH

 Final estimation of fixed effects:
 ----------------------------------------------------------------------
                                    Standard          Approx.
   Fixed Effect       Coefficient   Error    T-ratio   d.f.    P-value
 ----------------------------------------------------------------------
 For      INTRCPT1, B0
   INTRCPT2, G00       13.503827   0.221830   60.875    157    0.000
     SECTOR, G01        1.178035   0.364151    3.235    157    0.002
    MEANSES, G02        4.234930   0.474552    8.924    157    0.000
 For MINORITY slope, B1
   INTRCPT2, G10       -3.783326   0.307249  -12.314   7173    0.000
     SECTOR, G11        1.858083   0.423266    4.390   7173    0.000
    MEANSES, G12       -0.723968   0.498259   -1.453   7173    0.146
 For   FEMALE slope, B2
   INTRCPT2, G20       -1.250390   0.209528   -5.968   7173    0.000
     SECTOR, G21        0.064459   0.368228    0.175   7173    0.861
    MEANSES, G22        0.024325   0.447518    0.054   7173    0.957
 For      SES slope, B3
   INTRCPT2, G30        2.479777   0.151783   16.338   7173    0.000
     SECTOR, G31       -1.308003   0.231827   -5.642   7173    0.000
    MEANSES, G32        0.990517   0.288955    3.428   7173    0.001
 ----------------------------------------------------------------------


The outcome variable is  MATHACH

 Final estimation of fixed effects
 (with robust standard errors)
 ----------------------------------------------------------------------
                                    Standard          Approx.
   Fixed Effect       Coefficient   Error    T-ratio   d.f.    P-value
 ----------------------------------------------------------------------
 For      INTRCPT1, B0
   INTRCPT2, G00       13.503827   0.220136   61.343    157    0.000
     SECTOR, G01        1.178035   0.388637    3.031    157    0.003
    MEANSES, G02        4.234930   0.495913    8.540    157    0.000
 For MINORITY slope, B1
   INTRCPT2, G10       -3.783326   0.337783  -11.200   7173    0.000
     SECTOR, G11        1.858083   0.456644    4.069   7173    0.000
    MEANSES, G12       -0.723968   0.479575   -1.510   7173    0.131
 For   FEMALE slope, B2
   INTRCPT2, G20       -1.250390   0.219433   -5.698   7173    0.000
     SECTOR, G21        0.064459   0.387763    0.166   7173    0.868
    MEANSES, G22        0.024325   0.432989    0.056   7173    0.956
 For      SES slope, B3
   INTRCPT2, G30        2.479777   0.144943   17.109   7173    0.000
     SECTOR, G31       -1.308003   0.231415   -5.652   7173    0.000
    MEANSES, G32        0.990517   0.314886    3.146   7173    0.002
 ----------------------------------------------------------------------


 Final estimation of variance components:
 ----------------------------------------------------------------------
 Random Effect        Standard    Variance    df   Chi-square  P-value
                      Deviation   Component
 ----------------------------------------------------------------------
 INTRCPT1,     U0      1.36667     1.86780    157   516.15480   0.000
   level-1,    R       5.96755    35.61167
 ----------------------------------------------------------------------
```

```
Statistics for current covariance components model
--------------------------------------------------
Deviance                       = 46247.604169
Number of estimated parameters = 2
```

To interpret our coefficients, let's look at the table titled "Final estimation of fixed effects (with robust standard errors)":

```
Final estimation of fixed effects
(with robust standard errors)
-------------------------------------------------------------------------
                                      Standard            Approx.
    Fixed Effect        Coefficient   Error     T-ratio   d.f.    P-value
-------------------------------------------------------------------------
For        INTRCPT1, B0
    INTRCPT2, G00        13.503827    0.220136   61.343    157     0.000
      SECTOR, G01         1.178035    0.388637    3.031    157     0.003
     MEANSES, G02         4.234930    0.495913    8.540    157     0.000
For MINORITY slope, B1
    INTRCPT2, G10        -3.783326    0.337783  -11.200   7173     0.000
      SECTOR, G11         1.858083    0.456644    4.069   7173     0.000
     MEANSES, G12        -0.723968    0.479575   -1.510   7173     0.131
For    FEMALE slope, B2
    INTRCPT2, G20        -1.250390    0.219433   -5.698   7173     0.000
      SECTOR, G21         0.064459    0.387763    0.166   7173     0.868
     MEANSES, G22         0.024325    0.432989    0.056   7173     0.956
For       SES slope, B3
    INTRCPT2, G30         2.479777    0.144943   17.109   7173     0.000
      SECTOR, G31        -1.308003    0.231415   -5.652   7173     0.000
     MEANSES, G32         0.990517    0.314886    3.146   7173     0.002
-------------------------------------------------------------------------
```

Now, let's look at our main screen in HLM:

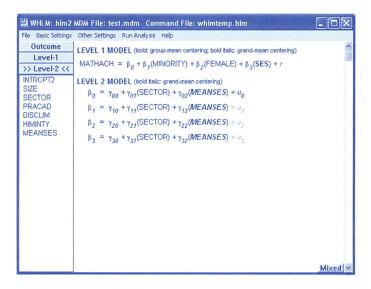

The equation for predicted math achievement can be represented as follows:

$$\text{Math Achievement} = \beta_0 + \beta_1(\text{Minority}) + \beta_2(\text{Female}) + \beta_3(\text{SES})$$

Or

Math Achievement $= [\gamma_{00} + \gamma_{01}(\text{Sector}) + \gamma_{02}(\text{Mean SES})]$
$+ [\gamma_{10} + \gamma_{11}(\text{Sector}) + \gamma_{12}(\text{Mean SES})][\text{Minority}]$
$+ [\gamma_{20} + \gamma_{21}(\text{Sector}) + \gamma_{22}(\text{Mean SES})][\text{Female}] + [\gamma_{30} + \gamma_{31}(\text{Sector})$
$+\gamma_{32}(\text{Mean SES})][\text{SES}]$

Based on the results of our analysis, the equation would be as follows:

Math Achievement $= [13.504 + 1.178(\text{Sector}) + 4.235(\text{Mean SES})]$
$+ [-3.783 + 1.858(\text{Sector}) + -0.724(\text{Mean SES})][\text{Minority}]$
$+ [-1.250 + 0.064(\text{Sector}) + 0.024(\text{Mean SES})][\text{Female}]$
$+ [2.480 + -1.308(\text{Sector}) + 0.991(\text{Mean SES})][\text{SES}]$

Our γ_{00} value is 13.504. This value represents our predicted value for the respondent's math achievement score if all our independent variables (*sector, meanses, minority, female,* and *SES*) were all zero. Our γ_{01} value of 1.178 represents the effect of sector on math achievement scores.

In our data set, the variable *sector* has been dichotomized between 0 and 1. Our value of 1.178 can be interpreted in the following way: Average math achievement scores in Sector 1 are 1.178 units higher than average math achievement scores in Sector 0. Our γ_{02} value was 4.235. This can be interpreted in the following way: For a 1 unit increase in *meanses*, math achievement scores are expected to increase by 4.235 units.

Next, I will interpret the coefficients corresponding to our *minority* Level 1 independent variable. First, we had a γ_{10} value of –3.783. In our data set, our minority variable was a dummy variable in which individuals who were a member of a minority race were coded 1 and others were coded 0. This value can be interpreted in the following way: Being a member of a minority race, when both of our Level 2 variables are equal to 0 (*sector* and *meanses*), is associated with a decrease in math achievement score by 3.783 units. Here, we are qualifying that our Level 2 variables must be equal to 0 because as you can see in the equation just presented both our Level 2 variables, *sector* and *meanses*, can alter the effect of minority on math achievement. In the example of *sector*, being in Sector 1 will serve to make the effect of *minority* on math achievement become less negative. Assuming that *meanses* is 0 for the purpose of this example, if a respondent resides in Sector 0, being a member of a minority race decreases their expected math achievement score by 3.783 points. However, if the respondent attends a school that is located in Sector 1, the new effect of minority race on math achievement score is –3.783 + 1.858(1), or –1.925. This new value can be interpreted in the following way: When *meanses* is equal to 0, out of those who attend schools residing in Sector 1, individuals of minority race are expected to have scores on math achievement 1.925 units lower than others. The value of *meanses* would also alter the effect of the minority race on math achievement scores in the same way. Likewise, as we can see in our equation, our Level 2 variables, *meanses* and *sector*, also alter the effect of our remaining Level 1 variables, *female* and *SES*, on math achievement scores. All these effects can be interpreted in the same way as our examples relating to minority race. Understanding hierarchical linear models and interpreting the results of these analyses is definitely more difficult than regressions or simpler statistical tests. However, with some practice and determination, all this will become second nature.

△   SECTION 3: SUMMARY

This chapter covered hierarchical linear modeling (HLM), which is a method that is used to analyze data that are "nested." While most data could be considered to be nested in some way, HLM is used specifically to analyze data in situations where the nested structure of the data is of particular importance. Data on schools are probably the most commonly used data in HLM analyses. The software program, also called HLM, is popularly used for HLM analyses and is quite user-friendly in regard to specifying and running hierarchical linear models. In this chapter, an example was presented in which math achievement scores were predicted using a set of Level 1 (individual level) and Level 2 (school level) independent variables.

RESOURCES

You can find more information about the HLM software program and how to purchase it by navigating to the following Web site: www .ssicentral.com/hlm/index.html

This book's Web site can be found at the following location: www .sagepub.com/kremelstudy

CHAPTER **10**

STRUCTURAL
EQUATION MODELING

OUTLINE OF CHAPTER

Section 1: Introduction

Section 2: AMOS

Introduction

Running a Model in AMOS

Modeling Nominal Variables

Running a Factor Analysis

Running a Model Using a Moderating Variable

Section 3: Summary

Resources

SECTION 1: INTRODUCTION

This final chapter covers structural equation modeling. While you will find
that structural equation modeling is in fact a very generalized statistical

model, I feel that it is similar to methods such as hierarchical linear modeling and factor analysis in that it tends to be used more often for particular types of models. Structural equation modeling is comparatively a very new statistical method and, while more powerful, is less often used than methods such as regression.

As a very general model, structural equation modeling can perform regressions and factor analysis, as well as other methods. However, if one is only performing a regression, for example, it is preferred to simply use that method itself as your statistical method, as the results will be easier to read and interpret. Structural equation modeling itself is preferred in situations where you want to run a model that cannot be run using simpler methods such as regression.

In structural equation modeling, you have two types of variables: exogenous variables and endogenous variables. First, let me present to you a simple model that will help explain the differences between these two types of variables.

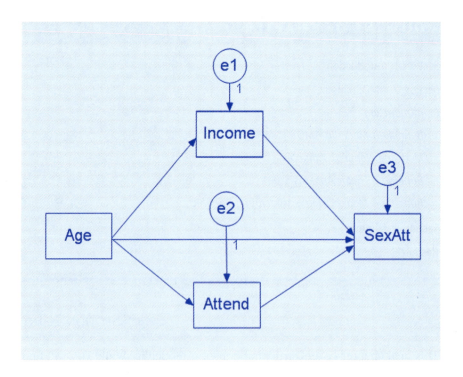

First, let me explain this model. In this model, our dependent variable is a single question that measures the respondent's permissiveness or nonpermissiveness about sex. We also have three predictor variables, the respondent's age, income, and religious attendance, which is a measure of how often the respondent attends religious services. As you can see, we have specified that age affects attitudes toward sex, age affects both income and religious attendance, and both income and religious attendance affect attitudes toward sex. As you can see, this is a more complex model that cannot be run simply using regression. While in a regression, you could specify a model in which attitude toward sex was predicted using income, age, and religious attendance, you could not specify a model in which one variable affects a second variable, which goes on to effect a third variable, as we have here in the case of age affecting income and religious attendance, which then affect attitudes toward sex. This type of model could also be analyzed using what is called path analysis. **Path analysis** is similar to structural equation modeling, although it can only include observed variables, or variables that are measured directly. This concept will be explained in more detail shortly. As path analysis is subsumed by structural equation modeling, it is not covered specifically in this book.

Now, to explain the difference between exogenous and endogenous variables. **Endogenous variables** are any variables that are specified to be predicted by one or more other variables. In this model, we have three endogenous variables. Sex attitudes is one endogenous variable because it is affected by income, age, and religious attendance. Income is also an endogenous variable because it is affected by age. Religious attendance is our third endogenous variable because it, too, is affected by age. On the other hand, **exogenous variables** are not predicted by any other variables. Our only exogenous variable in this model is the respondent's age, which is exogenous because there is no path leading into it from another variable.

Another aspect of this model are the three errors, which are represented by circles. As is customary within structural equation modeling, I have only specified errors for our endogenous variables. I will discuss errors in more detail in Section 2 of this chapter.

We have already covered one aspect of structural equation modeling that makes it unique: that you can specify one variable to affect a second variable, which then affects a third variable. In structural equation modeling, there is no limit to the number of "levels" that you can include in a model. A model such as the one below (variable names omitted) would not pose a problem within structural equation modeling.

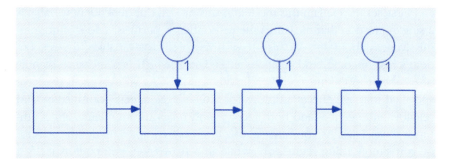

Another unique feature of structural equation modeling is the fact that it can incorporate what are called latent variables. Take, for example, the model presented below:

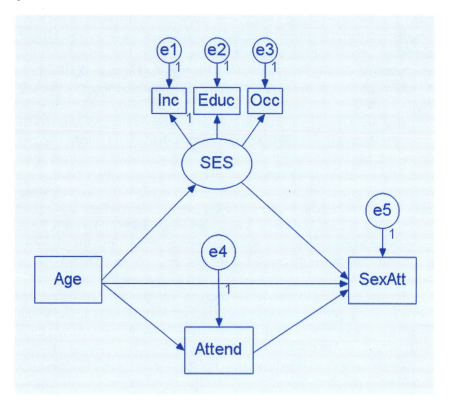

This is similar to the first model presented in this chapter, except that in this model, the respondent's income has been replaced with their socioeconomic status. In this model, socioeconomic status is the only **latent variable**, or variable that is not observed directly but instead consists of a series of observed variables. A latent variable can be thought of as a factor (as in factor analysis). The other variables in our model, age, income, education, occupational prestige, religious attendance, and sex attitudes are all **observed variables**, as they are measured directly. While in regression analysis, factor scores for a factor can be computed and then placed into an analysis, latent variables cannot be placed directly into a model as they can be in structural equation modeling. In structural equation modeling, latent variables are represented by circles or ovals, while observed variables are represented by squares or rectangles.

A third unique aspect of structural equation modeling is that it can be used to conduct a factor analysis. For example, the model below is an example of a factor analysis conducted on 10 variables that are specified to load on 2 factors (variable names omitted):

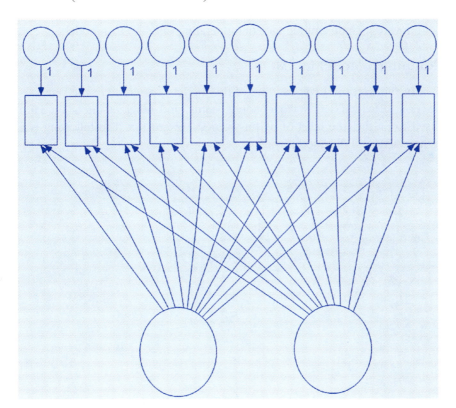

Introduction

There are several different programs that can be used for structural equation modeling, AMOS and LISREL being two of the most popular ones. I strongly recommend the use of AMOS over any other program for general work in structural equation modeling. You can find more information about the AMOS software program and how to purchase it by navigating to the following Web site: www.spss.com/AMOS/.

AMOS is very easy to use, and this program makes it very easy to correct problems with the specification of your model through the use of very user-friendly error messages. I have used LISREL in the past and find that it can be more difficult to use, especially for individuals new to statistics and structural equation modeling. Once you feel adept at structural equation modeling, LISREL may be worthwhile for you to look into.

In this chapter, I will first run you through how to specify a model in AMOS. I will then run the model. Finally, I will interpret its results. I will also cover how to conduct a factor analysis using structural equation modeling and how to include a moderator (a moderating variable) in a model.

Running a Model in AMOS

In this section, I will use one of the models presented in the previous section, in which age, socioeconomic status, and religious attendance are used to predict the level of permissiveness toward sex. The following is a reproduction of this model.

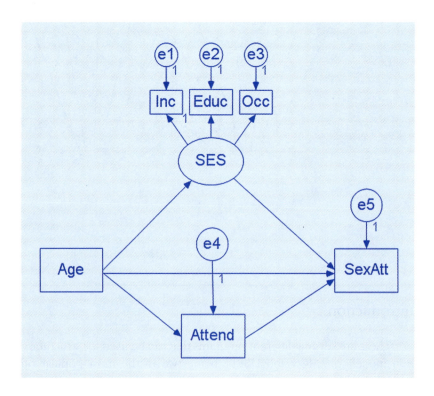

First, we will begin by opening the AMOS program. What we will see is the following screen:

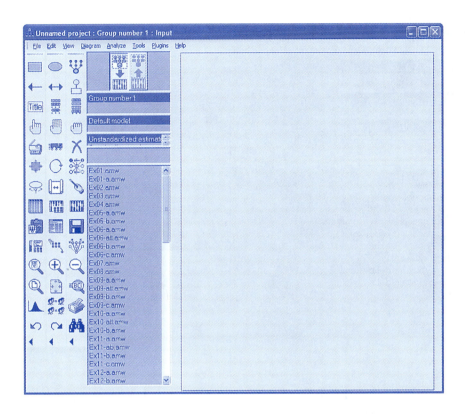

On the top bar, we have eight different menu selections. The three columns of pictures on the far left represent a number of different functions that are available to you in AMOS. The large area to the right taking up the majority of the screen is where you will specify your model within AMOS.

First, let's specify our age, religious attendance, and sex attitudes variables. As all these variables are observed variables, they are all represented by squares or rectangles. To make this selection, we will select the light blue rectangle in the far upper-left-hand corner of AMOS:

After this option has been selected, it will be highlighted, as you can see in the following picture:

Next, we can specify our age variable. To do this, we simply click and drag our mouse to form a rectangle somewhere in the general area of our workspace in AMOS:

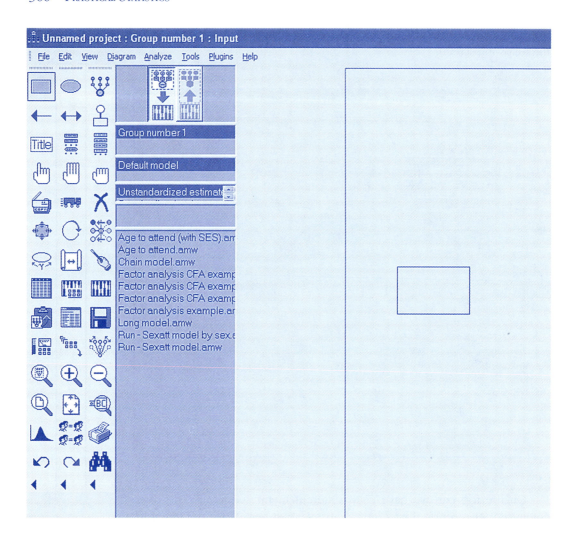

Next, to specify our religious attendance and sex attitudes variables, we can simply click our mouse two separate times. In AMOS, after creating a variable as we have just done, simply clicking the mouse additional times will create an identical copy of that same variable in terms of shape and size. To create another variable but represent it differently in regard to shape or size, simply click and drag the mouse as we have just done with our age variable. Following along with this model, we will click the mouse twice, generating something similar to the following image:

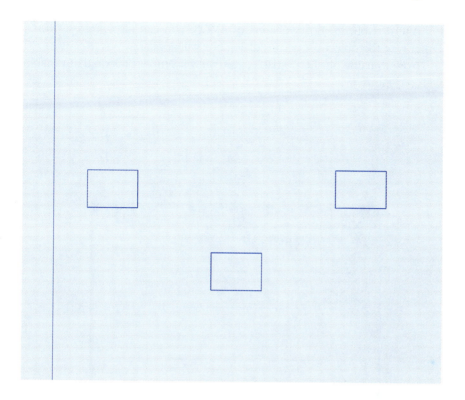

Now, before we get too far along in our model, let's name our three variables. The one on the far left is age, the one in the center is religious attendance, and the one on the right is sex attitudes. Copying our variable names from before, we'll name these variables *age*, *attend*, and *sexatt*. In AMOS, your observed variable names must always match the variables names as specified in your IBM SPSS file. To do this, first make the following menu selection:

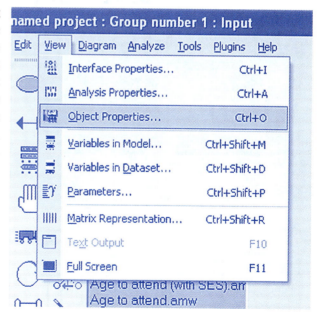

Alternatively, in most versions of AMOS, you can also press CTRL+O. Either way, the object properties dialog box will appear.

Now, to name our first variable, age, we will simply click on that variable with our mouse:

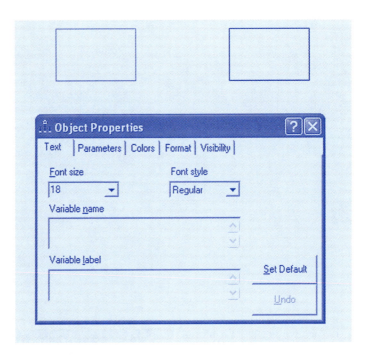

At this stage, we can type in our variable name:

As you can see, our model has now been updated to reflect this change. Next, we can click on the center variable and type "attend":

Finally, we will select the variable on the right and type "sexatt":

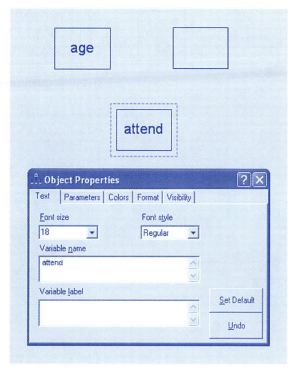

For now, we can close the *Object Properties* box. Our next step can be specifying our socioeconomic status latent variable in AMOS. Here, our first step will be to select the latent variable selection on the left.

Next, click and drag the mouse again to create a latent variable:

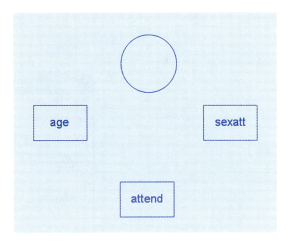

Now, click on this latent variable three times to create three indicators:

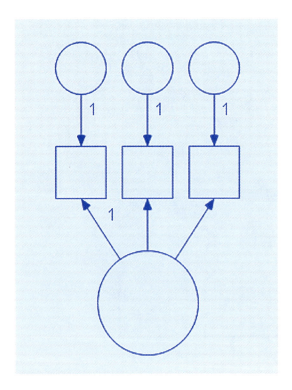

Now, let's name our four variables. First, open up the *Object Properties* dialog box again and click on our latent variable, naming it *SES*:

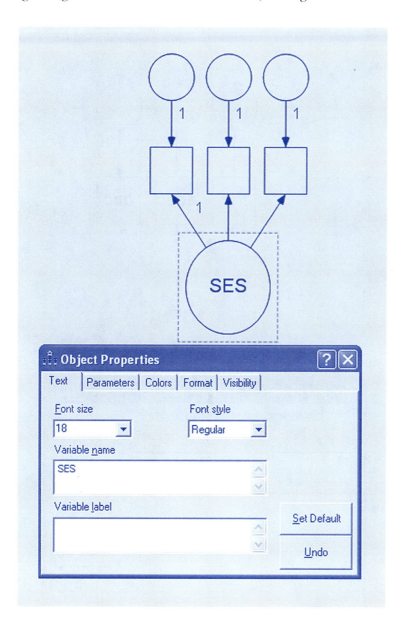

Unlike observed variables, we are allowed to name latent variables anything we like. Next, we can name each of our three indicators *inc*, *educ*, and *occ*:

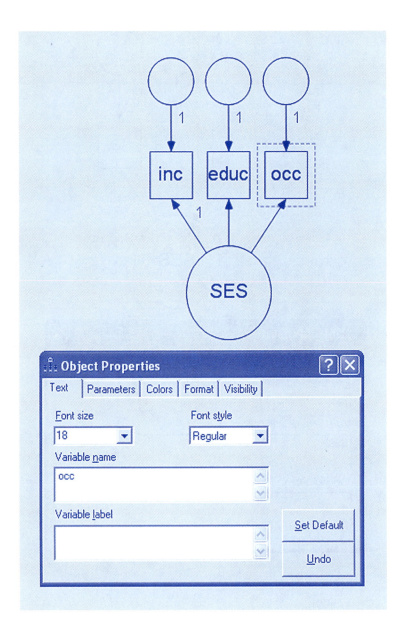

Now, let's specify and name our errors. Right now, we have the following model:

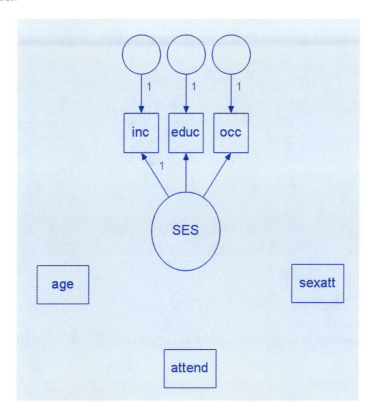

We already have errors for the three components of socioeconomic status—income, education, and occupational prestige. These were automatically specified by AMOS in our creation of the latent socioeconomic status variable. We now need to create errors for the remaining endogenous variables in our model, socioeconomic status, religious attendance, and sex attitudes. As mentioned previously, it is not customary within structural equation modeling to specify errors for exogenous variables, which in this model is the age variable. To specify our remaining errors, we will first make the following selection:

Next, we can click on the *attend* variable, creating the error:

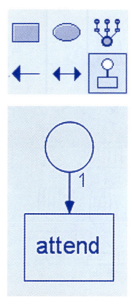

Now, we can simply click on our socioeconomic status latent variable and our sex attitudes variable:

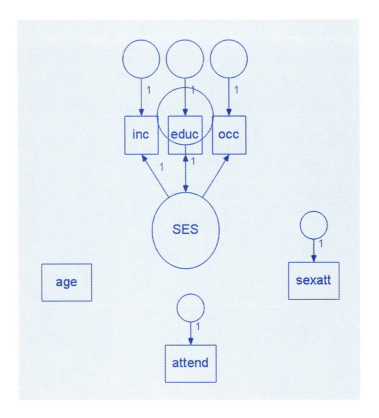

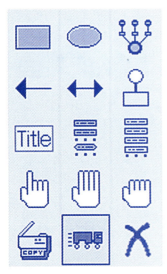

As you can see, the error for our socioeconomic status variable overlaps with the education variable. To fix this, we can simply move our error to the left. To do this, we will first select the button that looks like a train, which is used for moving objects:

Next, we can simply click and drag the error out of the way:

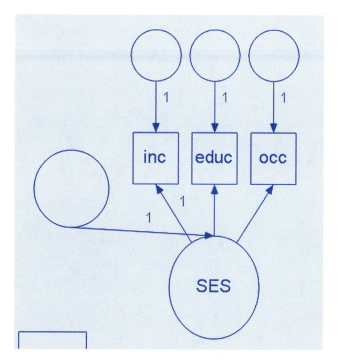

We can also move both sides of the arrow, again clicking and dragging either end, moving it:

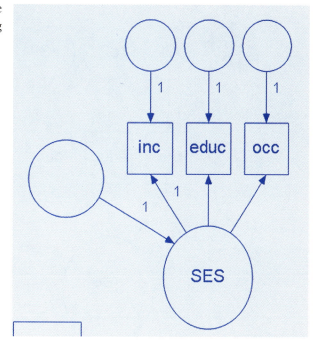

The *move* function can be very helpful in neatening our model up in AMOS. At this point, our model should look like this:

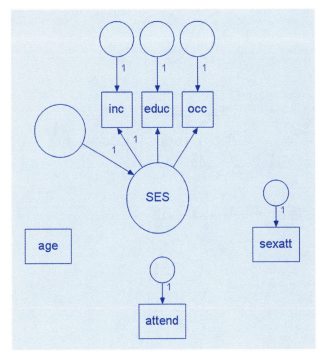

Now, we can name our errors. You can name your errors anything you wish, but I prefer to name them as *e1*, *e2*, *e3*, and so on just for the sake of simplicity. To do this, we'll once again open the *Object Properties* dialog box, either using the menus (*View→Object Properties*) or by pressing CTRL+O, and we can begin by naming the errors for income, education, and occupational prestige:

Next, we will name the error for socioeconomic status *e4*, the error for religious attendance *e5*, and the error for sex attitudes *e6*:

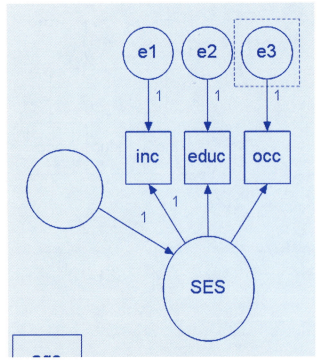

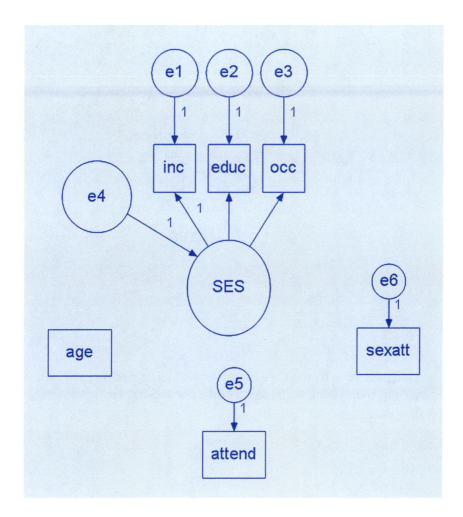

Now, the only thing we have left to do is to specify the paths between our variables. Specifically, we need to specify a path between age and socioeconomic status, between age and religious attendance, between socioeconomic status and sex attitudes, between religious attendance and sex attitudes, and between age and sex attitudes. First, we need to select the "Draw paths" button on the left:

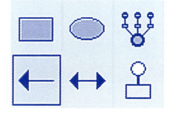

To draw the first path between age and socioeconomic status, we first need to click on our *age* variable and, holding our mouse button down, drag it to our *SES* variable, and then release the button. This will result in a path as shown here:

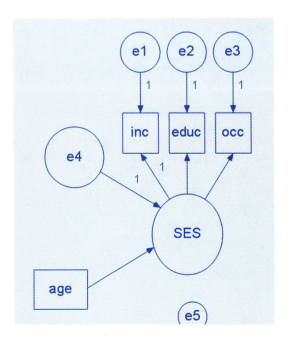

Using the same method, we can draw our four remaining paths. When completed, your model should look like the one shown here:

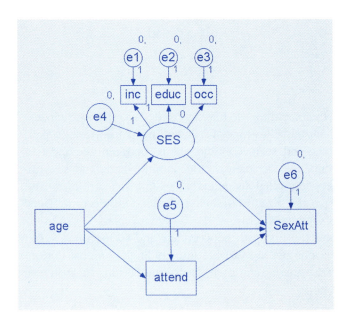

Of course, you do not need to specify the model in exactly the same order as we have in this section. For example, after drawing your variables, you can first draw the paths between your variables, then name them, then specify errors, and so on. At this point, we are finally able to run our model. Here, I will use data from the General Social Survey. If you wish to run the analysis yourself, go to this Web site: http://sda.berkeley.edu/cgi-bin/hsda? harcsda+gss04

Select *Download* and *Customized Subset*.

And choose to select the following variables: *year age educ prestg80 attend realrinc premarsx*

After downloading the file, we will rename our *prestg80* variable as *occ*, rename our *realrinc* variable as *inc*, and rename our *premarsx* variable as *sexatt*. We will also recode our variables so that respondents who replied with "not applicable," "don't know," and so on are recoded as missing. First, after saving our file, we will need to load it into AMOS. To do this, we'll make the following selection:

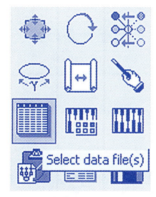

This will open the following dialog box:

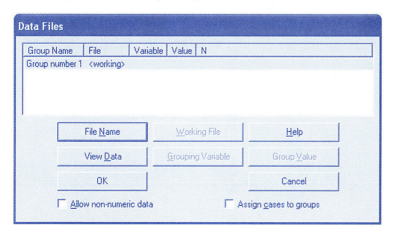

First, we will click on *File Name* and go to our IBM SPSS data file:

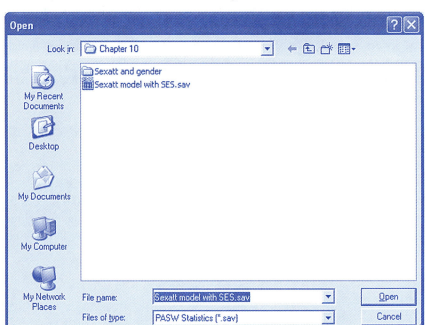

After selecting it and clicking *Open*, we can see that it has been loaded into AMOS:

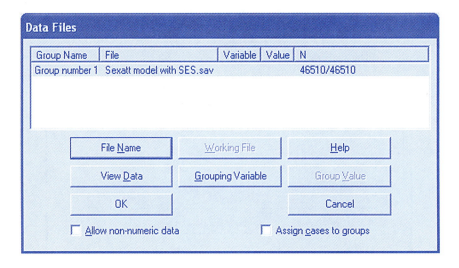

At this point, we can simply click *OK*. Clicking *View Data* in the dialog box just presented would open the data file within IBM SPSS.

Now, we're almost ready to run our model. As these data contain missing cases, we will first need to make a certain selection within AMOS. First, we will need to click on *View* and *Analysis Properties*:

Next, in the *Estimation* tab, we need to click the checkbox that says *Estimate means and intercepts*:

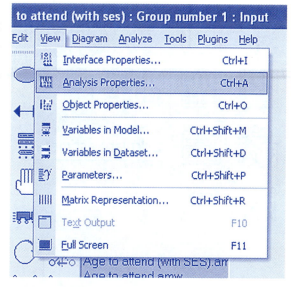

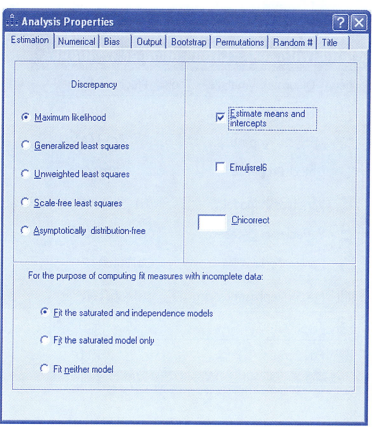

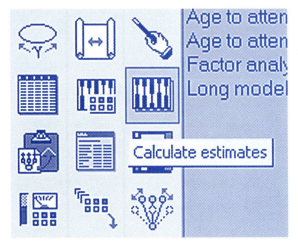

This always needs to be selected whenever you run a structural equation model in AMOS that contains missing data on one or more of the variables that are included in the model. If you forget, AMOS will simply remind you to make this selection.

Now, we can make the following selection to calculate estimates (run our model).

If all goes well, AMOS will not give us any error messages. If you do receive any error messages, they tend to be self-explanatory and easy to correct. After running the model, you can make the following menu selection to view the results of your analysis:

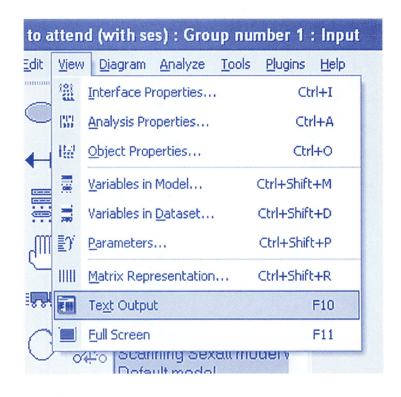

At first, you will see the following screen:

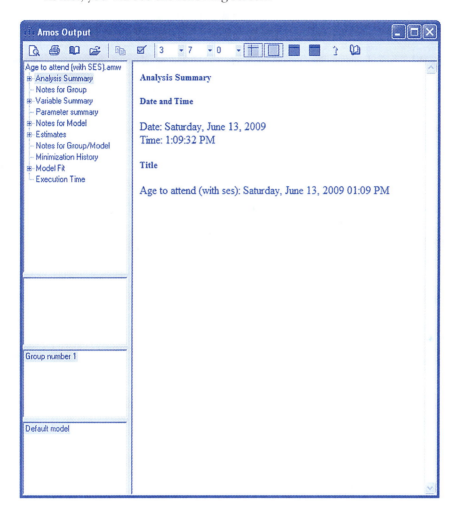

As you can see in the box in the top left-hand corner of the screen, there are a number of selections you can make when viewing your results. The selections that we will focus on in this section are the *Estimates* and *Model Fit* options.

With some older versions of AMOS, when viewing your output, you will commonly get the error:

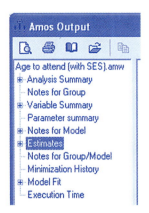

This is a bug in AMOS and can be safely ignored.
First, we will click on *Estimates*:
This will give us the main results of our analysis:

Estimates (Group number 1—Default model)
Scalar Estimates (Group number 1—Default model)
Maximum Likelihood Estimates
Regression Weights: (Group number 1—Default model)

Estimate			S.E.	C.R.	P	Label
attend	<---	age	.021	.001	29.317	***
SES	<---	age	-97.761	3.409	-28.680	***
SexAtt	<---	attend	-.180	.002	-73.565	***
SexAtt	<---	age	-.016	.000	-40.917	***
inc	<---	SES	1.000			
educ	<---	SES	.000	.000	33.906	***
occ	<---	SES	.001	.000	51.598	***
SexAtt	<---	SES	.000	.000	21.326	***

Means: (Group number 1—Default model)

Estimate	S.E.	C.R.	P	Label
age	45.267	.081	557.433	***

Intercepts: (Group number 1—Default model)

Estimate	S.E.	C.R.	P	Label
attend	2.948	.034	85.543	***

	Estimate	S.E.	C.R.	P	Label
SexAtt	4.247	.020	217.055	***	
inc	23845.642	198.317	120.240	***	
educ	14.661	.040	370.793	***	
occ	46.582	.171	272.999	***	

Variances: (Group number 1—Default model)

Estimate		S.E.	C.R.	P	Label
age	3 227.50	.2800	1522.25	***	
e5	7.084	.047	151.668	***	
e4	46854814.092	1919959.352	24.404	***	
e6	1.171	.010	117.374	***	
e1	395611474.253	3588135.904	110.255	***	
e2	-.710	.258	-2.757	.006	
e3	141.120	1.839	76.748	***	

The main set of results that we will focus on here are those listed under the *Regression Weights* heading:

Regression Weights: (Group number 1—Default model)

Estimate			S.E.	C.R.	P	Label
attend	<—-	age	.021	.001	29.317	***
SES	<—-	age	-97.761	3.409	-28.680	***
SexAtt	<—-	attend	-.180	.002	-73.565	***
SexAtt	<—-	age	-.016	.000	-40.917	***
inc	<—-	SES	1.000			
educ	<—-	SES	.000	.000	33.906	***
occ	<—-	SES	.001	.000	51.598	***
SexAtt	<—-	SES	.000	.000	21.326	***

These weights can be interpreted in the same way as unstandardized regression coefficients. Take, for example, the second estimate listed, which is the effect of age on socioeconomic status. The value of this estimate is −97.761. It can be interpreted in the following way: A one-year increase in age is associated with a decrease in socioeconomic status by 97.76 points. It could also be stated as follows: A one-year decrease in age is associated with an increase in socioeconomic status by 97.76 points. As you can see, this relationship is significant at the $p < .001$ level, signified by three asterisks. Let's look at the estimate of the relationship between age and sex attitudes. Here, we arrived at a value of −.016. This could be stated as follows: A one-year increase in age is associated with a decrease in premarital sex attitudes by 0.016 points. Of course, it is important to consider the directionality of your variables here, making sure to pay attention to, for example, whether a higher score on premarital sex attitudes means that the respondent is more permissive or less permissive. In this case, higher scores mean that the respondent was more permissive.

You can also instruct AMOS to calculate the **standardized coefficients** by navigating to the following menu selection:

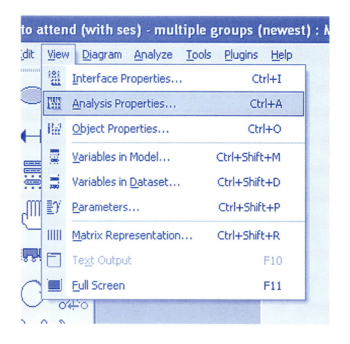

In the following dialog box, select the *Output* tab:

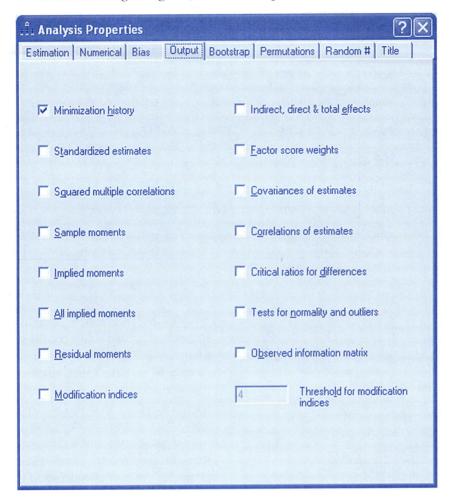

Here, all you need to do is to select the second option on the left-hand side, *Standardized estimates*. After running an analysis when this option is selected, AMOS will include a table of the standardized coefficients in your output under the *Estimates* selection.

Now, to return to the results of our analysis. Here, I have reproduced the table of our regression weights:

Regression Weights: (Group number 1—Default model)

Estimate			S.E.	C.R.	P	Label
attend	<---	age	.021	.001	29.317	***
SES	<---	age	-97.761	3.409	-28.680	***
SexAtt	<---	attend	-.180	.002	-73.565	***
SexAtt	<---	age	-.016	.000	-40.917	***
inc	<---	SES	1.000			
educ	<---	SES	.000	.000	33.906	***
occ	<---	SES	.001	.000	51.598	***
SexAtt	<---	SES	.000	.000	21.326	***

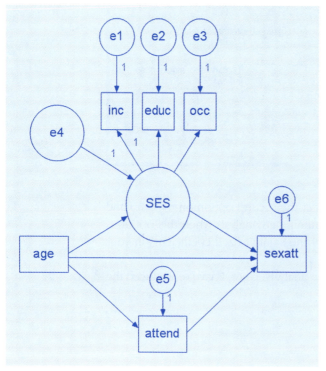

All the regression weights shown in the table above consist of what are called direct effects. A **direct effect** is simply that, an effect that one variable has directly on a second variable. An **indirect effect** is an effect that a variable has on a second variable through a third variable. To illustrate this, review the picture of our model as depicted in the following image:

As you can see, all the direct effects are modeled. One indirect effect is the effect of age on sex attitudes through socioeconomic status. Another indirect effect is the effect of age on sex attitudes through religious attendance. To get AMOS to calculate our indirect effects automatically, we can click on *View→Analysis Properties* and navigate to the *Output* tab, as shown here:

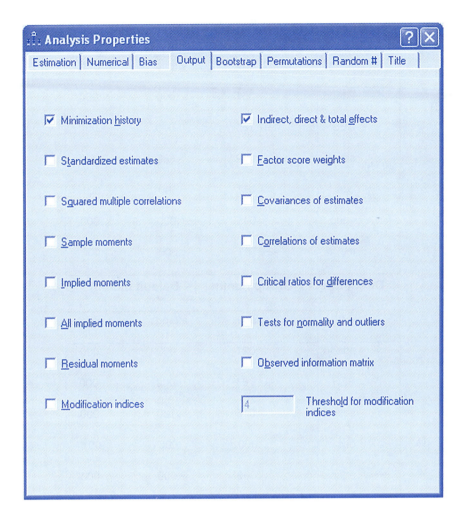

Here, we have simply selected the option on the top right: *Indirect, direct & total effects*. After running the model a second time, we will open the output and select the *Estimates* option. The tables are presented here:

Total Effects (Group number 1—Default model)

	age	attend	SES
attend	.021	.000	.000
SES	-97.761	.000	.000
sexatt	-.022	-.180	.000
occ	-.102	.000	.001
educ	-.045	.000	.000
inc	-97.761	.000	1.000

Direct Effects (Group number 1—Default model)

	age	attend	SES
attend	.021	.000	.000
SES	-97.761	.000	.000
sexatt	-.016	-.180	.000
occ	.000	.000	.001
educ	.000	.000	.000
inc	.000	.000	1.000

Indirect Effects (Group number 1—Default model)

	age	attend	SES
attend	.000	.000	.000
SES	.000	.000	.000
sexatt	-.006	.000	.000
occ	-.102	.000	.000
educ	-.045	.000	.000
inc	-97.761	.000	.000

Here, you can see that the total effect = the direct effect + the indirect effect. For example,

Total effect of age on attitudes = −.022

Direct effect of age on attitudes = −.016

Indirect effect of age on attitudes = −.006

Indirect effect + Direct effect = Total effect

−.016 + −.006 = −.022

−.022 = −.022

To calculate a single indirect effect yourself, which may be more useful, you can simply multiply the two direct effects together. For example,

Indirect effect of age on sex attitudes through attendance
= Effect of age on attendance × Effect of attendance on
sex attitudes = .021 × −.180 = −.00378

Also, you might have noticed that in our model, the path between SES and income is exactly 1. Let's review our model:

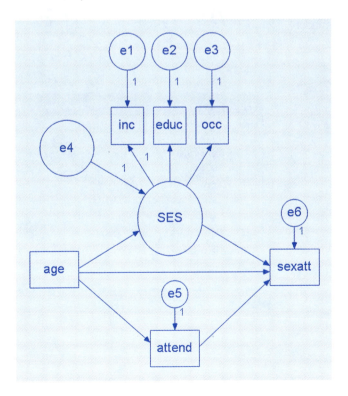

Here, we can see that the path between SES and income has already been specified to equal 1. In structural equation modeling, when including a factor in a model, either one of the indicators needs to be set to equal 1 or the factor variance needs to be set to equal 1. Setting one of the factor loadings to 1 tends to be more common. When doing this, it is best to choose the indicator that best represents your factor as well as the one that has the strongest correlations with the other indicators of your factor.

To specify which variable has a factor loading of 1, after creating the indicators for the factor, you could simply enter the name of the variable for which you wish to have a factor loading of 1 as the first indicator, as AMOS will automatically specify the first indicator to have a factor loading of 1. Alternatively, you could specify this yourself using the *Parameters* tab of the *Object Properties* dialog box. The factor loading is specified in the *Regression weight* field:

Next, let's look at our results under *Model Fit*:

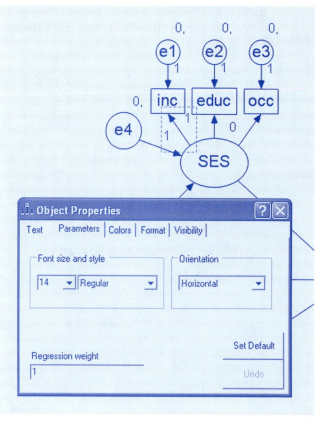

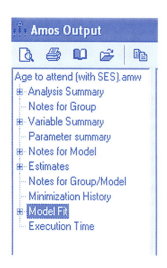

Model Fit Summary

CMIN

Model	NPAR	CMIN	DF	P	CMIN/DF
Default model	20	2787.000	7	.000	398.143
Saturated model	27	.000	0		
Independence model	6	24762.203	21	.000	1179.153

Baseline Comparisons

Model	NFI Delta1	RFI rho1	IFI Delta2	TLI rho2	CFI
Default model	.887	.662	.888	.663	.888
Saturated model	1.000		1.000		1.000
Independence model	.000	.000	.000	.000	.000

Parsimony-Adjusted Measures

Model	PRATIO	PNFI	PCFI
Default model	.333	.296	.296
Saturated model	.000	.000	.000
Independence model	1.000	.000	.000

NCP

Model	N PC	L 09 O	H 09 I
Default model	2780.000	2610.031	2957.276
Saturated model	.000	.000	.000
Independence model	24741.203	24226.788	25261.895

FMIN

Model	FMIN	F0	LO 90	HI 90
Default model	.060	.060	.056	.064
Saturated model	.000	.000	.000	.000
Independence model	.532	.532	.521	.543

RMSEA

Model	RMSEA	LO 90	HI 90	PCLOSE
Default model	.092	.090	.095	.000
Independence model	.159	.157	.161	.000

AIC

Model	AIC	BCC	BIC	CAIC
Default model	2827.000		2827.006	
Saturated model	54.000		54.008	
Independence model	24774.203		24774.205	

ECVI

Model	ECVI	LO 90	HI 90	MECVI
Default model	.061	.057	.065	.061
Saturated model	.001	.001	.001	.001
Independence model	.533	.522	.544	.533

HOELTER

Model	HOELTER .05	HOELTER .01
Default model	235	309
Independence model	62	74

These different measures of **model fit** measure how well our model accurately represents reality; that is, they are measures of how well the model that we specified accurately represents the different processes and relationships at work. While there are many different measures listed in this table, there are only a few that we need to focus on. The more popular measures of model fit include the significance level of our chi-square value, the ratio of chi-square divided by its degrees of freedom (**chi-square/*df* ratio**), **NFI (Normed Fit Index)** and **CFI (Comparative Fit Index)**, **RMSEA (root mean square error of approximation)**, and **Hoelter's critical *N***. The significance level of our chi-square value and the ratio of our chi-square divided by its degrees of freedom are presented in the first table:

CMIN

Model	NPAR	CMIN	DF	P	CMIN/DF
Default model	20	2787.000	7	.000	398.143
Saturated model	27	.000	0		
Independence model	6	24762.203	21	.000	1179.153

Here, we will want to look in the *Default model* row. Our actual chi-square value for the model is presented in the *CMIN* column. In our model, we had a chi-square value of 2787.0 with 7 degrees of freedom. This gave us a probability level of less than .001. In structural equation modeling, you actually want your chi-square value to not be significant. However, in models with larger sample sizes, you will almost always have a significant chi-square. So, in general, I would focus less on the significance value of your chi-square and more on the other popular methods of measuring model fit. Also, in this table, we have the ratio of chi-square divided by its degrees of freedom. This is listed in the final column under *CMIN/DF*. Our model achieved a value of 398.14. There are several different standards that are considered to be good model fit using this measure. Different authors have specified that 2, 3, or 5 be the upper limit for a model considered to have good model fit. Personally, I use the value 5, as I feel that the values of 2 and 3 are somewhat too conservative. Using this as a standard, models that have a value of 5 or less for the value of the chi-square divided by its degrees of freedom would be considered to have good model fit. As our model achieved a much higher value, that of 398.14, it would not be considered to have good model fit using this measure.

Next, NFI and CFI are also popular measures of model fit. Both of these measures range on a scale from 0 to 1. Both of these measures are listed in the second table and are reproduced here:

Baseline Comparisons

Model	NFI Delta1	RFI rho1	IFI Delta2	TLI rho2	CFI
Default model	.887	.662	.888	.663	.888
Saturated model	1.000		1.000		1.000
Independence model	.000	.000	.000	.000	.000

Our values for both NFI and CFI were .887 and .888, respectively. In general, models with scores for these measures of .9 or above are considered to have acceptable model fit, while models with scores of .95 or above are considered to have good model fit.

Possibly the most popular measure of model fit is RMSEA. This value is shown in the *RMSEA* table and is reproduced here:

RMSEA

Model	RMSEA	LO 90	HI 90	PCLOSE
Default model	.092	.090	.095	.000
Independence model	.159	.157	.161	.000

Our model achieved an RMSEA value of .092. This value indicates a marginal model fit. The following table presents the relationship between RMSEA values and model fit:

RMSEA	Model Fit
.05 or less	Good
.05 to .08	Acceptable
.08 to .10	Marginal
.10 or greater	Poor

Finally, the Hoelter's critical *N* is also used as an indicator of model fit. This table is the final one under *Model Fit*. It is reproduced here:

HOELTER

Model	HOELTER .05	HOELTER .01
Default model	235	309
Independence model	62	74

The Hoelter value refers to the sample size at which the significance level of our chi-square value crosses the .05 or .01 level. Using .05 as our standard, we achieve significance when our sample size is 235 or greater. This measure would only be used in situations where our chi-square is statistically significant, as it is here. To have acceptable model fit, this value should equal 200 or greater. As our value, 235, is greater than 200, the Hoelter value indicates that we have acceptable model fit.

As you can see, different measures of model fit give differing indications regarding how good or poor our model fit is. My preference is to look at these measures of model fit as a whole, while focusing especially on the ratio of our chi-square value to the degrees of freedom as well as the RMSEA value, which I believe to be two of the best indicators of model fit.

At this stage, we have specified our model, calculated estimates for the model, and reviewed both the calculated estimates for the paths in the model as well as the more popular measures of model fit. At this point in our analyses, we would perform what is called model trimming. **Model trimming** is a process in which the nonsignificant paths in our model are removed and the model is rerun until no more nonsignificant paths remain. After this process has been completed, we would review our final path estimates and model fit indicators and report this final set of results in our write-up or study.

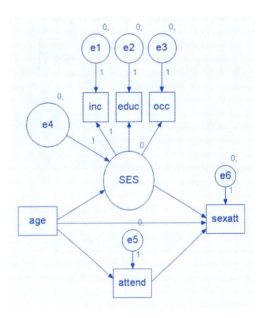

In the model that we ran, all our paths were significant. However, let's say that the path between age and sex attitudes was not significant at the .05 level. First, let's review our model:

Now, to remove the path between age and sex attitudes, we would first click on the following button:

Next, after we've made this selection, we would click on the path itself. The following should be your result:

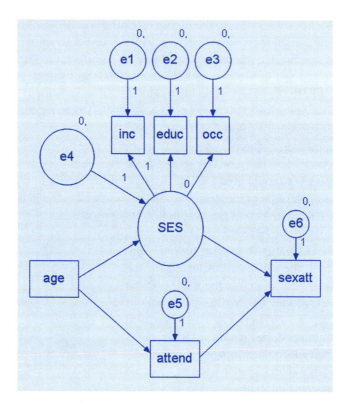

Next, we would simply rerun the model and view our results. Then, if we had any new nonsignificant paths, these paths would be removed and the model rerun. This process would be continued until we no longer had any nonsignificant paths. Finally, we would review and report our calculated estimates and measures of model fit.

In this example, our dependent variable was ordinal (categorical and ordered). For models that contain dependent or endogenous variables that are binary or dichotomous, MPLUS can be used, as AMOS is not able to handle binary endogenous variables. While your model will still run successfully in AMOS, the calculated results will be off.

Modeling Nominal Variables

If you remember from our chapter on regression, when including nominal independent variables (variables that are categorical and cannot be ordered) in a model, they need to be included as a series of dummy variables. To achieve this, one would select one of these categories as the comparison category and generate a series of dummy variables for each of the remaining categories. The same process would be conducted when running structural equation models. Take for example, race. In the chapter on linear regression, our race variable consisted of the following categories: white, black, and members of other races. White was selected as the comparison category, and dummy variables were created for blacks and for members of other races. Using the same example, if we wanted to include race as a variable in our model, we could first begin by choosing whites as the comparison category and create dummy variables for blacks and members of other races. As this topic has already been covered, I will not go through the process of creating dummy variables in detail. Simply for review, in this example, the dummy variable for blacks would equal 1 if the respondent was black and 0 if the respondent was not black. Also, the dummy variable for members of other races would equal 1 if the respondent was a member of another race and 0 if the respondent was not a member of another race. After these dummy variables have been created, we could include them in the model like this:

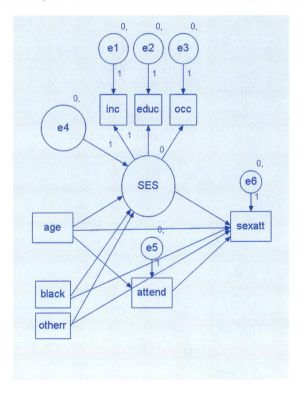

Just as in regression, we include the two dummy variables in our model but exclude the comparison category from our analysis. The results of such a model would show the effect of being black versus being white on both SES and sex attitudes as well as the effect of being a member of another race versus being white on both SES and sex attitudes.

Running a Factor Analysis

To run a factor analysis using structural equation modeling, you would first run a conventional factor analysis and determine the number of factors that you wish to keep. While you can also perform an exploratory factor analysis using structural equation modeling, I feel that you get a wider variety of information regarding how many factors you should keep when running a conventional factor analysis in a program such as IBM SPSS or Stata. After determining the number of factors to keep, you would specify your confirmatory factor analysis model in AMOS. While it is possible to specify particular parameters in regard to the factor loadings, the most common method is to simply let the factor loadings vary freely. Next, you would calculate your estimates for the model. It is also possible to compare several different models to determine which model of several has the best fit.

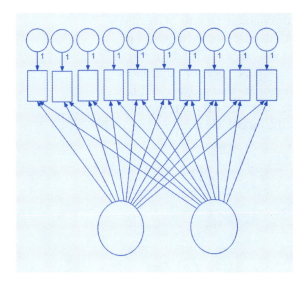

If you were to run an exploratory factor analysis in AMOS, it would look like the following model:

In the example just presented, there are 2 factors and 10 indicators, and paths are specified between both factors and all 10 indicators. A confirmatory factor analysis, on the other hand, would look like the model presented here:

In this confirmatory factor analysis, we have already identified not only the number of factors but also their components (i.e., which variables correspond to which factors). This is an example of a confirmatory factor analysis, which I will use in this section. In this example, we will study anti-Semitic attitudes.

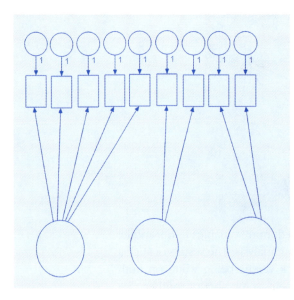

Here, I have first conducted a series of factor analyses with differing rotations in IBM SPSS and decided on varimax rotation.

Factor Analysis

[DataSet1] T:\Md book\#Data\Chapter 7\spss_data_final.sav

Communalities

	Initial	Extraction
farejews	1.000	.590
workjews	1.000	.567
influjew	1.000	.626
intljews	1.000	.515
patrjews	1.000	.402
violjews	1.000	.518
wlthjews	1.000	.591
livejews	1.000	.718
marjew	1.000	.692

Extraction Method: Principal Component Analysis.

Total Variance Explained

Component	Initial Eigenvalues			Extraction Sums of Squared Loadings			Rotation Sums of Squared Loadings		
	Total	% of Variance	Cumulative %	Total	% of Variance	Cumulative %	Total	% of Variance	Cumulative %
1	2.631	29.236	29.236	2.631	29.236	29.236	2.126	23.617	23.617
2	1.500	16.668	45.904	1.500	16.668	45.904	1.587	17.629	41.246
3	1.086	12.068	57.972	1.086	12.068	57.972	1.505	16.726	57.972
4	.870	9.667	67.639						
5	.703	7.816	75.455						
6	.630	7.001	82.456						
7	.551	6.123	88.579						
8	.540	6.004	94.584						
9	.487	5.416	100.000						

Extraction Method: Principal Component Analysis.

Component Matrix[a]

	Component		
	1	2	3
farejews	.766	-.021	.056
workjews	.750	-.029	.052
influjew	.313	-.282	.669
intljews	-.629	.064	.339
patrjews	.566	.204	-.201
violjews	-.484	.093	.524
wlthjews	.631	-.177	.401
livejews	.170	.817	.146
marjew	.085	.816	.139

Extraction Method: Principal Component Analysis.

a. 3 components extracted.

Rotated Component Matrix[a]

	Component		
	1	2	3
farejews	.596	.474	.101
workjews	.586	.464	.090
influjew	-.127	.776	-.089
intljews	-.710	-.096	.043
patrjews	.579	.102	.237
violjews	-.697	.124	.130
wlthjews	.288	.713	.003
livejews	.057	.003	.846
marjew	-.009	-.049	.830

Extraction Method: Principal Component Analysis.

Rotation Method: Varimax with Kaiser Normalization.

a. Rotation converged in 5 iterations.

Component Transformation Matrix

Component	1	2	3
1	.820	.554	.143
2	.002	-.253	.967
3	-.572	.793	.209

Extraction Method: Principal Component Analysis.

Rotation Method: Varimax with Kaiser Normalization.

This factor analysis uses principal component analysis for extraction and also uses varimax rotation. If you wish to follow along with this example, you can go to the following Web site: http://sda.berkeley.edu/cgi-bin/hsda?harcsda+gss04.

Select Download and Customized Subset

And choose to select the following variables: *farejews workjews influjew intljews patrjews violjews wlthjews livejews marjew*

These variables are nine separate measures of anti-Semitic attitudes. Specifically, they measure attitudes regarding Jews and welfare, Jews and work, the influence of Jews, the intelligence of Jews, the patriotism of Jews, the violence of Jews, the wealth of Jews, attitudes toward living in a Jewish neighborhood, and attitudes toward having a relative marry a Jew.

Based on the results of the factor analysis conducted in IBM SPSS, I have chosen to keep three factors. The first factor includes the following five variables: (1) Jews and welfare, (2) Jews and work, (3) the intelligence of Jews, (4) the patriotism of Jews, and (5) the violence of Jews. The corresponding variable names for these measures are *farejews, workjews, intljews, patrjews*, and *violjews*. The second factor includes the following two variables: the influence of Jews and the wealth of Jews. The corresponding variable names for these two measures are *influjew* and *wlthjews*. The third and final factor includes the following two measures: attitudes toward living in a Jewish neighborhood and attitudes regarding a close relative marrying a Jew. These two measures have the following variable names: *livejews* and *marjew*.

After specifying this model in AMOS, our path model should look like the following:

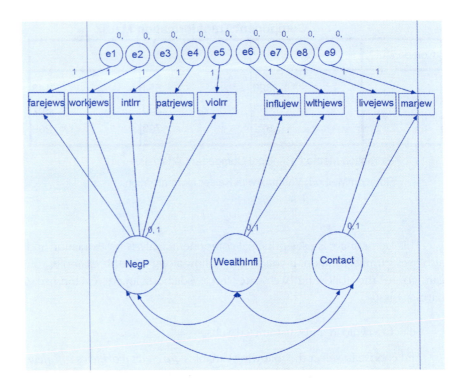

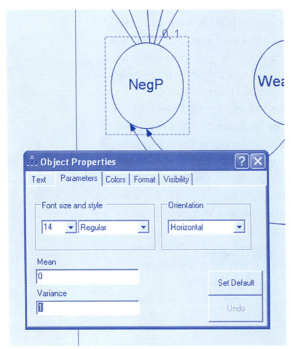

As you can see, I've named the three factors *NegP* (which stands for negative prejudices), *WealthInfl* (wealth and influence), and *Contact* (contact with Jews). I have also created flipped versions of the intelligence and Jews and Jews and violence variables, as these variables had negative factor loadings on Factor 1 as per our IBM SPSS factor analysis. In this example, instead of choosing one component of the factors to have a regression weight of 1, I have instead set the variance of each of the three factors to equal 1. This can be done simply by opening the *Object Properties* box, clicking on the *Parameters* tab, and clicking on the factor, as shown here:

I've also named the components of each of the three factors as well as named the errors of the indicators. Finally, I have also specified that each of the three factors be correlated with each of the others. To do this in AMOS, first make the following selection:

Next, simply click and hold the mouse button on one of the factors, drag it to the second factor, and release the mouse button. This would specify a correlation between these two factors.

At this point, I will load the data set into AMOS and calculate the estimates for this model after specifying *Estimate means and intercepts* under *View→Analysis Properties*, as this data set contains missing data. In this example, after we click *Calculate estimates*, AMOS may tell us that the three factors need to be uncorrelated and ask us whether we want to proceed or cancel the analysis:

Here, we can simply click *Proceed with the analysis*. Unless we find that we have specified the model incorrectly in some fashion, we can always click *Proceed with the analysis* if prompted by AMOS. After calculating the estimates, we get the following results for our estimates:

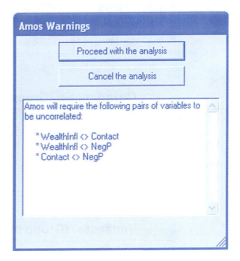

Estimates (Group number 1—Default model)

Scalar Estimates (Group number 1—Default model)

Maximum Likelihood Estimates

Regression Weights: (Group number 1—Default model)

Estimate			S.E.	C.R.	Label	
influjew	<---	WealthInfl	.205	.022	9.248	**
marjew	<---	Contact	.419	.071	5.938	**
livejews	<---	Contact	.862	.141	6.116	**
farejews	<---	NegP	.847	.034	24.939	**
workjews	<---	NegP	.886	.027	32.326	**
intlrr	<---	NegP	.719	.027	26.194	**
patrjews	<---	NegP	.639	.041	15.597	**
wlthjews	<---	WealthInfl	1.046	.074	14.192	**
violrr	<---	NegP	.411	.031	13.327	**

Intercepts: (Group number 1—Default model)

	Estimate	S.E.	C.R.	P	Label
farejews	2.377	.03176	.338	***	
workjews	2.954	.025118	.209	***	
intlrr	3.057	.025123	.391	***	
patrjews	3.076	.03783	.501	***	
violrr	3.314	.027124	.314	***	
influjew	1.919	.017110	.382	***	
wlthjews	2.983	.025119	.632	***	
livejews	2.747	.016167	.332	***	
marjew	2.789	.019149	.772	***	

Covariances: (Group number 1—Default model)

Estimate			S.E.	C.R.	P	Label
NegP	<—>	WealthInfl	.643	.047	13.774	***
WealthInfl	<—>	Contact	-.038	.024	-1.565	.118
NegP	<—>	Contact	.115	.030	3.795	***

Variances: (Group number 1—Default model)

Estimate	S.E.	C.R.	P	Label
WealthInfl	1.000			
Contact	1.000			
NegP	1.000			
e1	.647	.240	17.589	***
e2	.467	.037	20.729	***
e3	1.009	.036	27.711	***
e4	1.390	.064	22.477	***
e5	1.557	.047	33.287	***
e6	.334	.015	22.494	***
e7	.440	.149	2.954	.003
e8	−.026	.242	−.108	.914
e9	.750	.061	12.306	***

The first table, which shows the results of our path estimates, is reproduced here:

Regression Weights: (Group number 1—Default model)

Estimate			S.E.	C.R.	P	Label
influjew	<---	WealthInfl	.205	.022	9.248	***
marjew	<---	Contact	.419	.071	5.938	***
livejews	<---	Contact	.862	.141	6.116	***
farejews	<---	NegP	.847	.034	24.939	***
workjews	<---	NegP	.886	.027	32.326	***
intlrr	<---	NegP	.719	.027	26.194	***
patrjews	<---	NegP	.639	.041	15.597	***
wlthjews	<---	WealthInfl	1.046	.074	14.192	***
violrr	<---	NegP	.411	.031	13.327	***

In looking at this table, we can focus on the estimates for our factors. All the factor loadings are statistically significant, which is good. As we can see, for example, in regard to the negative prejudices factor, Jews and work has the highest factor loading, while the violence of Jews has the lowest loading. If we wanted to include these factors in a larger model, instead of creating new factor scores as we would in a customary factor analysis, we could simply include these latent variables in our model.

Next, we can view our covariances:

Covariances: (Group number 1—Default model)

Estimate			S.E.	C.R.	P	Label
NegP	<--->	WealthInfl	.643	.047	13.774	***
WealthInfl	<--->	Contact	-.038	.024	-1.565	.118
NegP	<--->	Contact	.115	.030	3.795	***

Here, we can see that while the covariance between negative prejudices and attitudes regarding wealth and influence is fairly strong, the other two covariances are quite weak. Also, the covariance between negative prejudices and attitudes toward wealth and influence as well as the covariance between negative prejudices and contact are both significant at the $p < .001$ level (indicated by ***), while the covariance between wealth and influence and contact is not statistically significant.

Finally, we should check our error variances for any negative values:

Variances: (Group number 1—Default model)

	Estimate	S.E.	C.R.	P	Label
WealthInfl	1.000				
Contact	1.000				
NegP	1.000				
e1	.746	.042	17.589	***	
e2	.764	.037	20.729	***	
e3	1.009	.036	27.711	***	
e4	1.390	.062	22.477	***	
e5	1.557	.047	33.287	***	
e6	.334	.015	22.287	***	
e7	.440	.149	2.954	.003	
e8	−.026	−.242	−.108	.914	
e9	.750	.061	12.306	***	

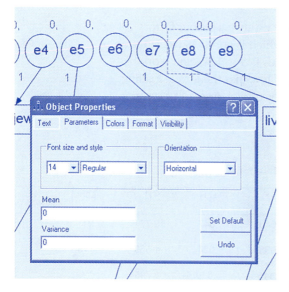

Here, we can see that our error variance for *e8*, which is the error for attitudes toward living in a Jewish neighborhood (*livejews*), is negative. Within structural equation modeling, this is also known as a **Heywood case**. We should correct this by going back to the model and setting its variance to 0. To do this, we would first open up the *Object Properties* dialog box, click on the *Parameters* tab, and finally click on *e8*. Then, we can simply set the variance equal to 0:

At this point, we would simply rerun our model and look at the new results.

Running a Model Using a Moderating Variable

At some point in your research, you may wish to run a model in which you hypothesize that the relationships between variables will differ depending on some categorical variable. For example, you might hypothesize that the relationship between drug use and risky sexual behavior will be different for males as compared with females or that it might differ between respondents of different religious affiliations. For example, you might hypothesize that drug use is more likely to lead to risky sexual behavior in males as compared with females. You might also hypothesize that higher levels of one variable would lead to higher levels of a second variable in one group but lead to lower levels of that second variable in another group. Using structural equation modeling, you can perform these types of tests, testing whether the estimates of your model are significantly different between different groups.

For an example, let's return to the example presented previously in this chapter in which the respondent's attitude toward premarital sex is predicted using their socioeconomic status, age, and religious attendance:

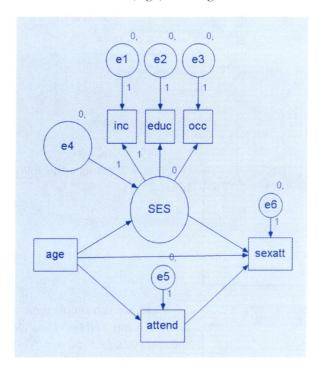

To test whether the estimates for this model differ between groups, we need to choose a categorical variable that will form the basis of our comparison. In this example, let's choose sex, testing whether this model differs between males and females.

First, I will download the data set from the following Web site: http://sda.berkeley.edu/cgi-bin/hsda?harcsda+gss04.

Next, I will select *Download* and *Customized Subset*.

I will choose to select the following variables: *year age educ prestg80 attend realrinc premarsx sex.*

As before, I will rename *prestg80* as *occ*, *realrinc* as *inc*, and *premarsx* as *sexatt*.

First, we will select *Analyze* and *Manage Groups*:

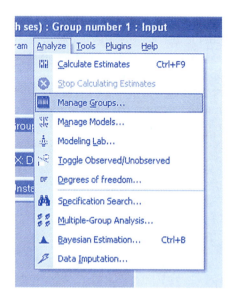

This will present the following dialog box:

Here, we can simply rename the group name "Group number 1" as "Male." To do this, simply select the text "Group number 1" and replace it with "Male." The dialog box should then appear as the one presented here:

Next, we will click on *New*. Then, we will specify the name of our new group to be "Female," as shown in the following image.

We will now select our "Male" group:

After selecting our "Male" group, we will select the "Select data file(s)" button:

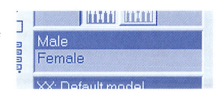

This will open the following dialog box:

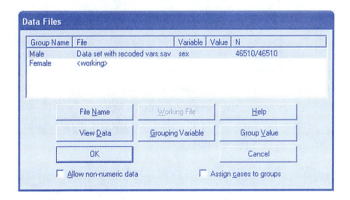

Now, we will select the *Grouping Variable* option. This will reveal the following dialog box:

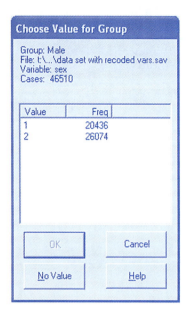

Here, we will select *sex* as our grouping variable and click *OK*. Back in the main dialog box, we'll now select *Group Value*. This will open the following dialog box:

In the General Social Survey, males are coded as 1, and females are coded as 2. As we are now defining our male group, we will select 1 under *Value* and click *OK*. After clicking *OK*, we will see that our *Data Files* dialog box has been updated:

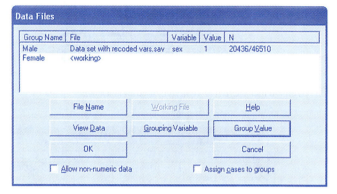

Now, we will have to define our female group. First, we will select the female group as shown in the previous image. Next, we will click *File name* and simply select the same data file that we used for our male group, as shown in the dialog box presented here:

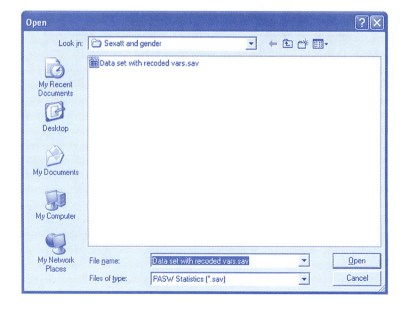

Then, we will once again click *Grouping Variable*, again selecting sex as our grouping variable:

We will then click *OK* and click *Group Value*. In the dialog box that appears, shown in the following image, we will select 2, as females are coded as 2, and click *OK*.

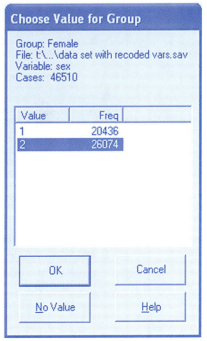

Finally, your *Data Files* dialog box should look like the one presented here:

Group Name	File	Variable	Value	N
Male	Data set with recoded vars.sav	sex	1	20436/46510
Female	Data set with recoded vars.sav	sex	2	26074/46510

Data Files

File Name | Working File | Help
View Data | Grouping Variable | Group Value
OK | | Cancel

☐ Allow non-numeric data   ☐ Assign cases to groups

Now, we can click on the *Multiple-Group Analysis* button:

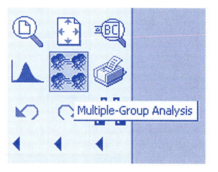

We can simply click *OK* when the following message appears:

Amos

The program will remove any models that you have added to the list of models at the left-hand side of the path diagram. It may also modify your parameter constraints.

OK   Cancel

Then, the following dialog box will appear, which shows the different models that will be analyzed in the multiple-group comparison. Along with these eight models, AMOS will also test the unconstrained model, a model in which no constraints are specified. As you can see in the following image, these eight constrained models progressively add more and more constraints to our model.

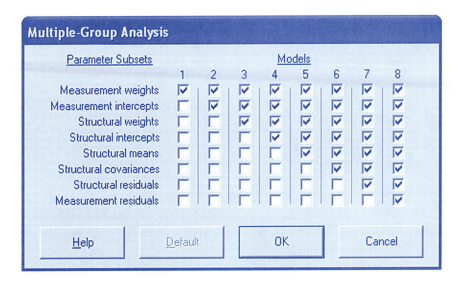

After clicking *OK*, we will see our model in AMOS updated as follows:

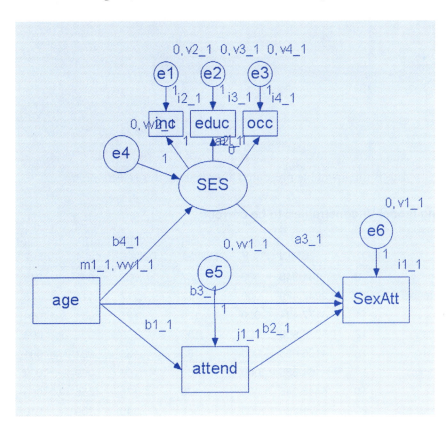

Next, we can click the *Calculate estimates* button:

After AMOS has finished calculating the estimates, we can open our output and click on the *Model Comparison* tab, which presents an overview of all the models analyzed in this analysis:

This is the first table presented after making this selection:

Assuming model Unconstrained to be correct:

Model	DF	CMIN	P	NFI Delta-1	IFI Delta-2	RFI rho-1	TLI rho-2
Measurement weights	3	181.940	.000	.007	.007	-.045	-.045
Measurement intercepts	7	2947.479	.000	.117	.117	.114	.115
Structural weights	11	3177.484	.000	.126	.126	.054	.054
Structural intercepts	12	4024.900	.000	.159	.160	.093	.093
Structural means	13	4106.955	.000	.163	.163	.081	.081
Structural covariances	14	164.835	.000	.165	.165	.069	.069
Structural residuals	16	4446.346	.000	.176	.176	.056	.056
Measurement residuals	20	8571.285	.000	.340	.340	.209	.210

The constrained models constrain values between males and females and are in essence simpler and more parsimonious models and therefore preferable to the unconstrained model. To test whether the constrained models can be used, we need to see whether the change in our chi-square value is significant based on the change in degrees of freedom. Our first constrained model is the constrained measurement weights model, in which the coefficients for the paths between our variables have been constrained between our male and female models. In the constrained measurement weights model, we see that the chi-square increased by 181.94 points, and the degrees of freedom increased by 3, as compared with the unconstrained model (in which everything is calculated separately for males and females). The critical chi-square for 3 degrees of freedom with a probability value of .05 is 7.82. Here, the difference between the unconstrained model and the constrained measurement weights model is statistically significant using the chi-square difference test. The unconstrained model has a lower chi-square value, which indicates that it is a significantly better fitting model as compared with the constrained measurement weights model. Because of this, we would have to prefer the unconstrained model to the constrained measurement weights model. At this point, we would stop here. If we did not find the unconstrained model to have significantly better fit as compared with the constrained measurement weights model, we would prefer the constrained measurement weights model. Next, we would compare the constrained measurement weights model with the constrained measurement intercepts model, which constrains the path coefficients as well as the intercepts. If the constrained measurement intercepts model did not have significantly worse fit as compared with the constrained measurement weights model, we would prefer the constrained measurement intercepts model to the constrained measurement weights model. We would continue with these comparisons, comparing each model only with the one directly below it, until we came to the point where the more constrained model was significantly worse than the less constrained model, at which point we would choose the less constrained model and end our comparisons.

The following table, under "Model Fit," shows the chi-square values and degrees of freedom for all models that were tested in this analysis:

CMIN

Model	NPAR	CMIN	DF	P	CMIN/DF
Unconstrained	40	3008.930	14	.000	214.924
Measurement weights	37	3190.870	17	.000	187.698
Measurement intercepts	33	5956.410	21	.000	283.639
Structural weights	29	6186.414	25	.000	247.457
Structural intercepts	28	7033.830	26	.000	270.532
Structural means	27	7115.885	27	.000	263.551
Structural covariances	26	7173.765	28	.000	256.206
Structural residuals	24	7455.276	30	.000	248.509
Measurement residuals	20	11580.215	34	.000	340.595
Saturated model	54	.000	0		
Inde pendence model	12	25235.754	42	.000	600.851

Just to illustrate, pretend that we have selected the measurement weights model as preferable to the unconstrained model. At this point, we will go back to the model comparison section. Now, we will focus on the second table shown, in which the measurement weights model is assumed to be correct.

Assuming model Measurement weights to be correct:

Model	DF	CMIN	P	NFI Delta-1	IFI Delta-2	RFI rho-1	TLI rho-2
Measurement intercepts	4	2765.540	.000	.110	.110	.160	.160
Structural weights	8	2995.544	.000	.119	.119	.099	.100
Structural intercepts	9	3842.961	.000	.152	.152	.138	.138
Structural means	10	3925.015	.000	.156	.156	.126	.126
Structural covariances	11	3982.895	.000	.158	.158	.114	.114
Structural residuals	13	4264.406	.000	.169	.169	.101	.101
Measurement residuals	17	8389.345	.000	.332	.333	.254	.255

As we can see here, all the models are significantly worse fitting than the measurement weights model. The first one shown, the constrained measurement intercepts model, has an increase in degrees of freedom of 4, but it has an increase in chi-square of well over 2,000. The critical chi-square value for 4 degrees of freedom with a probability level of .05 is only 9.49. As the constrained measurement intercepts model has an increase in chi-square of over 2,000 (and 2765.5 is greater than 9.49), this indicates significantly worse model fit. At this stage, we would select the constrained measurement weights model to be our best fitting model.

As can be seen from the following image (which was presented previously), each consecutive model adds additional constraints to the one presented previously.

In this hypothetical example, we preferred the constrained measurement weights model over the unconstrained model but did not prefer the constrained measurement intercepts model over the constrained measurement weights model. In the image above, we can see that the constrained measurement intercepts model constrained both the measurement intercepts and the measurement weights, keeping the constraints that were defined in the constrained measurement weights model but adding additional constraints as well. As you can see, each model tested progressively adds more constraints to the model.

△   Section 3: Summary

This chapter presented an overview of structural equation modeling, focusing on the ways in which structural equation models are uniquely different from the other statistical methods presented earlier in this book. Specifically, structural equation modeling allows what is called path analysis, in which it is possible to model the effect of one variable through a second variable on a third variable. Second, structural equation modeling allows the inclusion of what are called latent variables, or variables that are not measured directly but are instead constructed through the use of a number of indicators. One example of a latent variable is socioeconomic status, which can be measured through the use of the respondent's income, level of education, and occupational prestige. Finally, structural equation modeling uses a very general model that incorporates several statistical methods, including regression, factor analysis, and path analysis.

The second section of this chapter focused on the use of AMOS in structural equation modeling, which I feel is the best program for structural equation modeling in general. In this section, I covered how to run a model in AMOS, how to model nominal variables in AMOS (variables that are categorical but unordered), how to run a factor analysis using structural equation modeling in AMOS, and finally, how to run a multiple-group comparison using structural equation modeling.

This concludes our book on practical statistics. I hope that you use this foundation of knowledge as a launching base from which you will expand your expertise on statistical methods. For many people, especially when beginning their study, statistics can prove to be very difficult. However, regardless of the field that you are in or your topic of interest, you'll likely find knowledge of statistics to be very useful both in regard to the research that you conduct as well as the literature that you read. There's a wealth of knowledge on statistical methods, and most of the chapters in this book could easily be developed into 500+-page volumes. I hope that for you, statistics becomes not only an important tool, but a passion.

Resources

You can find more information about AMOS and how to purchase it by navigating to the following Web site: www.spss.com/AMOS/

This book's Web site can be found at the following location: www .sagepub.com/kremelstudy.

Appendix A

Selecting the Appropriate Test

Pearson's *r*: tests the correlation, or strength of the relationship, between two continuous variables

Chi-Square: tests the relationship between two categorical variables or whether a single variable conforms to some specific distribution

t-test: tests the differences between two groups on some continuous dependent variable

ANOVA: tests the differences between two or more groups on some continuous dependent variable

Regression: tests the effects of one or more predictor variables on some dependent variable

Type of Regression	Nature of Dependent Variable
Linear regression	Continuous
Logistic regression	Binary
Ordered logistic regression	Ordinal (categorical and ordered)
Multinomial logistic regression	Nominal (categorical and unordered)
Negative binomial regression	Count
Poisson regression	Count

Factor Analysis: tests whether a number of variables are interrelated or in essence are measuring a single factor or concept

Time-Series Analysis: a series of tests used to model how levels of a variable change over time as well as to predict the future values of some variable

Hierarchical Linear Modeling: a model used to analyze nested data, particularly useful for estimating the effect that higher-level variables have on the effect of lower-level variables on an outcome, or dependent variable

Structural Equation Modeling: a complex yet very general model that incorporates latent variables and path analysis

APPENDIX B

TABLES OF SIGNIFICANCE

The Chi-Square Distribution

Critical Values of Chi-Square

df	α Level of Significance			
	.05	.02	.01	.001
1	3.84	5.41	6.64	10.38
2	5.99	7.82	9.21	13.82
3	7.82	9.84	11.34	16.27
4	9.49	11.67	13.28	18.46
5	11.07	13.39	15.09	20.52
6	12.59	15.03	16.81	22.46
7	14.07	16.62	18.48	24.32
8	15.51	18.17	20.09	26.12
9	16.92	19.68	21.67	27.88
10	18.31	21.16	23.21	29.59
11	19.68	22.62	24.72	31.26
12	21.03	24.05	26.22	32.91
13	22.36	25.47	27.69	34.53
14	23.68	26.87	29.14	36.12
15	25.00	28.26	30.58	37.70

	α Level of Significance			
df	.05	.02	.01	.001
16	26.30	29.63	32.00	39.25
17	27.59	31.00	33.41	40.79
18	28.87	32.35	34.80	42.31
19	30.14	33.69	36.19	43.82
20	31.41	35.02	37.57	45.32
21	32.67	36.34	38.93	46.80
22	33.92	37.66	40.29	48.27
23	35.17	38.97	41.64	49.73
24	36.42	40.27	42.98	51.18
25	37.65	41.57	44.31	52.62
26	38.88	42.86	45.64	54.05
27	40.11	44.14	46.96	55.48
28	41.34	45.42	48.28	56.89
29	42.56	46.69	49.59	58.30
30	43.77	47.96	50.89	59.70

SOURCE: This table is taken from Table IV of Fisher and Yates (1995), *Statistical Tables for Biological, Agricultural, and Medical Research,* published by Longman Group Ltd., London (previously published by Oliver and Boyd, Ltd., Edinburgh).

NOTE: Reject the null hypothesis if the derived chi-square value is equal to or greater than the tabled chi-square value.

t Distribution

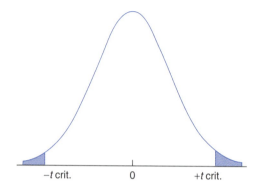

Two-Tailed or Nondirectional Test

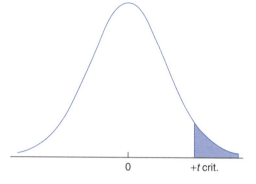

One-Tailed or Directional Test

	Level of Significance				Level of Significance		
df	.05	.01	.001	df	.05	.01	.001
1	12.706	63.657	636.62	1	6.314	31.821	318.31
2	4.303	9.925	31.598	2	2.920	6.965	22.326
3	3.182	5.841	12.924	3	2.353	4.541	10.213
4	2.776	4.604	8.610	4	2.132	3.747	7.173
5	2.571	4.032	6.869	5	2.015	3.365	5.893
6	2.447	3.707	5.959	6	1.943	3.143	5.308
7	2.365	3.499	5.408	7	1.895	2.998	4.785
8	2.306	3.355	5.041	8	1.860	2.896	4.501
9	2.262	3.250	4.781	9	1.833	2.821	4.297
10	2.228	3.169	4.587	10	1.812	2.764	4.144
11	2.201	3.106	4.437	11	1.796	2.718	4.025
12	2.179	3.055	4.318	12	1.782	2.681	3.930
13	2.160	3.012	4.221	13	1.771	2.650	3.852
14	2.145	2.977	4.140	14	1.761	2.624	3.787
15	2.131	2.947	4.073	15	1.753	2.602	3.733
16	2.120	2.921	4.015	16	1.746	2.583	3.686
17	2.110	2.898	3.965	17	1.740	2.567	3.646

	Level of Significance				Level of Significance		
df	.05	.01	.001	df	.05	.01	.001
18	2.101	2.878	3.922	18	1.734	2.552	3.610
19	2.093	2.861	3.883	19	1.729	2.539	3.579
20	2.086	2.845	3.850	20	1.725	2.528	3.552
21	2.080	2.831	3.819	21	1.721	2.518	3.527
22	2.074	2.819	3.792	22	1.717	2.508	3.505
23	2.069	2.807	3.767	23	1.714	2.500	3.485
24	2.064	2.797	3.745	24	1.711	2.492	3.467
25	2.060	2.787	3.725	25	1.708	2.485	3.450
26	2.056	2.779	3.707	26	1.706	2.479	3.435
27	2.052	2.771	3.690	27	1.703	2.473	3.421
28	2.048	2.763	3.674	28	1.701	2.467	3.408
29	2.045	2.756	3.659	29	1.699	2.462	3.396
30	2.042	2.750	3.646	30	1.697	2.457	3.385
40	2.021	2.704	3.551	40	1.684	2.423	3.307
60	2.000	2.660	3.460	60	1.671	2.390	3.232
120	1.980	2.617	3.373	120	1.658	2.358	3.160
∞	1.960	2.576	3.291	∞	1.645	2.326	3.090

F Distribution

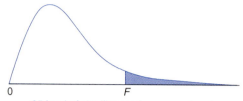

.05 level of significance (upper numbers)
.01 level of significance (lower numbers)

df₂	df₁									
	1	**2**	**3**	**4**	**5**	**6**	**7**	**8**	**9**	**10**
11	4.84	3.98	3.59	3.36	3.20	3.09	3.01	2.95	2.90	2.86
	9.65	7.20	6.22	5.67	5.32	5.07	4.88	4.74	4.63	4.54
12	4.75	3.88	3.49	3.26	3.11	3.00	2.92	2.85	2.80	2.76
	9.33	6.93	5.95	5.41	5.06	4.82	4.65	4.50	4.39	4.30
13	4.67	3.80	3.41	3.18	3.02	2.92	2.84	2.77	2.72	2.67
	9.07	6.70	5.74	5.20	4.86	4.62	4.44	4.30	4.19	4.10
14	4.60	3.74	3.34	3.11	2.96	2.85	2.77	2.70	2.65	2.60
	8.86	6.51	5.56	5.83	4.69	4.46	4.28	4.14	4.03	3.94
15	4.54	3.68	3.29	3.06	2.90	2.79	2.70	2.64	2.59	2.55
	8.68	6.36	5.42	4.89	4.56	4.32	4.14	4.00	3.89	3.80
16	4.49	3.63	3.24	3.01	2.85	2.74	2.66	2.59	2.54	2.49
	8.53	6.23	5.29	4.77	4.44	4.28	4.03	3.89	3.78	3.69
17	4.45	3.59	3.20	2.96	2.81	2.70	2.62	2.55	2.50	2.45
	8.40	6.11	5.18	4.67	4.34	4.10	3.93	3.79	3.68	3.59
18	4.41	3.55	3.16	2.93	2.77	2.66	2.58	2.51	2.46	2.41
	8.28	6.01	5.08	4.58	4.25	4.01	3.85	3.71	3.60	3.51

df$_2$	df$_1$									
	1	**2**	**3**	**4**	**5**	**6**	**7**	**8**	**9**	**10**
19	4.38	3.52	3.13	2.90	2.74	2.63	2.55	2.48	2.43	2.38
	8.18	5.83	5.01	4.50	4.17	3.94	3.77	3.63	3.52	3.43
20	4.35	3.49	3.10	2.87	2.71	2.60	2.52	2.45	2.40	2.35
	8.10	5.85	4.94	4.43	4.10	3.87	3.71	3.56	3.45	3.37
21	4.32	3.47	3.07	2.84	2.68	2.57	2.49	2.42	2.37	2.32
	8.02	5.78	4.87	4.37	4.04	3.81	3.65	3.51	3.40	3.31
22	4.30	3.44	3.05	2.82	2.66	2.55	2.47	2.40	2.35	2.30
	7.94	5.72	4.82	4.31	3.89	3.76	3.59	3.45	3.35	3.26
23	4.28	3.42	3.03	2.80	2.64	2.53	2.45	2.38	2.32	2.28
	7.88	5.66	4.76	4.26	3.94	3.71	3.54	3.41	3.30	3.21
27	4.21	3.35	2.96	2.73	2.57	2.46	2.37	2.30	2.25	2.20
	7.68	5.49	4.60	4.11	3.79	3.56	3.39	3.26	3.14	3.06
28	4.20	3.34	2.95	2.71	2.56	2.44	2.36	2.29	2.24	2.19
	7.64	5.45	4.57	4.07	3.76	3.53	3.36	3.23	3.11	3.03
29	4.18	3.33	2.93	2.70	2.54	2.43	2.35	2.28	2.22	2.18
	7.60	5.42	4.54	4.04	3.73	3.50	3.33	3.20	3.08	3.00
30	4.17	3.32	2.92	2.69	2.53	2.42	2.34	2.27	2.21	2.16
	7.56	5.39	4.51	4.02	3.70	3.47	3.30	3.17	3.06	2.98
32	4.15	3.30	2.90	2.67	2.51	2.40	2.32	2.25	2.19	2.14
	7.50	5.34	4.46	3.97	3.66	3.42	3.25	3.12	3.01	2.94
34	4.13	3.28	2.88	2.65	2.49	2.38	2.30	2.23	2.17	2.12
	7.44	5.29	4.42	3.93	3.61	3.38	3.21	3.08	2.97	2.89
36	4.11	3.26	2.86	2.63	2.48	2.36	2.28	2.21	2.15	2.10
	7.39	5.25	4.38	3.89	3.58	3.35	3.18	3.04	2.94	2.86
38	4.10	3.25	2.85	2.62	2.46	2.35	2.26	2.19	2.14	2.09
	7.35	5.21	4.34	3.86	3.54	3.32	3.15	3.02	2.91	2.82
40	4.08	3.23	2.84	2.61	2.45	2.34	2.25	2.18	2.12	2.07
	7.31	5.18	4.31	3.83	3.51	3.29	3.12	2.99	2.88	2.80

(Continued)

(Continued)

df₂					df₁					
	1	2	3	4	5	6	7	8	9	10
42	4.07	3.22	2.83	2.59	2.44	2.32	2.24	2.17	2.11	2.06
	7.27	5.15	4.29	3.80	3.49	3.26	3.10	2.96	2.86	2.77
44	4.06	3.21	2.82	2.58	2.43	2.31	2.23	2.16	2.10	2.05
	7.24	5.12	4.26	3.78	3.46	3.24	3.07	2.94	2.84	2.75
46	4.05	3.20	2.81	2.57	2.42	2.30	2.22	2.14	2.09	2.04
	7.21	5.10	4.24	3.76	3.44	3.22	3.05	2.92	2.82	2.73
48	4.04	3.19	2.80	2.56	2.41	2.30	2.21	2.14	2.08	2.03
	7.19	5.08	4.22	3.74	3.42	3.20	3.04	2.90	2.80	2.71
50	4.03	3.18	2.79	2.56	2.40	2.29	2.20	2.13	2.07	2.02
	7.17	5.06	4.20	3.72	3.41	3.18	3.02	2.88	2.78	2.70
55	4.02	3.17	2.78	2.54	2.38	2.27	2.18	2.11	2.05	2.00
	7.12	5.01	4.16	3.68	3.37	3.15	2.98	2.85	2.75	2.66
60	4.00	3.15	2.76	2.52	2.37	2.25	2.17	2.10	2.04	1.99
	7.08	4.98	4.13	3.65	3.34	3.12	2.95	2.82	2.72	2.63
65	3.99	3.14	2.75	2.51	2.36	2.24	2.15	2.08	2.02	1.98
	7.04	4.95	4.10	3.62	3.31	3.09	2.93	2.79	2.70	2.61
70	3.98	3.13	2.74	2.50	2.35	2.23	2.14	2.07	2.01	1.97
	7.01	4.92	4.08	3.60	3.29	3.07	2.91	2.77	2.67	2.59
80	3.96	3.11	2.72	2.48	2.33	2.21	2.12	2.05	1.99	1.95
	6.96	4.88	4.04	3.56	3.25	3.04	2.87	2.74	2.64	2.55
100	3.94	3.09	2.70	2.46	2.30	2.19	2.10	2.03	1.97	1.92
	6.90	4.82	3.98	3.51	3.20	2.99	2.82	2.69	2.59	2.51
125	3.92	3.07	2.68	2.44	2.29	2.17	2.08	2.01	1.95	1.90
	6.84	4.78	3.94	3.47	3.17	2.95	2.79	2.65	2.56	2.47
150	3.91	3.06	2.67	2.43	2.27	2.16	2.07	2.00	1.94	1.89
	6.81	4.75	3.91	3.44	3.14	2.92	2.76	2.62	2.53	2.44
200	3.89	3.04	2.65	2.41	2.26	2.14	2.05	1.98	1.92	1.87
	6.76	4.71	3.88	3.41	3.11	2.90	2.73	2.60	2.50	2.41

NOTE: Reject the null hypothesis if the derived F value is equal to or greater than the tabled F value. When $df_1 = \infty$ and $df_2 = \infty$, the tabled critical value of $F = 1.00$ at $p = .05$ and .01.

z Distribution

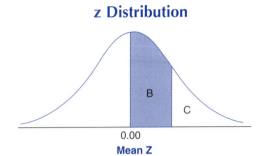

0.00
Mean Z

(A)	(B)	(C)	(A)	(B)	(C)	(A)	(B)	(C)
	Area	Area		Area	Area		Area	Area
	Between	Beyond		Between	Beyond		Between	Beyond
z	Mean and z	z	z	Mean and z	z	z	Mean and z	z
.00	.0000	.5000	.20	.0793	.4207	.40	.1554	.3446
.01	.0040	.4960	.21	.0832	.4168	.41	.1591	.3409
.02	.0080	.4920	.22	.0871	.4129	.42	.1628	.3372
.03	.0120	.4880	.23	.0910	.4090	.43	.1664	.3336
.04	.0160	.4840	.24	.0948	.4052	.44	.1700	.3300
.05	.0199	.4801	.25	.0987	.4013	.45	.1736	.3264
.06	.0239	.4761	.26	.1026	.3974	.46	.1772	.3228
.07	.0279	.4721	.27	.1064	.3936	.47	.1808	.3192
.08	.0319	.4681	.28	.1103	.3897	.48	.1844	.3156
.09	.0359	.4641	.29	.1141	.3859	.49	.1879	.3121
.10	.0398	.4602	.30	.1179	.3821	.50	.1915	.3085
.11	.0438	.4562	.31	.1217	.3783	.51	.1950	.3050
.12	.0478	.4522	.32	.1255	.3745	.52	.1985	.3015
.13	.0517	.4483	.33	.1293	.3707	.53	.2019	.2981
.14	.0557	.4443	.34	.1331	.3669	.54	.2054	.2946
.15	.0596	.4404	.35	.1368	.3632	.55	.2088	.2912
.16	.0636	.4364	.36	.1406	.3594	.56	.2123	.2877
.17	.0675	.4325	.37	.1443	.3557	.57	.2157	.2843
.18	.0714	.4286	.38	.1480	.3520	.58	.2190	.2810
.19	.0753	.4247	.39	.1517	.3483	.59	.2224	.2776

(Continued)

(Continued)

(A) z	(B) Area Between Mean and z	(C) Area Beyond z	(A) z	(B) Area Between Mean and z	(C) Area Beyond z	(A) z	(B) Area Between Mean and z	(C) Area Beyond z
.60	.2257	.2743	.85	.3023	.1977	1.10	.3643	.1357
.61	.2291	.2709	.86	.3051	.1949	1.11	.3665	.1335
.62	.2324	.2676	.87	.3078	.1922	1.12	.3686	.1314
.63	.2357	.2643	.88	.3106	.1894	1.13	.3708	.1292
.64	.2389	.2611	.89	.3133	.1867	1.14	.3729	.1271
.65	.2422	.2578	.90	.3159	.1841	1.15	.3749	.1251
.66	.2454	.2546	.91	.3186	.1814	1.16	.3770	.1230
.67	.2486	.2514	.92	.3212	.1788	1.17	.3790	.1210
.68	.2517	.2483	.93	.3238	.1762	1.18	.3810	.1190
.69	.2549	.2451	.94	.3264	.1736	1.19	.3830	.1170
.70	.2580	.2420	.95	.3289	.1711	1.20	.3849	.1151
.71	.2611	.2389	.96	.3315	.1685	1.21	.3869	.1131
.72	.2642	.2358	.97	.3340	.1660	1.22	.3888	.1112
.73	.2673	.2327	.98	.3365	.1635	1.23	.3907	.1093
.74	.2704	.2296	.99	.3389	.1611	1.24	.3925	.1075
.75	.2734	.2266	1.00	.3413	.1587	1.25	.3944	.1056
.76	.2764	.2236	1.01	.3438	.1562	1.26	.3962	.1038
.77	.2794	.2206	1.02	.3461	.1539	1.27	.3980	.1020
.78	.2823	.2177	1.03	.3485	.1515	1.28	.3997	.1003
.79	.2852	.2148	1.04	.3508	.1492	1.29	.4015	.0985
.80	.2881	.2119	1.05	.3531	.1469	1.30	.4032	.0968
.81	.2910	.2090	1.06	.3554	.1446	1.31	.4049	.0951
.82	.2939	.2061	1.07	.3577	.1423	1.32	.4066	.0934
.83	.2967	.2033	1.08	.3599	.1401	1.33	.4082	.0918
.84	.2995	.2005	1.09	.3621	.1379	1.34	.4099	.0901

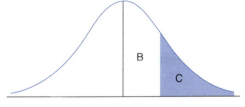

Mean Z

(A) z	(B) Area Between Mean and z	(C) Area Beyond z	(A) z	(B) Area Between Mean and z	(C) Area Beyond z	(A) z	(B) Area Between Mean and z	(C) Area Beyond z
1.35	.4115	.0885	1.70	.4554	.0446	2.05	.4798	.0202
1.36	.4131	.0869	1.71	.4564	.0436	2.06	.4803	.0197
1.37	.4147	.0853	1.72	.4573	.0427	2.07	.4808	.0192
1.38	.4162	.0838	1.73	.4582	.0418	2.08	.4812	.0188
1.39	.4177	.0823	1.74	.4591	.0409	2.09	.4817	.0183
1.40	.4192	.0808	1.75	.4599	.0401	2.10	.4821	.0179
1.41	.4207	.0793	1.76	.4608	.0392	2.11	.4826	.0174
1.42	.4222	.0778	1.77	.4616	.0384	2.12	.4830	.0170
1.43	.4236	.0764	1.78	.4625	.0375	2.13	.4834	.0166
1.44	.4251	.0749	1.79	.4633	.0367	2.14	.4838	.0162
1.45	.4265	.0735	1.80	.4641	.0359	2.15	.4842	.0158
1.46	.4279	.0721	1.81	.4649	.0351	2.16	.4846	.0154
1.47	.4292	.0708	1.82	.4656	.0344	2.17	.4850	.0150
1.48	.4306	.0694	1.83	.4664	.0336	2.18	.4854	.0146
1.49	.4319	.0681	1.84	.4671	.0329	2.19	.4857	.0143
1.50	.4332	.0668	1.85	.4678	.0322	2.20	.4861	.0139
1.51	.4345	.0655	1.86	.4686	.0314	2.21	.4864	.0136
1.52	.4357	.0643	1.87	.4693	.0307	2.22	.4868	.0132
1.53	.4370	.0630	1.88	.4699	.0301	2.23	.4871	.0129
1.54	.4382	.0618	1.89	.4706	.0294	2.24	.4875	.0125
1.55	.4394	.0606	1.90	.4713	.0287	2.25	.4878	.0122
1.56	.4406	.0594	1.91	.4719	.0281	2.26	.4881	.0119
1.57	.4418	.0582	1.92	.4726	.0274	2.27	.4884	.0116
1.58	.4429	.0571	1.93	.4732	.0268	2.28	.4887	.0113
1.59	.4441	.0559	1.94	.4738	.0262	2.29	.4890	.0110
1.60	.4452	.0548	1.95	.4744	.0256	2.30	.4893	.0107
1.61	.4463	.0537	1.96	.4750	.0250	2.31	.4896	.0104
1.62	.4474	.0526	1.97	.4756	.0244	2.32	.4898	.0102
1.63	.4484	.0516	1.98	.4761	.0239	2.33	.4901	.0099
1.64	.4495	.0505	1.99	.4767	.0233	2.34	.4904	.0096
1.65	.4505	.0495	2.00	.4772	.0228	2.35	.4906	.0094
1.66	.4515	.0485	2.01	.4778	.0222	2.36	.4909	.0091
1.67	.4525	.0475	2.02	.4783	.0217	2.37	.4911	.0089
1.68	.4535	.0465	2.03	.4788	.0212	2.38	.4913	.0087
1.69	.4545	.0455	2.04	.4793	.0207	2.39	.4916	.0084

(A) z	(B) Area Between Mean and z	(C) Area Beyond z	(A) z	(B) Area Between Mean and z	(C) Area Beyond z	(A) z	(B) Area Between Mean and z	(C) Area Beyond z
2.40	.4918	.0082	2.50	.4938	.0062	2.60	.4953	.0047
2.41	.4920	.0080	2.51	.4940	.0060	2.61	.4955	.0045
2.42	.4922	.0078	2.52	.4941	.0059	2.62	.4956	.0044
2.43	.4625	.0075	2.53	.4943	.0057	2.63	.4957	.0043
2.44	.4927	.0073	2.54	.4945	.0055	2.64	.4959	.0041
2.45	.4929	.0071	2.55	.4946	.0054	2.65	.4960	.0040
2.46	.4931	.0069	2.56	.4948	.0052	2.66	.4961	.0039
2.47	.4932	.0068	2.57	.4949	.0051	2.67	.4962	.0038
2.48	.4934	.0066	2.58	.4951	.0049	2.68	.4963	.0037
2.49	.4936	.0064	2.59	.4952	.0048	2.69	.4964	.0036

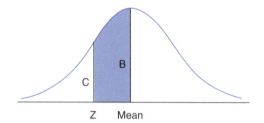

(A) z	(B) Area Between Mean and z	(C) Area Beyond z	(A) z	(B) Area Between Mean and z	(C) Area Beyond z	(A) z	(B) Area Between Mean and z	(C) Area Beyond z
2.70	.4965	.0035	2.95	.4984	.0016	3.20	.4993	.0007
2.71	.4966	.0034	2.96	.4985	.0015	3.21	.4993	.0007
2.72	.4967	.0033	2.97	.4985	.0015	3.22	.4994	.0006
2.73	.4968	.0032	2.98	.4986	.0014	3.23	.4994	.0006
2.74	.4969	.0031	2.99	.4986	.0014	3.24	.4994	.0006
2.75	.4970	.0030	3.00	.4987	.0013	3.30	.4995	.0005
2.76	.4971	.0029	3.01	.4987	.0013	3.40	.4997	.0003
2.77	.4972	.0028	3.02	.4987	.0013	3.50	.4998	.0002
2.78	.4973	.0027	3.03	.4988	.0012	3.60	.4998	.0002
2.79	.4974	.0026	3.04	.4988	.0012	3.70	.4999	.0001
2.80	.4974	.0026	3.05	.4989	.0011	3.80	.49993	.00007
2.81	.4975	.0025	3.06	.4989	.0011	3.90	.49995	.00005
2.82	.4976	.0024	3.07	.4989	.0011	4.00	.49997	.00003
2.83	.4977	.0023	3.08	.4990	.0010			
2.84	.4977	.0023	3.09	.4990	.0010			
2.85	.4978	.0022	3.10	.4990	.0010			
2.86	.4979	.0021	3.11	.4991	.0009			
2.87	.4979	.0021	3.12	.4991	.0009			
2.88	.4980	.0020	3.13	.4991	.0009			
2.89	.4981	.0019	3.14	.4992	.0008			
2.90	.4981	.0019	3.15	.4992	.0008			
2.91	.4982	.0018	3.16	.4992	.0008			
2.92	.4982	.0018	3.17	.4992	.0008			
2.93	.4983	.0017	3.18	.4993	.0008			
2.94	.4984	.0016	3.19	.4993	.0007			

Pearson's *r*

Critical Values of Pearson's *r*

	α Level of Significance			
One-Tailed:	0.05	0.025	0.005	0.0005
Two-Tailed:	0.1	0.05	0.01	0.001
df *				
1	0.9877	0.9969	0.9999	1.0000
2	0.9000	0.9500	0.9900	0.9990
3	0.8054	0.8783	0.9587	0.9911
4	0.7293	0.8114	0.9172	0.9741
5	0.6694	0.7545	0.8745	0.9509
6	0.6215	0.7067	0.8343	0.9249
7	0.5822	0.6664	0.7977	0.8983
8	0.5494	0.6319	0.7646	0.8721
9	0.5214	0.6021	0.7348	0.8470
10	0.4973	0.5760	0.7079	0.8233
11	0.4762	0.5529	0.6835	0.8010
12	0.4575	0.5324	0.6614	0.7800
13	0.4409	0.5140	0.6411	0.7604
14	0.4259	0.4973	0.6226	0.7419
15	0.4124	0.4821	0.6055	0.7247
16	0.4000	0.4683	0.5897	0.7084
17	0.3887	0.4555	0.5751	0.6932
18	0.3783	0.4438	0.5614	0.6788
19	0.3687	0.4329	0.5487	0.6652
20	0.3598	0.4227	0.5368	0.6524
21	0.3515	0.4132	0.5256	0.6402

22	0.3438	0.4044	0.5151	0.6287
23	0.3365	0.3961	0.5052	0.6178
24	0.3297	0.3882	0.4958	0.6074
25	0.3233	0.3809	0.4869	0.5974
26	0.3172	0.3739	0.4785	0.5880
27	0.3115	0.3673	0.4705	0.5790
28	0.3061	0.3610	0.4629	0.5703
29	0.3009	0.3550	0.4556	0.5620
30	0.2960	0.3494	0.4487	0.5541
40	0.2573	0.3044	0.3932	0.4896
50	0.2306	0.2732	0.3542	0.4432
100	0.1638	0.1946	0.2540	0.3211
150	0.1339	0.1593	0.2083	0.2643
200	0.1161	0.1381	0.1809	0.2298
500	0.0735	0.0875	0.1149	0.1464
1000	0.0520	0.0619	0.0813	0.1038
10000	0.0164	0.0196	0.0258	0.0329
100000	0.0052	0.0062	0.0081	0.0104

*NOTE: $df = N - 2$

APPENDIX C

ADDITIONAL STATISTICAL TESTS AND EQUATIONS

SECTION 1: INTRODUCTION

While the statistical tests covered in the previous chapters of this book are the tests most commonly used in the social sciences, there are a large number of less-commonly used statistical tests that nonetheless have their place in statistics and in this volume. Some are used at times as alternatives for tests we have discussed when certain issues with the data present

435

themselves, while others are simply more specialized tests that are just not used very frequently.

△ ## SECTION 2: NON-PARAMETRIC ALTERNATIVES

Briefly, **parametric tests** make the assumption that our data are normally distributed, while **non-parametric tests** do not assume that our data are normally distributed. In essence, if our data are in fact not normally distributed, the results obtained when conducting a parametric statistical test may in fact be in error. While some statistical texts will simply recommend that you conduct a non-parametric alternative if your data are not found to be normally distributed, this is in fact a very complex, nuanced area that cannot be reduced to a single general recommendation. Researchers commonly disagree on the "robustness" of parametric tests or the degree to which estimates will be accurate in the face of assumption violation (e.g., the assumption that your data are normally distributed). There are many other very important issues that relate to assumptions and assumption violation, and because this is such a complex area, I feel that briefly and superficially covering how to test assumptions and then instructing the reader to conduct a non-parametric alternative if an assumption is violated would do more harm than good. This area gets even more nuanced as even non-parametric tests have assumptions of their own. So in this section, I am simply presenting a number of the more-frequently seen non-parametric tests for your reference.

> *Wilcoxon signed-rank test:* This test is the non-parametric equivalent of the paired *t*-test. It does not assume a normal distribution.

> *Mann-Whitney U test:* This test is the non-parametric equivalent of the independent samples *t*-test. It does not assume a normal distribution.

> *Kruskal-Wallis one-way ANOVA:* This test is the non-parametric equivalent of the ANOVA. It does not assume a normal distribution.

△ ## SECTION 3: TESTING FOR NORMALITY

Part A: Introduction

As discussed in Section 2 of this appendix, many statistical tests, including the *t*-test and ANOVA, assume that your dependent variable is normally distributed. Some tests that can be used to test for normality are the Kolmogorov-Smirnov test, the Shapiro-Wilk test, the Anderson-Darling test, the Shapiro-Francia test, and many others.

Part B: SPSS

In SPSS, first make the following menu selection:

This will open the following dialog box:

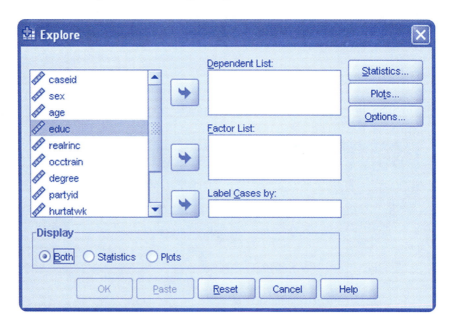

First, move your variable of interest into the *Dependent List* box, as shown here:

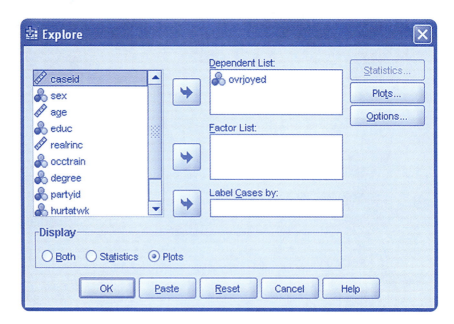

Next, click on the *Plots* button in the upper-right-hand corner. This will reveal the following dialog box:

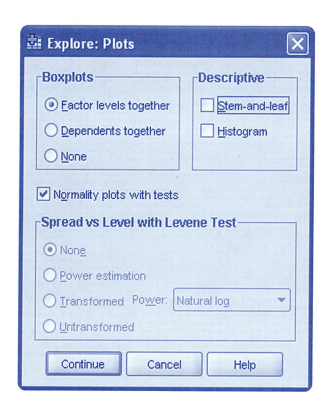

As shown, you will select *Normality plots with tests* and can deselect *Stem-and-leaf* under *Descriptive*. Then click *Continue* and *OK*. The relevant portion of the results are shown here:

Tests of Normality

	Kolmogorov-Smirnov[a]			Shapiro-Wilk		
	Statistic	df	Sig.	Statistic	df	Sig.
ovrjoyed	.229	1444	.000	.792	1444	.000

a. Lilliefors Significance Correction

In this example, both the Kolmogorov-Smirnov test as well as the Shapiro-Wilk test found this variable to be significantly nonnormal at the $p < .001$ probability level.

Part C: Stata

Stata supports the Shapiro-Wilk test, the Shapiro-Francia test, and it's own skewness-kurtosis test of normality. To run these tests in Stata, you can type the following commands, respectively:

```
swilk variable_name
sfrancia variable_name
sktest variable_name
```

Testing the *overjoyed* variable from a data set used earlier in this book, the following results were found:

```
. swilk ovrjoyed

                    Shapiro-Wilk W test for normal data
    Variable |    Obs         W          V          z       Prob>z
-------------+-----------------------------------------------------
    ovrjoyed |   1444     0.93355     58.583     10.22 8   0.00000


. sfrancia ovrjoyed

                    Shapiro-Francia W' test for normal data
    Variable |    Obs         W'         V'         z       Prob>z
-------------+-----------------------------------------------------
    ovrjoyed |   1444     0.93592     56.770     7.593    0.00001


. sktest ovrjoyed

                    Skewness/Kurtosis tests for Normality
                                        ------- joint ------
    Variable |  Pr(Skewness)   Pr(Kurtosis)   adj chi2(2)    Prob>chi2
-------------+-----------------------------------------------------
    ovrjoyed |     0.000          0.008            .          0.0000
```

In this final skewness-kurtosis test, the probability level is shown in the last row, under *joint* and *Prob>chi2*. The significant probability level found in all three of these tests indicates that this variable is significantly nonnormal.

SECTION 4: ADDITIONAL EQUATIONS △

This section includes a number of equations that are useful in specific situations. While you will most likely not find yourself using them too often, they are invaluable in situations where they are needed. They are also almost guaranteed to come up in more elementary statistics courses that you take.

Part A: The z Test and z Scores

The z test is used when one wishes to compare a single score with a group of scores or to compare two groups of scores. In short, z scores are used as a way to standardize scores and are also used to compare scores more easily. With z scores, the mean of scores will always be equal to 0, and the standard deviation will always be equal to 1. This is the way in which z scores are standardized. The z test is preferred over the t-test in situations where your sample size is greater than 30 *or* the population standard deviation is known.

When comparing a single score with a group of scores, one would use the following equation:

$$z = \frac{x - \mu}{\sigma}$$

where

z = the z score

x = the raw score, or original score

μ = the mean of the group of scores

σ = the standard deviation

For example, if you wanted to calculate the z score for an IQ score of 120, you would do the following:

$$z = \frac{x - \mu}{\sigma} = \frac{120 - 100}{15} = 1.33$$

Here, we plug in 120 for our raw or original score, and 100 and 15 for our mean and standard deviation, respectively, as IQ tests are standardized such that the mean is 100 and the population standard deviation is 15. If we were comparing a single score with a group that was not standardized in this way, we would first need to calculate the mean and standard deviation.

Now, looking at our z table in Appendix B, we see that for a z score of 1.33, we get a value of .4082. Our value of .4082 is the probability that an IQ score is between 100 (a z score of 0) and 120 (our raw score of 120/z score of 1.33). You could also say that 40.82% of individuals have an IQ score between 100 and 120. This is illustrated in the following image:

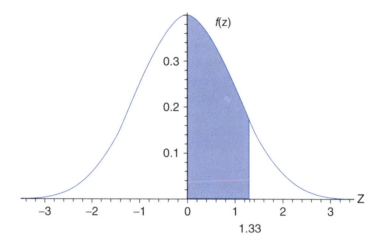

Here, the area shaded blue represents the area between the scores of 100 and 120 (raw), or between 0 and 1.33 (z scores). If we set the area under the entire normal curve equal to 1, this shaded green area would be equal to .4082. As mentioned in the previous paragraph, this could alternatively be stated in this way: The probability that an IQ score is between 100 and 120 (z scores of 0 and 1.33) is .4082. As you may have realized from the figure just presented, z scores and z tests assume that your data are normally distributed.

Here, our value of .4082 can be interpreted in the three following ways:

1. 40.82% of individuals have an IQ between 100 and 120.

2. .50 − .4082 = .0918; 9.18% of individuals have IQ scores more than 120.

    This is calculated by subtracting the area of the curve between 0 and 1.33 (.4082) from the entire area from 0 to infinity (.50).

3. .50 + .4082 = .9082; 90.82% of individuals have IQ scores between 0 and 120.

   This is calculated by adding the right half of the curve (from $z =$ negative infinity to $z = 0$), which is .50, to the area of the curve from $z = 0$ to $z = 1.33$ (.4082). The result is the percentage of individuals who have scores between the lowest score possible (a z score of negative infinity) and 120.

In this example, we simply used a z table to arrive at the value of .4082 for the area under the curve between the values of 0 and 1.33. While we would always normally simply use a z table to find these types of values, they are in fact calculated using the following equation:

$$\text{Area from } z_x \text{ to } z_y = \frac{1}{\sqrt{2\pi}} \int_{z=x}^{y} \ell^{\frac{-z^2}{2}} dz$$

where

z_x = the z score representing your lower boundary

z_y = the z score representing your upper boundary

e = the mathematical constant, approximately equal to 2.71828

π = the mathematical constant, approximately equal to 3.14159

This is a more complex equation that you would use a scientific calculator or computer to calculate. In the example just presented, the area under the curve from 0 to 1.33 would be calculated in the following way:

$$\text{Area from } z_0 \text{ to } z_{1.33} = \frac{1}{\sqrt{2\pi}} \int_{z=0}^{1.33} \ell^{\frac{-z^2}{2}} dz = 0.408241$$

The more general equation for the normal distribution is actually this:

$$\text{Area from } a_x \text{ to } a_y = \frac{1}{\sigma\sqrt{2\pi}} \int_{a=x}^{y} \ell^{\frac{-(a-\mu)^2}{2\sigma^2}} da$$

But in the case of the z distribution, where $\mu = 0$ and $\sigma = 1$, it reduces this:

$$\text{Area from } a_x \text{ to } a_y = \frac{1}{\sigma\sqrt{2\pi}} \int_{a=x}^{y} \ell^{-\frac{(a-\mu)^2}{2\sigma^2}} da = \frac{1}{1\sqrt{2\pi}} \int_{a=x}^{y} \ell^{-\frac{(a-0)^2}{2(1)^2}} da$$

$$= \frac{1}{\sqrt{2\pi}} \int_{a=x}^{y} \ell^{-\frac{a^2}{2}} da$$

When answering statistics problems, you will most likely never need to go to this level of complexity. However, I wanted to present the equation, in case you wanted a more detailed understanding of z scores.

To continue with our initial example, we can also determine the p value for the z test of whether our score of 120 differs significantly from the mean. What we can do is compare our z score with these standards:

z Score	p Level
±1.96	.05
±2.58	.01
±3.30	.001

Our p level for our z score of 1.33 was greater than .05, as 1.33 is not greater than our standard of 1.96, so it was not significantly different from the mean. To calculate the exact p level, we could simply double the value of the area of the curve in the "tail"—the area from $z = 1.33$ to infinity, which is .0918 × 2 or 0.1836.

If you think about it, you can use z scores and a z table to come up with much more. For example, say you wanted to find the percentage of individuals who had IQ scores between 120 and 130.

First, the z score for an IQ of 120:

$$z = \frac{x - \mu}{\sigma} = \frac{120 - 100}{15} = 1.33$$

Second, the z score for an IQ of 130:

$$z = \frac{x - \mu}{\sigma} = \frac{130 - 100}{15} = 2.0$$

This could be represented in the following way:

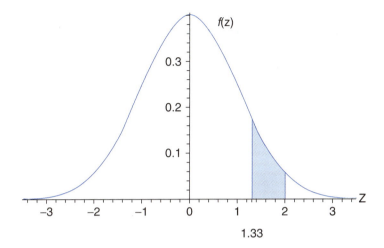

To determine the answer to our question, we need to calculate the area under the curve represented by the blue area in the previous figure. We could do this in the following ways:

1. [Area from $z = 0$ to $z = 2$] − [Area from $z = 0$ to $z = 1.33$] = [Area from $z = 1.33$ to $z = 2$]

This can represented pictorially as subtracting the dark blue area from the entire shaded area, leaving the light blue area:

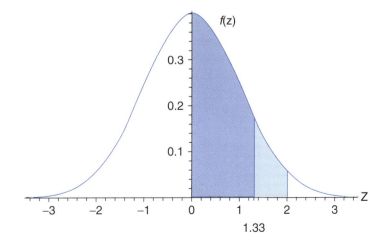

[Area from $z = 0$ to $z = 2$] − [Area from $z = 0$ to $z = 1.33$]
= 0.4772 − 0.4082 = 0.069 or 6.9%

Alternatively, we could do this:

2. [Area from $z = 1.33$ to $z =$ infinity] − [Area from $z = 2$ to $z =$ infinity] = [Area from $z = 1.33$ to $z = 2$]

This can represented pictorially as subtracting the dark blue area from the entire shaded area, leaving only the light blue area:

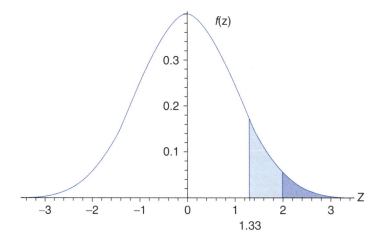

[Area from $z = 1.33$ to $z =$ infinity] − [Area from $z = 2$ to $z =$ infinity]
= .0918 − .0228 = 0.069 or 6.9%

As mentioned in the beginning of this section, z scores can also be used to compare two groups. Say we administer an IQ test to a class of 20 students, and we want to determine how they compare with the population (mean = 100, standard deviation = 15 for an IQ test). This is the equation we would use:

$$z = \frac{\bar{x} - \mu}{\sigma_{\bar{x}}} = \frac{\bar{x} - \mu}{\sqrt{\sigma/n}}$$

where

z = the z statistic

$\bar{x}$ = the mean of your sample

μ = the mean of your population

$\sigma_{\bar{x}}$ = the standard error of the mean

σ = the standard deviation of your population

n = the sample size

Say our mean was 120. Plugging our values into this equation, we would get the following:

$$z = \frac{\bar{x} - \mu}{\sigma_{\bar{x}}} = \frac{\bar{x} - \mu}{\sqrt{\sigma^2/n}} = \frac{102 - 100}{\sqrt{15/20}} = \frac{2}{.8660} = 2.31$$

Looking at our z table, the area from 0 to 2.31 is .4896. So the probability of a sample of this size having a mean between 0 and 2.31 is .4896 or 48.96%. The probability of a sample of this size having a mean anywhere below 2.31 is .5 + .4896 = .9896 or 98.96%, and the probability of a sample of this size having a mean above 2.31 is .5 − .4896 = .0104 or 1.04%.

Looking at the table from earlier,

z Score	p Level
±1.96	.05
±2.58	.01
±3.30	.001

We can see that the difference in scores between our sample and the population is significant at the $p < .05$ level, as our calculated z score of 2.31 is greater than the 1.96 standard at the $p = .05$ level. However, our result is not also significant at the $p < .01$ level.

Part B: The *t*-Test and *t* Scores

As mentioned earlier, the determination of a z score depends on knowing the population standard deviation. Within the study of the social sciences, this tends to be rare. If you do not know the population standard deviation, then the t statistic would be preferred over the z statistic. However, with larger sample sizes, a t value obtained from a t table will approximate a z value at the same probability level or level of significance.

A common rule of thumb is to prefer the t statistic when you have sample sizes less than 30 and to prefer the z statistic when you have sample sizes of 30 or greater. So in essence:

1. Population standard deviation known, $n < 30$: z statistic

2. Population standard deviation known, $n > 30$: z statistic

3. Population standard deviation unknown, $n < 30$: t statistic

4. Population standard deviation unknown, $n > 30$: z statistic

In the first two cases, we prefer the z statistic because the population standard deviation is known. In the fourth case, we use the z statistic as since the sample size is greater than 30, use of the t statistic is unnecessary as the t statistic approximates the z statistic in larger sample sizes. In the third case, where the population standard deviation is unknown and the sample size is less than 30, we prefer the t statistic.

The t statistic for a sample mean uses the following equation:

$$t = \frac{\bar{x} - \mu}{\left(\frac{s}{\sqrt{n}}\right)}$$

$$df = n - 1$$

where

t = the t score

$\bar{x}$ = the mean of the sample

μ = the mean of the population

s = the standard deviation of the sample

n = the sample size

As an example of calculating the t-statistic for a sample, if you administered an exam to 15 students, and the average score for these 15 students was 97 with a standard deviation of 57 and a population mean of 92, the t-score would be computed in the following way:

$$t = \frac{\bar{x} - \mu}{\left(\frac{s}{\sqrt{n}}\right)} = \frac{97 - 92}{\left(\frac{57}{\sqrt{15}}\right)} = \frac{5}{14.72} = 0.34$$

Now, while we would prefer to use the t statistic in this example as the population standard deviation is unknown and since the sample size is less than 30, I will also calculate the z statistic, plugging in our sample standard deviation in place of the population standard deviation and plugging in our sample mean in place of the population mean simply to illustrate the differences between the calculated t statistic and the z statistic in this example.

$$z = \frac{x - \mu}{\sigma} = \frac{97 - 92}{57} = 0.09$$

As you can see, there is a substantial difference between our calculated t statistic and our z statistic.

Part C: Confidence Intervals—The z Statistic

To explain what a confidence interval is, I will first describe the meaning of a point estimate. A **point estimate** is a single numerical estimate of some measure. An example of a point estimate might be, for the average yearly income among working Americans, $35,426. While our estimate may be close to the true value of this measure, it will almost definitely be off by some degree. In many cases, a **confidence interval** proves to be more useful than a point estimate of a measure as it specifies a range of values in which the true value is likely to lie as well as giving you the probability that the true value lies within your confidence interval or range.

Let's continue with the measure of the average yearly income among working Americans as an example of how to calculate a confidence interval for the population mean using a sample mean. In this example, our sample mean will consist of the average income in a random sample of 40 working Americans. Our population will consist of the entire American working population. This is the equation that we will use to calculate a confidence interval of the population mean:

$$95\% \text{ Confidence interval} = \bar{x} \pm 1.96\sigma_{\bar{x}} = \bar{x} \pm 1.96\left(\frac{s}{\sqrt{n}}\right)$$

So, if our mean was $34,596, our variance was $9,246, and if we had a sample size of 40 individuals, our 95% confidence interval would be:

$$95\% \text{ Confidence interval} = \bar{x} \pm 1.96\sigma_{\bar{x}} = \bar{x} \pm 1.96\left(\frac{s}{\sqrt{n}}\right)$$

$$= 34596 \pm 1.96\left(\frac{9246}{\sqrt{40}}\right) = 34596 \pm 2865.37$$

Upper limit of the 95% confidence interval = 34596 + 2865.37 = 37461.37

Lower limit of the 95% confidence interval = 34596 − 2865.37 = 31730.64

So we can say with a 95% degree of confidence that the population mean for the average yearly income of working Americans is between \$31730.64 and \$37461.37. As you might have noticed, the 1.96 value used in the previous equations is the equivalent z score at the .05 probability level as presented in a previous table, which is reproduced here:

z Score	p Level
±1.96	.05
±2.58	.01
±3.30	.001

By simply plugging the two other values into the equation just presented, we are able to calculate the confidence interval for the population mean at either a 99% or 99.9% level of confidence. For example, to determine the 99% confidence interval, you would simply use the following equation:

$$99\% \text{ Confidence interval} = \bar{x} \pm 2.58\sigma_{\bar{x}} = \bar{x} \pm 2.58\left(\frac{s}{\sqrt{n}}\right)$$

And to calculate the 99.9% confidence interval, you would use this equation:

$$99.9\% \text{ Confidence interval} = \bar{x} \pm 3.30\sigma_{\bar{x}} = \bar{x} \pm 3.30\left(\frac{s}{\sqrt{n}}\right)$$

As you may have noticed, there is a simple way to determine the equation for any percentage confidence interval. All we need to do is determine the corresponding z score for the probability level or confidence interval that we are interested in. For example, say we wanted to find the 80% confidence interval for some population mean. We could find the corresponding z score and hence the equation in one of two ways:

1. First, convert 80% into a probability by simply dividing it by 100. This would give us the value of .80. Next, divide this value by two. Our quotient of .40 represents the area under the curve from $z = 0$ to the z score that we will use to plug into our equation. Looking at a z table, the corresponding z score for an area of .40 is approximately 1.28. So now, you'll simply plug that value into the equation to determine the equation for the 80% confidence interval:

$$80\% \text{ Confidence interval} = \bar{x} \pm 1.28\sigma_{\bar{x}} = \bar{x} \pm 1.28\left(\frac{s}{\sqrt{n}}\right)$$

This equation is exactly the same as the ones presented previously except for the z value used in the equation.

2. First, convert 80% into a probability by dividing it by 100, giving us the probability of .80. Next, subtract this value from 1, giving us a difference of 0.20. Next, divide this value by 2. This gives us a quotient of 0.10. Now, looking at a z table, we need to look up the corresponding z value for the area under the curve equivalent to 0.10 looking at the "area beyond z" column. Basically, you need to find the specific z value that corresponds to an area under the curve of 0.10 starting from the z value that you are looking for to infinity. Looking at a z table, this corresponds to a z value of approximately 1.28. Now, simply plugging this value into the equation to determine the equation for the 80% confidence interval:

$$80\% \text{ Confidence interval} = \bar{x} \pm 1.28\sigma_{\bar{x}} = \bar{x} \pm 1.28\left(\frac{s}{\sqrt{n}}\right)$$

This equation is in the same format as the ones presented previously with the exception of the z value used in the equation.

Either of these methods will work fine for determining equations for alternative confidence intervals. Simply choose the method that is more comfortable for you.

Part D: Confidence Intervals—The t Statistic

Confidence intervals can also be calculated for the t statistic. As presented earlier, the equation for the t score of a sample can be computed using the following equation:

$$t = \frac{\bar{x} - \mu}{\left(\frac{s}{\sqrt{n}}\right)}$$

Say, for example, we have a random sample of 10 respondents with data on their political views, which is measured on a scale from 0 (most liberal) to 10 (most conservative). To calculate the 95% confidence interval, we would use the following equation:

$$95\% \text{ Confidence interval} = \bar{x} \pm t s_x = \bar{x} \pm t \frac{s}{\sqrt{n}}$$

$$df = n - 1.$$

Say that we calculated a mean of 3.4 and a variance of 2.2. Our degrees of freedom would be our sample size minus 1, or simply 9. Looking at a t table, the t value for a two-tailed test at the 0.05 level of significance (which corresponds to our 95% confidence interval) is 2.262. Plugging this value into the previous equation, we would get the following result:

$$95\% \text{ Confidence interval} = \bar{x} \pm t s_x = \bar{x} \pm t \frac{s}{\sqrt{n}}$$

$$= 3.4 \pm 2.262 \left(\frac{2.2}{\sqrt{10}}\right) = 3.4 \pm 1.57$$

Upper limit of the 95% confidence interval = 4.97

Lower limit of the 95% confidence interval = 1.83

So we know with 95% confidence that the population mean for political views is between 1.83 and 4.97. To calculate other confidence intervals, such as a 99% or 99.9% confidence interval, we would simply look up the corresponding t score from a t table. For example, to continue with our example, to calculate the 99% confidence interval, we would simply find the corresponding t value: here, it would be the t score corresponding to the .01 level of significance for a two-tailed test with 9 degrees of freedom. Looking at a t table, this corresponds to a t value of 3.250. Then, we would simply calculate the 99% confidence interval using the following equation:

$$99\% \text{ Confidence interval} = \bar{x} \pm t s_x = \bar{x} \pm t \frac{s}{\sqrt{n}}$$

$$= 3.4 \pm 3.250 \left(\frac{2.2}{\sqrt{10}}\right) = 3.4 \pm 2.26$$

Upper limit of the 99% confidence interval = 5.66

Lower limit of the 99% confidence interval = 1.14

Here, we can state with 99% confidence that the population mean for political views is between 1.14 and 5.66. Once again, as we increase the certainty of our confidence we lose precision, having a wider range of potential values. Calculating the 99.9% confidence interval would be done in the same way and would be computed as follows.

$$99.9\% \text{ Confidence interval} = \bar{x} \pm ts_x = \bar{x} \pm t \frac{s}{\sqrt{n}}$$

$$= 3.4 \pm 4.781 \left(\frac{2.2}{\sqrt{10}} \right) = 3.4 \pm 3.33$$

Upper limit of the 99.9% confidence interval = 6.73

Lower limit of the 99.9% confidence interval = 0.74

Based on our calculations, we can state that with 99.9% confidence, the population mean for political views is between 0.74 and 6.73.

Part E: Proportions

While many of the simpler statistical tests presented in this book rely on sample means, you may sometimes come across data that consist of a proportion instead. There are a number of methods that can be used to generate meaningful data from one or more proportions.

Calculating a confidence interval based on a proportion is done similarly to the calculation of a confidence interval using a z statistic or a t statistic. For example, to calculate the 95% confidence interval of a proportion, you would use the following equation:

$$95\% \text{ Confidence interval} = P \pm 1.96s_p = P \pm 1.96 \sqrt{\frac{P(1-P)}{n}}$$

For example, say we wanted to calculate the 95% confidence interval for the proportion of people who plan to vote in the next presidential election. We took a random sample of 50 individuals, 40% of whom said that they plan to vote in the next presidential election. Our value of 40% would correspond to the proportion of 0.40. To calculate the 95% confidence interval of the population proportion of individuals who plan to vote in the next presidential election, we would simply plug these values into the following equation:

$$95\% \text{ Confidence interval} = P \pm 1.96 s_p = P \pm 1.96 \sqrt{\frac{P(1-P)}{n}}$$

$$= 0.40 \pm 1.96 \sqrt{\frac{0.40(1-0.40)}{50}} = 0.40 \pm 0.136$$

Upper limit of the 95% confidence interval = 0.536

Lower limit of the 95% confidence interval = 0.264

So we can state with 95% confidence that the population proportion lies between 0.264 and 0.536. As you may notice, the value of 1.96 is the same value we used when calculating the 95% confidence interval using z scores. In calculating the 95% confidence interval for a proportion, we will simply use the corresponding z score that we would use when calculating the confidence interval for a z score. So the equation for the 99% confidence interval for a proportion is as follows:

$$99\% \text{ Confidence interval} = P \pm 2.58 s_p = P \pm 2.58 \sqrt{\frac{P(1-P)}{n}}$$

And, the equation for the 99.9% confidence interval of a proportion would simply be as follows:

$$99.9\% \text{ Confidence interval} = P \pm 3.30 s_p = P \pm 3.30 \sqrt{\frac{P(1-P)}{n}}$$

To calculate any other confidence interval for a proportion, you can simply look up and use the corresponding z score and substitute that value in place of the z score of 1.96, 2.58, or 3.30.

The **difference in proportions test** is used to test whether a certain proportion is statistically different between two samples. To test this, we would use the following series of equations:

$$P^* = \frac{N_1 P_1 + N_2 P_2}{N_1 + N_2}$$

$$s_{p_1 - p_2} = \sqrt{P^*(1 - P^*)\left(\frac{N_1 + N_2}{N_1 N_2}\right)}$$

$$z = \frac{P_1 - P_2}{s_{P_1 - P_2}}$$

where

$P*$ = the weighted sample proportion

N_1 = the sample size of the first proportion

N_2 = the sample size of the second proportion

P_1 = the value of the first proportion

P_2 = the value of the second proportion

$s_{p_1 - p_2}$ = the standard error of the difference in proportions

z = the calculated z score

As an example, say we had two classes of students, both of whom were going on a field trip. The first class consisted of 20 students of whom 80% were planning to attend. The second class consisted of 25 students of whom 90% were planning to attend. These equations will allow us to determine whether there is a statistically significant difference in these two proportions. This would be calculated as shown here:

$$P* = \frac{N_1 P_1 + N_2 P_2}{N_1 + N_2} = \frac{(20)(.80) + (25)(.90)}{20 + 25} = 0.8556$$

$$s_{p_1 - p_2} = \sqrt{P*(1 - P*)\left(\frac{N_1 + N_2}{N_1 N_2}\right)}$$

$$= \sqrt{0.8556(1 - 0.8556)\left(\frac{20 + 25}{(20)(25)}\right)} = 0.1055$$

$$z = \frac{P_1 - P_2}{s_{P_1 - P_2}} = \frac{.80 - .90}{0.1055} = -0.9482$$

To determine whether these two proportions are statistically significantly different, we need to compare our calculated z score with a critical z score. The critical z scores corresponding to the probability levels of .05, .01, and .001 are reproduced here:

z Score	p Level
±1.96	.05
±2.58	.01
±3.30	.001

As we can see, the difference between our two proportions was not found to be significant at the .05 level as our calculated z score of -0.9482 was not lower than the critical z score of -1.96. In this case, where our calculated z score is negative, the results would be statistically significant if the calculated z score is *less than* the critical z score. Alternatively, we could take the absolute value of the calculated z score (just make it positive) and then compare this value with the positive critical z score of 1.96. To determine our exact probability level, as discussed earlier, we can simply find our z value on a z table and double the value found in the "area beyond z" column. Our z score of -0.9482 would give us an "area beyond z" of approximately 0.1711. To look this value up on a table as it is negative, we can simply look up the value corresponding to 0.9482. As the z distribution is based on a normal curve, and since a normal curve is symmetrical, it does not matter whether we use the negative or positive value. Doubling this value gives us a product of 0.3422. This means that our probability level is .3422 or 34.22%. Hence, the probability that this difference in proportions is simply due to random variation or error is .3422, while the probability that there is a true difference between these two proportions is one minus this value, or .6578.

Part F: Correlations

While this book focused on Pearson's correlation coefficient, there are a number of other types of correlations that can prove to be very useful in certain circumstances. The first one I will discuss is called the **partial correlation coefficient**. This is similar to Pearson's correlation coefficient, with the exception that the partial correlation coefficient allows you to determine the correlation between two variables while controlling for a third variable. In this respect, you can view it as being similar to a regression with two independent variables; we will determine the correlation between one of the independent variables and the dependent variable while the second independent variable is controlled for or held constant. The equation for the partial correlation coefficient between two variables, notated as x and y, controlling for the variable z, is as follows:

$$r_{xy.z} = \frac{r_{xy} - r_{xz}r_{yz}}{\sqrt{1 - r^2_{xz}}\sqrt{1 - r^2_{yz}}}$$

where

$r_{xy.z}$ = the partial correlation coefficient between variables x and y controlling for variable z

r_{xy} = the Pearson correlation coefficient between variables x and y

r_{yz} = the Pearson correlation coefficient between variables y and z

r_{xz} = the Pearson correlation coefficient between variables x and z

While computationally more complex, the partial correlation between two variables controlling for more than one additional variable can easily be computed using IBM SPSS or Stata.

An additional alternatives measure of correlation is Spearman's rank correlation coefficient, or Spearman's rho. **Spearman's correlation** coefficient can be used in place of Pearson's r when one or both variables are ordinal (categorical and ordered). That is, it can be used to estimate the correlation between two ordinal variables or one continuous and one ordinal variable. Spearman's rank correlation coefficient is similar to Pearson's r in that it is used to detect a linear correlation between two variables. Say, for example, we wanted to determine the correlation between socioeconomic status, coded as low, medium, and high, and the amount of time spent in the past week reading for five individuals. In terms of socioeconomic status, low would be coded as "1," medium as "2," and high as "3." In regard to the amount of time spent reading in the past week, this would be ranked from 1, the lowest, through 5, the highest. Our data would look something like the following:

SES Rank	Reading Rank
1	1
2	2
2	3
3	5
3	4

As you can see, under socioeconomic status, we have two ties (two values that have the rank of two and two values that have the rank of three).

To determine the rank in situations where there is a tie, you will add the ranks together and divide by the total number of ties. First, you would do the following:

SES Rank	Numerical Rank
1	1
2	2
2	3
3	4
3	5

Here, I have forced socioeconomic status to have a distinct and unique numerical ranking for each individual. To determine the new unique ranks, we will add the two new ranks together and divide by the total number of ties. For an original SES of 2, we simply add 2 and 3 together to get 5, divide it by 2 (the total number of ties), giving us 2.5. For an SES of 3, we will add 4 and 5 together to get 9, divide it by 2 (the total number of ties) giving us 4.5. The new ranks that we will use to calculate Spearman's rank correlation coefficient are shown in the table below in the third column:

SES Rank	Numerical Rank	New Rank
1	1	1
2	2	2.5
2	3	2.5
3	4	4.5
3	5	4.5

Putting everything together, these are the data that we will use to calculate Spearman's rank correlation coefficient:

SES Rank	Reading Rank
1	1
1.5	2

1.5	3
4.5	5
4.5	4

The equation for Spearman's rank correlation coefficient is as follows:

$$\rho = 1 - \frac{6 \sum d^2}{n(n^2 - 1)}$$

where

ρ = Spearman's rank correlation coefficient

d = the distance in ranks between the two variables

n = the sample size

and

$$z = \rho \sqrt{n - 1}$$

is used to calculate the z score and determine the statistical significance of the correlation.

To calculate Spearman's rank correlation coefficient for our example, we would simply plug our values into the equation:

$$
\begin{aligned}
\rho &= 1 - \frac{6 \sum d^2}{n(n^2 - 1)} \\
&= 1 - \frac{6 \left[(1 - 1)^2 + (1.5 - 2)^2 + (1.5 - 3)^2 + (4.5 - 5)^2 + (4.5 - 4)^2 \right]}{5(5^2 - 1)} \\
&= 1 - \frac{18}{120} = 0.85
\end{aligned}
$$

We find a high positive correlation between socioeconomic status and the amount of time spent reading in the past week. To determine whether this correlation is statistically significant, we would use the following equation:

$$z = \rho \sqrt{n - 1} = 0.85 \sqrt{5 - 1} = 1.7$$

Then, again, the table of critical z scores:

z Score	p Level
±1.96	.05
±2.58	.01
±3.30	.001

While our Spearman's rank correlation coefficient of 0.85 was quite high, it was not found to be statistically significant at the .05 probability level, as our calculated z score of 1.7 was not greater than the critical z score of 1.96. Most likely, the correlation between socioeconomic status and the amount of time spent reading in the past week would have been found to be statistically significant if our sample size had been greater.

Kendall's tau is also used to estimate the correlation between two ordinal variables or one ordinal and one continuous variable. It is calculated using the following equation:

$$\tau = \frac{n_c - n_d}{\frac{1}{2}n(n-1)}$$

where

τ = Kendall's tau

n_c = the number of concordant pairs

n_d = the number of discordant pairs

n = the sample size

While computationally more complex, Kendall's tau tends to be preferred over Spearman's rho.

At some point, you'll most likely find yourself in the situation where you wish to determine the correlation between two variables, one or both of which may be ordinal (categorical and ordered), nominal (categorical and unordered), or binary/dichotomous (only consists of two categories). As you may remember from earlier, Pearson's correlation coefficient is designed to test the correlation between two continuous variables. While it can be used in some other situations, you will prefer an alternative method of determining the correlation in many situations.

The **point-biserial correlation coefficient** is used to determine the correlation between one continuous and one dichotomous or binary variable. This correlation coefficient can be used both in situations where the dichotomous variable is naturally dichotomous (such as sex of the respondent) as well as situations where the dichotomous variable was converted from a continuous variable into a dichotomous variable. Interestingly, the formula for the point-biserial correlation coefficient will give you a result exactly equal to the Pearson's correlation coefficient for correlations between one continuous and one binary variable. Therefore, Pearson's correlation coefficient could simply be used in these situations, and the point-biserial correlation coefficient can be viewed as a special case of Pearson's correlation coefficient.

The equation for the point-biserial correlation coefficient is as follows:

$$r_{pb} = \frac{M_1 - M_0}{s_{n-1}} \sqrt{\frac{n_1 n_0}{n(n-1)}} = \frac{M_1 - M_0}{\sqrt{\frac{1}{n-1} \sum\limits_{i=1}^{n} (x_i - \bar{x})^2}} \sqrt{\frac{n_1 n_0}{n(n-1)}}$$

where

r_{pb} = the point-biserial correlation coefficient

M_0 = the mean of scores of the continuous variable when the binary variable equals 0

M_1 = the mean of scores of the continuous variable when the binary variable equals 1

s_{n-1} = the sample standard deviation

n_0 = the number of cases when the binary variable equals 0

n_1 = the number of cases when the binary variable equals 1

n = the total sample size

$\bar{x}$ = the mean of scores for the continuous variable

x = the individual continuous variable scores

Unlike Pearson's correlation coefficient when calculated between two continuous variables, the point-biserial correlation coefficient will generally have a more constrained range, not achieving the normal Pearsonian range of −1 to +1. Instead, the range will tend to be fairly more restricted, and this restriction will increase as the dichotomous variable moves further away from an even 50/50 split.

There are a number of correlation coefficients that can be used to calculate the correlation between two nominal or ordinal variables. Several of these correlations can be used in situations where you also calculate the chi-square statistic. The **phi coefficient** is used to determine the correlation between two binary variables. As the relationship between two binary variables can be represented in a 2 × 2 table, it is common for the phi coefficient to be used alongside the chi-square statistic. The phi coefficient can be computed in the following way:

$$\phi = \sqrt{\frac{\chi^2}{n}}$$

where

ϕ = the phi coefficient

χ^2 = the chi-square statistic

n = the total sample size

The phi coefficient can also be calculated using the following equation, which does not require you to calculate the chi-square statistic first:

$$\phi = \frac{bc - ad}{\sqrt{(a+b)(c+d)(a+c)(b+d)}}$$

where $a, b, c,$ and d come from a 2 × 2 table as shown here:

| | | **Variable One** | |
		Category One	**Category Two**
Variable	Category One	a	b
Two	Category Two	c	d

Like the point-biserial correlation coefficient, the phi coefficient will commonly not be able to achieve the full range of values between −1 and +1. For this reason, a modified phi value, called **phi adjusted**, can be calculated using the following equation:

$$\phi_{max} = \frac{\sqrt{p_j - p_j p_i}}{\sqrt{p_i - p_i p_j}}$$

$$\phi_{adj} = \frac{\phi}{|\phi_{max}|}$$

where

p_j = the row or column with the lowest proportion

p_i = the row or column with the second lowest proportion

ϕ_{max} = the maximum possible phi value

ϕ_{adj} = the adjusted phi value

To determine the two p values, you will first find the proportions of the four row and column totals by dividing these four values by the total number of cases. Next, select the row with the lowest proportion and the column with the lowest proportion. The lower of these two becomes p_j, while the greater of these two becomes p_i. Then, simply plug these values into the first equation to calculate ϕ_{max}, then plug that value along with the original phi value into the second equation to determine the phi adjusted value. The significance of your phi value is equivalent to the significance of your chi-square.

In practice, values obtained for the phi coefficient are equivalent to those generated using the equation for Pearson's correlation coefficient for dichotomous or binary variables. In this way, the phi coefficient is a special case of Pearson's correlation coefficient. While the phi coefficient can be calculated for tables greater than 2×2 using the first equation presented, phi will have a maximum potential value greater than one, and interpretation becomes more difficult. For these reasons, the phi coefficient is not preferred for variables with more than two categories.

The **contingency coefficient** (also called **Pearson's Contingency Coefficient** or **Pearson's C**), represented as C, is like the phi coefficient in that it can be used to determine the correlation between two categorical variables, either nominal or ordinal. However, unlike phi, it is not restricted to only two dichotomous or binary variables. The contingency coefficient can be viewed as a generalized version of the phi coefficient and can be applied to 2×2 or larger tables. It is calculated using the following equation:

$$C = \sqrt{\frac{\chi^2}{\chi^2 + n}}$$

The maximum possible value of the contingency coefficient approaches 1 and serves as a better estimate of the correlation between two categorical variables for larger tables (i.e., between two categorical variables with a greater number of categories). When used to determine the correlation between two categorical variables with a smaller number of categories, the contingency coefficient will underestimate the true correlation, having a maximum possible value less than 1. A more accurate version of the contingency coefficient is **Sakoda's adjusted contingency coefficient**, which can be calculated in the following way:

$$C^* = \frac{C}{C_{max}} = \frac{C}{\sqrt{\frac{k-1}{k}}}$$

where

C^* = Sakoda's adjusted contingency coefficient

C_{max} = the maximum possible contingency coefficient value

k = the number of rows or columns, whichever is smaller

As you can see from the above equation, the maximum potential value of the contingency coefficient will vary by the number of rows and columns that you have. In a 2×2 table, the maximum value for the unadjusted contingency coefficient is approximately 0.7071. In a 3×3 table, the maximum value is approximately 0.8165. The significance of the contingency coefficient or the Sakoda's adjusted contingency coefficient is equivalent to the significance of the chi-square statistic. One limitation of both the contingency coefficient and Sakoda's adjusted contingency coefficient is that the maximum potential value is equal to 1 only in situations where the number of rows and columns are equal (i.e., both variables have the same number of categories).

One popular measure of the correlation between two categorical variables, either nominal or ordinal, is **Cramer's V**. Cramer's V is sometimes considered to be superior to the contingency coefficient as it does not suffer from the limited maximum potential value based on table size as does the contingency coefficient. However, tables with a different number of rows and columns will serve to reduce the maximum potential value of Cramer's V, with the magnitude of reduction being directly related to the degree of difference between the number of rows and columns. Cramer's V is calculated using the following equation:

$$V = \sqrt{\frac{\chi^2}{n(k-1)}}$$

where

χ^2 = the chi-square statistic

n = the total sample size or number of observations

k = the number of rows or columns, whichever is smaller

The significance of Cramer's V is equivalent to the significance of the chi-square statistic. As you might have noticed, the value of Cramer's V will be equal to the phi coefficient in cases where $k = 2$:

$$V = \sqrt{\frac{\chi^2}{n(k-1)}} = \sqrt{\frac{\chi^2}{n(2-1)}} = \sqrt{\frac{\chi^2}{n}} = \phi$$

Another popular correlation coefficient used to estimate the correlation between two categorical variables is **Goodman and Kruskal's lambda**, or simply **lambda**. While lambda is defined differently than the correlation coefficients we have covered so far, it can be viewed similarly to them. Lambda is what is known as a **proportionate reduction in error measure**, which is a measure of the degree to which the error in predicting one variable is reduced by incorporating a second variable. In that sense, when using the lambda measure, one of the variables will be considered to be the independent variable, while the other variable will be considered to be the dependent variable. Lambda is computed using the following equation:

$$\lambda = \frac{\sum (f_i) - F_d}{n - F_d}$$

where

λ = lambda

f_i = the largest cell value for each category of the independent variable

F_d = the largest marginal total among the categories of the dependent variable

n = the total sample size

For example, if you had the following data:

		Parent's SES			
		Low	Middle	High	Totals
	Low	65	20	12	97
SES	Middle	22	48	18	88
	High	8	15	53	76
	Totals	95	83	83	n = 261

We would consider the parent's socioeconomic status to be the independent variable and the individual's socioeconomic status to be the dependent variable, as we would be trying to predict the individual's socioeconomic status based on the socioeconomic status of the parent. We would compute the lambda measure as follows:

$$\lambda = \frac{\sum (f_i) - F_d}{n - F_d} = \frac{65 + 48 + 53 - 97}{261 - 97} = \frac{69}{164} = 0.4207$$

So knowing the socioeconomic status of the parent reduces the error in predicting the individual's socioeconomic status over simply guessing by 42.07%. Determining the significance of lambda is complex and the equation is not reproduced here. However, IBM SPSS calculates the significance of lambda when the lambda measure is calculated. A module for Stata allows for the calculation of lambda, but it does not calculate its significance.

Finally, two measures of the correlation between two categorical variables that are conceptualized as being underlying continuous variables are the polychoric correlation and the tetrachoric correlation. The **polychoric correlation** is used to estimate the correlation between two categorical variables that are viewed as being underlying continuous variables. The **tetrachoric correlation** is a special case of the polychoric correlation and is used to estimate the correlation between two dichotomous variables that are viewed as being underlying continuous variables. There is a module for Stata that can be downloaded for free which allows one to calculate the polychoric or tetrachoric correlation between variables.

Part G: Chi-Square—Corrections and Alternative Tests

One modification of the chi-square statistic is called **Yates' correction for continuity** or simply **Yates' correction**. This correction would be used in situations where you have a 2 × 2 table that includes cells with an expected frequency of less than five. In these situations, the chi-square statistic tends to be inflated (i.e., more likely to be significant without justification), hence the reason for Yates' correction. This test tends to be fairly conservative in the sense that it has been viewed as potentially overcorrecting for chi-square inflation. The equation for Yates's correction for continuity is as follows:

$$\chi^2_{Yates} = \sum_{i=1}^{n} \frac{(|O_i - E_i| - 0.5)^2}{E_i}$$

And the original equation for chi-square:

$$\chi^2 = \sum_{i=1}^{n} \frac{(O_i - E_i)^2}{E_i}$$

So basically, when implementing Yates' correction for continuity, instead of simply squaring the difference between observed and expected values, one first takes the absolute value of the difference, subtracts 0.5, then squares this value. So in essence, the magnitude of the difference between observed and expected values is decreased by 0.5 before being squared.

For example, if we had the following 2 × 2 table:

		Variable One		
		Category One	**Category Two**	**Total**
Variable	Category One	2	7	9
Two	Category Two	15	9	24
	Total	17	16	$n = 33$

The chi-squared value would be this:

$$\chi^2 = \sum_{i=1}^{n} \frac{(O_i - E_i)^2}{E_i} = \frac{(2 - 4.6364)^2}{4.6364} + \frac{(7 - 4.3636)^2}{4.3636}$$
$$+ \frac{(15 - 12.3636)^2}{12.3636} + \frac{(9 - 11.6364)^2}{11.6364} = 4.2515$$

While with Yates' correction, it would be as follows:

$$\chi^2_{Yates} = \sum_{i=1}^{n} \frac{(|O_i - E_i| - 0.5)^2}{E_i} = \frac{(|2 - 4.6364| - 0.5)^2}{4.6364}$$
$$+ \frac{(|7 - 4.3636| - 0.5)^2}{4.3636} + \frac{(|15 - 12.3636| - 0.5)^2}{12.3636} +$$
$$\frac{(|9 - 11.6364| - 0.5)^2}{11.6364} = 2.7918$$

And for both equations

$$df = (\text{Rows} - 1)(\text{Columns} - 1) = (2 - 1)(2 - 1) = 1$$

The critical chi-square value for $df = 1$, $p = .05$: 3.84.

As you can see, while the original chi-square statistic was found to be significant at the .05 level as its calculated value is greater than 3.84, the Yates' correction for continuity value was not found to be significant, not being greater than the critical value of 3.84.

The Mantel-Haenszel chi-square test can be preferred in situations where you are trying to determine the dependence between two ordinal (categorical and ordered) variables. It is calculated using the following equation:

$$Q_{MH} = (n - 1)r^2$$

where

Q_{MH} = The Mantel-Haenszel chi-square statistic

n = the total sample size

r = Pearson's r

Fisher's exact test is another test sometimes used in place of Pearson's chi-square. It may be preferred in situations with small sample sizes and is typically used only for 2 × 2 tables. It can also be preferred in situations where you have expected values for cells less than 5. What Fisher's exact test does is to compute the probability of finding a 2 × 2 table with an association between the two variables as strong or stronger than you have observed. To illustrate, take the following example:

		Variable One		
		Category One	Category Two	Total
Variable	Category One	3	1	4
Two	Category Two	1	3	4
	Total	4	4	$n = 8$

Fisher found that the probability of finding any unique set of values could be calculated using the following equation:

$$p = \frac{\begin{pmatrix} a+b \\ a \end{pmatrix}\begin{pmatrix} c+d \\ c \end{pmatrix}}{\begin{pmatrix} n \\ a+c \end{pmatrix}} = \frac{(a+b)!(c+d)!(a+c)!(b+d)!}{n!a!b!c!d!}$$

where

n = the total sample size

a, b, c, d are as follows:

		Variable One	
		Category One	Category Two
Variable	Category One	a	b
Two	Category Two	c	d

Also:

$$x! = x(x-1)(x-2)\cdots(2)(1)$$

$1! = 1$
$0! = 1$

For example:
$5! = 5 \times 4 \times 3 \times 2 \times 1 = 120$

For example, the probability of achieving the data in the table presented earlier would be the following:

$$p = \frac{\binom{a+b}{a}\binom{c+d}{c}}{\binom{n}{a+c}} = \frac{(a+b)!(c+d)!(a+c)!(b+d)!}{n!a!b!c!d!}$$

$$= \frac{4!4!4!4!}{8!3!1!3!1!} = \frac{(24)(24)(24)(24)}{40320(6)(1)(6)(1)} = .2286$$

To calculate the one-sided Fisher's exact test, we would next need to specify the next stronger 2×2 table. We do this by "strengthening" the strong diagonal by one, reducing the "weak diagonal" also by one, like so:

		Variable One		
		Category One	Category Two	Total
Variable	Category One	4	0	4
Two	Category Two	0	4	4
	Total	4	4	n = 8

Next, we would calculate the probability for this new table:

$$p = \frac{\binom{a+b}{a}\binom{c+d}{c}}{\binom{n}{a+c}} = \frac{(a+b)!(c+d)!(a+c)!(b+d)!}{n!a!b!c!d!}$$

$$= \frac{4!4!4!4!}{8!4!0!4!0!} = \frac{(24)(24)(24)(24)}{40320(24)(1)(24)(1)} = .0143$$

Since we cannot "strengthen" this table any further, as there is at least one "0" in the weak diagonal, we stop here. Otherwise, we would continue strengthening the table and calculating each unique probability until we could no longer strengthen the table any further.

To calculate the one-sided probability for Fisher's exact test, we simply add all the previous probabilities together:

$$p_{\text{one-tailed}} = .2286 + .0143 = .2429$$

This one-sided test is used to calculate the probability of randomly selecting data with an association between the two variables as strong or stronger than what was observed in the direction that it was observed in. As this value is not less than .05, we have failed to find a significant relationship between these two variables. The value of .2429 can be interpreted in the following way: The probability of randomly selecting data with an association between these two variables as strong or stronger than what was observed is .2429 or 24.29%.

If we had wanted to calculate the two-sided probability for Fisher's exact test, we would need to systematically strengthen the table in the opposite direction and add to the probability score each unique probability score for every instance of the table that is as strong or stronger than our original, observed table. This two-sided test would be used to calculate the probability of randomly selecting data with an association between the two variables as strong or stronger than what was observed in either direction.

Finally, the **G test** or **likelihood ratio chi-square test** can be used to compare the distribution of a nominal variable with its expected or predicted distribution. While it can be used to test the level of association between two nominal variables, in practice it is generally used to test the distribution of a single nominal variable with its expected or hypothesized distribution. It will generally give you similar results to Pearson's chi-square. The G test is calculated as follows:

$$G = 2 \sum_{i=1}^{n} O_i \ln\left(\frac{O_i}{E_i}\right)$$

where

O_i = the observed value

E_i = the expected value

n = the total sample size

ln = the logarithm in base e (≈ 2.71828). Basically, the value for $\ln(x)$ would equal the number that e would have to be raised to to equal x.

For example, say we had the following data:

	Observed	Expected
Males	37	50
Females	63	50

In this example, we are expecting an equal proportion of males and females; however, we observe 37 males and 63 females. The chi-square statistic for this distribution would be calculated in the following way:

$$\chi^2 = \sum_{i=1}^{n} \frac{(O_i - E_i)^2}{E_i} = \frac{(37 - 50)^2}{50} + \frac{(63 - 50)^2}{50} = 6.76$$

While using a G test would give the following result:

$$G = 2 \sum_{i=1}^{n} O_i \ln\left(\frac{O_i}{E_i}\right) = 2\left[37 \ln\left(\frac{37}{50}\right) + 63 \ln\left(\frac{63}{50}\right)\right]$$
$$= 2[37(-0.3011) + 63(0.2311)] = 6.8383$$

For both the chi-square statistic and the G test:

Degrees of freedom = Number of categories − 1 = 2 − 1 = 1

The critical value for a G test is identical to that of the chi-square statistic, and in this example would equal 3.84 at the .05 probability level. As you can see, while both the chi-square test and the G test found the distribution of gender to be significantly different from the equal proportions that we had expected, there was a slight difference between the two statistics. Also, you may have noticed that the ratio of the observed to the expected value can never equal zero for the G test equation, as it is impossible to raise e, or any other number, to a number that gives you a result of zero. Therefore, if any cell has an observed or expected value of zero, it would not be included in the equation for the G test. Similarly, while it would be extremely rare to have an expected value of zero, as it would require either a row or column total of zero, such a result would give you an undefined quotient when using the chi-square equation, and such a cell would not be included in the equation for the chi-square statistic.

Finally, the **Kolmogorov-Smirnov test** is used to test the equivalency of a sample with a population (the one-sample Kolmogorov-Smirnov test) or to test the equivalency of two samples (the two-sample Kolmogorov-Smirnov test). It can also be used to test for normality.

Part H: ANCOVA, MANOVA, and MANCOVA

There are a number of statistical tests that are similar to the ANOVA but add on to it in some way. In the **ANCOVA** (analysis of covariance), you will study the relationship between a continuous dependent variable and one or more categorical independent variables. However, with the ANCOVA, you will be able to control for one or more continuous variables, called covariates. In this way, it combines some of the elements of an ANOVA with linear regression. For example, if you wanted to study the effect of a number of treatments on lifespan while controlling for age, you could conduct an ANCOVA. A **MANOVA** (multiple analysis of variance), a generalized version of the ANOVA, can be used in situations where you have two or more related dependent variables. Finally, the **MANCOVA** (multiple analysis of covariance) is a generalized version of the ANCOVA and can be used in situations where you have multiple related dependent variables and you wish to control for one or more continuous covariates.

Part I: Probability Distributions

In this section, I will present several of the more commonly used equations for probability distributions. The **binomial distribution** is used in situations where you want to calculate the probability of achieving a specific result or a specific set of results among a number of trials that have a binary outcome. For example, the binomial distribution could be used to calculate the probability of achieving a passing score (a specific set of results, a grade from 65% to 100%) on a true or false exam (a binary outcome). The binary outcome does not need to be an even 50/50 split to use the equations for the binomial distribution. For example, it could also be used to calculate the probability of achieving a passing score on a multiple-choice exam, where the probability of getting a correct answer on any one answer is 1/4, .25, or 25%. The equation for what is called the probability mass function of the binomial distribution is as follows:

$$\Pr(K = k) = \binom{n}{k} p^k (1-p)^{n-k} = \left[\frac{n!}{k!(n-k)!}\right] p^k (1-p)^{n-k}$$

where

$\Pr$ = the probability

K = the number of successes

k = the exact number of successes that you are trying to calculate the probability of

n = the total number of trials

p = the probability of a success

Say, for example, we wanted to calculate the probability of achieving a score of exactly 90% on a 20-question multiple-choice exam that had four options for each question. The score of 90% on a 20-question exam translates into a value of 18 for the exact number of successes that we will calculate the probability of. Since this is a 20-question exam, 20 is our total number of trials. Finally, our value for the probability of a success is .25, as the probability of guessing the correct answer on a multiple-choice question with four possible options is 1/4. This probability would be calculated in the following way:

$$\Pr(K = k) = \left[\frac{n!}{k!(n-k)!}\right] p^k (1-p)^{n-k}$$

$$= \left[\frac{20!}{18!(20-18)!}\right] .25^{18}(1-.25)^{20-18} = 1.5552 \times 10^{-9}$$

The resulting probability is extremely small and has been expressed in scientific notation. Now, say that we want to calculate the probability that we would get a least a C on the same exam. Since it is a 20-question exam, the equivalent of a 70% grade is 14 out of 20 questions correct. To calculate this, we could simply calculate the sum of the probabilities of getting 14 through 20 questions correct:

$$\Pr(K \geq 14) = \sum_{k=14}^{20} \left(\left[\frac{n!}{k!(n-k)!}\right] p^k (1-p)^{n-k} \right)$$

$$= \sum_{k=14}^{20} \left(\left[\frac{20!}{k!(20-k)!}\right] .25^k (1-.25)^{20-k} \right) = .00002951$$

In this example, the probability of achieving at least a 70% grade on this exam was calculated to be .00002951. By dividing this number by one, we convert this result into a "1 in x" probability. To illustrate, 1 divided by .00002951 is equal to approximately 33,887. So instead of stating that the probability of achieving a grade of 70% or greater on this exam is .00002951, you could alternatively say that the probability of achieving a grade of 70% or greater on this exam is 1 in 33,887.

The **hypergeometric distribution** is used in similar situations to the binomial distribution, in which you are trying to calculate the probability of getting a specific number of successes out of a total number of trials. However, the binomial distribution is used in situations where your trials are done with replacement. For example, if you had a large pot filled with blue and red marbles, and after every time you selected a marble you would put it back into the pot before selecting another one, that would be considered **sampling with** replacement, and would use the binomial distribution. Likewise, the example presented in the previous section, that of a multiple-choice exam, would also be considered sampling with replacement in the sense that the probability of achieving a correct guess on any question is independent of the number of correct or incorrect guesses that you have already made. In the blue and red marble example, if you were to not put the marbles you have selected back into the pot, this would be considered sampling without replacement, as you are not "replacing" the marbles you have selected back into the pot. In essence, sampling without replacement implies dependence between previous selections and the probability of a current success or failure. If you had an equal number of blue and red marbles in a pot and were sampling without replacement, if your first five selections were all blue marbles, the current probability of selecting a blue or red marble is no longer an even 50/50 split, but now is more than .5 for red marbles as there are currently more red marbles than blue marbles in the pot, while it is now less than .5 for blue marbles as there is currently five fewer blue marbles than red marbles. If we had done sampling with replacement, in which the selected marble was placed back into the pot before selecting the next marble, the probability would remain .5 for selecting either a blue or red marble at any trial, and computing probabilities in this type of situation would necessitate use of the binomial distribution. However, if we didn't put the selected marbles back into the pot, this would be sampling without replacement, and would necessitate use of the hypergeometric distribution.

To calculate the probability of a certain number of successes out of a certain number of trials when sampling from a population of a certain size, when sampling is done without replacement, you would use the probability mass function of the hypergeometric distribution:

$$P(X = k) = \frac{\binom{m}{k}\binom{N-m}{n-k}}{\binom{N}{n}} = \frac{\left[\frac{m!}{k!(m-k)!}\right]\left[\frac{(N-m)!}{(n-k)!(N-m-(n-k))!}\right]}{\left[\frac{N!}{n!(N-n)!}\right]}$$

where

X = the number of successes

k = the specific number of successes that you are calculating the probability of

m = the number of possible successes

N = the total sample size

n = the number of trials

For example, say we bought a collection of 50 very old videocassettes, and we know that 10 out of the 50 are working, but we do not know which ones. If we were to select three videocassettes, the probability that two of the three were working would be calculated in the following way:

$$P(X = k) = \frac{\binom{m}{k}\binom{N-m}{n-k}}{\binom{N}{m}} = \frac{\left[\frac{m!}{k!(m-k)!}\right]\left[\frac{(N-m)!}{(n-k)!(N-m-(n-k))!}\right]}{\left[\frac{N!}{n!(N-n)!}\right]} =$$

$$\frac{\left[\frac{10!}{2!(10-2)!}\right]\left[\frac{(50-10)!}{(3-2)!(50-10-(3-2))!}\right]}{\left[\frac{50!}{3!(50-3)!}\right]} = \frac{\left[\frac{10!}{2!8!}\right]\left[\frac{40!}{1!39!}\right]}{\left[\frac{50!}{3!47!}\right]} = .0918$$

If you wanted to calculate the probability that at least one of the three videocassettes was working, we could calculate that in the following way using a summation:

$$P(X > 1) = \sum_{k=1}^{3}\left[\frac{\binom{m}{k}\binom{N-m}{n-k}}{\binom{N}{n}}\right]$$

$$= \sum_{k=1}^{3}\left[\frac{\left[\frac{10!}{k!(10-k)!}\right]\left[\frac{(50-10)!}{(3-k)!(50-10-(3-k))!}\right]}{\left[\frac{50!}{3!(50-3)!}\right]}\right] = .4959$$

So the probability of selecting at least one functioning videocassette in our sample of three is nearly .50 or 50%. Likewise, by dividing 1 by our calculated probability of .4959, we can see that the probability of selecting a least one functioning videocassette in our sample of three is equal to a chance of approximately 1 in 2.017.

The **Poisson distribution** is used to calculate the probability of a specific number or range of events occurring within a specified period of time when the average number of events occurring within that period of time is known. It is assumed that the length of time to the next event is independent of how long ago the last event occurred. Say, for example, that on average, you meet three new friends a year. Using the Poisson distribution, you can calculate the probability of meeting five new friends, the probability of meeting five or more new friends, and so on in 1 year. The equation for what is called the probability mass function of the Poisson distribution is as follows:

$$f(k; \lambda) = \frac{\lambda^k \ell^{-\lambda}}{k!}$$

where

$f(k;\ \lambda)$ = the probability

λ = the expected, or average, number of occurrences that occur during the given time period

k = the number of occurrences that you wish to calculate the probability of

e = the mathematical constant, approximately equal to 2.71828

So to continue with the above example, if we normally meet three new friends every year, the probability of meeting five friends in a year would be calculated as follows:

$$f(k; \lambda) = \frac{\lambda^k \ell^{-\lambda}}{k!} = \frac{3^5 \ell^{-3}}{5!} = .1008$$

So the probability is .1008, or 10.08%. Now, to calculate the probability of meeting five friends or greater, we would simply calculate the sum of meeting five or more friends:

$$p = \sum_{k=5}^{\infty} \frac{\lambda^k \ell^{-\lambda}}{k!} = \frac{3^5 \ell^{-3}}{5!} + \frac{3^6 \ell^{-3}}{6!} + \frac{3^7 \ell^{-3}}{7!} + \cdots + \frac{3^{\infty} \ell^{-3}}{\infty!} \approx .1847$$

Here, we have calculated the probability to be approximately equal to .1847. Dividing 1 by this number, we get a value of approximately 5.41. Therefore, we could also state that the probability of meeting five friends or greater within 1 year is approximately equal to a chance of 1 in 5.41.

An exponential distribution is used to determine the probability of a certain time or range of times occurring between two events for types of events that occur continuously and are independent of each other. The equation that you can use to calculate the probability of the time between two events being of a certain value, called the probability density function of an exponential distribution, is shown here:

$$f(x; \lambda) = \lambda \ell^{-\lambda x}$$

where

$f(k; \lambda)$ = the probability

x = the amount of time

λ = the rate parameter, equal to one divided by the mean

e = the mathematical constant, approximately equal to 2.71828

For example, say you work as a freelance translator, and the average time between getting two jobs is 4 days. The probability of having the time between two jobs be equal to 7 days would be computed as follows:

$$f(x; \lambda) = \lambda \ell^{-\lambda x} = \frac{1}{\mu} \ell^{-\frac{1}{\mu}x} = \frac{1}{4} \ell^{-\frac{1}{4}(7)} = .0434$$

In this example, the probability of the amount of time between two jobs being equal to 7 days is equal to .0434 or 4.34%. If we wanted to find the probability of the amount of time between two jobs being equal to 2 through 5 days, we could use one of two methods. First, we could take the integral of the probability density function, like so:

$$\int_{x=2}^{5} \lambda \ell^{-\lambda x} = \int_{x=2}^{5} \frac{1}{4} \ell^{-\frac{1}{4}x} = .3200$$

Alternatively, we could use the cumulative distribution function, which calculates the probability of achieving any value from zero through the value that you specify. This equation is as follows:

$$F(x; \lambda) = 1 - \ell^{-\lambda x}$$

Using the cumulative distribution function, we would calculate the probability of the length of time between two jobs being between the values of 0 and 5 days and then subtract from this value the calculated probability of the length of time between two jobs being between 0 and 2 days, leaving us with the probability of the length of time between two jobs being between 2 and 5 days:

$$p = \left(1 - \ell^{-\lambda x}\right) - \left(1 - \ell^{-\lambda x}\right) = \left(1 - \ell^{-0.25(5)}\right) - \left(1 - \ell^{-0.25(2)}\right)$$
$$= .7135 - .3934 = .3200$$

The **gamma distribution**, like the exponential distribution, can be used to calculate the probability of a certain amount of time or range of times occurring between two events, as long as the length of time between the events are independent of each other and the events occur continuously. It is used especially in situations where the time between two events is equal to the sum of one or more independent exponentially distributed variables. The probability density function of the gamma distribution would be used to calculate the probability of the time between two events being of a specific value and is presented here:

$$f(x;k;\theta) = x^{k-1}\frac{\ell^{-x/\theta}}{\theta^{k}\Gamma(k)} = x^{k-1}\frac{\ell^{-x/\theta}}{\theta^{k}(k-1)!}$$

where

$f(x; k; \theta)$ = the probability

x = the amount of time

k = the shape parameter (number of instances of the event occurring)

θ = the scale parameter (equal to the average length of waiting time)

$\Gamma(k)$ = the gamma function of k, equal to $(k-1)!$

e = the mathematical constant, approximately equal to 2.71828

Here, let us continue the example used in the previous section on the exponential distribution in which we worked as a freelance translator with an average time between getting two jobs being equal to 4 days. Using the gamma distribution, the probability of the length of time between two jobs being equal to 7 days would be computed as follows:

$$f(x;k;\theta) = x^{k-1}\frac{\ell^{-x/\theta}}{\theta^{k}\Gamma(k)} = x^{k-1}\frac{\ell^{-x/\theta}}{\theta^{k}(k-1)!} = 7^{1-1}\frac{\ell^{-7/4}}{4^{1}(1-1)!} = .0434$$

As we can see, the exponential distribution gives an identical result when $k = 1$:

$$f(x;\lambda) = \lambda\ell^{-\lambda x} = \frac{1}{\mu}\ell^{-\frac{1}{\mu}x} = \frac{1}{4}\ell^{-\frac{1}{4}(7)} = .0434$$

as

$$f(x;k;\theta) = x^{k-1}\frac{\ell^{-x/\theta}}{\theta^{k}\Gamma(k)} = x^{k-1}\frac{\ell^{-x/\theta}}{\theta^{k}(k-1)!} = x^{1-1}\frac{\ell^{-x/\theta}}{\theta^{1}(1-1)!}$$

$$= \frac{\ell^{-x/\theta}}{\theta} = \frac{1}{\mu}\ell^{-x/\mu} = \lambda\ell^{-\lambda x} = f(x;\lambda)$$

The **Pareto distribution** is used to model certain types of data that consist of many small cases and only a few large cases. It could be applied to individual wealth or income, the sizes of towns/cities, the length of time spent on papers/class assignments, and so on. The probability density function, used to calculate the probability of selecting something of one specific size, is the following:

$$f(x; k, x_m) = \frac{kx_m^k}{x^{k+1}}$$

where

$f(x; k, x_m)$ = the probability

k = a constant

x = the specific value that you are calculating the probability of

x_m = the smallest possible value

To calculate the probability that x is greater than some specific value, we could use the following equation:

$$\Pr(X > x) = \left(\frac{x}{x_m}\right)^{-k}$$

Finally, the equation of the cumulative distribution function can be used to calculate the probability of achieving any value between x_m and x:

$$F_x(x) = 1 - \left(\frac{x}{x_m}\right)^{-k}$$

For example, say that we found the number of employees in a corporation to follow a Pareto distribution (i.e., there were many small corporations and only a few large corporations). Also, say we determined the value of the constant k to be equal to 1.2. Choosing as the minimum value of x_m to be 2, we can calculate the probability of a corporation having more than three employees in the following way:

$$\Pr(X > x) = \left(\frac{x}{x_m}\right)^{-k} = \left(\frac{3}{2}\right)^{-1.2} = .6147$$

So in this example, the probability of a corporation having more than three employees is .6147 or 61.47%.

The **geometric distribution** is used to determine the probability of the number of trials needed to achieve a success for processes that have a single unique probability of success. For example, if we were taking a multiple-choice exam, we can calculate the probability that a certain question, or "trial," would be our first correct answer if we were guessing randomly. This would be calculated using the probability mass function of the geometric distribution, shown here:

$$\Pr(Y = k) = (1 - p)^{k-1} p$$

where

$\Pr(Y = k)$ = the probability

p = the probability of success

k = the specific trial number

If our multiple-choice exam had four possible answers for each question and we were guessing randomly, the probability of success on any question would be 1/4, or .25. The probability that our fifth question would be the question with the first correct answer would be calculated in this way:

$$\Pr(X = k) = (1 - p)^{k-1} p = (1 - .25)^{5-1}(.25) = .0791$$

where

p = the probability of success

k = the trial number

Equivalently, the probability that we have four incorrect guesses before our first correct guess could be calculated like this:

$$\Pr(Y = k) = (1 - p)^{k} p = (1 - .25)^{4}(.25) = .0791$$

where

p = the probability of success

k = the number of failures

Calculating the probability that our first correct guess will lie somewhere between the first question and our fifth question could be calculated using the cumulative density function, shown here:

$$\Pr(X \le k) = 1 - (1 - p)^k$$

This calculation would be as follows:

$$\Pr(X \le k) = 1 - (1 - p)^k = 1 - (1 - .25)^k = .7627$$

So the probability that our first correct answer will lie somewhere between our first and fifth answer is .7627, or 76.27%.

The **negative binomial distribution** can be used to calculate the probability of a specific number or range of unsuccessful trials before a certain number of successes has been achieved, as long as the probability of achieving a success is constant. This probability is calculated using the probability mass function of the negative binomial distribution:

$$f(k;r,p) = \binom{k+r-1}{r-1} p^r (1-p)^k$$

where

$f(k; r; p)$ = the probability

p = the probability of success

k = the number of failures or unsuccessful trials

r = the number of successes

For example, if guessing on a multiple-choice exam with four possible answers for each question, the probability of having seven incorrect answers before three correct answers have been achieved would be calculated in the following way:

$$f(k;r,p) = \binom{k+r-1}{r-1} p^r (1-p)^k = \binom{7+3-1}{3-1} .25^3 (1-.25)^7$$

$$= \binom{9}{2} .25^3 (.75)^7$$

$$= \frac{9!}{2!(9-2)!} .25^3 (.75)^7 = .0751$$

The probability of having from one through seven incorrect answers before achieving three correct answers could be calculated in the following way:

$$\text{Pr} = \sum_{k=1}^{7} \binom{k+r-1}{r-1} p^r (1-p)^k$$

$$= \sum_{k=1}^{7} \binom{k+2}{2} (.25)^3 (.75)^k = .4589$$

Permutations and combinations are also used in the field of probability and are also useful for calculating the probability of certain types of events. Permutations are used to calculate the total possible number of arrangements when selecting a subset of items from a set of items. The formula is shown here:

$$P(n,r) = \frac{n!}{(n-r)!}$$

where

$P(n, r)$ = the number of possibilities

n = the total sample size

r = the size of the subset

For example, the total possible number of poker hands (5 cards) using a deck of 52 cards and counting the same hand twice even if the cards are just arranged differently would be done in the following way:

$$P(n,r) = \frac{n!}{(n-r)!} = \frac{52!}{(52-5)!} = \frac{52!}{47!}$$
$$= 52 \times 51 \times 50 \times 49 \times 48 = 311,875,200$$

To illustrate this example, when we select our first card, there are 52 possible options. After the first card is selected, there are only 51 cards left to choose from. This continues until we select our fifth card, at which point there are only 48 cards left in the deck to choose from, as we have already selected 4 cards. As you can see in the above calculation, this is exactly how this permutation is calculated.

As mentioned previously, two identical hands that simply have different arrangements of the cards would be counted twice using a permutation, but not using a combination, which will be covered next. For example, with a permutation, the following hands would be all counted separately as unique possibilities, with the cards ordered from the first selection to the fifth selection:

$$2\heartsuit, 7\clubsuit, 9\heartsuit, J\blacklozenge, A\spadesuit$$

$$A\spadesuit, 7\clubsuit, 9\heartsuit, 2\heartsuit, J\blacklozenge$$

$$7\clubsuit, J\blacklozenge, 9\heartsuit, A\blacklozenge, 2\heartsuit$$

Using a **combination**, the three hands listed above, all the same but ordered differently, would not be counted separately. This is the distinction between permutations and combinations. The formula for a combination is shown here:

$$C(n,k) = \binom{n}{k} = \frac{n!}{k!(n-k)!}$$

where

$C(n, k)$ = the number of possibilities

n = the total sample size

k = the size of the subset

To continue with our poker example, you can use a combination but not a permutation to calculate the number of unique 5-card hands when picked from a 52-card deck using a combination. This would be calculated in the following way:

$$C(n,k) = \binom{n}{k} = \frac{n!}{k!(n-k)!} = \frac{52!}{5!(52-5)!} = 2,598,960$$

As you can see, this value is much lower than the one calculated using a permutation. So, while there are almost 312 million possible poker hands if the same hand simply having a different ordering of cards were counted twice, there are only approximately 2.6 million unique poker hands.

Part J: All Equations

This section lists all the equations presented in the book.

Measures of central tendency and variability
Mean:

$$\bar{x} = \frac{1}{n}\sum_{i=1}^{n} x_i = \frac{1}{n}(x_1 + \cdots + x_n)$$

Variance:

$$s^2 = \frac{\sum_{i=1}^{n}(x_i - \bar{x})^2}{n - 1}$$

Standard deviation:

$$s = \sqrt{\frac{\sum_{i=1}^{n}(x_i - \bar{x})^2}{n - 1}}$$

Pearson's r:

$$r = \frac{\sum xy - N\bar{x}\bar{y}}{\sqrt{(\sum x^2 - N\bar{x}^2)(\sum y^2 - N\bar{y}^2)}}$$

$$t = \frac{r\sqrt{N - 2}}{\sqrt{1 - r^2}}$$

$$\text{Degrees of freedom} = N - 1$$

$$R\text{-squared} = r^2$$

The chi-square statistic:

$$\chi^2 = \sum_{i=1}^{n}\frac{(O_i - E_i)^2}{E_i}$$

One sample:

$$\text{Degrees of freedom} = \text{Number of response categories} - 1$$

Two sample:

$$\text{Degrees of freedom} = (\text{Rows} - 1)(\text{Columns} - 1)$$

$$E_i = \frac{(\text{Row total})(\text{Column total})}{\text{Grand total}}$$

t-test:

Independent samples, unequal sample sizes:

$$t = \frac{\bar{X}_1 - \bar{X}_2}{\sqrt{\left[\frac{SS_1 + SS_2}{n_1 + n_2 - 2}\right]\left[\frac{1}{n_1} + \frac{1}{n_2}\right]}} = \frac{\bar{X}_1 - \bar{X}_2}{\sqrt{\left[\frac{\sum x_1^2 - \frac{\left(\sum x_1\right)^2}{n_1} + \sum x_2^2 - \frac{\left(\sum x_2\right)^2}{n_2}}{n_1 + n_2 - 2}\right]\left[\frac{1}{n_1} + \frac{1}{n_2}\right]}}$$

$$df = n_1 + n_2 - 2$$

Independent samples, equal sample sizes:

$$t = \frac{\bar{X}_1 - \bar{X}_2}{\sqrt{\left[\frac{SS_1 + SS_2}{n_1 + n_2 - 2}\right]\left[\frac{1}{n_1} + \frac{1}{n_2}\right]}} = \frac{\bar{X}_1 - \bar{X}_2}{\sqrt{\frac{SS_1 + SS_2}{n^2 - n}}}$$

$$df = n_1 + n_2 - 2$$

Dependent samples/within subjects:

$$t = \sqrt{\frac{n - 1}{\left(\frac{n \sum D^2}{\left(\sum D\right)^2}\right) - 1}}$$

$$df = n - 1$$

ANOVA:

$$F = \frac{MS \text{ between}}{MS \text{ within}} = \frac{\frac{SS \text{ between}}{df \text{ between}}}{\frac{SS \text{ within}}{df \text{ within}}} = \frac{\frac{SS \text{ between}}{df \text{ between}}}{\frac{SS \text{ total} - SS \text{ between}}{df \text{ within}}} =$$

$$\frac{\left(\frac{\sum \frac{\left(\sum x\right)^2}{n} - \frac{\left[\sum\left(\sum x\right)\right]^2}{N}}{n(\text{Groups}) - 1}\right)}{\left(\frac{\left[\sum\left(\sum(x^2)\right) - \frac{\left[\sum\left(\sum x\right)\right]^2}{n}\right] - \left[\sum \frac{\left(\sum x\right)^2}{n} - \frac{\left[\sum\left(\sum x\right)\right]^2}{N}\right]}{N - n(\text{Groups})}\right)}$$

Linear regression, one independent variable:

$$\alpha = \bar{y} - \beta \bar{x}$$

$$\beta = \frac{n(\sum xy) - (\sum x)(\sum y)}{n(\sum x^2) - (\sum x)^2}$$

$$R^2 = 1 - \frac{SS_{\text{error}}}{SS_{\text{total}}} = 1 - \frac{\sum (y - f)^2}{\sum (y - \bar{y})^2}$$

$$\text{Adjusted } R^2 = 1 - \left(1 - R^2\right)\left[\frac{n - 1}{n - k - 1}\right]$$

Linear regression, two independent variables:

$$\alpha = \bar{y} - \beta_1 \bar{x}_1 - \beta_2 \bar{x}_2$$

$$\beta_1 = \left[\frac{r_{x_1y} - \left(r_{x_2y}\right)\left(r_{x_1x_2}\right)}{1 - \left(r_{x_1x_2}\right)^2}\right] \times \left[\frac{s_y}{s_{x_1}}\right]$$

$$\beta_2 = \left[\frac{r_{x_2y} - \left(r_{x_1y}\right)\left(r_{x_1x_2}\right)}{1 - \left(r_{x_1x_2}\right)^2}\right] \times \left[\frac{s_y}{s_{x_2}}\right]$$

The z statistic:
For a population:

$$z = \frac{x - \mu}{\sigma}$$

For a sample:

$$z = \frac{\bar{x} - \mu}{\sigma_{\bar{x}}} = \frac{\bar{x} - \mu}{\sqrt{\frac{\sigma^2}{n}}}$$

$$\text{Area from } z_x \text{ to } z_y = \frac{1}{\sqrt{2\pi}} \int_{z=x}^{y} \ell^{-\frac{z^2}{2}} dz$$

$$\text{Area from } a_x \text{ to } a_y = \frac{1}{\sigma\sqrt{2\pi}} \int_{a=x}^{y} \ell^{\frac{-(a-\mu)^2}{2\sigma^2}} da$$

The t statistic:
For a sample:

$$t = \frac{\bar{x} - \mu}{\left(\frac{s}{\sqrt{n}}\right)}$$

$$df = n - 1$$

Confidence intervals: The z statistic:

$$95\% \text{ Confidence interval} = \bar{x} \pm 1.96\sigma_{\bar{x}} = \bar{x} \pm 1.96\left(\frac{s}{\sqrt{n}}\right)$$

$$99\% \text{ Confidence interval} = \bar{x} \pm 2.58\sigma_{\bar{x}} = \bar{x} \pm 2.58\left(\frac{s}{\sqrt{n}}\right)$$

$$99.9\% \text{ Confidence interval} = \bar{x} \pm 3.30\sigma_{\bar{x}} = \bar{x} \pm 3.30\left(\frac{s}{\sqrt{n}}\right)$$

$$x\% \text{ Confidence interval} = \bar{x} \pm [z_{p/2}]\sigma_{\bar{x}} = \bar{x} \pm [z_{p/2}]\left(\frac{s}{\sqrt{n}}\right)$$

Confidence intervals: the t statistic:

$$95\% \text{ Confidence interval} = \bar{x} \pm ts_x = \bar{x} \pm t\frac{s}{\sqrt{n}}$$

$$df = n - 1$$

Generally,

$$x\% \text{ Confidence interval} = \bar{x} \pm ts_x = \bar{x} \pm t\frac{s}{\sqrt{n}}$$

where

t = the t score corresponding to your desired probability level.

Proportions:
Confidence intervals:

$$95\% \text{ Confidence interval} = P \pm 1.96s_p = P \pm 1.96\sqrt{\frac{P(1-P)}{n}}$$

$$99\% \text{ Confidence interval} = P \pm 2.58s_p = P \pm 2.58\sqrt{\frac{P(1-P)}{n}}$$

$$99.9\% \text{ Confidence interval} = P \pm 3.30s_p = P \pm 3.30\sqrt{\frac{P(1-P)}{n}}$$

Difference between two proportions:

$$P^* = \frac{N_1 P_1 + N_2 P_2}{N_1 + N_2}$$

$$s_{p_1 - p_2} = \sqrt{P^*(1 - P^*)\left(\frac{N_1 + N_2}{N_1 N_2}\right)}$$

$$z = \frac{P_1 - P_2}{s_{P_1 - P_2}}$$

Correlations: Additional:

Partial correlation coefficient:

$$r_{xy.z} = \frac{r_{xy} - r_{xz}r_{yz}}{\sqrt{1 - r^2_{xz}}\sqrt{1 - r^2_{yz}}}$$

Spearman's rank correlation coefficient:

$$\rho = 1 - \frac{6\sum d^2}{n(n^2 - 1)}$$

$$z = \rho\sqrt{n - 1}$$

Kendall's tau:

$$\tau = \frac{n_c - n_d}{\frac{1}{2}n(n - 1)}$$

Point-biserial correlation coefficient:

$$r_{pb} = \frac{M_1 - M_0}{s_{n-1}}\sqrt{\frac{n_1 n_0}{n(n - 1)}} = \frac{M_1 - M_0}{\sqrt{\frac{1}{n-1}\sum_i^n (x_i - \bar{x})^2}}\sqrt{\frac{n_1 n_0}{n(n - 1)}}$$

Phi coefficient:

$$\phi = \sqrt{\frac{\chi^2}{n}}$$

$$\phi = \frac{bc - ad}{\sqrt{(a + b)(c + d)(a + c)(b + d)}}$$

Phi adjusted:

$$\phi_{max} = \frac{\sqrt{p_j - p_j p_i}}{\sqrt{p_i - p_i p_j}}$$

$$\phi_{\text{adj}} = \frac{\phi}{|\phi_{\text{max}}|}$$

The contingency coefficient:

$$C = \sqrt{\frac{\chi^2}{\chi^2 + n}}$$

Sakoda's adjusted contingency coefficient:

$$C^* = \frac{C}{C_{\text{max}}} = \frac{C}{\sqrt{\frac{k-1}{k}}}$$

Cramer's V:

$$V = \sqrt{\frac{\chi^2}{n(k-1)}}$$

Goodman and Kruskal's Lambda:

$$\lambda = \frac{\sum (f_i) - F_d}{n - F_d}$$

Chi-square: Corrections and additional tests:
Yates's correction for continuity:

$$\chi^2_{Yates} = \sum_{i=1}^{n} \frac{(|O_i - E_i| - 0.5)^2}{E_i}$$

Mantel-Haenszel chi-square test:

$$Q_{\text{MH}} = (n-1)r^2$$

Fisher's exact test:

$$p = \frac{\binom{a+b}{a}\binom{c+d}{c}}{\binom{n}{a+c}} = \frac{(a+b)!(c+d)!(a+c)!(b+d)!}{n!a!b!c!d!}$$

The probability value for Fisher's exact test is calculated using a sum of these probabilities and is outlined earlier in this appendix.

The *G* test:

$$G = 2 \sum_{i=1}^{n} O_i \ln \left(\frac{O_i}{E_i} \right)$$

Probability equations:
The binomial distribution:

$$\Pr(K = k) = \binom{n}{k} p^k (1 - p)^{n-k} = \left[\frac{n!}{k!(n - k)!} \right] p^k (1 - p)^{n-k}$$

The hypergeometric distribution:

$$P(X = k) = \frac{\binom{m}{k} \binom{N - m}{n - k}}{\binom{N}{n}} = \frac{\left[\frac{m!}{k!(m-k)!} \right] \left[\frac{(N-m)!}{(n-k)!(N-m-(n-k))!} \right]}{\left[\frac{N!}{n!(N-n)!} \right]}$$

The Poisson distribution:

$$f(k; \lambda) = \frac{\lambda^k \ell^{-\lambda}}{k!}$$

The exponential distribution:

$$f(x; \lambda) = \lambda \ell^{-\lambda x}$$

$$\Pr(a \leq x \leq b) \int_{x=a}^{b} \lambda \ell^{-\lambda x}$$

$$F(x; \lambda) = 1 - \ell^{-\lambda x}$$

$$\Pr(a \leq x \leq b) = \left(1 - \ell^{-\lambda b} \right) - \left(1 - \ell^{-\lambda a} \right)$$

The gamma distribution:

$$f(x; k; \theta) = x^{k-1} \frac{\ell^{-x/\theta}}{\theta^k \Gamma(k)} = x^{k-1} \frac{\ell^{-x/\theta}}{\theta^k (k - 1)!}$$

The Pareto distribution:

$$f(x; k, x_m) = \frac{k x_m^k}{x^{k+1}}$$

$$\Pr(X > x) = \left(\frac{x}{x_m}\right)^{-k}$$

$$F_x(x) = 1 - \left(\frac{x}{x_m}\right)^{-k}$$

The geometric distribution:

$$\Pr(X = k) = (1-p)^{k-1}p$$

$$\Pr(Y = k) = (1-p)^{k}p$$

$$\Pr(X \leq k) = 1 - (1-p)^{k}$$

Negative binomial distribution:

$$f(k;r,p) = \binom{k+r-1}{r-1}p^{r}(1-p)^{k}$$

A permutation:

$$P(n,r) = \frac{n!}{(n-r)!}$$

A combination:

$$C(n,k) = \binom{n}{k} = \frac{n!}{k!(n-k)!}$$

GLOSSARY

Adjusted R-Squared: A modification of the R-squared equation that helps protect against artificial inflation of the R-squared value, which can happen when including a larger number of independent variables in a model.

AMOS: A statistical software program that is used to run structural equation models.

ANCOVA (Analysis of Covariance): Similar to the ANOVA, this test is used to study the relationship between a continuous dependent variable and one or more categorical independent variables. However, with the ANCOVA, it is possible to control for one or more continuous variables, called covariates.

ANOVA (Analysis of Variance): A statistical test that is used to test whether there is a difference in the mean of some continuous variable between two or more groups or to test the level of a continuous variable in a single group of respondents that were tested at two or more points in time. It can be used to test the difference between two groups; in this case, results would be identical to a t-test. Also, see one-way ANOVA, factorial ANOVA, and repeated measures ANOVA.

ARIMA (Autoregressive Integrated Moving Average) Models: A method in time-series analysis which is used to model changes over time as well as predict the future values of a variable.

Bar Charts: A type of chart in which the number of cases in each response category of a variable is represented as a bar. Bar charts are used for categorical variables and have spaces between each bar.

Beta Coefficient: In regression analysis, the value that is multiplied by the value of the independent variable in the regression equation to ascertain the predictive value of your dependent variable. Within regression, you will have as many beta coefficients as there are independent variables in your model, not including your y-intercept. For every one-unit increase in the value of an independent variable, the predicted value for the dependent variable increases by the value of the independent variable's unstandardized beta coefficient.

Binary Variable: A variable that only has two possible response categories and is typically coded as 0 or 1 (also known as a dichotomous variable).

Binomial Distribution: A probability distribution that is used in situations where you want to calculate the probability of achieving a specific result or specific set of results among a number of trials that have a binary outcome. For example, the binomial distribution could be used to calculate the probability of achieving a passing score on a true or false or multiple-choice exam. The binomial distribution is used in situations where you are sampling with replacement.

Brown's Linear Trend: In time-series analysis, a type of model that is used when there are no seasonal effects but there appears to be a linear trend in the data.

Case: One single respondent (individual, school, etc.) from a study. This term is used mainly in the context of data sets themselves, in which a single case is represented as a row.

Categorical Variable: A variable that consists of a number of discrete categories.

Cattell Scree Test: In factor analysis, a test that uses a scree plot to help determine the number of factors to keep. Specifically, the "elbow" of the curve in the scree plot, or the point at which the curve begins to level off, would be ascertained, and this determination would equal the number of factors you would keep.

Causation/Causality: Refers to a situation in which a change in one variable causes the value of another variable to change, either directly or indirectly.

Cell: The intersection of a single row and column in a table that includes two categorical variables. For example, in a table that includes both sex and political affiliation, one cell would consist of male liberals, another cell would consist of female moderates, and so on. Assuming two categories for sex and three for political affiliation, we would have six cells altogether.

CFI (Comparative Fit Index): A popular measure of model fit in structural equation modeling. This measure ranges on a scale from 0 to 1. Models with a CFI of .9 or above are considered to have acceptable model fit, while models with scores of .95 or above are considered to have good model fit.

Charts: A series of methods within descriptive statistics that is used to pictorially represent your data. Bar charts, histograms, and pie charts are some of the most commonly used charts in statistics.

Chi-Square/df Ratio: A popular measure of model fit in structural equation modeling.

Models with a chi-square/*df* ratio of less than five are considered to have a good model fit. The standards of less than two and less than three are also used but are more conservative.

Chi-Square Test or Chi-Square Statistic: A test used to measure the level of relatedness between one categorical variable and a known distribution or the relatedness between two categorical variables.

Combination: In the field of probability, this represents the total possible number of subsets when selecting a subset of items from a set of items. With combinations, subsets containing the same exact items but which are arranged differently are *NOT* counted separately.

Comparison Category: One single category of a categorical variable that is omitted from analyses. For example, if race was coded as white, black, and Hispanic and was to be included in a regression analysis as an independent variable, dummy variables for black and Hispanic could be created, leaving white as the comparison category. In this example, only the dummy variables for black and Hispanic would be included in the analysis, and results for the black and Hispanic variables would be as compared with white respondents.

Confidence Interval: An estimated range of values in which the true value is likely to lie along with the probability that the true value lies within this range of values.

Confirmatory Factor Analysis: A method of factor analysis in which you predetermine the final number of factors. Also, the variables that are associated with each factor are also typically predetermined when using confirmatory factor analysis.

Contingency Coefficient (also called Pearson's Contingency Coefficient or

Pearson's C): A correlation coefficient that is used to determine the correlation between two categorical variables, either nominal or ordinal.

Continuous Variable: A variable that does not consist of a number of discrete categories. Examples of continuous variables include age, IQ, height, weight, and years of education completed.

Correlation: A number of measures that estimate the strength and direction of the relationship between two variables.

Count Variable: A variable that measures the number of times an event has occurred. An example of this would be the number of times the respondent went to a doctor in the past year.

Covariance: A measure of the strength of the relationship between two variables.

Cramer's V: A correlation coefficient used to measure the correlation between two categorical variables, either nominal or ordinal.

Curve Fitting: A method in time-series analysis that uses regression methods to determine how well a series of different curves, which are specified by equations, "fit" your data.

Damped Trend: In time-series analysis, a type of model that is used when there is no seasonality, and there is a linear trend that is decreasing in magnitude.

Data Point: One particular piece of data. For example, a data point could be the level of education for one specific individual in your sample. If you are studying schools instead of individuals, the length of time that one specific school has been in operation would also be an example of a data point.

Data Set: A collection of data in the format of a statistical software program, such as SPSS/PASW, Stata, or Excel. Within these programs, data are represented as a table, with rows representing individual cases (e.g., individuals) and columns representing individual variables.

Dependent Samples *t*-Test: A type of *t*-test that is used to test whether the mean of some continuous variable is significantly different across two groups that have been matched or paired on some important variable. It is also used to test whether the mean of some continuous variable is significantly different within a group of respondents at two different points in time.

Dependent Variable: The variable that you are trying to predict in a statistical analysis using one or more independent or predictor variables.

Descriptive Statistics: A set of statistical methods that is used to simply describe your data.

Dichotomous Variable: A variable that only has two possible response categories and is typically coded as 0 or 1 (also known as a binary variable).

Difference in Proportions Test: A statistical test used to determine whether a certain proportion is statistically different between two samples.

Direct Effect: An effect that one variable has directly on a second variable.

Direct Oblimin Rotation: In factor analysis, a method of oblique rotation.

Directional Hypothesis: A hypothesis that specifies the direction of the relationship between two or more variables. For example, the hypothesis that males have higher incomes than females would be a directional hypothesis. In these cases, a one-tailed test can be but does not have to be used. The hypothesis that the average income will simply differ between males and females would be an example of a nondirectional hypothesis.

Dummy Variable: A variable consisting of only two outcomes, 0 and 1, in which "1" represents being a member of some category, while "0" represents not being a member of that category. For example, a dummy variable for white respondents would be equal to 1 if the respondent was white and be equal to 0 if the respondent was nonwhite. Dummy variables are often used in statistical analyses that incorporate categorical variables. In these situations, one dummy variable for each category of the categorical variable would be included in the analysis except for one category, which is called the comparison category.

Eigenvalue: In factor analysis, values that are used to help decide the number of factors to keep. Using the Kaiser criterion, only factors with eigenvalues of 1 or higher would be kept.

Endogenous Variables: In structural equation modeling, variables that are specified to be predicted by one or more other variables. In a path model, endogenous variables would consist of all variables that have arrows leading into them.

Exogenous Variables: In structural equation modeling, variables that are not predicted by any other variables. In a path model, exogenous variables are those that consist of all variables that do not have any arrows leading into them.

Exploratory Factor Analysis: A method of factor analysis in which you do not predetermine the number of factors or predefine which variables will load on which factors.

Exponential Distribution: A probability distribution that is used to determine the probability of a certain time or range of times occurring between two events for types of events that occur continuously and are independent of each other. For example, if you

work as a freelance translator and know that the average time between getting two assignments is 4 days, the exponential distribution could be used to calculate the probability of the time between two jobs being equal to 7 days.

Exponential Smoothing: A method of time-series analysis that is used for very short-term prediction or forecasting, specifically being used for the forecasting of the very next value in your series of data.

Factor: In factor analysis, a variable that consists of multiple related variables.

Factor Analysis: A method in statistics that is used to determine whether a larger number of variables can be reduced to a smaller number of factors.

Factor Extraction: In factor analysis, a number of differing methods that are used to extract factors from a set of variables. The two most common forms of factor extraction include principal components analysis (PCA) and principal factor analysis (PFA).

Factor Loading: In factor analysis, a measure of how heavily an individual variable weighs on a factor.

Factorial ANOVA: A type of ANOVA in which you have two or more categorical predictor variables (compare with one-way ANOVA).

Fisher's Exact Test: A measure similar to Pearson's chi-square that may be preferred in situations with small sample sizes and is typically used only for 2 × 2 tables. It can also be preferred in situations where you have expected values for cells less than 5. This test is used to compute the probability of finding a 2 × 2 table with an association between the two variables as strong or stronger than you have observed.

G Test or Likelihood Ratio Chi-Square Test: A test similar to Pearson's chi-square for one variable in which the distribution of a nominal variable is compared with its expected or predicted distribution. It is also sometimes used to test the level of association between two nominal variables.

Gamma Distribution: A probability distribution that is used to calculate the probability of a certain amount of time or range of times occurring between two events, as long as the length of time between the events are independent of each other and the events occur continuously. It is used in situations similar to those used with the exponential distribution. It is used especially in situations where the time between two events is equal to the sum of one or more independent exponentially distributed variables.

Generalizability: The ability to generalize the results of your analyses from your sample to a larger population. This is possible when your sample is representative of a larger population.

Geometric Distribution: A probability distribution that is used to determine the probability of the number of trials needed to achieve a success for processes that have a single unique probability of success. It can also be used to calculate the probability that the first success will lie between a specific range of trials. For example, the geometric distribution could be used to calculate the probability that a certain question would be our first correct answer if we were guessing randomly on a multiple-choice exam. It could also, for example, be used to calculate the probability that our first correct guess will lie somewhere between the first question and the fifth question.

Goodman and Kruskal's Lambda: A correlation coefficient used to estimate the correlation between two categorical variables. This correlation coefficient is what is known as a proportionate reduction in error measure.

Grand Centered: In hierarchical linear modeling, when the grand or total mean is subtracted from each individual score in order to create a new variable that is used in the analysis.

Graphs: A series of methods within descriptive statistics that are used to pictorially represent your data. Line graphs and scatter plots are some of the most commonly used graphs in statistics.

Group Centered: In hierarchical linear modeling, when the group mean is subtracted from each individual score in order to create a new variable that is used in the analysis.

Heywood Case: In structural equation modeling, a situation where the error variance for a variable is negative. In these cases, the error variance would customarily be set equal to 0.

Histograms: A type of chart in which the number of cases in each response category of a variable is represented as a bar. Histograms are used for continuous variables and do not have spaces between each bar.

HLM (Hierarchical Linear Model/Modeling): A statistical model that is used to analyze nested data. It can be used in situations where members of the same group are predicted to be more similar as compared with members of different groups. For example, students in the same classroom would be expected to have more similar scores compared with students in two different classrooms. HLM also refers to a specialized statistical software program that is used to run HLM models.

Hoelter's Critical N: A popular measure of model fit in structural equation modeling. The calculated value refers to the sample size at which the significance level of the chi-square value for your model crosses the .05 or .01 probability threshold. This measure is only used in situations where the chi-square value for your model is statistically significant. Having a calculated value for Hoelter's critical N at the .05 probability level of 200 or greater indicates acceptable model fit.

Holt's Linear Trend: In time-series analysis, a type of model that is used when there are no seasonal effects, but there appears to be a linear trend in the data.

Hypergeometric Distribution: A probability distribution that is used in situations similar to the binomial distribution in which you are trying to calculate the probability of getting a specific number of successes out of a total number of trials. However, the hypergeometric distribution is used in place of the binomial distribution in situations where you are sampling without replacement.

Hypothesis: A prediction about the relationship between two or more variables.

IBM SPSS: A general-purpose statistical software package.

Incidence Rate Ratio: A measure that is used in negative binomial and Poisson regression and is interpreted in the following way: With one additional unit (of some independent variable), the average value of the dependent variable increases by a factor (of the incidence rate ratio value). With incidence rate ratios, a value of 1 indicates no relationship, while a value of greater than 1 indicates a positive or direct relationship, and a value of less than 1 indicates a negative or inverse relationship.

Independent Samples *t*-Test: A type of *t*-test that is used to test whether the difference in the mean of some continuous variable is significant across two groups that have not been matched or paired.

Independent Variable: A variable that you are using to predict a dependent variable in a statistical analysis.

Indirect Effect: An effect that one variable has on a second variable through a third variable.

Inferential Statistics: A set of statistical methods that are used to test hypotheses that relate to relationships between variables. These methods allow you to make inferences about your data, including testing whether the relationship between variables is statistically significant.

Interquartile Range: A measure of variability that is defined as your 75th percentile score minus your 25th percentile score.

Inverse Relationship: See negative relationship.

Kaiser Criterion: In factor analysis, a method of determining the number of factors to keep. Using the Kaiser criterion, only factors that have eigenvalues of 1 or higher would be kept.

Kendall's Tau: A correlation coefficient used to estimate the correlation between two ordinal variables or one ordinal and one continuous variable.

Kolmogorov-Smirnov Test: A test that is used to test the equivalency of a sample with a population (the one-sample Kolmogorov-Smirnov test) or to test the equivalency of two samples (the two-sample Kolmogorov-Smirnov test). It can also be used to test for normality.

Kruskal-Wallis One-Way ANOVA: The nonparametric equivalent of the ANOVA. It does not assume a normal distribution.

Latent Variable: In structural equation modeling, a variable that is not observed directly but instead consists of a series of observed variables. An example would be a socioeconomic status latent variable that includes education, income, and occupational prestige as indicators or components. Latent variables can be thought of as factors (as in factor analysis). In a path model, latent variables are represented by circles or ovals.

Line Graphs: A type of graph that is typically used to plot the mean of one variable as a line against a second variable.

Linear Regression: A method of regression that is used when your dependent variable is continuous.

Logistic Regression: A method of regression that is used when your dependent variable is binary or dichotomous (consisting of only two categories).

MANCOVA (Multiple Analysis of Covariance): A generalized version of the ANCOVA that can be used in situations where you have multiple related dependent variables and you wish to control for one or more continuous covariates.

Mann-Whitney U Test: The non-parametric equivalent of the independent samples t-test. It does not assume a normal distribution.

MANOVA (Multiple Analysis of Variance): A generalized version of the ANOVA that can be used in situations where you have two or more related dependent variables.

Mantel-Haenszel Chi-Square Test: A version of the chi-square test that can be preferred in situations where you are trying to determine the dependence between two ordinal variables.

Mean: Commonly referred to as the average or average score, this is a commonly used measure of central tendency.

Measures of Central Tendency: A set of measures within descriptive statistics that are used to try to determine the "average" or "middle" score. The most common measures of central tendency are the mean, median, and mode.

Measures of Variability: A set of measures within descriptive statistics that is used to show the degree of variability or range within your data. The most common measures of variability are the range, standard deviation, variance, and interquartile range.

Median: A measure of central tendency that is defined as the middle score when scores are arranged from lowest to highest.

Menu/Menu Bar: The row of options, generally starting with *File*, that you see near the top of a program. When running analyses in statistical software packages, you can choose to use either syntax or menus.

Missing Data: Data for some individual or entity that does not exist, generally because the respondent refused to answer a question. For example, surveys on income or those that ask sensitive questions tend to have a large amount of missing data due to respondents not wanting to answer those questions.

Mode: A measure of central tendency that is defined as the most common score among a group of scores.

Model Fit: In structural equation modeling, a number of measures that measure how well your model accurately reflects reality or how well your model fits your data. Popular measures of models fit include the significance level of your chi-square value, the ratio of chi-square divided by its degrees of freedom, NFI and CFI, RMSEA, and Hoelter's critical N.

Model Trimming: In structural equation modeling, a process in which the nonsignificant paths in your model are removed, and the model is rerun until no more nonsignificant paths remain.

Multinomial Logistic Regression: A type of regression that is used if your dependent variable is categorical and cannot be ordered in any meaningful way.

Multiple Linear Regression: A linear regression in which there are two or more independent variables.

Negative Binomial Distribution: A probability distribution that is used to calculate the probability of a specific number or range of unsuccessful trials before a certain number of successes have been achieved, as long as the probability of achieving a success is constant. For example, if guessing on a multiple-choice exam, the negative binomial distribution could be used to calculate the probability of having seven incorrect answers before the first three correct answers have been achieved. It could also be used to calculate the probability of having from one through seven incorrect answers before achieving three correct answers.

Negative Binomial Regression: A type of regression that is used when your dependent variable is a count variable. Oftentimes, linear regression is used instead, depending on the nature of the dependent variable.

Negative Relationship (also called an Inverse Relationship): A relationship between two variables that can be described in the following way: As one variable increases, the other decreases; also, as one variable decreases, the other increases.

Nested Data: Data that can be grouped into higher-order categories. For example, data on students' test scores can be viewed as being nested in that students can be grouped into classrooms, which can be grouped into schools. Data of this nature can, but do not necessarily need to, be analyzed using hierarchical linear modeling.

NFI (Normed Fit Index): A popular measure of model fit in structural equation modeling. This measure ranges on a scale from 0 to 1. Models with an NFI of .9 or above are considered to have acceptable model fit, while models with scores of .95 or above are considered to have good model fit.

Nominal Variable: A variable that consists of a number of discrete categories that cannot be ordered. Examples include race, college major, sex, region of residence, and religion.

Nondirectional Hypothesis: A hypothesis that does not specify the direction of the relationship between two or more variables. For example, the hypothesis that the average income differs between males and females would be an example of a nondirectional hypothesis. In these instances, a two-tailed test would be used.

Non-Parametric Tests: Statistical tests that do not assume that our data or that the dependent variable is normally distributed.

Nonseasonal Model: In time-series analysis, a type of model that is used to model data that do not present any regular, periodic patterns.

Normal Distribution: See normally distributed data.

Normally Distributed Data: Data in which the majority of cases falls close to the mean, and as you go further and further from the mean, you see fewer and fewer cases. Graphically, normally distributed data resemble a bell, which is why a graph of normally distributed data is sometimes referred to as a "bell curve." Many statistical tests assume that data are normally distributed. Tests for normality include the Kolmogorov-Smirnov test, the Shapiro-Wilk test, the Anderson-Darling test, and the Shapiro-Francia test.

Oblique Rotation: In factor analysis, a method of rotation in which the factors are allowed to correlate with each other.

Observed Variables: In factor analysis, variables that are measured directly. In a path model, observed variables are represented by squares or rectangles.

Odds Ratio: A measure that is used in logistic and ordered logistic regression and is interpreted in the following way: one additional unit (of some independent variable) increases the odds of having the dependent variable equal one by a factor (of the odds ratio value). With odds ratios, a value of 1 indicates no relationship, while a value of greater than 1 indicates a positive or direct relationship, and a value of less than 1 indicates a negative or inverse relationship.

One-Sample t-Test: A type of t-test that is used to test whether a group's mean on some continuous variable is significantly different from a comparison mean, which can be any value. A one-sample t-test is preferred to a z test in situations where the sample size is less than 30 and the population standard deviation is unknown.

One-Tailed Test: A method of determining statistical significance that can be used when testing a directional hypothesis. One-tailed tests of significance are less conservative than two-tailed tests.

One-Way ANOVA: A type of ANOVA in which there is only one categorical predictor variable (compare with factorial ANOVA).

Ordered Logistic Regression: A type of regression that is used when your dependent variable is categorical and can be ordered from lowest to highest in some meaningful way.

Ordinal Variable: A variable that consists of a number of discrete categories that can be ordered (examples include highest degree completed and social class).

Outliers: Scores that are very high or very low compared with the average score. Outliers can have a tendency to exert a greater influence on values, such as the mean. In that case, they should and sometimes are removed from the calculations.

Overdispersion: Used to describe variables that have greater variance than expected. This can also be applied more specifically to

variables having a variance greater than its mean.

Paired Samples t-Test: See dependent samples t-test.

Parametric Tests: Statistical tests that assume that our data or that the dependent variable is normally distributed.

Pareto Distribution: A probability distribution that is used to model certain types of data that consist of many small cases and only a few large cases. It can be applied to individual wealth or income, the sizes of towns/cities, the length of time spent on papers/class assignments, and so on. It is used specifically to calculate the probability of selecting something of one specific size or between a range of two sizes.

Partial Correlation Coefficient: A correlation coefficient similar to Pearson's correlation coefficient that allows you to determine the correlation between two variables while controlling for a third or additional variables.

Participant: See respondent.

Path Analysis: A statistical method that can be viewed as a special case of structural equation modeling in which both direct and indirect effects can be ascertained but in which latent variables cannot be included.

Pearson's Correlation Coefficient or Pearson's r: A measure used to estimate the level of correlation or the relationship between two continuous variables. The value of Pearson's correlation coefficient ranges from negative one (a perfect negative relationship) to positive one (a perfect positive relationship), with zero representing no linear relationship.

Permutation: In the field of probability, this represents the total possible number of arrangements when selecting a subset of items from a set of items. With permutations, subsets containing the same exact items but which are arranged differently are counted separately.

Phi Adjusted: A modified equation for the phi coefficient that does not suffer from the restricted range of the phi coefficient to as great of an extent.

Phi Coefficient: A correlation coefficient that is used to determine the correlation between two binary or dichotomous variables.

Pie Charts: A type of chart in which the percentage of cases within the response categories of a variable are represented as slices of a pie, where the size of the slice is proportional to the percentage of cases within the particular response category that that slice represents.

Point-Biserial Correlation Coefficient: A correlation coefficient that is used to determine the correlation between one continuous and one dichotomous or binary variable. It is used both in situations where the dichotomous variable is naturally dichotomous as well as in situations in which the dichotomous variable was converted from a continuous variable into a dichotomous variable. The formula for the point-biserial correlation coefficient will give you a result exactly equal to the Pearson's correlation coefficient for correlations between one continuous and one dichotomous variable.

Point Estimate: A single numerical estimate of some measure.

Poisson Distribution: A probability distribution that is used to calculate the probability of a specific number or range of events occurring within a specified period of time when the average number of events occurring within that period of time is known. This distribution assumes that the length of time to the next event is independent of how long ago the last event occurred. For example, if you meet on average three new friends a year, the Poisson distribution could be used to calculate the probability of meeting five or more new friends in 1 year.

Poisson Regression: A type of regression that is used when your dependent variable is a count variable. Oftentimes, linear regression is used instead, depending on the nature of the dependent variable.

Polychoric Correlation: A correlation coefficient that is used to estimate the correlation between two ordered categorical variables that are viewed as being underlying continuous variables.

Population: A larger body of individuals (or schools, states, etc.) whom a sample was selected from and whom you may be able to describe using the results of analyses conducted on the sample. This is possible if the sample was representative of the population.

Positive or Direct Relationship: A relationship between two variables that can be described in the following way: As one variable increases, the other also increases; also, as one variable decreases, the other also decreases.

Predictor Variable: See independent variable.

Principal Components Analysis: A method of factor extraction that is typically used when conducting an exploratory factor analysis.

Principal Factor Analysis: A method of factor extraction that is typically used when conducting confirmatory factor analysis.

Probability: An area of mathematics that can be used to estimate the chance of an event occurring or not occurring.

Probability Level or p-Level: The probability that the relationship between the variables is actually due to random variation, chance, or error (also referred to as the significance level or the alpha level).

Proportionate Reduction in Error Measure: A measure of the degree to which the error in predicting one variable is reduced by incorporating a second variable. An example of this is Goodman and Kruskal's lambda.

Pseudo R-Squared: An estimate of the linear regression *R*-squared value that is used in nonlinear regression (logistic, ordered logistic, multinomial logistic, etc.). This is used in place of *R*-squared as *R*-squared can only be calculated in linear regression. Pseudo *R*-squared formulas do not directly calculate the percent variance in the dependent variable explained by the independent variable(s) and should not be interpreted as such.

R-Squared: A statistical measure that represents the proportion of variance in the dependent variable that is explained by the independent variable(s).

Random Sample: A sample in which every person in the population had an equal chance of being selected for participation in the study.

Randomness: See random sample.

Range: A measure of variability that is defined as the difference between the highest score and the lowest score.

Recoding Data: The process of changing the response categories of a variable.

Regression: A statistical technique that allows you to ascertain the effect of a variable on the dependent variable while holding constant any number of other variables. Types of regression include linear regression, logistic regression, ordered logistic regression, multinomial logistic regression, Poisson regression, and negative binomial regression.

Relative Risk Ratio: A measure that is used in multinomial logistic regression and is interpreted in the following way: One additional unit (of some independent variable) increases the odds of having that particular category of the dependent variable as compared with the comparison category of the dependent variable by a factor (of the relative risk ratio value). With relative risk ratios, a value of 1 indicates no relationship, while a value of greater than 1 indicates a positive or direct relationship, and a value of less than 1 indicates a negative or inverse relationship.

Repeated Measures ANOVA: A type of ANOVA that analyzes differences in scores between two or more points in time.

Representative(ness): A characteristic of random samples. A random sample could be said to be representative of a larger population, allowing for results obtained through running analyses on the sample to be applied to the larger population.

Respondent: An individual who participates in the study.

Response Categories: The set of all possible values for a categorical variable. For example, for a variable measuring the respondent's sex, the response categories consist of male and female. When measuring political orientation, you might have three response categories: liberal, middle-of-the-road, and conservative.

RMSEA (Root Mean Square Error of Approximation): A popular measure of model fit in structural equation modeling. Models with RMSEA values of .05 or less are considered to have good model fit, while models with values of .05 to .08 are considered to have acceptable model fit. Models with RMSEA values of .08 to .10 are considered to have marginal model fit, while models with values of .10 or greater are considered to have poor model fit.

Rotation: A number of methods used in factor analysis of fitting your data to factors. Methods of rotation include varimax rotation and direct oblimin rotation (an oblique method of rotation).

Sakoda's Adjusted Contingency Coefficient: A modification of the contingency coefficient that helps account for the fact that the contingency coefficient will underestimate the true correlation when used to determine the correlation between two categorical variables with a smaller number of categories.

Sample: The group of individuals (or schools, states, etc.) who were selected for participation in the study.

Sampling With Replacement: A type of sampling in which the probability of achieving a success or failure on your current trial is independent of the outcome of any and all previous trials. When sampling is conceptualized as selecting items out of a group of items, sampling with replacement would constitute putting back the selected items into the group after each trial.

Sampling Without Replacement: A type of sampling in which the probability of achieving a success or failure on your current trial is dependent on the outcome of any and all previous trials. When sampling is conceptualized as selecting items out of a group of items, sampling without replacement would constitute not putting back the selected items into the group after each trial.

Scatter Plots: A type of graph in which two variables, generally continuous, are plotted against each other with individual data points represented as dots, crosses, or similar characters.

Scree Plot: In factor analysis, a line graph that plots your factors with their eigenvalues. Specifically, the factors would occupy the *x*-axis, beginning with the first factor, while their eigenvalues would be plotted on the *y*-axis. The scree plot is used to help determine the number of factors to keep in a factor analysis in what is known as the Cattell scree test.

Seasonal Model: In time-series analysis, a type of model that is used to model data that is patterned, that is having some specific element, like a spike, appear at regular time intervals. For example, the price of a stock that always appears to spike in January would be modeled using a seasonal model.

Simple Linear Regression: A linear regression in which there is only one independent variable.

Simple Model: In time-series analysis, a model that is used when there are no seasonal effects and there is no apparent trend in the data.

Spearman's Rank Correlation Coefficient or Spearman's rho: A correlation coefficient that can be used in place of Pearson's *r* when one or both variables are ordinal.

Standard Deviation: A measure of variability that measures the amount of dispersion within your data. It is equal to the square root of the variance.

Standardized Coefficient: Refers to a coefficient in statistics (e.g., a beta coefficient) in which the units of the independent and dependent variable have been modified to reflect units of standard deviation as opposed to their original unit. For example, running a regression with years of education as the independent variable and income as the dependent variable, if income was coded in thousands of dollars, a standardized beta coefficient of .5 for years of education would mean that an increase in level of education by one standard deviation is associated with an increase in predicted income by .5 standard deviations. Likewise, a decrease in level of education by one standard deviation is associated with a decrease in predicted income by .5 standard deviations.

Stata: A general-purpose statistical software package.

Statistically Significant: This term is used to describe a result of a statistical analysis that has a probability level of less than .05. Alternatively, the standards of .1, .01, and .001 are sometimes used.

Statistics: An area of mathematics that can be used to describe data as well as provide evidence for a relationship, or a lack of a relationship, between two or more variables.

Structural Equation Modeling: A very general statistical model that allows one to determine both direct and indirect effects and also allows for the inclusion of latent variables.

Stat/Transfer: A program that is used to transfer data sets between SPSS format, Stata format, Excel format, and a variety of other formats.

Syntax: Written instructions that are used by programs such as SPSS/PASW and Stata to perform operations (e.g., creating new variables, recoding variables, creating charts and graphs, and running analyses). SPSS/PASW and Stata syntax are very distinct and cannot be used interchangeably. Syntax looks similar to computer code.

***t*-Test**: A statistical test that is used to test whether the difference in the mean of some continuous variable is significant between two groups.

Table: A method of summarizing your data by category, using rows for a single variable or rows and columns for two variables. When used for a single variable, the tables show you the number of respondents or cases in each response category of the variable. When used for two variables, the tables show you the number of respondents or cases for every possible combination of the two variables.

Tetrachoric Correlation: A correlation coefficient that is used to estimate the correlation between two dichotomous variables that are viewed as being underlying continuous variables.

Time-Series Analysis: A set of statistical methods that is used to model changes in variables that occur over time. These methods include exponential smoothing, ARIMA models, and curve fitting.

Two-Tailed Test: A method of determining statistical significance that is used when testing a nondirectional hypothesis. A two-tailed test is more conservative than a one-tailed test.

Uncentered: In hierarchical linear modeling, when a variable that is included in a model is left unmodified.

Unrotated Solution: In factor analysis, a solution that does not use any method of rotation.

Unstandardized Coefficient: Refers to a coefficient in statistics (e.g., a beta coefficient) in which the units of the independent and dependent variable have not been modified. For example, running a regression with years of education as the independent variable and income as the dependent variable, if income was coded in thousands of dollars, an unstandardized beta coefficient of 0.5 for years of education would mean that for every additional year of education, predicted income is expected to increase by $500.

Variable: Anything that can be measured or coded quantitatively (with numbers). Variables can be directly measured (as with age) or can be a concept that is only indirectly measured (e.g., attitudes).

Variance: A measure of variability that measures the amount of dispersion within your data. It is equal to the square of the standard deviation.

Varimax Rotation: In factor analysis, a method of rotation that commonly makes small factor loadings smaller and large ones larger, making it easier to associate specific variables with the factor that they load on.

Wilcoxon Signed-Rank Test: The non-parametric equivalent of the paired t-test. It does not assume a normal distribution.

x-Axis: In a graph, the horizontal line on which a variable is plotted.

y-Axis: In a graph, the vertical line on which a variable is plotted.

y-Intercept: In regression analysis, the y-intercept is interpreted as the predicted value for your dependent variable when your independent variable(s) are all equal to 0.

Yates' Correction for Continuity or Yates' Correction: A modification of the chi-square equation that is used in situations where you have a 2×2 table that includes cells with an expected frequency of less than five. This helps account for the fact that the chi-square statistic tends to be inflated in these situations.

INDEX

Supporting researchers for more than 40 years

Research methods have always been at the core of SAGE's publishing program. Founder Sara Miller McCune published SAGE's first methods book, *Public Policy Evaluation*, in 1970. Soon after, she launched the *Quantitative Applications in the Social Sciences* series—affectionately known as the "little green books."

Always at the forefront of developing and supporting new approaches in methods, SAGE published early groundbreaking texts and journals in the fields of qualitative methods and evaluation.

Today, more than 40 years and two million little green books later, SAGE continues to push the boundaries with a growing list of more than 1,200 research methods books, journals, and reference works across the social, behavioral, and health sciences. Its imprints—Pine Forge Press, home of innovative textbooks in sociology, and Corwin, publisher of PreK–12 resources for teachers and administrators—broaden SAGE's range of offerings in methods. SAGE further extended its impact in 2008 when it acquired CQ Press and its best-selling and highly respected political science research methods list.

From qualitative, quantitative, and mixed methods to evaluation, SAGE is the essential resource for academics and practitioners looking for the latest methods by leading scholars.

For more information, visit **www.sagepub.com**.